Leveling the Playing Field

Leveling the Playing Field

Transnational Regulatory Integration and Development

Edited by

László Bruszt and Gerald A. McDermott

OXFORD
UNIVERSITY PRESS

OXFORD

UNIVERSITY PRESS

Great Clarendon Street, Oxford, OX2 6DP,
United Kingdom

Oxford University Press is a department of the University of Oxford.
It furthers the University's objective of excellence in research, scholarship,
and education by publishing worldwide. Oxford is a registered trade mark of
Oxford University Press in the UK and in certain other countries

© Oxford University Press 2014

The moral rights of the authors have been asserted

First Edition Published in 2014

Impression: 1

Published in the United States of America by Oxford University Press
198 Madison Avenue, New York, NY 10016, United States of America

British Library Cataloguing in Publication Data
Data available

Library of Congress Control Number: 2014938930

ISBN 978–0–19–870314–3

Printed and bound by
CPI Group (UK) Ltd, Croydon, CR0 4YY

Preface

Emerging market countries face the dual challenge of attempting to define and incorporate transnational regulations into their societies while attempting to build their own versions of regulatory capitalism, a process by which public and private actors of a relevant domain contest one another's institutional experiments. In a world where the euphoria of globalization has given way to lurching from one crisis to another, how can emerging market countries even imagine meeting this challenge? Is there a single unique path to transnational regulatory integration and local prosperity or is there a variety of paths and strategies? Moreover, to the extent there is variety, how can we identify the strategies that might facilitate or impede both regulatory integration and local institutional upgrading and how might countries from different regions of the world learn from one another?

These were some of the core questions we began asking several years ago as we observed the seemingly divergent experiences of institutional and economic upgrading in East Europe, Latin America, Asia, and Africa over the past 20 years. It was no surprise to find that emerging market countries were often pursing very different national policies and institutional experiments. But it was becoming increasingly evident that countries and many of their industries were ever more embedded in fundamentally different integration regimes with different constellations of rules, resources, and goals. That is, transnational integration was increasingly less about simply liberalizing trade and finance but rather about integrating often conflicting systems of regulation. Moreover, emerging market countries had significantly different public and private capacities to regulate economic activities, let alone manage the attendant negative and positive externalities. A closer examination of the patterns of transnational regulatory integration revealed not only a variety of roles of governments, multinational corporations (MNCs), international NGOs, and trade associations, but especially how different integration strategies could impact domestic institutional and economic upgrading in the developing world as well as shape the sustainability of transnational regulatory frameworks themselves.

This book aims to offer a fresh perspective in reconciling the seemingly incompatible goals of transnational regulatory integration and development.

It offers a new analytical framework and a set of case studies that helps forge (a) a comparative analysis of integration and development and (b) the identification of the mechanisms that can foster both lasting transnational integration settlements and broad-based domestic institutional upgrading. To do so, it draws on a set of ongoing research from scholars across the disciplines who analyze these issues from a variety of regions around the world and in industries and domains ranging from food safety, manufacturing, telecommunications, finance, as well as labor and environmental rights.

This book has emerged from a series of conversations and debates among the contributors that participated in two workshops co-organized by the Global Governance Program of the European University Institute, the Inter-American Development Bank, and the Center for International Business Education and Research of the University of South Carolina. These workshops have benefited the volume in two unique ways. First, the workshops fostered debates about the ways to rethink the different mechanisms that link transnational regulatory integration and fundamental development problems. Second, the workshops offered the participants the opportunity to learn how integration strategies varied across regions and domains and how they might be compared with novel approaches. This volume incorporates many of these lessons that we think can aid both students and policy-makers in linking the creation of cross-border regulatory systems with the process of domestic institution building in emerging market countries.

The first lesson that emerged was that conventional approaches to transnational integration and development often led scholars to view outcomes as binary—either formal market integration and development were advancing or not. Rather, when one combined recent work on these issues, one found a great variety of outcomes of integration attempts in terms of the institutionalization of transnational rules and of the extent to which key public and private stakeholder groups were benefiting or losing out. The second was that these apparent outcomes were not permanent but rather unstable, as relevant foreign and domestic actors continued to experiment with different regulatory arrangements and local capacity-building projects. The third was that sustainable market and thus regulatory integration across borders was clearly linked to the domestic politics of institution building and economic upgrading in emerging market countries. New transnational standards could set in motion divisive conflicts in developing countries, but they also can act as catalysts of initiating new public-private experiments to improve local regulatory capacities, firm capabilities, and social conditions. Even when formally adopted, they could create significant barriers to institutional change, benefiting relatively few stakeholder groups while marginalizing the majority. In turn, each of the chapters in this book explores the constraints that lead to the latter situation as well as the mechanisms that create paths toward the former outcome.

We are greatly indebted to the aforementioned institutions for their generous financial and organizational support. We are especially grateful to Antoni Estevadeordal, director of the Trade and Integration Division of the IADB. He and his team are relentless in their efforts to foment new thinking and generate pragmatic approaches to resolving the interlinked problems of transnational integration and local development. Their enthusiasm and insights greatly benefited not only the debates and lessons manifested in this book but also the creation of a new international network of scholars and practitioners dedicated to finding solutions to the ongoing challenges discussed herein. Realizing the workshops also would not have been possible without the support of Miguel Maduro, director of the Global Governance Program of the EUI, as well as Kendall Roth and Mike Shealy at the Moore School of Business.

The debates at the workshops and the arguments made in this volume greatly benefited from the comments and criticisms from Barbara Stallings, Fabrizio Cafaggi, Marie-Laure Djelic, Eun Mee Kim, Layna Mosley, Paolo Giordano, Fernando Ocampo, Grant Aldona, Andres Rebolledo, Antonio Ortiz Mena, Eric Miller, Carlo Pietrobelli, Philippe Schmitter, Tim Bartley, and, of course, the contributors to this volume. David Musson and his team at Oxford University Press have been extraordinarily generous with their time and support for helping this book see the light of day. We are also greatly indebted to Hye Sun Kang, Kurt Norder, Metria Harris, Stefano Palestini Céspedes, and Gergő Medve-Bálint for their research and editing assistance.

Finally, we are eternally grateful to Emese, Sandra, Miranda, and Jazmin for all their intellectual and spiritual support as well as their unending patience during the lunacy of researching, writing, and organizing this book.

L.B.

G.A.M.

Florence and Columbia

December 2013

Contents

Contents

List of Figures

List of Tables

List of Contributors

Liliana B. Andonova is Professor and Chair of the Political Science/IR Department and Academic Director of the Center for International Environmental Studies at the Graduate Institute of International and Development Studies, Geneva. She has been named Giorgio Ruffolo Fellow in Sustainability Science at Harvard University and Jean Monnet Fellow at the European University Institute. Andonova is the author of *Transnational Politics of the Environment. EU Integration and Environmental Policy in Eastern Europe* (MIT Press, 2003) and co-author of *Transnational Climate Change Governance* (Cambridge University Press, 2014). Her research and publications focus on international institutions, public-private partnerships, European integration, environmental governance, transnational governance, and the interplay between international and domestic politics.

Mark Aspinwall is Professor of International Studies at the Centro de Investigación y Docencia Económicas (CIDE) in Mexico City, and Professor of Politics at the University of Edinburgh, Scotland. He received his Ph.D. in International Relations at London School of Economics and Political Science. From August 2010 until December 2012, he was Head of the Department of Politics and International Relations at Edinburgh. His research interests are in the impact of regional organizations on domestic politics in North America and the European Union. His recent book, *Side Effects: Mexican Governance under NAFTA's Labor and Environmental Agreements* (Stanford University Press, 2013) concerns the capacity-building effect of the NAFTA environmental and labor side agreements on Mexican politics. He is also working on correlates to rule of law and on US–Mexico cooperation in the war on drugs.

Belem Avendaño Ruiz is Professor at the School of Economics and International Relations, of the Autonomous University of Baja California, Mexico. She received her Ph.D. in Agrifood Economics from the CIESTAAM-University of Chapingo. Her research focuses on the implementation of regulations and standards in Mexican agriculture. She specializes in measuring the impact of food safety policy on the fresh produce sector and the development and competitiveness of the Mexican agrifood sector. In 2013, she was appointed as the Director of Inspection, Health and Food Safety for the State Government of Baja California.

László Bruszt is Professor of Sociology at the Department of Social and Political Sciences of the European University Institute, Firenze. He was Head of Department from 2009 to 2013. His earlier research on the economic and political transformation in the post-communist countries resulted in several scholarly articles and the award-winning book (with David Stark) *Post-Socialist Pathways* (Cambridge University Press, 1998). His current work on the interplay between transnationalization, institutional development, and economic change has resulted in articles in such scholarly journals as *Review of International Political Economy* and *Studies in Comparative International Development* as well as the edited volume (with Ronald Holzhacker) *The Transnationalization of States, Economies and Civil Societies: New Modes of Governance in Europe* (Springer, 2009).

Moises Costa is a doctoral student in the Department of Political Science at Brown University. He holds a MPA from the Romney Institute at Brigham Young University and previously worked as an executive for the Volkswagen Group in the area of International Government Relations. He has been a visiting scholar and affiliate faculty at the Kennedy Center for International Studies at Brigham Young University, in Provo, Utah. His research focuses on governance, regionalism, globalization, and the automotive sector.

Valentina Delich is Professor of International Economic Law and Intellectual Property at FLACSO, Argentina. She holds a Ph.D. in International Law from the University of Buenos Aires. Her research interests are in the areas of international regulations, globalization, and economic integration. Her works usually focus on developing countries, Latin America in particular. Her recent publications include the book *Asimetrías, conflictos comerciales e instituciones internacionales* (Eudeba, 2011) and the chapter "Multilateralismo, incertidumbre y reputación. Las disputas argentinas en la OMC," in L. M. Donadio Linares (ed.), *Controversias en la OMC: Protagonismo y estrategias de los países desarrollo* (Buenos Aires: Editorial FLACSO-Argentina, 2013).

Wade Jacoby is the Mary Lou Fulton Professor of Political Science and Director of the Center for the Study of Europe at Brigham Young University in Provo, Utah. Jacoby is the author of *Imitation and Politics: Redesigning Modern Germany* (Cornell University Press, 2000) and *The Enlargement of the EU and NATO: Ordering from the Menu in Central Europe* (Cambridge University Press, 2004). He is co-editor of *The Politics of Representation in the Global Age: Identification, Mobilization, Adjudication* (Cambridge University Press, 2014). Jacoby has published articles in many journals including *World Politics, Comparative Political Studies, Politics and Society*, the *Review of International Political Economy*, the *Review of International Organizations*, and the *British Journal of Industrial Relations*. Winner of a number of research fellowships, Jacoby received the DAAD Prize for his scholarship on Germany. He is co-editor of *German Politics* and serves on the editorial boards of *Governance* and *European Security*.

Jacint Jordana is Professor of Political Science and Public Administration at the Universitat Pompeu Fabra. He has a Ph.D. in Economics (Universitat de Barcelona, 1992). He has been visiting fellow at the Australian National University, Wissenschafts Zentrum Berlin, University of California (San Diego), and Konstanz University. From 2005 to 2010 he was co-chair (together with David Levi-Faur) of the ECPR standing group on Regulatory Governance. Currently, he is director of the Institut Barcelona d'Estudis Internacionals (IBEI), an inter-university research institute devoted to international studies. His research focuses on regulatory policy and regulatory governance.

Julia Langbein is senior research fellow at the Center for European Integration at Freie Universität Berlin and scientific coordinator of a FP7-funded research project which investigates the consequences of current and future EU enlargements for the Union's internal and external integration capacity. She holds a Ph.D. from the European University Institute in Florence and degrees in Political Science from Freie Universität Berlin and the European University at St Petersburg. Her research interests include European integration (special foci: EU enlargement and the European Neighborhood Policy), transnationalization, political economy of Eastern Europe. Her research has been published in the *Journal of European Public Policy, Journal of Common Market Studies, Europe-Asia Studies,* and *Osteuropa.*

Miguel F. Lengyel is currently Director of the Argentine campus of the Facultad Latinoamericana de Ciencias Sociales (FLACSO). Between 2006 and 2009, he served as Principal Analyst at the Office of the Resident Coordinator System of the United Nations in Argentina. He was previously the Executive Director of the Latin American Trade Network (LATN), a network of scholars working on trade and development matters. He holds a law degree and a Master's in International Relations from the UB, Argentina, and is a Ph.D. (c) in Political Science from the Massachusetts Institute of Technology (MIT). He has been a consultant for IADB, the World Bank, ECLAC, and the Harvard Business School. His recent publications include: "La política industrial: que hay de nuevo?"; "Desarrollo tecnológico, innovación y cambio climático: Nuevas oportunidades de mercado para la producción agrícola"; "The Co-Production of Innovation: Insights from Argentina's Industry."

David Levi-Faur is Associate Professor at the School of Public Policy and the Department of Political Science at the Hebrew University of Jerusalem. He received his Ph.D. in Political Science from University of Haifa. He is a founding editor of *Regulation and Governance*, a scholarly journal that is a leading platform for the study of regulation and governance in the social sciences. He has held research and teaching positions at the University of Haifa, the University of Oxford, the Australian National University, and the University of Manchester, and visiting positions in the London School of Economics, the University of Amsterdam, FU Berlin, University of Utrecht, and University of California (Berkeley).

Gerald A. McDermott is Associate Professor of International Business at the Darla Moore School of Business of the University of South Carolina and is a Senior Research Fellow at IAE Business School in Argentina. He was previously Assistant Professor of Multinational Management at the Wharton School of the University of Pennsylvania for seven years. He specializes in international business and political economy, mainly on issues of institutional change, innovation, risk, and corporate strategy in emerging market countries, particularly East-Central Europe and Latin America. McDermott received his Ph.D. from the Massachusetts Institute of Technology (MIT). His has published articles in many of the leading scholarly journals in management, international business, and politics. His book, *Embedded*

Politics: Industrial Networks and Institutional Change in Post-Communism (University of Michigan Press, 2002), was a finalist for APSA's 2003 Woodrow Wilson Foundation Award for the Best Book on government, politics, and international affairs.

Christine Overdevest is an Associate Professor of Sociology and Criminology and Law at the University of Florida. Her current interests include new public transnational regulations to control trade in illegal timber and their interaction with other public and private regulations. She is also interested in the theory of experimentalist governance. She is the author of "Assembling an Experimentalist Regime: Transnational Governance Interactions in the Forest Sector," *Regulation and Governance* (co-authored with Jonathan Zeitlin, 2014), and "Towards a More Pragmatic Theory of Markets," *Theory and Society* (2011), among other papers. She has taught environmental and economic sociology at the University of Florida since 2005.

Michael J. Piore is David W. Skinner Professor of Political Economy Emeritus at the Massachusetts Institute of Technology (MIT) and was a MacArthur Prize Fellow. He is a labor economist who has worked on a variety of labor problems including employment, technological change, trade union organization and behavior, and work regulations. His focus is primarily upon the United States, but he has also studied labor institutions closely in France and Mexico. His influential books and papers include *Birds of Passage: International Migration and Industrial Society; Beyond Individualism, Internal Labor Markets and Manpower Analysis* (with Peter Doeringer); *The Second Industrial Divide* (with Charles Sabel), *Dualism and Discontinuity in Industrial Society* (with Suzanne Berger), and *Innovation: the Missing Dimension* (with Richard Lester). He is currently working on a book on competing models of labor and work regulation with Andrew Schrank.

Katharina Pistor is Michael I. Sovern Professor of Law at Columbia Law School, director of Columbia Law School's Center on Global Legal Transformation, and founding member of Columbia University's Committee on Global Thought. Her research focuses on comparative law with emphasis on emerging markets, the legal construction of financial markets, and law and development. She has published widely in leading law and social science journals and has co-authored and edited several books. In 2012 she was co-recipient of the Max Planck Research Award on International Financial Regulation. She is also the recipient of research grants by the Institute for New Economic Thinking and the National Science Foundation. She serves on several editorial boards, including Columbia's *Journal of Transnational Law*, the *American Journal of Comparative Law*, and the *European Business Organization Law Review*.

Andrew M. Schrank received his Ph.D. from the University of Wisconsin in 2000 and is currently Professor of Political Science and Sociology at the University of New Mexico in Albuquerque. He studies the organization, regulation, and performance of business—especially in Latin America. His articles have appeared in journals like the *American Journal of Sociology*, the *Journal of Politics*, *World Development*, and *Social Forces*. He is currently working on a book on competing models of labor and work regulation with Michael Piore.

Aneta Spendzharova is Assistant Professor of Political Science at Maastricht University. She holds a Ph.D. in Political Science from the University of North Carolina at Chapel Hill. Her research interests are in the areas of comparative political economy, banking sector supervision, and regulatory governance in the European Union and Central and Eastern Europe. She is currently working on a book manuscript, *Through Crisis and Boom: Regulating Banks in Central and Eastern Europe* (Palgrave Macmillan). Her research has been published in the *Journal of Common Market Studies*, the *Journal of European Integration*, and the *Review of International Political Economy*.

Ioana A. Tuta is a Ph.D. candidate in Political Science and International Relations at the Graduate Institute of International and Development Studies in Geneva. Her current work explores the business and human rights agenda, with a focus on the processes of socialization of multinational companies into human rights norms. She has completed a Master's degree in Political Science at the Graduate Institute and worked on issues related to environmental governance, with a focus on biodiversity conservation and protected areas, and the transformative dynamics of Europeanization. She has previously worked in the Treaty Division of the United Nations Office of the High Commissioner for Human Rights and with the International Advocacy Programme of Amnesty International.

Milada Anna Vachudova is Associate Professor of Political Science at the University of North Carolina at Chapel Hill. She received her Ph.D. in Politics from University of Oxford. Her book, *Europe Undivided: Democracy, Leverage and Integration After Communism* (Oxford University Press) analyzes how the leverage of an enlarging EU has influenced domestic politics and facilitated a convergence toward liberal democracy among credible future members of the EU in Central and Eastern Europe. It was awarded the XIIth Stein Rokkan Prize for Comparative Social Science Research. Professor Vachudova has held fellowships and research grants from, among others, the European University Institute, the Center for European Studies at Harvard University, the Center for International Studies at Princeton University, the National Science Foundation, the Woodrow Wilson Center, IREX, and the National Council for Eurasian and East European Research.

Jonathan Zeitlin is Professor of Public Policy and Governance, Distinguished Faculty Professor, and Jean Monnet Chair in European and Transnational Governance at the University of Amsterdam. He is also Scientific Director of the Amsterdam Centre for Contemporary European Studies (ACCESS EUROPE). His current research interests focus on experimentalist governance within and beyond the European Union. Recent publications include: "Assembling an Experimentalist Regime: Transnational Governance Interactions in the Forest Sector," *Regulation and Governance* (co-authored with Christine Overdevest, 2014); "Experimentalist Governance" (co-authored with Charles Sabel), in David Levi-Faur (ed.), *The Oxford Handbook of Governance* (Oxford University Press, 2012); *Experimentalist Governance in the European Union* (co-edited with Charles Sabel, Oxford University Press, 2010).

1

Introduction: The Governance of Transnational Regulatory Integration and Development

László Bruszt and Gerald A. McDermott

1.1 Introduction

Long gone are the days when the creation of transnational or global markets was framed largely as a function of trade and financial liberalization. The twenty-first century is undoubtedly about transnational and global regulations (Baldwin 2011; Braithwaite 2008; Jordana and Levi-Faur 2004). International organizations like the WTO, regional regimes like the EU, NAFTA, CAFTA, or the MERCOSUR, and a host of non-state actors, including multinational corporations (MNCs) and international NGOs, are attempting to create transnational regulations. Motivations for these efforts vary, ranging from the goal to integrate national markets by harmonizing diverging and conflicting domestic regulations, the aspiration to manage the social or environmental externalities of more open markets, to the desire to weaken competitors (Vogel 1997; Braithwaite and Drahos 2000).

These efforts by international organizations, intergovernmental negotiations, together with the dramatic growth of private standards have led less to uniform, harmonized global rules and more to a "patchwork" of transnational public and private regulations, further segmenting rather than integrating markets (Djelic and Sahlin-Andersson 2006; Kobrin 2002). Differences in regulatory norms are increasingly seen as the key barriers to the growth of regional and global markets, and regulatory disputes make up some of the most contentious issues in world politics (Drezner 2007; Estevadeordal et al. 2009). Controversies ranging from the 2008 global financial crisis to the breakdown of the Doha Round of trade negotiations to the life-threatening working conditions in Third World garment factories have simply made ever more salient core questions about which regulations matter, who makes the rules, and which socio-economic groups win and lose.

Regulation has long been central to the study of market making across the disciplines. Whether one views regulation as the rules that reduce transaction costs or that protect weaker members of society from negative externalities, regulations shape the distribution of opportunities and wealth as well as the allocation of rights and obligations among socio-economic actors (Büthe and Mattli 2011; Mattli and Woods 2009; Sunstein 1990). Seemingly simple changes in regulations might deprive thousands of producers of their livelihood, or alternatively, increase their market power and dramatically boost their economic opportunities (Dunn 2003; Braithwaite and Drahos 2000; Bruszt and Stark 2003). In turn, market regulation remains the locus of ongoing contestation by public and private actors that vary in their capacities to shape the definition of rules, the way they are implemented, and the distribution of their attendant costs and benefits.

This book examines how the extension of regulatory integration to developing countries affects the nature of these contestations and their outcomes in terms of both the spread of coordinated transnational regulations and their developmental outcomes. We use here the label "developing" as shorthand for low- and middle-income countries outside of the core of most developed countries. The dramatic increase in the attempts at regulatory integration involving less developed market economies brings a special twist into the patterns of contestation and the accompanying scholarly debates. The traditional concerns over transaction costs, social reproduction, and economic order are now linked to issues of differences in the capacities of advanced and developing countries to shape transnational rule making and benefit from the attendant redistribution of rights and obligations. As much as transnational regulatory integration could foster domestic reforms of regulatory institutions in the developing world, it could as easily foster resistance and repellence (Braithwaite 2008; Drezner 2007). Indeed, as John Ruggie (1982) suggested over thirty years ago, integration could leave the "regime takers" marginalized or force the "regime makers" to adjust their goals and the way they use their powers.

In considering developmental outcomes, this book argues that transnational markets do not emerge in a sustainable fashion by merely liberalizing trade or by imposing the same rules on countries at the different levels of development. Rather, integration strategies can decrease the negative and increase the positive developmental consequences of transnational regulations. The strategies that aim to create sustainable common rules should make transnational rules a common good. Such strategies have to face the problem of differences in domestic institutional conditions that prevent many of the private and public actors in less developed countries from implementing and benefiting from new transnational rules. While actors in more developed and more powerful countries might gain from finding ways to link the issue of transnational regulatory integration with concerns about development, the transnational institutions that could help solve the attendant coordination problems are often not present.

The details of the strategies that could integrate sectors and national markets previously regulated by incompatible rules will differ region-by-region and sector-by-sector because of differences in the starting domestic and transnational institutional conditions. The different combinations of these conditions set the starting parameters of integration strategies. Successful strategies alter pre-existing institutional endowments in order to increase the capacities of actors in weaker countries both to implement and to benefit from the common rules. We offer here an analytical framework that identifies the diverse starting conditions that can shape the various paths of initial regulatory integration attempts. The framework then identifies the components of regulatory integration strategies that could address the interlinked requirements of moving ahead with the creation of common market rules and making them a common good.

The contemporary debate on creating a "level playing field" reflects some of the dilemmas of integrating "rule makers" and "rule takers" but has often viewed outcomes as binary—markets are harmonized with a uniform set of regulations or integration is blocked. On the one hand, many proponents of regulatory integration argue that imposing the same rights, obligations, and rules—from finance to labor to food safety to the environment—for all market players will reduce transaction costs and increase trade flows with broad welfare gains. On the other hand, critics argue that such an approach can easily conserve backwardness in the global East and South, or indeed disassociate many of the economic actors in the developing countries from international markets. In emerging market economies, governments often lack the capacities to enforce transnational regulations as well as monitor and manage their developmental effects (Stiglitz and Charlton 2006; Ismail 2007). Even if access to richer markets is offered, the new standards impose costs that most public and private actors with limited resources and capabilities cannot meet (Dunn 2003). These views, however, can overlook the much larger variation in institutional and economic outcomes, and thus miss how different approaches to transnational integration can impede or promote local adaptation.

This book takes as a point of departure the rather stark variation in the outcomes of transnational integration attempts within and across regions, policy domains, and economic sectors. In many cases, governments or alliances of private actors in less developed countries successfully resist accepting or implementing transnational standards. In other cases, more developed countries or regional hegemons simply impose their rules on the weaker countries. In a few cases, governments and private actors can negotiate settlements that result in the spread of common rules that could bring benefits to various domestic actors in less developed countries. But attempts at arriving at such settlements many times fail to bring about encompassing market integration. Instead, MNCs and NGOs may mobilize to implement their own standards in specific sectors or policy fields in ways that combine upgrading regulatory and firm practices but benefit just a few stakeholder groups (Bartley 2010; Locke 2013). Lastly, governments might accept transnational rules on the books, but key domestic players can shape implementation to create various forms of local conversion or hybridization of transnational rules.

Such variation raises several important issues for students of integration and development. Why is it more likely to find resistance and repellence in some domains or regions, marginalization of "rule-takers" in others, and the proactive management of developmental externalities in still others? To what degree is variance simply a product of domestic institutional capacities or how can different approaches to transnational integration improve or worsen those conditions? What role do transnational public and private actors play in shaping both the approaches and the local outcomes?

This book offers analytical tools to answer these questions in two ways. First, we advance a comparative analysis by bringing together in a novel way the seemingly distinct literatures on transnational regulatory integration and development. The literature on transnational regulatory capitalism (Braithwaite 2008; Drezner 2007; Mattli and Woods 2009; Büthe and Mattli 2011) rarely considers the impact of this process on emerging market countries or the regional integration regimes in which they are embedded. In contrast, by bringing developmental issues and the mediating roles of regional regimes to the forefront, we help identify the conditions under which attempts at transnational regulatory integration are more or less sustainable.

Second, our framework helps identify dynamics—how different approaches to integration can alter or conserve regulatory quality and the distribution of their benefits. Building on research about transnational public and private regulation (Bartley 2010, 2011; Locke 2013; Mattli and Woods 2009), we note how pre-existing transnational and domestic institutional conditions can vary and shape in different ways the starting opportunities of the actors participating in transnational rule making. We also argue, however, that many of the attendant initial outcomes represent unstable equilibriums. Interests of the diverse private and public participants or the balance of power among them change over time (Keohane and Victor 2011). The outcomes of the first rounds of transnational regulations might "spill over" to other policy fields, mobilizing new actors to renegotiate them. More powerful actors in transnational rule making might learn that they can lose potential gains if they do not invest in increasing the capacities of weaker actors to implement and/or to gain from regulatory integration. Actors from countries at different levels of development might learn that uncoordinated actions can have welfare effects that are inferior to solutions based on collaborative exploration of opportunities to change pre-existing domestic and/or transnational institutions. Based on the recognition of their interdependence, actors from more and less developed countries can combine and jointly search for ways to alter domestic and transnational institutions, increase the capacities of domestic public and private actors in emerging market countries, and enlarge the scope for sustainable regulatory change.

The book thus offers a dynamic, transformative approach, analyzing different combinations of transnational integration strategies that could alter the parameters of the starting institutional conditions and in this way change the outcomes of the integration attempts. We draw on previous studies that have offered analytical tools to evaluate various modes of governing collective action for transnational regulations (Keohane and Victor 2011; Keohane and Ostrom 1995; Sabel and Zeitlin 2008). We extend their approaches by highlighting how problems linked to domestic institutional weaknesses in less developed countries change the nature of the dilemmas that govern the joint search for common rules with broad-based benefits.

With this perspective, we focus on the strategies that can reduce the potential negative and increase the potential positive developmental externalities of regulatory integration in the less developed countries. As the relevant actors come to recognize their interdependence, either through conflict or deliberation, one can analyze transnational regulatory attempts in terms of coordination problems of creating common goods in the transnational arena (Keohane and Ostrom 1995). Transnational hierarchies have limited capacities to solve such coordination problems. The information about the constraints in implementing transnational rules in developing countries or the relative success of interventions to alter domestic capacities is dispersed, and external actors might lack capacities to incorporate this. Potential domestic beneficiaries of these rules and changes often lack capacities to voice and enact their claims. Weak institutional capacities can also prevent various stakeholder groups from recognizing the different ways in which the rules can be adopted in a beneficial manner (Locke 2013; Schrank 2013b).

On the other hand, the inclusion and empowerment of diverse domestic private and public actors, their embedding in a multiple network of transnational supporting and monitoring institutions, can dramatically improve the success of regulatory integration and its developmental effects (Bruszt and McDermott 2012). The more complex the interactions among diverse actors, with potentially conflicting interests and beliefs, the harder it is to create encompassing solutions without the use of strategies that prefer joint problem-solving and recursive learning (Sabel and Zeitlin 2012; Overdevest and Zeitlin in this volume). Strategies that broaden the range of interlinked policy issues related to regulatory change and organize negotiations and agreements around a bundle of policies at the inception can better associate diverse interests and create more lasting settlements (Bruszt and McDermott 2012; Hoekman 2013).

The key argument that we make in this volume is that variation in the choice of such strategies largely determines whether the outcomes will be closer to a patchwork of regulations that just increase the segmentation of transnational markets, or alternatively whether actors can level the playing field and extend the scope of transnational markets by assembling encompassing settlements supported and reproduced by a wide diversity of beneficiaries both from the most developed and the less developed economies.

This book purposively analyzes different combinations of transnational integration strategies with the aim of identifying the hindering and enabling effects on emerging market countries. Its comparative nature offers a rare opportunity for policy-makers and scholars to consider how diverse approaches to integration from different regions of the world have significant impacts on the quality of regulatory institutions and on the variance of the types of state and non-state actors that both shape and benefit from these changes. The lessons of the chapters have implications for many developing regions, industries, and policy domains, as our cases examine some of the most salient integration issues in regulatory domains as food safety, labor, environment, finance, telecommunications, and manufacturing supply chains and compare experiences from countries in Latin America and East-Central Europe. At the same time, we restrict our regional analysis to the most prominent and advanced arrangements in regional political-economic integration, such as NAFTA, CAFTA, MERCOSUR, and the EU accession and neighborhood arrangements

The next section offers a typology of the outcomes of regulatory integration attempts in terms of the institutional capacity to implement international standards and in terms of their distributional effects on the ground. Sections 1.3 and 1.4 offer an analytical framework for the variation in these outcomes. We first focus on institutional statics, deriving different starting conditions for regulatory integration attempts based on two factors: pre-existing domestic institutional conditions and the properties of the pre-existing regional transnational regimes. The starting conditions, we argue, represent different opportunities and constraints for domestic and transnational agency to move integration attempts in the directions of the diverse outcomes described in section 1.2. We then turn to dynamics and offer an analytical basis for the evaluation of strategies that transnational actors use to depart from the initial status quo.

1.2 Mapping Outcomes of Regulatory Integration Attempts

Regulatory institutions are mechanisms for coordinating diverse interests and considerations with the goals to extend economic transactions and to cope with the related externalities. They establish binding settlements, of varied temporality, among, for instance, producers and consumers, employers and employees, often to balance the perceived requirements to compete internationally and to fulfill domestic needs (Bruszt and Stark 2003). Transnational regulations include rules and standards derived from pure intergovernmental agreements as well as those derived from interactions among domestic and external private actors that may or may not be codified and enforced by national- or supranational-level public actors (Cafaggi 2006; Djelic and Sahlin-Andersson 2006). The former are found typically in bilateral trade agreements, WTO agreements, and regional trade and integration regimes, such as the EU, NAFTA, and MERCOSUR. The latter often emerge from the expansion of global value chains, where private actors—firms, associations, and NGOs—attempt to set standards governing such issues as products, working conditions, and the environment.

Transnational regulatory integration is the process by which public and private actors from different countries attempt to create and implement common rules or standards that govern cross-border transactions and their potential positive and negative externalities. These regulations are ideally constructed to be compatible with relevant national laws and non-discriminatory. This process aims at bringing about convergence in norms, rules, and policies between sectors and across countries (Stone Sweet and Sandholtz 1997). Deepening integration means extending normative convergence from a limited regulatory framework, such as for contract enforcement or the removal of certain non-tariff barriers, to a more complex one, including regulations in various non-economic domains. Regulatory fragmentation occurs when integration fails to bring about a common set of rules and results instead in multiple conflicting rules within the same sector, policy field, or territorially bounded market.

When considering outcomes involving emerging market countries, we move beyond the international relations and political economy literatures by capturing both failed integration attempts and the developmental consequences. We classify four ideal-type outcomes according to two dimensions. The first dimension assesses the degree to which transnational rules are adopted and enforced domestically. We distinguish between attempts at common rule making in terms of whether they result in codified adjustment of national standards that are monitored and enforced by domestic institutions. For the sake of simplicity, no enforcement includes not adopting the rule or only adopting the rule on the books but not enforcing it.

The second dimension is the degree to which the successful or failed transnational regulatory integration attempt benefits a relatively broad or narrow set of domestic constituents in the developing countries. At its most basic level, this variable captures the proportion or distribution of firms that could stay in the market and gain greater value-added opportunities or be excluded from these opportunities. By extension, this captures the distributional effects on firm stakeholders, such as the positive or negative externalities borne by socio-economic groups linked to the industry or domain. Although our first point of reference is the firm, the relational theory of the firm established in comparative political economy (Hall and Soskice 2001) allows us to incorporate the distributional effects on stakeholder groups in such areas as labor and environmental standards.

The combination of these two dimensions reveals four ideal-type outcomes as presented in Table 1.1. In Outcomes 1 and 2, regulatory integration attempts succeed in bringing about common enforced rules or standards in a particular domain. They differ, however, in their distributive effects, namely whether a broad or narrow group of firms have the capabilities to implement the standards. We assume that if many actors, e.g. firms, can implement the standards, then they have created the new organizational capabilities necessary to participate in new market opportunities and to extend the benefits of new practices to a broader set of stakeholder groups (Bartley 2010; Locke 2013; Schrank 2013b).[1]

Outcome 1 is when the transnational rules are enforced and implemented in ways that benefit a broad constituency of the relevant industry or domain

Table 1.1 Ideal-type outcomes of transnational regulatory integration attempts

		Distribution of benefits	
		Broad	Narrow
Formal adoption and enforcement	Full enforcement	Outcome 1 Common Interest Regulation	Outcome 2 Transnational Regulatory Capture
	No enforcement	Outcome 3 Resistance	Outcome 4 Stasis

[1] Nonetheless, we do not distinguish at this point between firms that can or cannot increase their value-added production even if they have met the basic international standards.

domestically. This is akin to Mattli and Woods's (2009) "common interest regulation." It is usually reserved for integration attempts involving advanced countries with robust domestic institutions, such as among advanced countries in the EU. Examples in our chapters that appear to be reaching this outcome include the cases of Polish dairy farmers implementing new food safety standards and East-Central European countries meeting new environmental regulations. In both cases, the countries have been able to monitor and enforce the rules and help many firms in implementing the new standards.

Outcome 2 is "transnational regulatory capture" and often occurs when a dominating external actor succeeds in imposing transnational rules that imply, from the perspective of developing countries, a highly asymmetrical distribution of the costs and gains of regulatory change (Mattli and Woods 2009: ch. 1). Here the country adopts and enforces the new international rules, but only relatively few firms can actually implement them. In turn, few firms can partake in the economic benefits of the more sophisticated markets or few stakeholder groups can benefit from a rule that would potentially improve their working or environmental conditions. For instance, chapters in this volume and work by Dunn (2003) show how the imposition of new food safety standards in East-Central Europe via the EU and in Mexico via NAFTA creates significant entry barriers that large firms can overcome but small and medium size producers often cannot.

In Outcomes 3 and 4, attempts at creating a common set of enforced rules across the relevant countries have failed, and regulatory fragmentation is more likely to emerge. These outcomes differ from one another in terms of whether a broad or a narrow set of domestic actors benefits from the failure to bring about common transnational rules.

Outcome 3 can be called "resistance" when the rules are not adopted but there remains a preservation of benefits to a broad constituency. We find this when diverse domestic actors who might lose benefits from rule enforcement rally the state and society to block the new transnational rules. This outcome can limit regional or global regulatory integration but prevents losses to key actors in targeted countries. The case of the Multilateral Agreement on Investment is a classic example of joint action by a transnational coalition of civil society organizations and governments from the global South preventing a harmful transnational regulation initiated from the global North (Cohn 2007; Neumayer 1999).

Outcome 4 can be called "low equilibrium stasis," when transnational rules are not adopted and the skewed distribution of benefits in the relevant domain remains. This results in the preservation of the status quo with little integration of standards and limited advances in changing domestic institutions (Duina 2006). These are cases for lost opportunities to benefit from positive externalities of regulatory integration.

Outcomes 3 and 4 are arguably the most common in the global South, especially in South–South arrangements. The resistance to international rules can often begin as appearing to fit in Outcome 3, protecting local producers and groups from rules that would create immediate large disadvantages for their survival or that would remove local traditions. For instance, as we will see in chapters on the MERCOSUR, domestic resistance to enforcing new international standards in such industries as automotive and agriculture can allow local actors time to adapt. Jordana and Levi-Faur (2005) have also shown how domestic interests in Latin America thwart regulatory models promulgated by European and US MNCs. But in both instances, it is less clear whether the distribution of benefits might expand. Some private actors may be strong enough to initiate cross-border regional standards in particular industries or sectors, like in automotive, dairy, and grains. These standards could help expand the number of suppliers and beneficiaries. But often it can lead to those few private actors controlling entry to domestic or cross-border markets, which would be closer to Outcome 4. Duina (2006) has described how the MERCOSUR has attempted to create and implement transnational standards in many areas of trade and social policy on paper, but failed to translate them into national laws or practices on the ground. In their respective work on Latin America and Asia, Locke (2013) and Bartley (2010, 2011) have shown how transnational networks of NGOs and MNCs have had limited success in filling this void with private regulatory models and codes of conduct, especially for the potential benefit of relevant stakeholder groups.

Failed attempts at formal regulatory integration do not necessarily mean that integration is completely blocked or reversed. Rather, well organized or resource-strong non-state actors often attempt to create new transnational standards with or without the assistance of governments. Several chapters in this volume, especially those on the MERCOSUR and on the telecommunications and financial sectors, reveal coalitions of large domestic firms and MNCs promoting a variety of private standards and regulatory models. This sphere of ambiguity often results in regulatory fragmentation and severe implementation problems for relevant public and private actors. In many ways, this is similar to what scholars studying the advanced world have called "regime complexity": a proliferation of regulatory schemes operating in the same policy domain, supported by different combinations of public and private actors, including states, international organizations, businesses, and NGOs (Keohane and Victors 2011; Overdevest and Zeitlin in this volume).

The four ideal-types are used in this volume to better locate cases which at a specific point in time might be navigating between two outcomes or stuck in a sphere of fragmentation. They force one to consider the factors responsible for such divergence in outcomes and the strategies that could lead them towards more stable and encompassing regulatory integration with broad-based benefits. For instance, why do countries with similar levels of economic and institutional development vary in terms of their formal incorporation of transnational standards and their distribution of benefits? How might one country or region shift from one outcome to another? We now critically review how different analytical approaches address these concerns.

1.3 Explaining Outcomes: Domestic Agency and Transnational Public Power—The Static Approach

The literature on transnational regulatory integration seeks to explain regulatory outcomes in two main ways. The static approaches focus on pre-existing institutional endowments to identify factors that could help or hinder private and public actors with conflicting beliefs and interests to advance their own version of regulatory change. The dynamic approaches help explain why initial regulatory outcomes may not be stable and might lead to a renovation of the original institutional endowments. Also, the latter approaches offer criteria to evaluate the various strategies in terms of their abilities to move outcomes toward more encompassing regulatory settlements with better distribution of benefits. We combine and somewhat modify these two approaches to build our own analytical framework. Our static approach considers diverse starting conditions that could define the most likely initial outcomes of regulatory integration attempts, as well as the strategic dilemmas of regulatory change in dramatically different local and transnational contexts. We modify both the static and dynamic approaches in order to consider the more specific problems of less developed countries.

Static approaches mainly seek to explain why one regulatory regime or set of standards wins out over another and why then certain national governments might conform or integrate these rules into domestic institutions. They often portray the emergence of transnational regulation as a distributional game among national governments, key dominant firms, and occasionally international NGOs (Mattli and Woods 2009; Büthe and Mattli 2011; Simmons 2001; Drezner 2007). The outcomes depend in part on the employment and organization of financial and political resources that certain groups, most often MNCs, can use to influence governments and international organizations. Hence, a common argument is that transnational regulations usually reflect the preferences of the larger MNCs and the strongest public actors, such as the US or EU (Drezner 2007; Simmons 2001). An alternative is that the determinism of hegemons is mediated by a combination of domestic and transnational institutional factors (Büthe and Mattli 2011; Mattli and Woods 2009). To the extent that the forums for transnational rule making allow for transparency and the participation of a diversity of actors, then the rules can reflect a more balanced distribution of costs and benefits, even for weaker countries. But these effects also depend on the strength of domestic demand—the degree to which a broad set of relevant public and private actors has adequate knowledge and material resources.

As much as these works push us to consider domestic and transnational institutional conditions, their focus on largely successful transnational regulatory agreements among advanced countries creates explanatory problems when considering emerging market countries. For instance, as suggested in the previous section, to the extent that the growth of transnational standards penetrates less developed countries, they have limited reach and often lead to market fragmentation. Moreover, domestic implementation varies, with governments either blocking or being incapable of enacting new rules, while non-state actors initiate their own standards.

These difficulties point to two problems in specifying the structural conditions for emerging market countries when they engage in transnational regulatory integration. One problem is a mis-specification of the domestic institutional conditions. The vast majority of the research tends to focus on the integration games or processes among advanced industrial nations and their respective firms and NGOs. Differences among countries in institutional capacities, if they are mentioned, are used to account for the range of interests that will be taken into account in accepted and implemented transnational rules and not whether and to what extent a common rule could come about in the first place. It tends to overlook that developing countries often lack institutional capacities needed for the definition and implementation of rules, while diverse state and non-state actors lack the organizational capacities to promote and access certain information and ideas (Abbott and Snidal 2010). Many of these countries do not have the resources and capacities to capitalize on the opportunities of regulatory integration, let alone monitor and manage the developmental effects of the attendant rules (Stiglitz and Charlton 2006; Ismail 2007).

A second problem is that much of this literature tends to overlook the fact that many developing countries are either already integrated or are in the process of integrating themselves into *regional, public* multidimensional regimes. These regional Transnational Integration Regimes (TIRs), such as NAFTA, CAFTA, MERCOSUR, and the EU accession and neighborhood agreements, have their own mediating affects on transnational rule creation and adoption regardless of the specific industry domain (Bruszt and McDermott 2012; Bruszt and Greskovits 2010). Countries with similar domestic starting conditions but embedded in different TIRs might vary in the ways they link transnational rules from one domain to another or link rule implementation with the recognition of claims from different actors.

In sum, in order to account for the variation in initial integration outcomes, one must consider the variation of both the domestic institutional conditions across countries and the variety of transnational integration regimes across regions.

1.3.1 *An Alternative Framework: The Static Stage*

We develop the static part of our framework to account for probable initial outcomes, by specifying two dimensions that account for domestic and transnational institutional conditions. The first dimension considers the relative strength of *domestic agency* in emerging market countries. Domestic agency here refers to the capacities of domestic actors to define, implement, and enforce transnational rules. Relatively strong domestic agency allows domestic actors to adjust transnational rules to domestic needs, and/or adjust domestic institutions to the requirements of transnational rules, cope with the attendant negative developmental externalities, and broaden the range of local actors that could benefit. The strengths and weaknesses of private and public actors are strongly interlinked in shaping domestic development agency in most of the cases. Relatively weak public capacities can result in an inability to enforce new rules, to anticipate or mitigate their potential negative developmental consequences, and to support a variety of non-state actors' capabilities to implement them. On the other hand, many non-state groups might lack the organizational capacities to promote different claims and regulatory models, while a few resource-rich, entrenched actors might have the capacities to advance their own private standards. While the capacities of private and public actors do not always correlate, for the sake of simplicity here, we treat them as interlinked aspects of domestic agency.

Our second dimension considers *regional institutional capacities* to create and sanction binding rules as well as solve the attendant collective action problems in various local contexts. Regional TIRs vary in the degree to which they are based on significant political and economic power asymmetries (e.g. a hegemon) or based on more balanced, if not fragmented power structures that allow greater room for member vetoes and self-protection. Transnational hierarchies might be better able to define and impose rules and ensure compliance via side payments (Abbot and Snidal 2009; Kahler and Lake 2009; Suwa-Eisenmann and Verdier 2007). Mere imposition of the rules, however, rarely creates lasting regulatory institutions. Rather, TIRs may be more or less capable at assisting domestic actors in improving their institutions to enable compliance and manage the attendant negative externalities of the new rules (Orenstein et al. 2008; Schimmelfennig and Sedelmeier 2005; Tallberg 2002;

Bruszt and McDermott 2012). Similar to Mann's "infrastructural power," this capacity allows the actors in transnational regimes to combine their resources and provide centrally organized services or regional public goods (Mann 1984).

We depict our framework in simplified form in Figure 1.1. Each axis is viewed as a continuum, and the combinations of the supranational and domestic institutional characteristics allow us to identify ideal-type outcomes and stages of regional regulatory integration. The vertical Y-axis is a continuum describing the relative strength of public and private capacities for *domestic agency* in a country. Moving from low to high implies that the country is increasing its capacities to monitor and enforce the new regulations as well as the capacities to ensure that a relatively broad set of stakeholder groups can participate in and benefit from the implementation of the new regulations.

The horizontal X-axis is a continuum describing the variation in *regional institutional capacities*. On the right side, one finds relatively loose institutional arrangements among countries where there are no strong power asymmetries between the participating actors who have relatively weak regulatory implementation capacities. Moving from the right to the left we find not only the increased importance of a regional hegemon, vis-à-vis the emerging market country, for imposing common regional rules but also an increase in the capacities of the TIR to resolve related collective action problems in adjusting the rules to local contexts. This also implies that regulatory integration increases in complexity. Toward the right side, transnational settlements result in common rules solely at the level of specific sectors or policy areas. Toward the left side, regional arrangements are able to integrate national economies that might have prior conflicting regulatory systems.

Hence, toward the left side of the figure, one finds the world of regional TIRs with hegemons, but with different transnational public capacities. The EU stands out not just as the largest but also as the one with significant capacities for regulatory convergence and empowering institutional change in the post-communist countries of East-Central Europe. NAFTA and CAFTA also have hegemonic structures but with limited integration capacities. The emerging TIRs in Latin America, East Asia, and Africa would be found toward the right side, as they lack a capable hegemon and the capacity to coordinate and/or impose regional regulatory norms. In this world, TIRs are less coherent and have limited ability to mediate the seemingly more dominant industry- or issue-specific transnational private regulatory networks, often known as Transnational Regulatory Regimes (TRRs) (Jordana and Levi-Faur 2005).

Combining the two dimensions yield several dramatically different institutional contexts to attempts at regulatory integration. While not being

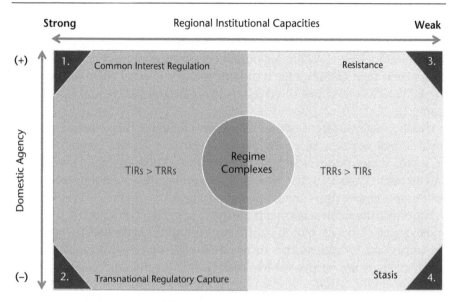

Strong   Regional Institutional Capacities   Weak

(+)

Domestic Agency

1. Common Interest Regulation

Resistance 3.

Regime Complexes

TIRs > TRRs

TRRs > TIRs

(−)

2. Transnational Regulatory Capture

Stasis 4.

Figure 1.1 Domestic and supranational dimensions of regulatory integration attempts

deterministic, they greatly delimit the space in which firms, NGOs, and governments can strategize to conserve or change the regulatory status quo. In the four corners of the Figure 1.1 we find the four ideal-typical outcomes discussed in section 1.1. In the upper left corner, we find Outcome 1, "common interest regulation," which emerges from the combination of relatively strong domestic public and private capacities for domestic agency with a TIR that has strong public capacities. A typical example for that could be the integration of Northern European countries into the EU. The more advanced stages of the integration of some of the most developed East-Central European countries are moving to this outcome as well.

Outcome 2, "transnational regulatory capture," is in the bottom left corner and is a combination of weak domestic agency with a strong regional hegemon with limited capacities to produce regional public goods. The initial stages of the regulatory integration of East-Central Europe and the integration of Mexico into NAFTA are cases that are the closest to this corner.

In the upper right corner, we have Outcome 3, "resistance." The combination of relatively strong domestic agency and the absence of a regional hegemon provides for a context in which domestic actors might have the capacity to block the imposition of non-beneficial rules, but lack the transnational institutional environment that could help them advance coherent attempts in regional rule harmonization. It is more likely that transnational coordination is limited to attempts at relatively narrow regulatory integration at the level of well-organized sectors. In the MERCOSUR, the auto sector and parts of the agriculture industry are attempting to move in this direction, whereby a limited number of strong domestic firms and MNCs create their own cross-border standards and try to have them validated at the MERCOSUR level (see the chapters by Costa and Jacoby, and Delich and Lengyel).

Finally, the lower right corner represents Outcome 4, the least congenial institutional context for regulatory integration, with the combination of very weak domestic developmental agency and a TIR with fragmented power and no public capacities. In this setting, the probability of even the initiation of attempts at regulatory integration is very low.

The only truly stable settlements are in the upper left corner where domestic and external actors have both the incentives and the capacities to reproduce the status quo. Outside of this corner we find diverse institutional contexts in which there are significant weaknesses in institutional capacities and/or developmental outcomes. In turn, key groups might have strong incentives and opportunities to alter the parameters of their context and employ strategies that can move outcomes away from an unstable equilibrium. We will discuss these conditions and strategies in the next section.

Figure 1.2 provides a sampling of our cases in a variety of intermediate spaces, including indications of paths of movement between outcomes. On the left side, TIRs have relatively stronger impacts on rule-taking countries than TRRs. The TIRs provide the key architecture for transnational private and

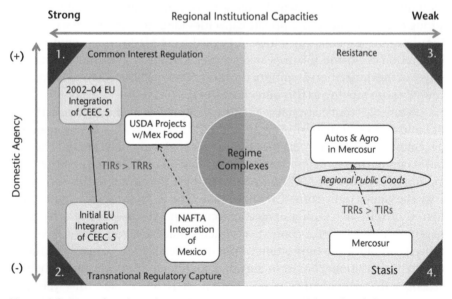

Figure 1.2 Examples of regulatory integration attempts with paths of change

public actors to alter domestic socio-economic and institutional conditions in *rule-taking countries* and potentially move these countries upward. Examples could be the complex institution-building programs of the EU in the Eastern and Central European countries applying for EU membership, or in a much more limited way, the various developmental programs in Mexico and Central America described in several chapters in this volume (Bruszt and McDermott 2012; and see the chapters by Spendzharova and Vachudova, Andonova and Tuta, Bruszt and Langbein, McDermott and Avendaño, Schrank and Piore).

In the space between the lower and upper right corners, there are no regional TIRs that could help public and private actors to solve complex problems of coordination (see the chapter of Jordana and Levi-Faur and, as a contrast, the chapter by Andonova and Tuta). Attempts at regulatory harmonization might have only a weakly defined territorial dimension and are more sector- or domain-based, allowing TRRs to multiply and fragment markets. For instance, the chapters by Jordana and Levi-Faur, Costa and Jacoby and Lengyel and Delich provide examples of the attempts at regulatory integration by industry-based networks, like telecoms in Latin America, and autos and agriculture in the MERCOSUR. Possibilities for broader regulatory harmonization and improved domestic agency more often than not come from institutional bootstrapping strategies initiated by transnational networks of regulators, business associations, MNCs, NGOs, and governments. Although there are not many, typical examples are regional public goods programs supported by the Inter-American Development Bank that focus on creating new regional systems of infrastructure and standards while improving the relevant domestic capacities (Estevadeordal et al. 2004).

Finally, the large space in the middle of the figure is where we find the highest degree of regulatory fragmentation of transnational markets, or "regime complexes," the proliferation of regulatory schemes operating in the same policy domain, supported by varying combinations of public and private actors, including states, international organizations, businesses, and NGOs. While many have described this space as one of the most difficult for the initiation of coherent regulatory integration, the chapters by Overdevest and Zeitlin and Pistor explain how this very regulatory uncertainty can give rise to patterns of experimental governance that can induce pathways toward settlements linking regulatory harmonization with domestic developmental agency.

1.4 Assembling Transnational Markets: Integration Strategies and Domestic Developmental Agency

In this section, we analyze how different integration strategies can improve domestic development agency and, in turn, provide the basis for more encompassing and sustainable transnational regulatory arrangements. We argue that moving towards regulatory arrangements that can integrate transnational markets implies a search for ways to upgrade domestic agency in developing countries with the goal to increase domestically the potential benefits of incorporating transnational rules while decreasing their potential negative consequences. The more complex domestic institutional problems are, the greater will be the need to assist domestic institutional change via external intervention.The latter, the external governance of domestic institutional change, requires transnational institutional capacities that in most of the cases are not at hand. Assembling transnational markets via common rules thus has the dilemma of how to upgrade domestic institutions and create simultaneously transnational capacities to govern domestic change successfully.

As discussed in the previous section, with the exception of the upper left corner of Figure 1.2, several of the actors participating in or affected by regulatory integration might have limited incentives to stick to the status quo and might have strong incentives to search for solutions that could yield more encompassing regulations with a better distribution of its gains. Such expectations about change are increasingly commonplace in the literature on integration. For instance, the institutional parameters that have shaped initial outcomes might change: balance of power or the way actors define their interests might change, dominating actors might see their net gains increase if they depart from the status quo (Keohane and Victor 2011). More powerful actors in transnational rule making might learn that they cannot "externalize" the costs of regulatory harmonization and might lose potential gains if they do not invest in increasing the capacities of weaker actors to implement and/or to gain from regulatory integration. Similarly, neo-functionalists have called attention to the various ways in which prior rounds of transnational regulations might "spill over" to other policy fields, mobilizing resistance and bringing in new actors to contest previous settlements (Haas 1958; Niemann and Schmitter 2009). Constructivists have also shown how transnational networks and communities of private actors or public regulators might help actors to learn about alternative ways to settle regulatory conflicts; they might offer forums for deliberations that could lead to the reframing of the goals of regulatory change and redefine the preferences of the participating actors (Djelic and Quack 2010).

While these schools of thought emphasize different sources of instability to integration attempts, they also increasingly stress that these very breakdowns or uncertainties can give rise to increased recognition by the relevant actors of their interdependencies (Sabel and Zeitlin 2010). Actors from countries at different levels of development might learn either as a result of lasting conflicts or via deliberations that uncoordinated actions might have outcomes that are inferior to solutions that are based on collaborative exploration of opportunities to create common transnational rules. The closer they get to recognizing their interdependence, the more likely the creation of the common rules becomes linked to the coordination problems of producing common goods in transnational arenas, more specifically, common regulations with broad-based distribution of benefits (Keohane and Ostrom 1995; see also the chapter by Overdevest and Zeitlin in this volume).

We have argued that significant structural factors might constrain attempts at solving such coordination problems—capacity and resource limitations that impede key public and private actors in developing countries from accessing vital information, mobilizing around alternative ideas, or implementing and enforcing new regulations. Altering these structural constraints is at least as important as changing beliefs, principles of learning, or processes of altering interests and time horizons—factors cited by the mentioned literature dealing with transnational coordination problems.

In earlier works, we suggested studying such structural constraints in developing countries by differentiating between problems linked to the demand and supply sides of building domestic institutions that could help developing countries to benefit from regulatory integration attempts (Bruszt and McDermott 2012). On the demand side, public and private actors that might have an interest in new institutional capacities and might be potential beneficiaries of regulatory change often lack the resources and channels to gain the sustained attention of the state. Entrenched groups maintain the status quo not only because they profit from it but also because there are no encompassing structures to facilitate horizontal ties to weaker groups, which can open new possibilities for experimentation and create win-win solutions (Schneider 2004; Tendler 1997).

On the supply side, states often lack the capacity needed for coordinating institutional upgrading, while many non-state actors lack the material and knowledge resources to undertake their own initiatives (McDermott 2007). Adaptation and enforcement of transnational rules in local contexts, as well as enabling local actors to benefit from these rules, need specific state capacities. But many states in developing countries do not have the requisite skills, knowledge, or resources, and have no capacity to coordinate diverse stakeholder groups who together have complementary resources and information. At the same time, the benefits of this coordination can be sacrificed if the groups lack the power and processes with which to contest one another's claims or models (Evans 2004; McDermott 2007; Tendler 1997).

Notice that framing blockage to both institutional change and regulatory integration in these terms, rather, say than reference to purely state capture or culture, highlights a few core dilemmas in the governance of institutional change for an external actor—be it an MNC, a multilateral agency, or a regional hegemon. One is that, without dedicated empowerment of different key public and private (often weaker) actors, the benefits and sustainability will be limited. Another is that the variety of combinations of the specific demand and supply side constraints in countries at different levels of development limit a universal solution or design while demanding a flow of information to external actors to adapt their approaches and coordinating efforts to specific contexts. Domestic configurations of power can frustrate, amplify, or distort the application of transnational regulatory standards in particular places, might conflict with them, and might thus result either in rejection, partial fulfillments, or some form of local conversion or hybridization (Bartley 2010, 2011). These concerns are echoed in recent critiques of externally induced institutional change, be they in the form of aid packages, imposed market reforms, or private regulations from MNCs and NGOs. On the one hand, an emphasis on universal solutions prevents external actors from developing capacities to track why certain models fail or succeed and what adjustments can be made (Easterly 2006; Evans 2004). On the other hand, seeing regulatory integration solely as a function of positive and negative incentives overlooks the need to empower diverse stakeholder groups to search for solutions that combine implementation with expanded benefits (Locke 2013).

Assembling transnational markets via common rules must account for these dilemmas and more often than not it presupposes change in the capacities of transnational actors who want to further domestic institutional change. This latter point may not be directly obvious, as it goes beyond simply the overt power and incentive packages usually provided by the external actors. For instance, as we have discussed, even if a TIR has the capacity to impose externally invented solutions, it might have weak capacities to detect why certain solutions worked or not and how it could coordinate, assist, and monitor institutional change in a variety of local contexts.

To summarize, we have identified key governance dilemmas of domestic institutional change that involve external actors. There are no universal recipes for the right way to adjust the requirements of furthering common transnational rules with the need for institutional upgrading in diverse local contexts.. Information on what could work is dispersed and in many cases it can only be collected by the empowering of local actors. Potential problems of implementation are not known ex ante. Transnational actors might have weak capacities to coordinate, assist, and monitor institutional change. To this list we can add a final one: regulatory norms across regulatory domains are interlinked and the more narrow regulatory integration attempts are the more likely will they yield resistance by stakeholders in other regulatory fields. Altering regulation of competition or state aid, for example, might have effects on other regulatory domains like environment or labor standards. Bundling efforts of regulatory change in diverse domains, therefore, might help to increase their sustainability.

Based on this characterization of the governance dilemmas, we will outline the main components of integration strategies highlighting their specific goals and means and the way they can facilitate or impede (1) changes in domestic developmental agency and (2) the capacity of transnational actors to govern domestic institutional change.

1.4.1 *The Goals and Means of Integration Strategies*

We can contrast the various strategies based on *two components of their goals and two components of their means*. The former are the scope and depth of the goals of institutional change. The latter are whether monitoring and assistance are dyadic or multiplex and the degree to which they are based on principles of checklist compliance or joint problem-solving. Figure 1.2 portrays the different paths and mixes of these components found in our cases.

Scope refers to the different policy domains in which the attempts at regulatory integration require institutional changes from participating countries. This can be rather narrow, focusing on a few economic trade rules, or quite extensive, reaching into social and political domains. But even if the scope is narrow, it is likely that the changes will have spillover effects into other domains and upon a variety of stakeholder groups (Haas 1958; Niemann and Schmitter 2009). Goals that have relatively broad scope affecting related domains and organize negotiations around a bundle of policies can potentially incorporate these groups at inception, offering them opportunities to shape and "own" reforms that can account for the constraints they face due to regulatory integration (Hoekman 2013).

Depth refers to the emphasis placed on building different types of domestic capacities. Most often the goals are shallow, with simply an emphasis on changes in rules. Relatively greater depth means improving the capacities to enforce and monitor new regulations (Schimmelfennig and Sedelmeier 2005; Stiglitz and Charlton 2006) and to enable a broad variety of stakeholder groups to benefit from these changes. Relatively shallow goals assume that rules changes will trigger incentives for further domestic changes; relatively deeper goals target implementation with a focus on institutional change that could allow for decreasing negative and increasing positive externalities of regulatory integration.

The *means of integration* are assistance (i.e. resources) in helping the target country meet the designated goal and monitoring the degree to which the country meets the goals. These means vary not simply in size or quantity but especially according to two qualitative components: the structure of transnational horizontal relationships and the nature of information feedback loops.

The first component is the degree to which the interactions between relevant external and domestic actors can be *dyadic*, involving solely two institutional actors (eg, state to state), or *multiplex*, including a variety of public and private actors to create ongoing professional relationships (Padgett and Ansell 1993). Some integration strategies that promote mainly dyadic relationships assume that general economic and political incentives will foster transnational relationships between peer groups or actors. In contrast, other integration strategies purposively support multiplexity by using legal triggers and resources to foster transnational relationships among a variety of groups relevant to the domain, such as NGOs, associations, firms, and subnational governments. Promoting multiplexity offers the external actors a greater variety of information and experiments related to domestic changes, while many domestic actors are empowered via new alliances, resources, and knowledge (Andonova 2004; Jacoby 2004; Tallberg 2002). For both sides, if the transnational horizontal linkages have relatively greater multiplexity, then it is less likely that there would be single gatekeeper in the developing country controlling resources, contacts, and information about the given policy domain.

The second component of the means is the *relative emphasis on checklist compliance or joint problem-solving,* denoting the ways in which the relevant external and domestic actors share and analyze information within and across policy domains to reveal shortcomings and how to address them (Carothers 2003; Easterly 2006; Sabel and Zeitlin 2008). Feedback via checklist compliance means that information is used simply to determine whether a country meets the designated goal, but not much else. This assumes that such revelations would give incentives to the relevant domestic actors to take corrective action. Feedback via joint problem-solving principles emphasizes the need for relevant external and domestic actors to evaluate shortcomings with the aim of generating alternative solutions to be followed. Even if assistance and monitoring criteria are non-negotiable and inflexible, repeated information about why the country is falling short in one domain can force deliberations in several directions, such as revising the sequencing of steps within the domain, altering the type of assistance being delivered, or targeting resources toward particular groups better suited to undertake the given reform (Jacoby 2004; Vachudova 2005). When multiplexity and joint problem-solving are combined, they can greatly improve accountability and the legitimacy among all parties as they become part of a "community of practice" that instills ownership and adherence to common norms (Bartley and Smith 2010).

The combination of these goals and means helps one compare and contrast transnational integration strategies and evaluate their resulting paths of change, such as those presented in Figure 1.2. The case studies in this volume demonstrate this in two important ways. First, movement up and to the left in Figure 1.2 comes in the context of integration strategies that place relatively strong emphasis on broad-based capacity-building in their goals and on multiplexity and joint problem-solving. In contrast, the weaker outcomes appear to remain when integration strategies emphasize goals that are narrow and shallow, along with means that stress dyadic ties and checklist compliance principles. Second, integration strategies often vary in their combinations of components, and pilot projects can lead to broader changes in regulatory regimes. The cases of integration taking place outside of EU accession show great variation in their strategies and their paths of changes. We find that many attempts at moving away from the status quo and upwards on the right side of Figure 1.2 are initiated by non-state actors of a particular industry or domain with rather narrow goals, but make progress by emphasizing capacity-building and joint problem-solving. Such results and those from NAFTA and CAFTA (on the right-hand side) also suggest how key public and private actors in different domains are discovering more or less optimal combinations of goals and means, and in turn, are confronted with promoting significant further experiments in the governance of TIRs and TRRs.

1.4.2 Statics and Dynamics in Regional TIRs with Rule Takers and Hegemons

Part I of the book compares and contrasts the different approaches to regulatory integration in the most advanced TIRs, where the less developed new member countries must accept the rules and standards of the more advanced member countries. These are cases that can potentially move upward on the left-hand side of Figure 1.2. They focus on NAFTA, CAFTA, and the EU Eastern accession process and such regulatory domains as food safety, environmental protection, corruption, and labor rights. The chapters highlight how the TIRs vary in defining institutional goals, utilize horizontal professional networks, and adapt the strategies of the hegemon. These differences lead to variations in terms of regulatory capacity, the participation of non-state actors, and the upgrading of practices on the ground.

In their analysis of the impact of NAFTA on development of public and private food safety regulations in Mexico, McDermott and Avendaño argue that NAFTA has induced two parallel paths of adjustment. With NAFTA's limited emphasis on scope and depth but a stronger emphasis on dyadic and checklist compliance, the dominant path for Mexico is a weak decentralized system of regulation and dominance of large exporting firms. In the less dominant, emerging path, Mexican and US authorities have in certain instances collaborated with sectoral associations to improve both regulatory institutions and firm practices in medium-sized firms. These gains, however, depend largely on former corporatist associations, which constrain broad-based participation and institutional change. At the same time, the progress with pilot projects signals a potential shift in the integration strategies within food safety, with US agencies focusing increasingly on administrative capacities and joint problem-solving principles of evaluation in Mexico.

In contrast, the chapter by Bruszt and Langbein shows how the EU adjusted its strategies of food safety regulatory integration during the Eastern enlargement, with its greater emphasis on building elementary state capacities to regulate and develop a sector in a country where both domestic private and public actors were weak. In Poland the EU faced well-organized private actors in developmental alliance with an effective state, and EU assistance could focus on furthering an inclusive developmental strategy. In Romania, with the combination of a disorganized economic sector and an insulated weak state, the EU had to create basic elements of sectoral state organization and could address the distributive aspects of market integration to a much lesser degree, resulting in the dissociation of many domestic producers from the market in the process of integrating the sector.

Piore and Schrank analyze how Mexico and Central American countries have responded to integration in terms of fortifying labor market regulations and labor practices in the firm. NAFTA's reliance on shallow institutional goals and market incentives has constrained both regulatory and firm upgrading. But the authors also show in certain cases how greater emphasis on administrative capacities and joint problem-solving can reverse this trend. In particular, they reveal how regulatory improvements can lead to improved practices and firm performance when labor inspectorates collaborate with firm support agencies and stakeholder groups, lining deterrence with upgrading and empowerment.

Aspinwall then examines two sides of the NAFTA approach: the weakness of the reliance on market incentives, the dominant mechanism, and the potential strength of linking integration with both capacity-building and the empowerment of transnational NGO networks. On the one hand, the NAFTA side agreement on labor allowed for a re-entrenchment of the old guard. On the other hand, the side agreement on environment induced domestic investments into regulatory capacity and the expansion of the components of multiplexity and joint problem-solving, which in turn empowered non-state actors in the reform process.

The remaining chapters on EU Eastern expansion reinforce our framework and the claims of Bruszt and Langbein. The chapter by Andonova and Tuta explains how the EU utilizes transnational networks (multiplexity) to improve the capacities of relevant domestic public and private actors to enforce and implement its environmental standards. They find that the variation in environmental policy in Romania and Bulgaria, two countries with ex ante limited public and private institutional capacities, depends largely on key differences in their policy networks, namely the types of non-state actors that are empowered membership and the organizational structure.

Vachudova and Spendzharova analyze how the EU adapts its goals and means to integration so as to reply to new challenges and to compensate for weaknesses in domestic capacities to fight corruption in countries with weak judiciaries and political accountability. In Bulgaria and Romania, the EU implemented a novel monitoring instrument, called the Cooperation and Verification Mechanism (CVM) that expanded the components of scope, multiplexity, and joint problem-solving. CVM had a positive impact by giving domestic elites stronger incentives to pursue reform, especially when progress on CVM benchmarks has been linked to goods that voters in Bulgaria and Romania highly value. The EU then applied these lessons to adapt its integration approach in the new candidate countries in the Western Balkans.

1.4.3 *Emerging TIRs in the Global South: Blockage and Coordination in the MERCOSUR*

Part II analyzes the most advanced attempt at market integration after the EU and NAFTA and especially for the south–south world—the MERCOSUR. The chapters consider this TIR in comparative perspective, emphasizing not simply its well-known limitations, but especially the emerging forms of transnational coordination for creating and implementing common rules and standards. Because of its overall level of development and its structural power balance, the MERCOSUR can be viewed as a laboratory of lessons for other emerging regional TIRs in the developing world and where TRRs are relatively stronger. In particular, the chapters highlight the interaction between three forces: the discretion that public and private actors have in shaping if not blocking outright key rules; the weakness of supranational public capacities and domestic state capacity; and the skewed distribution of domestic non-state actors to participate in the rule-making process.

Costa and Jacoby compare how different public–private standards in the auto industry emerge as part of different integrations approaches in East-Central Europe and in the MERCOSUR. Their comparison reveals how TIRs can have informal spillover effects outside their formal territorial and sectoral scope. The TIRs can effectively create different impacts on TRRs, but MNCs can still gain the upper hand in defining transnational standards and paths of regional regulatory integration. In particular, the chapter outlines different strategies that the MNCs pursue to potentially improve the capacities of the TIR, even in the MERCOSUR case.

The chapter by Lengyel and Delich explores how weaknesses in the formal integration goals and means of the MERCOSUR are creating space for alternative mechanisms for the cross-border coordination and local adoption of international food safety standards. With limited capacities at the MERCOSUR and state levels, governments have difficulty reconciling the use of "inclusive" standards for local firms with more "exclusive" standards to compete in international markets. These constraints have opened three simultaneous patterns of creating transnational standards and local capabilities. First, with its growing economic and political power, Brazil has increased its ability to define regional standards. Second, large dominant firms build their own multiple and joint problem-solving linkages to define exclusive private standards. Third, local public–private alliances use joint problem-solving principles to improve the capacities of smaller firms.

1.4.4 *Fragmentation and Regime Complexity in TRRs*

The third and final part of the book provides alternative views about the more common approach to the transnationalization of markets: those focusing on the emergence of cross-border industry or domain-based rules and standards or TRRs. Although the chapters focus on very different domains (finance, environment, and telecoms), they highlight two common arguments in the book. First, they all show how emerging market countries confront competing models of regulation, with conflicting forms of governance and distributional effects on the ground. Second, they also highlight alternative combinations of the aforementioned components of regulatory integration that can impede or facilitate domestic capacity-building, broad-based adoption of international standards, and the empowerment of a variety of local state and non-state actors.

Overdevest and Zeitlin explain how novel transnational regulatory governance mechanisms can further adoption and enforcement of international standards in highly complex regulatory environments. They show that an increasingly comprehensive transnational regime can be assembled by strategies that accommodate local diversity and foster recursive learning from decentralized implementation experience even in situations where interests diverge and no hegemon can impose its own will. Based on the design principles of experimentalist governance, they identify a variety of pathways and mechanisms that promote productive interactions in regime complexes. Although there is no hegemon, adaptive transnational integration and local capacity-building can emerge when there is greater emphasis on multiplexity, symmetry, and joint problem-solving.

The chapter by Jordana and Levi-Faur analyses how competing TRRs in telecommunications impact regulatory integration in Latin America and the reform of sectoral regulation domestically. This is a world where there are only fledgling TIRs. These TIRs have weak capacity to help transnational networks to solve their coordination problems. Unlike within the EU, TIRs in Latin America have extremely limited capacity to frame and assist attempts of transnational regulatory networks at furthering regulatory integration (see the chapter by Andonova and Tuta for a contrasting case). The authors suggest that Latin American networks in telecommunications reflect the institutional weaknesses of the region and remain exposed to particular forms of dependent governance. While institutions within the region and outside it often support and nurture them, they are alive and contribute to an intense exchange of information and policy experiences within the countries in the region.

Lastly, Pistor argues that three distinct TRRs are emerging in the world of finance, with special attention to the potential resolution of the euro crisis. The contending "governance regimes" combine both public and private actors, but differ greatly in their mechanisms of problem-solving and coordination, impacts on domestic capacity-building, and normative understanding of markets and regulation. The chapter identifies three types of governance regimes that have been tried and tested in the past or are up for testing now: a laissez-faire regime, a *coordinative*, and a *centralized* regime. Each of these regimes relies on distinct combinations of goals and means.

1.5 Concluding Remarks

If the recent global financial crisis has taught us anything, it is that the transnationalization of markets is fraught with fragility, which makes domestic institutional development that much more contingent on the interaction between local and foreign approaches to regulatory integration. In opening their economies to accelerate growth and upgrade their capabilities, societies of the developing world have known this all too well. The framework presented here and the chapters in this book strive to define the contours of this contingency by linking the approaches to transnational regulatory integration with the domestic process of institution-building in emerging market countries. They show how these countries face different types of political constraints due to both domestic variation in institutional capacities and the supranational regimes in which they find themselves increasingly embedded. But these factors are not static or immutable. As our framework suggests, the chapters also explain how different combinations of the goals and means of TIRs and TRRs can reify or reshape the constraints and opportunities that domestic and external actors face as they forge distinct paths of transnational regulatory integration and domestic regulatory renovation.

In combining advances in comparative and international political economy, the approach advanced in this book makes two basic claims. First, sustained regulatory integration depends in large part on the capacities of domestic public and private actors to incorporate, adapt, and implement international rules and standards at the formal regulatory level and at the firm or organizational level in a broad-based manner. The process of capacity-building, however, can take different paths and cannot be read off a generic template and thus induced by arm's length incentives or a largess of foreign resources. Rather, it is a process of contestation and experimentation, in which public and private actors often recombine resources to experiment with new formal and informal regulatory models and challenge one another's claims about the attendant costs, benefits, and legitimacy. Hence, the second argument advanced here is that the variation in the goals and means of intersecting integration approaches can empower different public and private actors on the ground, in turn shaping the process of contestation and experimentation at the local and regional levels. Rather than separating the external from the internal or the public from the private in tracking regulatory integration, the chapters here suggest that scholars and policy-makers pay closer attention to the ways in which assistance and monitoring in integration approaches can stimulate or impede horizontal linkages, accountability, and problem-solving among a broader set of local and outside actors.

The arguments advanced in this book naturally have their limits. Any interactive framework has difficulty clarifying the causality of political and strategic choices of the relevant public and private actors as well as specifying the sequencing of choices that can lead to a particular outcome of institutional upgrading and regulatory integration.

Nonetheless, our framework and cases should provide a basis to compare integration approaches and their outcomes. While not all encompassing, the chapters in this book do examine the core issues at the intersection of transnational and domestic regulatory change in emerging market countries. Moreover, by analyzing these issues across and within industries, domains, and regions that are some of the more relevant to these types of countries and that have made some of the most concerted efforts in transnational integration, the chapters highlight how certain integration strategies can impede or facilitate regulatory change for the few or the many, and thus can be applied to other contexts. At the same time, the comparative nature of this book and our framework should open debate about which types of mechanisms of integration can stimulate broad-based cross-border, coordinated experiments in regulatory institutions and adoption of new standards. If anything, the chapters here should compel scholars to examine more closely how more or less hierarchical approaches to regulatory integration combine distinct goals and means and in turn empower or constrain the relevant state and non-state actors to contest one another's institutional experiments on the ground.

Part I
Statics and Dynamics in Regional TIRS with Rule Takers and Hegemons

2

The Dual Paths of Transnational Integration and Institutional Upgrading for Mexican Food Safety

Gerald A. McDermott and Belem Avendaño Ruiz

2.1 Introduction

This chapter analyzes the conditions under which internal and external forces facilitate or impede the broad-based upgrading of regulatory institutions and firm practices in food safety in Mexican fresh produce over the past twenty years. Following the discussion and framework laid out in the introductory chapter of this volume, this case in particular highlights the interactive roles of two key transnational forces shaping the incentives and capabilities of domestic public and private actors. First, as a member of NAFTA, Mexico is effectively a rule-taker. In order to gain access to a vast North American market and reap the benefits of foreign investment, Mexico has to comply with the rules presented by the regional hegemon, namely the United States (Abbott 2000; Duina 2006). This has been particularly the case for Mexican fresh produce exports, which must adhere with the regulations of the US to gain market entry. As such, Mexico finds itself in a TIR, in which the regional hegemon has the capacities to enforce its transnational rules, but does not appear to have the public capacities to deepen transnational integration—to shape directly the expansion of food safety regulation and its benefits to a broad set of relevant public and private actors. Second, food safety is a leading case for the diffusion of transnational private regulation (Henson and Humphrey 2009; Henson and Reardon 2005; Lee et al. 2012). Because of the dependence of lesser developed countries on agricultural exports, the rise of cross-border food value chains, and the expansion of international supermarkets into emerging markets, foreign and domestic actors have significant economic incentives and the resources to compel domestic producer-suppliers to implement international practices and thus adhere to newly imported product standards.

In many ways Mexico could be viewed as an ideal case for the forces of transnational market integration leading to robust and broad-based regulatory integration at both the institutional and firm levels. The combination of NAFTA rules, the country's reliance on agricultural exports to the US, especially in produce, and the penetration of international buyers into the sector gives producers and regulators alike strong incentives to upgrade their capabilities. Nonetheless, similar to trends in many other domains across Mexico, upgrading at the two levels has not been broad-based (Lederman et al. 2005). Rather, we see two paths of adaptation emerging. In the dominant path, Mexico has changed its laws and developed supply chains for exports and modern domestic supermarkets, yet implementation on the ground has been confined to a limited set of firms with domestic regulatory spillovers at best a patchwork. In a nascent path, producer organizations are building new regulatory and assistance institutions with the collaboration of subnational governments and even certain US agencies. This latter path presents a possible shift in US policy toward transnational regulatory integration with Mexico, in that certain US agencies are increasingly engaged in joint problem-solving and capacity building with Mexican actors.

In explaining these two paths, this chapter makes two claims. First, beneficial paths of regulatory and firm upgrading do not emerge necessarily from the sudden creation of a strong state with skilled regulators or the commitment from lead firms, but rather through a recombination of institutional and organizational resources embodied in actors that regulate and assist firms. That is, similar to recent work on the diffusion of international labor standards in developing countries (Bartley 2011; Locke 2013; Piore and Schrank in this volume) and the chapter by Bruszt and Langbein (in this volume) on food safety in EU Accession countries, the creation of producer associations is critical to building the collective knowledge resources and collaborative ties that underpin government responsiveness and standards adoption. Also, similar to these works, both upgrading and collective action are constrained to the prior distribution of economic and political resources. In the case of Mexico, the federal government's reliance on the market and reluctance to invest in new comprehensive regulatory structures has made the ability of firms to organize collectively and regional politics of capacity building dependent on its corporatist legacies (Shadlen 2004; Snyder 1999). Second, the strategies of transnational integration attendant to a TIR, in this case NAFTA, can constrain or expand these learning communities. Relying on market incentives and checklist compliance mechanisms limits this process to include mainly large firms and those with strong associations. Even in the nascent path, subnational governments and US agencies are partnering with former corporatist associations. But partially because of these experiences, the US agencies are gradually shifting their mechanisms of transnational integration toward joint problem-solving and capacity building with the Mexican government, at least in food safety matters.

In turn, we argue that the learning communities needed to forge a synthesis between regulation and upgrading depend largely on the politics surrounding the creation of producer associations and the empowerment of local public agencies. Without the expansion of these institutional actors, the use of standards as tools of upgrading becomes the realm of a privileged few. This is the dominant effect of NAFTA, but recent crises in food safety have begun to open an alternative path of development.

2.2 Rule Takers and Institutional Change

When concerning emerging market countries, much of the literature on regulatory integration stresses the ways in which external political-economic incentives and asymmetric power can induce the rapid adoption of a standards or a regulatory model domestically. Whether the channels of delivery are through bilateral treaties or regional arrangements, scholars have emphasized how the combination of reputation effects and the threat of denial of material and political benefits allows elite "reformists" to insulate themselves from particularistic interests in order to implant on society a set of new governance designs (Levitsky and Way 2010; Pevehouse 2005). This view is complemented by the work on global value chains and private regulation, which argues that the international adoption of quality standards depends on the coercive and isomorphic pressures from MNCs (as global buyers or local FDI), international NGOs, or business associations, and intense trade relations with advanced countries on local firms (Lee et al. 2012; Perez-Aleman 2011).

Such pressures and models appear in the development of food safety standards and regulations that reach across national boundaries and influence both public and private actors in emerging market countries. At the supranational level, governments via international organizations like the WTO, WHO, and FAO have negotiated technical standards (like the Codex Alimentarius). These standards have two purposes: (1) to use generally agreed upon scientific standards and methods to ensure food safety of products crossing borders and (2) to ensure that national import and export regulations do not become means of discriminating against countries, while harmonizing the terms of compatible national regulations. Within this architecture, firms and governments have rapidly changed and expanded their own rules and standards to govern international food supply chains. Governments have often incorporated private standards into regulating imported food products, ranging from rules on safety and quality to guidelines on processes and traceback procedures in order to limit both biological and environmental hazards (Henson and Reardon 2005; Lee et al. 2012; Perez-Aleman 2011). For instance, the creation of NAFTA has given Mexico strong economic incentives to comply with and imitate US food safety regulations. More than 85 percent of Mexican exports of fruits and vegetables and 65 percent of meat products have relied on the US market (Cruz and Rindermann 2009). Indeed, in response to tightening of US import regulations in 1997–8, Mexico changed its food safety laws to reflect these standards.

Nonetheless, the work on transnational regulation in less developed countries reveals that reliance on arm's length incentives via mechanisms of external enforcement and MNC commitment misconstrues the institution-building process. For instance, the growing research on the role of MNCs and INGOs in promoting international labor and environmental standards in developing countries has argued that, even when we find powerful MNCs governing the supply chain, transparent monitoring information, and strong incentives to promote changes, compliance on the ground greatly varies (Bartley 2010; Locke 2013). Transnational standards and rules rarely transcend domestic institutions, but are layered upon local laws and configurations of public and private regulatory capacities and power (Bartley 2011).

This layering problem can be seen in two ways. First, both the stricter import regulations and the private standards in supply chains push the cost of adoption onto developing firms, restricting the accessibility of SMEs to more advanced markets and chains. Large established firms of developing countries tend to have more resources and stronger international professional ties that aid them with adopting new practices and technology, while small- and medium-size firms (SMEs) are often forced to exit the market or turn to local retailers with lower standards and profit margins (Cafaggi 2011; Henson and Humphrey 2009). The implementation of new standards is impeded by the relatively low skills and knowledge resources of local suppliers, a gap which can be very costly for any single firm, even an MNC, to overcome (Perez-Aleman 2011).

Second, there are also higher adjustment and coordination costs for government. As Cafaggi and Janczuk (2010) argue, the beneficial co-evolution of private and public and regulation in food safety often depends on a strong public regulatory framework at the domestic and transnational levels. But as Abbott and Snidal (2009a) note, governments from emerging market countries may well lack the capacities or interest in order to effectively participate in the supranational game let alone monitor, enforce, and implement the standards domestically.

To explain how these public and private capacity gaps might be reinforced or overcome, we link recent work on upgrading with the framework of this volume. First, recent work from economic sociology and evolutionary schools suggests that the upgrading of firm and formal regulatory capabilities emerges from combining complementary knowledge and capacities of relevant public and private actors in the given domain. The work on upgrading in global value chains (GVCs) increasingly argues that emerging market firms meet international standards through incremental experiments of adaptation with practical examples from the local context, rather than relying on institutions promoting pioneering technologies and practices (Pietrobelli and Rabellotti 2011; Perez-Aleman 2011). Similarly, the work on labor regulation stresses how labor standards tend to take hold through incremental joint problem-solving of root causes between "inspectors as teachers," managers and workers (Amengual 2010; Locke 2013). The common line is that the implementation of international standards is a process of multi-party experimentation and learning to adapt them to local conditions. Broad-based learning comes from multiple actors (local and foreign) recombining knowledge and resources through a network of complementary, previously isolated organizations, that together create collective knowledge resources and collaborative ties (McDermott 2007). Here, the adaptation of practices does not simply emerge from MNC commitment to knowledge transfer or from auditors with new skills, but rather from the existing knowledge resources of producer associations and public extension services being put to new uses (Piore and Schrank in this volume; Tendler 1997).

Second, the work on institutional layering (Thelen 2003; Bartley 2011) suggests that the contours of potential learning communities are shaped by legacies of formal government power and laws, namely how membership is defined by authorized certifications and resources. Just as foreign governments define the baseline rules and actors for determining entry into their markets, domestic governments conserve or delegate the resources and authority to different public and private actors in standards implementation. The work on Latin American political economy has stressed that economic reforms in the 1990s were often mediated by the vestiges of the corporatist system, which offered certain business associations, related firms, and subnational politicians critical institutional resources (Schneider 2004; Snyder 1999). To the extent that upgrading and regulation are localized collective actions, those who have an organizational advantage can be gate keepers for the ways in which rules are adapted and learning communities are developed.

These two factors suggest that firm and regulatory upgrading in Mexican food safety emerges from the formation of learning communities, which are constrained by both firm resources and formal institutional legacies, particularly corporatism. The question then is what types of transnational integration strategies might relieve or reinforce these constraints. The framework offered in the Introduction of this volume unpacks of the *goals and means* of TIRs that mediate the forces of global supply chains. In using this framework in the remaining sections of this chapter, we will show how NAFTA—the main TIR in which Mexico is embedded—has given birth to two paths of food safety regulatory integration. The dominant path has allowed the incentives of the US market and the regulations of the US government to spur upgrading and imitation by both Mexican firms and government agencies, but also reinforces significant domestic economic and political constraints to their broad adoption. At the same time, we find a nascent path based on organizational experiments at the subnational levels to overcome these constraints. On the one hand, these experiments are constrained because both Mexican public actors and US agencies limit their actions to partnerships with formerly corporatist sectoral associations. On the other hand, the progress gained from these experiences has led US and Mexican agencies to launch pilot projects of transnational regulatory integration based on mechanisms of joint problem-solving and capacity building rather than just check list compliance and legal changes.

2.3 NAFTA and Mexico

In terms of the *scope and depth* of its integration goals, NAFTA for Mexico is relatively narrow and shallow, but with precise rules and high levels of obligation (Abbott 2000; Duina 2006). NAFTA focuses mainly on economic and trade policy domains, with additional agreements in environmental protection and labor rights. (See also the chapters by Aspinwall and Piore and Schrank.) NAFTA emphasizes making the laws and standards of member countries compatible, so as to limit discrimination against foreign products and investors. For Mexico, compliance to the agreed upon terms of NAFTA is mandatory, and private actors aiming to take advantage of the new market opportunities must also adopt the standards set by US and Canadian actors. Although compliance is effectively ex-post for Mexico, it can be ongoing. The NAFTA commission can authorize retroactive penalties, such as fines or temporary trade restrictions, for violations in the standards. Moreover, because of the economic dominance of the United States, Mexican firms have to adapt their product standards to those of US regulatory agencies to gain market entry and their governance standards to access US capital markets. However, beyond the limited number of domains specified in NAFTA, NAFTA emphasizes as its institutional purpose the adoption by Mexico of rules and standards but not necessarily of the capacity to do so. As Abbott (2000) and Duina (2006) have argued, NAFTA's emphasis on precision and obligation, but avoidance of predefining issues in many domains and delegating many powers to the Secretariat makes NAFTA reactive to instead of preventive of institutional problems and puts a premium on the mechanism of conflict to mobilize public and private actors to identify weaknesses and seek resolution.

In being reactive, assistance and monitoring in NAFTA are ever present but their *structure is dyadic* and *feedback is largely checklist compliant*. Although the NAFTA commission is a standing body with oversight powers, it is mainly an intergovernmental forum with limited resources. In turn, in addition to turning to the multilateral agencies for assistance, Mexico has increasingly sought direct, limited assistance from relevant agencies in Canada and the US on an ad hoc basis, largely as part of intergovernmental discussions to resolve a particular trade problem. Those problems emerge from the NAFTA-level intergovernmental working groups that monitor the activities of member countries via annual reports to the Commission about their respective policy domains. The working groups meet at most twice a year, although several were suspended by 2001–3. The annual reports largely catalogue possible areas of dispute and trade discrimination, including grievances from private actors, with minimal attention to problem-solving and identification of root causes (Studer and Wise 2007). Like the EU, NAFTA strove to increase transparency, with open databases on standards and violations to stimulate accountability (Gilbreath and Ferretti 2004). The precise rules in NAFTA are not meant to predefine the harmonization of standards and regulations but trigger further change via public and private actors contesting existing regulations and resolving disputes first through bilateral consultation and then through the NAFTA commission (Duina 2006; Studer and Wise 2007). In turn, NAFTA creates incentives for governments and private groups to monitor violations, but with limited formal support for using transnational horizontal ties or acting on violations other than to penalize the offense. National governments have the main responsibilities to monitor standards and directly resolve trade violations. For Mexico, this effectively means responding directly to the demands of the Canadian and US regulators.

These characteristics of NAFTA for Mexico can be seen in incentives guiding changes in private and public food safety regulations. Article 722 defined a full set of international food standards, mimicking the principles of the GATT and the WTO, phased out many subsidies and tariffs, and established a new Committee on Sanitary and Phytosanitary Measures (SPS Committee) largely as an intergovernmental body to ensure non-discriminatory compliance with national regulatory standards for imports (Bredahl and Holleran 1997). As Caswell and Sparling (2005) emphasize, nearly all of the regulatory integration activities among the NAFTA countries on SPS standards fall into the category of "policy coordination," as the countries aim to gradually reduce differences in policy, often based on voluntary adherence to international codes of practice. The SPS Committee has a mandate to facilitate the enhancement of food safety and the improvement of SPS in member countries; the adoption of international standards and the use of equivalence agreements; technical cooperation and consultation in the development, application, and enforcement of SPS standards. But with the SPS committee meeting just once a year, including the suspension by 2003 of several key working groups, the principal intergovernmental relationships were between the USDA and FDA, as the regulators of the largest market, and their Mexican counterparts in SAGARPA (the Ministry of Agriculture) and its food safety secretariat, SENASICA (Green et al. 2006). Although NAFTA promoted the creation of the non-profit Fruit and Vegetable Dispute Resolution Corporation (DRC) in 1999, its activities focus on US–Canadian commercial disputes. Indeed, as of 2009, only 23 of the almost 1,300 member firms are from Mexico.

In turn, with the structure of its rules and Mexico's growing reliance on the US market and FDI, Article 722 would reinforce mechanisms of economic incentives and institutional isomorphism for the transmission of largely US standards and regulations into the Mexican food system. We now show how the rule changes led to reorganization of private value chains but with limited standards adoption by the vast majority of producers because of resource and organizational constraints.

2.4 The Dominant Path for Regulatory Integration via Market Actors

To comply with NAFTA and advance its own market-based reforms, the Mexican government in the 1990s, eliminated price controls, drastically reduced subsidies, privatized state agricultural companies, eliminated virtually all of the old regulatory agencies, eliminated the old corporatist rules on associations, allowed the old communal ejidos of land to be converted into private farms, and opened up trade and investment (Avendaño et al. 2006; Chavez 2009; Snyder 1999). Common to other developing countries, these reforms allowed the transmission of new standards to occur largely through private retail value chains, run mainly by MNCs—as global buyers sourcing Mexican products for the US market and as local buyers establishing new, modern supermarket chains in Mexico (Lee et al. 2012; Henson and Humphrey 2009). In both types of value chains, suppliers are required to comply with a mix of private standards and public regulations. Differentiation for local supermarkets and entry into the US market effectively has meant complying with international, namely US, food safety regulations. These require the product to be free of certain diseases, microbial and chemical contaminants, pests, etc., which in turn requires that the supplier make significant investments in new practices of quality control and transportation as well as growing and harvesting processes, such as systems of HACCP, refrigeration, storage, pest control.

The force of these avenues has been noteworthy in Mexico. In the 1990s, exports of their food products grew significantly, particularly to the US. Fruits and vegetables dominated Mexican agricultural exports, growing from about 60 percent in 1994 to over 74 percent in 2006 (FAO 2006).[1] But the legacy of highly fragmented producers with weak resources to implement international standards remains.

By 2001, MNCs controlled an estimated 75 percent of the new supermarket chains in Mexico (Chavez 2009). By 2003, four companies controlled 50 percent of the food market (Cervantes-Godoy 2007). Nonetheless, despite the growth of these retailers, they accounted in 2005 for 25–30 percent of fruit and vegetable sales. The large modern chains, such as Walmart, Costco, Gigante, Soriana, and Comercial Mexicana bypass the traditional wholesale markets, using their own distribution centers, which account for about 80 percent of their sold produce; 95 percent of this is supplied by large firms (Cervantes-Godoy et al. 2008). Most farmers sell directly or via middlemen into one of the 60 CEDAs (Central de Abasto)—wholesale markets that were trusts created with federal, state, and municipal resources in the 1980s and operated by private companies, of which about 10 percent control the vast majority of product flows. CEDAs account for about 50 percent of the produce required by large supermarkets and 95 percent by smaller chains.

The default development path for regulatory and firm upgrading in food safety confines diffusion to global buyers and MNCs requiring relatively few local suppliers to meet international standards, with limited spillovers into the domestic institutions (Lee et al. 2012). Although there are no systematic data, the most recent estimates based on surveys suggest that the effects of this path in Mexico have reinforced an industry structure of relatively few large participants and a vast majority of small unintegrated firms. Cervantes-Godoy et al. (2008) estimated that of the 4.5 million farms in Mexico in 2005, 76 percent are for subsistence, 19 percent are in transition, and only 6 percent are commercial. The FAO recently estimated that about 2 percent of fruit and vegetable farmers participate in export markets or supply chains and about 17 percent participate in both export markets and sales to big supermarket chains (FAO 2012). In a study of US imports of Mexican winter vegetables from one of the most advanced, developed border states

[1] Bilateral agricultural terms of trade would decline due mainly to a large growth in grain imports from the US (Chavez 2009).

in Mexico, Calvin and Barrios (1998) found that about three-quarters of a shipper's volume came from its largest grower, usually its own farms. Indeed, in sectors as varied as mangoes, kiwi, green onions, avocados, strawberries, melons, and other vegetables, survey and field studies have also shown that a majority of producers are still unaware of international standards or even the new national norms.[2]

Part of the reason such weak structure and diffusion standards persist concerns the economics of upgrading. The evidence to date has shown that producers, if they were to link into the supply chains for exports or for the large supermarket chains in Mexico, would have to agree under contract to upgrade their operations extensively—from installing new fixed equipment for watering, harvesting, and storage to new inputs and fertilizers to implementing Good Agricultural Practices (GAPs) and Good Management Practices (GMPs) in both the fields and packing houses to reduce microbial and pest hazards. In return the producers would receive better prices, timely payments, and potentially technical assistance. There is no doubt that many firms have responded positively to these changes. Nonetheless, three economic barriers to adoption remain.[3]

The first barrier to adaptation is cost. Avendaño and colleagues (2005, 2009, 2013) have undertaken several studies in the northern states of Mexico, where producers have been highly oriented to the US market. On average, fresh fruit and vegetable producers face a fixed cost increase of $700,000 to $1.5million, and a continuing annual cost (for training, inputs, regular third-party inspectors and certifiers, like Primus Labs, etc.) of $15,000 to $28,000. Such costs are prohibitive for most small and medium-sized producers. A second barrier is the distribution of retained value and costs in the supply chain. The greatest retention of income comes from controlling downstream parts of the value chain. In turn, vertical integration and size highly correlate to profitability. Indeed, because of storage and transportation costs, small and many medium-sized producers tend to prefer the use of middlemen that come to receive and pay for goods on site, although the middleman cuts significantly into the retained earning of the producer. A third barrier is market volatility in prices. Due to the attraction of potentially higher prices for higher quality goods, most sectors in the 1990s experienced a surge in supply, which over

---

[2] Extensive studies can be found at Avendaño et al. (2006), Coemel (2005), FAO (2006), and Chavez (2009). In their 2004–5 survey of fresh vegetable producers in three of the most export-oriented states, Avendaño et al. (2009) reveal that although over 80 percent of respondents were aware of the new US standards, less than half complied with them and the vast majority were not aware of the Mexican government's food safety laws or its support programs.

[3] We draw here on our own interviews and the following case studies: FAO (2005, 2006) Cervantes-Godoy (2007), Avendaño et al. (2009), Avendaño and Rinderman (2005), COEMEL (2005), and Calvin (2003).

time reduced market prices significantly, in turn, leading producers to return to the local traditional outlets or exit altogether.

The MNCs and large affiliated Mexican buyers have tried to address these problems in a number of ways. There is considerable evidence that these actors have used contracts and other means to experiment with credit assistance, input packages, and direct assistance. Nonetheless, the administrative and coordination costs are large. In cases as varied as supplying fresh produce to frozen vegetables, the trend over time is for the buyer to reduce the number of suppliers and focus on larger partners. Hence, it is not surprising to see the estimates given earlier about the relatively low participation of the vast majority of producers in the relatively more publicly and privately regulated supply chains. These figures are supported by smaller survey samples. For instance, in their study of fresh vegetable producers in the northern Mexicali Valley, Avendaño and Rindermann (2005) found that at the time of market liberalization in the early 1990s there were about 200 producers, 30 percent of which exported to the US and 86 percent of which were small firms. By 2002, there were only 25 firms exporting, 40 percent of which were large and the rest medium-sized. Similar trends can found across a variety of fresh produce and meat export sectors. The most notorious case is that of cantaloupes, in which after a US import suspension in 2002 and a new certification process (discussed below) Mexico saw a 40 percent decrease in its US market share, with only 13 producers certified to export as of 2009 (Avendaño et al. 2009; COEMEL 2005). Although the state of Michoacán accounts for 40 percent of the world's avocados, only 8 percent growers were export certified for the US by 2001 (Stanford 2002). In an exhaustive search, Cervantes-Godoy (2007) found only about 2,500 small producers in all of Mexico selling to the modern supermarkets.

The few systematic statistical analyses of regulation awareness and implementation of Mexican large and small producers reveal also a dependence on collective knowledge and material resources. For instance, in their survey analysis of small producers from mostly relatively poorer states selling to the domestic modern supermarkets, Cervantes-Godoy et al. (2008) found that obtaining credit, technical assistance, and critical information on product and process standards, in turn gaining consistent sales to the supermarkets, depended on whether the firm belonged to a collective producer organization. Alcantar (2010) surveyed the 343 fruit and vegetable producers in the export-oriented northeast states of Mexico that were affiliated to any of the state-level producer associations. Her network analysis found that the most important sources of knowledge and assistance for upgrading practices and technological adoption were not private certifiers and only moderately the buyers; rather they were other growers, the state-level producer associations, the public-private state committee on SPS, as well as the state-level offices of SENESICA and occasionally the national agriculture research institute.

These findings coincide with a growing literature arguing that the intersection of regulation and upgrading is largely a collective action problem requiring an institutional shift that rarely individual firms or the state alone can generate (McDermott 2007; Perez-Aleman 2011). On the one hand, the common problem of regulation is not per se one of a level playing field but one of economic necessity: if one producer shirks then all bear the costs since the disease or pests can spread easily to others or can lead to a negative reputation effect on the whole region of producers. On the other hand, implementation is largely about adoption of standards in the local context, which requires time-consuming and costly investments in field experiments, skills, and equipment. In the studies just mentioned and our own interviews, we found that the associations were critical for pooling knowledge about practices, monitoring members about their compliance with agreed upon standards, and instigating the support of the local public institutions for technical assistance, R&D, worker training, and transforming standards into laws. The role of the public institutions at the state level was triggered in many ways by the organizational power of the local associations and key producers. These institutions had the material resources and extensive knowledge on standards and techniques from different regions, which the firms and associations lacked on their own, and also had the authority to reinforce standards into active regulations.

In sum, while creating learning communities with collective resources presents itself as a possible solution to the regulation-upgrading nexus, the integration mechanisms of NAFTA would appear to leave their creation dependent on pre-existing collective organizations, which can act as gate keepers to new markets and resources. We now analyze how the Mexican government responded to more stringent US food safety import regulations. Although they implemented new laws and policies, their emphasis on decentralizing implementation would leave upgrading constrained largely by the ability of producers to collectively organize and the legacies of Mexican corporatism.

2.5 The Dominant Path in the Federal Government's Approach to Food Safety

Mexico's federal government and the peak-level agriculture confederation (CNA) did not view food safety regulations as strategic for Mexico in NAFTA negotiations, other than try to limit their affects as barriers for entry to the US market for some of their most concentrated sectors (Studer and Wise 2007).

As one outside expert notes, "the concept of safe domestic food supply for the Mexican people does not appear to exist as an explicit policy" (Knutson 2009: 13). Indeed, COFEPRIS, the domestic food safety agency under the Ministry of Health, has about only 30 employees in its national office (FAO 2005).

A turning point for the government came in 1997, when the US passed the US Produce and Imported Food Safety Initiative, which heightened enforcement of imported food standards and also placed greater emphasis on producers using preventive practices like GAPs and GMPs. The ongoing concern from the US grew out of pressure from local growers and concerns over recurring problems of pests and food-borne disease outbreaks linked to imported Mexican fresh fruits and vegetables. The USDA and FDA then suspended the import of a variety of fresh fruits and vegetables because of problems of microbial hazards (in some cases leading to severe illness in the US) and pests over the following years.[4] The Mexican government passed two sets of legislation between 1999 and 2001 that aimed to make food safety laws, their regulation, and implementation meet US standards. Indeed, outside experts have noted that the related reorganization of SAGARPA and SENASICA in many ways mimicked the USDA and FDA (FAO 2005; Knutson 2009). The challenge was daunting. A government study revealed at the time that less than 53 percent of firms in fruits and vegetables had identified the need to establish a system of GAPs and GMPs, 34 percent had the minimal infrastructure to implement these practices, and only 11 percent had adapted international practices (Avendaño et al. 2006: 63).

The government's "Master Plan" for food safety explicitly emphasized export value chains without attention to broader regulatory implementation for the domestic market. Leaders from major confederations involved in the legislation, like CNA and CAADES, confirmed that this was consistent with their view at the time, as standards still meant barriers. However, without a comprehensive approach, resources and legal authority for monitoring and implementation would be constrained and inconsistent, leading to a reliance on the initiative and mobilization of local actors (Avendaño et al. 2006).

This lack of coherence is reflected in both the budgets and organizational structure of the related public programs and regulations. After significant declines in public spending on agriculture in the 1990s, the Fox

---

[4] Major cases of import suspensions include strawberries, green onions, avocados, mangos, tomatoes, and melons. Some of the most newsworthy cases of food-borne illness in the US caused by imported Mexican fruits and vegetables are: the 1997 Hepatitis A outbreaks caused by strawberries (leading apparently to over 200 illnesses), the 1998 *Shigella sonnei* outbreak from parsley and cilantro, the 1999 outbreak of the pathogen *S. baildon* in raw tomatoes, the 2003 Hepatitis A outbreak from green onions, and recurring outbreaks of Salmonella in 1991, 1997, 1998, and 2000 from cantaloupe melons. See Avendaño et al. (2013).

administration slightly increased and stabilized it after 2000 to about 10 percent of the total budget (Cruz and Rinderman 2009). Alianza Para el Campo contained the main programs to aid the competitiveness and capacities of the agricultural industry, and under the Fox administration it captured 13–15 percent of the agricultural budget. Within Alianza, the overarching program for food safety and SPS monitoring and support (Programa de Sanidad e Inocuidad Agroalimnetaria or PSIA) gradually gained increased federal funding, rising to 14.5 percent of the Alianza budget in 2006. The specific subprogram on food safety practices, which were finally put into legislation as norms in 2002, accounts for less than 5 percent of the PSIA budget (FAO 2005).

But the key weaknesses in the public regulatory changes appear to be rooted in the decentralized nature of financing and operationalizing the laws, especially PSIA. For instance, from 2001 to 2005, on average about 42 percent of PSIA funding came from the federal budget, while the rest came from the state governments (25 percent) and the producers themselves via fees (33 percent). SENASICA was left with limited resources and legal authority to coordinate and supervise subnational actors, let alone build the infrastructure for testing, trace-back, certification, and training (FAO 2005, 2006). The main unit for phytosanitary regulation of SENASICA has 250 employees at the central office, while the unit for food safety practices has 40 employees. The former has legal authority to issue obligatory norms for controlling the eradication of harmful pests, such as fruit flies, and has certified to date 12 third-party laboratories for testing on its behalf. The latter has no legal obligatory powers. Their norms are voluntary.

Both SENASICA units rely on two decentralized organizations for operations and manpower. First, they rely on the offices and personnel of SAGARPA, located in each of the 32 Mexican states. The designated SAGARPA employees handle several policy portfolios, causing SENASICA to lack dedicated experts at the state level. Second, each state has an OAS (Auxiliary Sanitary Organism), comprised of a SENASICA representative and then representatives of the given state government and the local producers. The latter are elected from local/municipal juntas (JLSVs), of which there are 224 today in the whole country. JLSV boards are comprised of local producers and municipal functionaries. Although SENASICA sets overarching priorities and rules for campaigns of prevention, testing, certification, and training of producers in new practices, it relies heavily on the OAS and JLSV to set annual goals and operational plans, including reliance on funding from the states—the governments and producers.

These conflicting lines of authority have caused the FAO (2005, 2006) to identify significant flaws in SENASICA's ability to create a consistent, coherent implementation strategy for monitoring and standards adoption at the level of the firm. For starters, state governments, which historically have limited resources and vary tremendously in wealth, are unlikely to put in more resources in the PSIA while the main legal competencies for rule making and enforcement are held federally. Indeed, an earlier program to transfer legal authority in areas such as inspections to state governments has been halted due to the lack of required capacities at the state level (FAO 2006: 48). But SENASICA relies heavily on the OAS and JLSV to implement, monitor, and anticipate programs. For instance, both the sanitary and food safety practices units rely on about 350 third-party, contracted auditors and certifiers, who are paid mainly from local OAS budgets and represent a significantly weak capacity for coverage of such a large country. SENASICA has limited resources to conduct follow up analyses of compliance for certified firms and regions. It also lacks the mechanisms to have the OAS coordinate priorities which concern multiple states, such as the recurring problems of pests that naturally can cross state borders. Its central staff must review annual plans for four different PSIA programs from the 32 state offices and only has 20 days to respond. Finally, besides having the authority to order and finance campaigns to fight pests once an outbreak is detected, SENASICA often is in conflict with the OAS priorities, which attend largely to local interests and funds—i.e. mainly the interests of large local firms (FAO 2006).

At the same time, there is a need for decentralization and coordination since the eradication of pests and microbial hazards requires constant scouting at the farm level for plant diseases and maintaining traps in the field, in turn demanding participation from regional OAS employees, state officials, and JLSV, as well as the producers and their organizations. Knutson (2009) and the FAO (2006) have argued that, though limited, the authority of SENASICA and the funds and programs from the PSIA have been able to induce some of this cooperation. For instance, in its extensive review of plant safety programs, the FAO (2006, 2007) noted that the SENASICA had made important gains in their campaigns to eradicate pests and flies that have historically plagued many regions, but most consistently in the more advanced north than the poorer south and in targeted export value chains. SENASICA also has gradually expanded its best practices certification programs, at times working with large retailers like Costco and Walmart. Nonetheless, by 2008 only about 240 fruit and vegetable producers were certified and maintained compliance in GAPs, while a limited number large firms, with the resources and foreign commercial ties, dominated export value chains.[5]

Reflecting our discussion so far, these limited advances by the federal actors reveal the two sides of the emergence of new forms of regulation and

---

[5] Certification data come from SENASICA, Subdirecion de Inocuidad Agricola, 24 June 2008. See also FAO (2006).

upgrading. On the one hand, the need to combine complementary skills, authority, and resources at the local level is more likely to be an effective process than one based on top-down laws and incentives. On the other hand, it inevitably opens the process to regional and sectoral variation and potential conflicts of interests. The question is whether the institutional and political conditions are more likely to drive the experimental process towards expansion or exclusion.

NAFTA created strong incentives for the Mexicans to comply with US food safety standards. But NAFTA does not have strong mechanisms to support new Mexican institutional capacities or empower a diversity of groups for collective action. The latter is left to the market. This has meant that collective action in regulation and upgrading is shaped by a skewed distribution of past resources and power in Mexico. The federal government's limited approach to building state capacity for food safety regulation or clarifying the terms of multi-level governance makes institutional development and upgrading increasingly dependent on the longstanding legacies of market reregulation by governors and powerful associations (Snyder 1999). That is, the available institutional infrastructure comes often not simply from market forces or an all-dominating central state, but the historically organized sectors and their associations. We now examine this tension in greater detail through three types of public-private coordination to resolve regulatory gaps.

2.6 The Nascent Path of Regulation of Fresh Produce Exports: Local Collective Action and US Intervention

This section analyzes failed and successful cases of public-private solutions to improving regulation and upgrading in response to US standards. Successes depended on two conditions: the creation of effective producer associations by a limited number of firms with similar interests and past social ties; empowerment by the state via granting of exclusive resources, rights, and authority in a domain. The former condition was shaped by the legacies of corporatism. The latter was shaped by policy choices by certain Mexican state-level governments and by US agencies. The increasing role of the US agencies signals a possible shift in the integration mechanisms in NAFTA.

Although Mexican scholars are finding growing evidence of the critical role of producer organizations creating, monitoring, and implementing standards across a variety of product sectors, their use and numbers remain sparse. For instance, in the aforementioned study of small growers selling to modern supermarkets, Cervantes-Godoy (2007) could only identify 12 producer organizations in all of Mexico. Ruiz (2001) estimated that 80 percent of Mexican growers did not belong to a producer organization. Alcantar (2010) estimated that only 343 producers in the whole northeast region, where agricultural exports are historically an important component of the economy, were affiliated with associations. Larger studies confirm low participation rates elsewhere in the country (Cervantes-Godoy 2007; COEMEL 2005).

A major explanation for this low mobilization rate is historical aversion to associations because of their linkage to the corporatist era before the 1990s. For decades, the Mexican government used associations both to enact policy and maintain socio-political order. Only official associations were allowed, as they had exclusive rights over a territory and/or sector to administer planting and transport permits, quotas, and policy resources for firms. While the associations were controlled by elite few who were closely tied to national or state-level politicians, they mediated the paternalistic relationship between government and farmers in exchange for political support (Schneider 2004; Snyder 1999). This had three related legacies in the past 20 years since the liberalization of the economy and associations.

First, firms in general abandoned them, with the vast numbers of small and medium-sized firms treating them with suspicion and entrepreneurs viewing them as constraints (Shadlen 2004). As of 2003, there were registered about 2,500 associations in agriculture, grouped under 38 "unions," but it is estimated that less than 30 percent are actively functioning (Claridades 2006). Second, the past left the vast majority of producers with no organizing experience, as it had always been a top-down decision (Cervantes-Godoy 2007). Third, and conversely, the few that remained active composed some of the only available institutional infrastructure especially at state levels to implement new policies. Indeed, Snyder (1999) argues that state-level variation in the reregulation of the coffee industry in the 1990s was due to the interaction between the organizational capabilities of small holders and large firms and the preference by governors to reuse existing corporatist organizations.

In turn, while NAFTA depends on Mexican actors organizing to change institutions and firm capabilities, the attendant collective action is greatly shaped by the legacies of corporatism. In all the cases here, exports were threatened by enforcement of US regulations and a lack of producer compliance. Where we see a long-term negative decline in performance, producers were unable to organize effectively and the federal government imposed a new regulation. The remaining players are mainly a few large firms and their reinvented old association. Where regulation and growth did occur, producer associations worked closely with state agencies and even the US government, but the diffusion of benefits and standards have been limited to relatively few firms controlling the relevant associations. Ironically, despite the efforts of neo-liberalism to dismantle the old structure, the need to control hazards for exports has meant Mexican governments and the US agencies re-empowering some former corporatist associations.

2.6.1 *Cantaloupe Exports—Regulation without Coordination*

Cantaloupe production is historically widespread in Mexico, with numerous producers of all sizes exporting from 13 different states.[6] Exports to the US consistently rose through the 1990s, reaching $72 million in 1999, accounting for about 30 percent of cantaloupe imports in the US. At the same time, the number of rejections by the FDA of Mexican cargo sampled at the border increased 92 percent due to contamination with illegal pesticide residues and microbial contaminants such as salmonella and shigella. In cooperation with the Mexican government, the FDA conducted farm investigations from 2000 to 2002, determining that the contamination from salmonella came from unhygienic conditions in cultivating and packaging the product, mainly in the state Guerrero. The FDA issued an import alert and then a total ban in 2002. Mexican producers would be allowed to re-enter the US market after October 2003, after the new system to be described here. But as late as 2008 export sales never rose above $10 million, with import market share at 3 percent (Avendaño et al. 2013; Calvin 2003).

The reaction by Mexican authorities was delayed, as they first tried to fight the ban at the WTO. To save their exports the government then worked with the FDA to develop new strict guidelines for food safety practices. They were presented in the form of an official Mexican norm and adoption of it was, and remains, obligatory for all businesses who wish to export cantaloupes to the US. The official Mexican norm, *"NOM-EM-038-FITO-2002: Requirements for the application and certification of good agricultural practices and of control for the production and packaging of the cantaloupe melon as an emergency measure,"* was published in the official daily of the Federation (*DOF*) on 13 November 2002. This specific certification must be renewed annually and is issued directly by SENASICA, which uses its network of contracted inspectors.

The regulation gives very detailed GAPs and GMPs, including specific hygienic conditions on the farm, methods of harvest, packaging, and transport, and cold storage. By extension, in order to be prepared for audits, the firm must implement systems of constant testing and monitoring using internal systems and third-party private inspectors. The standards were not only costly but required significant changes in the organization and skills of the firms and their employees. The vast majority of producers could not respond adequately. Most of these producers are small, in relatively backward regions. For instance, in a 2004 survey of producers in the state of Colima, over 60 percent have only a primary education, 90 percent lacked basic managerial capabilities, 17 percent had access to credit, and 77 percent had never

---

[6] In addition to the sources cited, these sections draw on 27 interviews with officials and producers from the relevant sectors and functionaries in the relevant Mexican and US agencies.

received any government assistance or program. 96 percent did not apply the GAPs. Even the packers, which are usually larger, more experienced firms had never participated in a government program (COEMEL 2005). A separate survey in 2007 found similar trends. For instance, 88 percent of growers were still using water from rivers, which increases microbial risks, but only 59 percent reported ever having the water tested. 71 percent did not know the implications of GAPs, while 41 percent revealed that lack of information was the main reason for not implementing GAPs (Avendaño et al. 2009).

A key reason for the inability to find the means to upgrade and even become adequately informed of the regulations is the lack of collective organization of the producers. For instance, in 2004, 94 percent of cantaloupe producers in Colima did not belong to any type of collective organization (e.g. cooperative, association etc.). In that state, there is little history of producer organizations or active government programs and infrastructure in educating and training producers, let alone monitoring food safety. At the same time, there is no encompassing melon producer association for the country, as the producers are historically fragmented and small throughout many states.

By 2009, only 13 producers were certified to export to the US, with one from Colima, two from Michoacán, and 10 from Sonora. These are all relatively large firms, with internal integration of growing, packaging, and storage. All processes are documented, made available for clients and auditors of SENASICA and FDA, which usually visit three times during preparation, harvest, and packing. The shift of production to the northern state of Sonora also is not surprising. This is a relatively prosperous state, with large experienced diversified agricultural firms, involved with associations, like the historically strong AOANS, which was created in 1963 in the corporatist era and works actively with the state commissions and SAGARPA offices.[7] These traits will be highlighted in our next case.

2.6.2 *Green Onions and Tomatoes in the North: Rapid Response by Strong Associations and Allied State Agencies*

During the 1990s, Mexico became the most important exporter of green onions to the US. Production is concentrated in 25 firms located in neighboring valleys in the states of Baja California and Sonora. In November 2003, the FDA reported outbreaks of Hepatitis A linked to green onions consumed in four US states. The FDA traced some of the cases to four producers in this region. In December, in cooperation with SAGARPA, the FDA and CDC

[7] AOANS Organismos Agricolas is the Association of Agriculture Organs of Northern Sonora. It represents the agriculture sector in the regions of Guaymas, Hermosillo, and Caborca, comprised of six local associations, three integradoras, and a cooperative.

(Center for Disease Control) investigated these and other producers in the region. They issued a report identifying several quality-control problems that could have allowed the disease to emerge, including poor sanitary conditions, inadequate hygiene facilities, poor maintenance by employees, and questionable quality of the water used in the fields, packing and cold storage (Calvin et al. 2004).

Cognizant of the reputational damage and the events in the cantaloupe sector, the producers, under the leaders of UARPH, the Agriculture Union of Producers of the Region of Mexicali Valley, immediately called on the Secretariat of Agriculture of Baja California (SEFOA) and SENESICA to create a comprehensive set of standards for all green onion export producers. UARPH is a holdover confederation from decades past, representing seven producer associations of the region. In close consultation with UARPH, SEFOA, and the Agriculture Union of Producers of Rio Colorado (in adjoining Sonora), SENESICA created a voluntary protocol specifically for GAPs and GMPs for the production of green onions in the two valleys. Published in the official registry in Baja California in August 2004, the protocol details strict guidelines and practices for production, harvesting, and packaging of green onions; it also requires that any exporter must be audited regularly by SENESICA and certified by a third-party private firm. The protocol sought to utilize the resources and authority of SENESICA and adhere to the preference by US importers for internationally recognized certifiers.

The state office of SENESICA (the OAS), via the JLSVs of the region, committed also to training SENESICA employees and their contracted certifiers in the details of the GAPs and GMPs and customizing a program of technical support for standards adoption and regular monitoring. SEFOA committed funds to these programs and also enlisted the aid of regional universities and institutes to help the growers implement new practices and technology and utilize laboratories. The two aforementioned unions and their relevant member associations committed resources in co-financing the programs and also personnel in a new monitoring system. The firms in these unions accounted for 85 percent of production. By 2006, 20 firms were certified. From 2003 to 2010, exports increased by about 60 percent.

A similar case concerns Mexican tomato exports, which almost doubled during 1995–2005. Baja California accounts for about 75 percent of the exports. During this period, these producers have been subject to several rounds of negotiations regarding certification protocols and alerts. In 2008, the FDA reported an outbreak of Salmonella Saint Paul linked to tomatoes founds in several US states. Although the FDA did not identify the actual source of the hazard, it put Mexico on the list of possible contaminated suppliers. Within four days, the governor of the state of Baja California petitioned the FDA to exclude the producers of Baja California from this list.

Backed by a detailed report on tomato exports, the mechanism for exclusion was a new protocol that would be required of any tomato exporter in Baja California.

The producers, this time through two main associations CAADES and CABC (linked as well to UARPH), worked closely with SENESICA, SEFOA, and the JLSVs to design a protocol that required an exporter to certify the origin of the tomatoes (only from Baja California) and to follow numerous detailed GAPs and GMPs from farm to transport (similar to the types already mentioned). The protocol also established that SEFOA would be the government authority issuing the certificates. The FDA reviewed and approved the protocol, and excluded Baja California from the alert list. As of 2011, of the 34 tomato producers in Baja California, 21 were up to date on their certification; tomato exports sales from the state to the US increased 50 percent between 2005 and 2010 and 8 percent between 2008 and 2010. Most of the producers are relatively large with their own farms and packing houses.

There are two points to highlight from these cases. First, the processes of upgrading and regulating are closely linked, requiring close coordination and joint action between the relevant public and private actors. These cases reveal that such cooperation appears more likely when there is a relatively small group of experienced, resourceful producers who have a well-organized association that then has a working relationship with the key public institutions (Shadlen 2004). This is naturally a concern. While upgrading and learning communities must start from the resources they have, it is not clear how the circle will grow. Indeed, the network study by Alcantar (2010) mentioned earlier was conducted in these northern states, and they found that only 343 firms across many sectors were members of producer associations, almost all of which came from the corporatist era.

Second, it is noteworthy that the key public actors come from the state level. In both cases, the leaders were a combination of producer associations and state agencies. This may not be a surprise since Baja California and Sonora have rather active agricultural institutions, with state committees on plant safety composed of representatives of the associations and the secretariats. These state actors then turned to the federal actors, the regional offices of SENESICA, for complementary expertise, knowledge, and authority.

2.6.3 *The Transnational State as Initiator of Mexican Public-Private Regulation*

In these cases, the US FDA was playing an indirect role in shaping paths of transnational regulatory integration via enforcement and encouraging relevant Mexican public and private actors to improve joint problem-solving and capacities. In the following cases, the role of the US government, specifically the USDA agency APHIS, the regulator of plant and vegetable safety, has a much more direct role. In contrast to the FDA, APHIS has the authority to evaluate and certify another country's producers and its regulators. This authority, coupled with the threat of pests hazards to US growers, has led APHIS to create pre-certification programs for exports in several key fruit sectors, such as mango, citrus, avocado, papaya, and guava. Due to growing problems with certain flies and with import restrictions, APHIS has provided an avenue for stable market access for Mexican producers. The design and evolution of the programs, as we will see, has also resulted in coordination and learning opportunities in regulation and upgrading not only between US and Mexican actors but also between Mexican public and private actors at the state and federal levels. At the same time, and similar to these cases, the spillover effects on domestic regulation and upgrading are constrained by program design and the exclusive rights the APHIS grants to the non-state partners.

The programs require that relevant packers be paying members of an association that partners with APHIS. APHIS has created agreements with one association for each of aforementioned sectors, and only their members who comply with all the stipulations of the agreements can then be certified to export the given product to the US. The agreements require the Mexican packers (in some cases their supplying producers) to follow strict plans for the eradication of pests and treatment of products in packing houses. APHIS has 90 employees, mostly Mexican nationals, based in Guadalajara, who regularly inspect the packing houses and treatment centers, and certify for export the compliant packers (and by extension, their producers). The Mexican firms, via their association, pay for these employees, while the associations are the intermediaries for the financial management of the program and in any disputes, such as decertification or suspensions of particular firms. Each association representing packers in the aforementioned sectors came from the corporatist era, although each renamed itself and also has changed its governance rules and roles, in part adapting to the APHIS work plans. SENESICA is also a signatory to the annual work plans, though its role is less direct. The strength of this approach for the Mexicans has been the institutionalization of cross-border public-private regulation, the transfer of standards and practices, and stable growth in exports. We now describe the two most prominent programs, those for mango and avocado exports, which reveal the variation in approaches to regulation and in the roles of the public and private actors.

The mango program started in earnest in the early 1990s, when APHIS contracted with EMEX, the association for Mexican Mango Exporters (Alvarez 2006). Before 1991, EMEX was known as ANEPMM, a corporatist association for mango packers. From 1992 to 2010, the number of participating packers has grown from 30 to 58, with export sales and volumes growing by about 200 percent.

APHIS employees annually certify and regularly monitor each packing house, in turn each shipment, and the required hot water treatment to eradicate fruit flies. The annual work plans specify fees, standards, and roles. To be certified, a packer must pay a set of fees to EMEX to cover the costs of all inspections and certification. This payment makes one a member of EMEX. The work plan specifies all the mandatory procedures and schedules for treatment and inspections. SENESICA employees accompany the APHIS inspectors to packing houses as observers and mediators. The work plans have evolved to specify also the GAPs to be used by producers and how producers are to be registered. APHIS however does not have a direct role with the producers and has no authority to visit, without invitation, orchards or the JLSVs.

This program has revealed opportunities and limits for regulatory and firm upgrading. On the one hand, EMEX and SENESICA are gradually expanding their roles and learning how to adapt the APHIS requirements for regulatory expansion. EMEX, though only with a full-time staff of six people, has developed capabilities for export promotion, collecting and sharing information on regulations, practices, and producers, and working with SENESICA and the JLSVs to update GAPs and programs for aiding packers, and somewhat producers. SENESICA, in turn, has incorporated APHIS standards and methods into its own certification and monitoring systems and directed greater resources over time to encourage JLSVs to upgrade the pest monitoring methods. SENESICA now maintains a detailed database on all producers it certifies as suppliers to the designated packers, and also occasionally invites APHIS employees to meetings with the JLSV to explain new requirements and techniques in packing that it has learned elsewhere.

On the other hand, there are clear constraints to expansion and upgrading. First, because of the program design, SENESICA does not work with APHIS directly in the fields and responds mainly to firm demands. For instance, while EMEX has helped coordinate some changes in monitoring and assistance programs between SENESICA and producer associations, these are mostly limited to the states of Nayarit and Sinaloa, where most member packers are located and where there are historically strong associations, such as CAADES. Indeed, the president of EMEX made clear to us his frustration with the JLSV and the producers, remarking that implementation of GAPs, monitoring, and assistance is the responsibility of the local producers and the JLSV, not EMEX. Hence, expansion and upgrading of local infrastructure and producers are still subject to the local politics and organizational issues already discussed. Those constraints may be the reason that certified producers in the export value chain are limited to mainly two states, although mango production is across ten states, and that 90 percent of EMEX packers are supplied mostly from their own orchards. Second, in 2005 EMEX changed the member voting rules to allow the number of votes per packer/member to correspond to the volume of shipments. This has allowed about 20 members to hold a majority of the votes (Alvarez 2006).

The avocado program shows both more opportunities and constraints. This program was created through negotiations between the USDA and SAGARPA to resolve a long-running conflict over the entry of Mexican avocados into the US. In turn, this program not only has a similar structure to the one just outlined but also a Mexican law authorizing it and defining its terms. Starting in 1995, APHIS signed an agreement with SAGARPA/SENESICA and APEAM, the association of avocado exporters from the state of Michoacán. Only avocados from this state are allowed into the program. APEAM grew out of a decades-old association, represents only packers, not producers, and governs itself like EMEX. The number of packers has grown from a handful to 38 as of 2010. Each pays fees to APEAM to cover the costs of the program, promotion, and APHIS employees. The number of producers certified as suppliers has grown, especially in the past six years, to include over 9,000, with 19 of 38 municipalities certified by SENESICA (their office at the state-level OAS) as pest free. Exports to the US have grown by 250 percent over the past 15 years, though only about 20 percent of avocado production is exported.

This program follows a systems approach, whereby APHIS monitors and certifies the packers as well as includes in the work plan detailed practices for control of pests and microbial hazards in the orchard. APHIS employees also inspect orchards twice per year. Because of this approach, the roles of APEAM and SENESICA are more directly expansive, as they both are involved, via the agreement and de facto incentives, in promoting GAPs and GMPs not only with packers but also with growers. This also allows much closer relationships with and learning opportunities from APHIS employees. For instance, APHIS employees are in regular contact with the OAS and work together on updating standards, identifying weakness in the monitoring systems, and encouraging more Mexican resources. SENESICA, APEAM, and APHIS representatives have regular meetings to update databases and plan certification of more municipalities. Indeed, this relationship has led APHIS to trust SENESICA professionals more, as they now use SENESICA labs for analyses of pests.

At the same time, SENESICA and SAGARPA employees have learned to work more closely with APEAM and state-level actors to expand certification, monitoring, and assistance programs. Over the years, the three have designed an economical monitoring and training package for growers, which greatly interests Michoacán officials in increasing the number of certified municipalities. They have pooled resources to increase the number of full-time dedicated inspectors and certifiers to 138 for the state. More recently, they have created coordination agreements with the state university's agronomy faculty to access their laboratories, perform regular studies, and send graduate students to test and aid producers.

As with mangos, this and other programs still face important constraints. First, these programs are a delicate balance between tight control of SPS hazards in the supply chain and gradual export growth. For instance, as of 2009, the total number of number of certified packers for mangos, avocados, guava, and citrus are, respectively 49, 28, 5, and 7. More detailed data on the number of producers certified are not publicly available. But just to give an idea about the bottleneck the programs have created, there are over 61,000 mango producers, 49,000 lemon producers, and 122,000 orange producers in Mexico. The avocado program is restricted to the state of Michoacán, which accounts for about 33 percent producers and 69 percent of production nationally. The most generous estimates of coverage would have the APHIS avocado program including 35 percent of Michoacán producers but only 11 percent of Mexican producers and 24 percent of Mexican production. Six export distributors accounted for 72 percent of the total avocado exports (by volume) to the US between 2005 and 2010.[8]

Second, these programs have purposively aimed to begin with relatively small groups in order to utilize the institutional infrastructure at hand. This means that a handful of associations are still the gate keepers and the cost of membership is nontrivial. At the same time, it depends on finding active public partners at the state level. As the dominant producer of avocados, the state of Michoacán clearly has a very strong interest in participating in the program and working with the others to expand certification and related infrastructure. Whether other states, with fewer resources, less direct incentives, and weaker associations can do so is less clear.

Third, while the USDA and APHIS continue to work closely with Mexican partners, their representatives have made clear to us that they are not in the institutional development business (but rather protecting US consumers) and that they are not interested in transferring pre-clearance authority to SENESICA. While there have been positive developments in SENESICA over the past ten years, they still see it as having weak resources and authority, subject to the variations in interest groups and infrastructure at the state and local levels. Indeed, a repeated concern is the continued lack of a corps of highly trained SENESICA inspectors instead of third-party private, "recognized" inspectors, who face potential conflicts of interest.

[8] Data are available at <http://www.sagarhpa-export.gob.mx>.

2.7 In Lieu of a Conclusion: A Shift in US–Mexican Integration?

These last cases reveal both opportunities and constraints for significant changes in the strategies toward US–Mexican regulatory integration and broad-based implementation in food safety. These experiences, on the one hand, appear to have nudged the US and Mexican government agencies to explore deeper regulatory integration via the principles of capacity building and joint problem-solving along three overlapping paths. First, the FDA opened a new office in Mexico City in 2011, and the 2010 Food Modernization and Safety Act in the US gives the FDA the authority to certify whether a country's food safety institutions have equivalency status. This could lead to the FDA regularly evaluating Mexican food safety regulatory institutions comprehensively rather than on a product-by-product basis. At the same time, APHIS plans to expand its activities in Mexico. The combination of these changes has led to greater regular contact between US and Mexican authorities as well as new working groups tasked with identifying areas of common goals for food safety implementation.

Second, in 2008 APHIS and Mexico launched a five-year joint plan for eradication of several fruit fly species in Mexico (APHIS 2008a, b). While APHIS has jointly built with Mexico several outposts in the past 15 years, the new plan is much more comprehensive in scope and depth. For instance, the plan focuses on the overall institutional capacity of many areas for data gathering, tracking, prevention, and eradication. The plan calls for significant joint investments in new facilities and personnel in Mexico. Moreover, all aspects of plan development and implementation emphasize putting in place joint problem-solving working groups to create joint standards, methods, and mechanisms. In short, a sub-theme of the plan is loss of confidence by US authorities in Mexican data and capacities that can only be addressed via jointly coordinated efforts and investments into new capacities.

Third, Mexico initiated recently new negotiations with the FDA and APHIS to improve and expand the aforementioned limited export certification programs for producers. A priority for the Mexicans is having SENASICA take a much greater role in these programs, including actual program management and certification procedures. There is already some evidence that SENASICA is stepping up its role in the APHIS programs. For instance, the renewed work plans for the APHIS pre-clearance and irradiation programs requires SENASICA to provide up-to-date, publicly available information of the programs and the firms and farms that are both certified and suspended. SENASICA employees regularly accompany APHIS employees for inspections, maintain regular working groups, and have increasingly paid joint visits to OAS (state offices) meetings to help come up with new solutions to recurring implementation problems. Moreover, APHIS is increasingly working with relevant JLSVs (the local committees) to have the latter take on greater responsibilities in conducting field inspections in such sectors as mangos and avocados.

The constraints to these shifts in regulatory integration are both external and internal for Mexico. The former will be largely determined by how the US government views food safety issues as broader regional risks and whether greater intervention and joint action with the Mexicans is warranted. The latter will continue to concern the linking of regulatory integration to local producer organizational capacities. As we have highlighted in this chapter, the co-evolution of regulation and upgrading depends less on optimal incentives and state largess, and more on process of joint problem-solving, knowledge sharing, resource pooling. The creation of new regulatory institutional capacities to integrate and monitor rules and the ability of firms to adapt practices and upgrade processes are functions of relevant public and private actors recombining existing knowledge and material resources while coordinating ongoing organizational experiments. However, such a process is shaped by the institutional resources at hand, particularly those that enable or constrain the ability of producers to organize collectively and collaborate with subnational government agencies to invest in both regulatory capacities and upgrading assistance programs.

In the case of Mexican food safety, while the federal government eventually created laws and agencies reflecting international standards, namely those of the US, its reluctance to invest in comprehensive capacities for enforcement and assistance made implementation often a function of state- and sectoral-level politics and organizational resources. Common to many countries in Latin America (Schneider 2004; Shadlen 2004), these latter factors have been greatly shaped by the corporatist legacies of privileged associations and fragmented producers. The cases of the different fresh fruit and vegetable sectors reflect these legacies. Proactive responses to regulatory crises in many ways came from those regions and sectors where a limited number of firms within existing associations created a common regulatory and upgrading system, with often state-level public agencies, with which they had longstanding professional relationships. At the same time, these legacies can reinforce exclusion as the associations have been granted particular rights and resources with limited incentives or governance rules to enhance inclusion.

The core issue going forward is how SAGARPA and SENESICA, most likely with concerted assistance from their US counterparts, might expand regulatory and firm upgrading by complementing local initiatives with resources to assist small and medium-size firms to improve practices and tap into the existing upgrading communities while transferring lessons from the success cases to other sectors.

3

Strategies of Regulatory Integration via Development

The Integration of the Polish and Romanian Dairy Industries into the EU Single Market

László Bruszt and Julia Langbein

3.1 Introduction

This chapter analyzes the conditions under which the interventions of the same transnational regulatory regime, in this case the EU, yield similar levels of rule compliance but dramatically different developmental outcomes. Agricultural producers in Poland and Romania, the two cases analyzed in this chapter, had to comply with the non-negotiable rules of the EU. While enforcing the EU food safety regulations to the same degree in both countries, the EU had different goals and used different strategies to shape the distribution of benefits of regulatory compliance, yielding widely diverging developmental outcomes. The analysis of these cases allows us to highlight the role played by pre-existing distribution of organizational capacities and economic and political resources in shaping the goals and the developmental effects of the interventions of the regional hegemon.

The transnational regime that the EU developed to govern the economic and political integration of the Central and Eastern European (CEE) countries had to deal with a wide range of countries and sectors within these countries, with dramatically different institutional endowments. The regulations imposed by the EU on the CEE countries were initially developed for West European economic actors who had abundant economic resources, robust political organization, and were serviced by capable states. The imposition of these rules on countries and sectors that only had some or none of these properties involved the risk that successful rule imposition would go hand in hand with the exclusion of accession country economic actors from the European markets (Bruszt and Stark 2003). By examining compliance towards European food safety standards in the Polish and Romanian dairy industries, we show that better organized sectors working in developmental alliance with domestic state authorities could use the EU in a proactive way. By contrast, weakly organized, fragmented economic sectors and an insulated state were not capable of formulating an inclusive development strategy and could not play an active developmental role in using EU assistance. In the latter case, the EU had to create the basic elements of sectoral state organization so EU intervention could address the distributive aspects of market integration to a much lesser degree.

The study of variation in the implementation of transnational rules in rule-taking countries is not new. Students of compliance, primarily coming from the field of European studies, focused their analysis on the "paths to compliance" (Tallberg 2002), i.e. the factors triggering variation in rule adoption, implementation, and enforcement (see also Börzel 2000; Knill and Lenschow 2005; Börzel et al. 2010). Yet, the analysis of developmental outcomes is still a neglected key dimension of these studies despite the fact that it is the unique feature of the EU to employ encompassing strategies to address problems linked to developmental externalities of regulatory integration, as noted in the introductory chapter of this volume. While imposing its rules on the CEE countries, the EU went way beyond the managerial perspective on compliance (Tallberg 2002) by using various forms of assistance and resource transfers that targeted the capacity of actors to govern compliance with EU market rules in a way that could benefit a larger group of economic actors.

Our goal in this chapter is to understand variation in the developmental outcomes of these EU strategies in the new member states. We conceptualize developmental outcomes of compliance in terms of an economic and a social dimension. With regard to the former, compliance with transnational rules can help to alter the position of domestic economies in transnational/regional markets by contributing to increased capacity to export and move up the level of sophistication of exports towards the high-end markets. Alternatively, regulatory integration might weaken the competitive standing of domestic players and turn whole sectors into net importers and/ or exporters of low value-added products (Gereffi and Lee 2009). Regarding the social dimension, some scholars would expect compliance with transnational rules and standards to benefit only a narrow group of economic actors and trigger large-scale economic exclusion, particularly of small producers or firms (Dunn 2003; Dolan and Humphrey 2004). However, we find that the same regulatory requirement may result in inclusive market integration when competitive asymmetries among diverse producers or firms can be successfully mitigated.

In this chapter we argue that domestic developmental outcomes of transnational market integration were the function of the dynamic interplay between domestic organization and the type of external intervention. In sectors where economic actors were weak or fragmented, the domestic state had weak or no capacity to administer, regulate, and develop the sector, and only the strongest economic actors had access to the state, the EU's proactive strategy had to be adjusted to the domestic context. More specifically, the EU had to focus on the bringing about of the minimum necessary conditions of rule compliance simultaneously with the generation of elementary state capacities to produce developmental policies that could cope with at least some of the developmental externalities of regulatory integration. In a way, the EU had to substitute for the missing domestic demand and supply side of institutional development. By contrast, in an economy where domestic economic actors were better organized and where a cohesive developmental alliance between private actors and a capable state existed, the strategies of regional regulatory integration could focus assistance toward sectoral upgrading, increased competitiveness, and reduced economic exclusion.

To demonstrate these arguments, we present two cases with similar initial conditions in 1989 that ended with dramatically different developmental outcomes. We focus our analysis on the Polish and Romanian dairy industries because both cases were characterized in the 1990s by rural backwardness, weak production capacity, and fragmented industry structure. Upon accession in 2004 and 2007, both Poland and Romania transposed the relevant EU laws into their national legislation. However, the dairy sectors of these two countries displayed divergent outcomes by 2010 in terms of economic and social developmental effects. While Poland turned into a net exporter of dairy products and managed to export high-value-added products, such as cheese and curd, to the rest of the EU, Romania turned into a net importer of high-quality milk and dairy products (van Berkum 2009). Furthermore, in Poland, modernization and market integration of the dairy sector created development opportunities for small, medium, and larger milk-producing farms. Despite the fact that the Polish dairy sector is still more fragmented than the average of the EU-15 (van Berkum 2009), all Polish milk farms producing for the market comply with EU quality and safety requirements. In Romania's fragmented dairy sector, only a few larger milk producers situated in the Bucharest area managed to comply with European standards and the smaller and most medium-sized farms were excluded from the high-end market and subjected to transition periods negotiated between the EU and the Romanian government (Pieniadz et al. 2010).

In the next section we build our theoretical foundation. We subsequently discuss in section 3.3 why the Polish and Romanian dairy industries were selected as cases to scrutinize the factors shaping diverse developmental outcomes. Sections 3.4 and 3.5 then turn to the empirical analysis of the two case studies. We finish with some concluding remarks and discuss the implications of our findings for future studies on the impact of transnational market integration on developmental outcomes in evolving market economies.

3.2 Domestic Organization and Strategies of Regulatory Integration

Standards and regulations are settlements, contested and temporarily valid accommodations of interests among diverse categories of economic and political actors (Bruszt and Stark 2003; Bartley 2007). Meeting transnational quality standards and regulatory requirements and achieving industrial upgrading, we argue, is shaped by two variables: the nature of domestic organization of a particular economy or sector and the regional strategy of fostering regulatory integration in a particular transnational market.

3.2.1 Domestic Organization

Coordination for economic and social development depends on the input of well-organized economic actors as well as on the support of domestic state actors. With regard to the former, complex forms of organizing are needed among diverse categories of firms in a production chain to facilitate both the compliance with transnational rules and further industrial upgrading (Gereffi and Lee 2009; Cafaggi 2010). Greater fragmentation between producers, processing firms, and retailers in a given sector, in combination with limited conditions that could help them to solve complex collective action problems, yields a lower likelihood that they will be able to meet transnational regulatory requirements (Gereffi and Lee 2009).

In particular, regulations that imply risk management, like food safety, require solutions to complex coordination problems. Hanf and Pieniadz (2007) show that food quality management systems must perform at least two main tasks that go far beyond a firm's boundaries. The first task concerns compliance with the "legally-demanded commitments of providing transparency and traceability of any food item" (Hanf and Pieniadz 2006: 460). The installment of tracking systems and labeling technologies across the entire food supply chain requires intense organizing and comprehensive communication systems between the individual business partners. The second task concerns the creation of positive reputation, which can only be realized if all food and feed operators throughout the supply chain can rely on one another because of their compliance with safety and quality requirements. Interestingly, Hanf and Pieniadz (2007) noted that this also includes public authorities in charge of risk management, since they need to communicate any upcoming risks in a timely and efficient manner. The authors stress that permanent food quality management needs a collective strategy among firms as well as between firms and the state since each quality decision by individual actors has direct effects on the entire supply chain. In a similar vein, Cafaggi (2010: 19) notes that EU food safety control has turned from a "public command and control system, based on (ineffective) on-site inspections, to a mainly private monitoring system, placing higher responsibility on the supply chain within a co-regulatory scheme that involves state agencies or ministries" (see also Wendler 2008; Giorgi and Lindner Friis 2009).

State authorities must therefore have the ability to nurture and monitor the reorganization of production and need the capacity to oversee and enforce transnational regulations. The coming about of some of these state capacities is linked to such bureaucratic features of the state as meritocratic selection, professionalism, or stable and predictable carrier paths (e.g. Evans 1995). The same literature also stresses the role of intensive ties linking the state to diverse producer groups. The evolution of dense ties between the state and private actors might allow the state to get intimate knowledge of the potential effects of its policies in time to foster developmental alliances between the state and sectoral private actors.

Finally, the third potential actor in sectoral institutional change are the multinational enterprises (MNEs) that might also have incentives to develop, however selectively, the capacities of domestic private and public actors in order to gain access to new markets and/or minimize negative externalities of free trade on their home markets by promoting regulatory convergence (Andonova 2004; Jacoby 2010). Either way, MNEs are likely to facilitate technology transfer and vertical integration. In doing so, they contribute not only to the upgrading of production facilities. MNEs may also help in creating integrated production chains that are better suited than atomized economic actors to address complex coordination problems which are at the core of transnational market regulations.

The previous discussion suggests that individual economic actors in a sector along with the state must have domestic organization to implement transnational integration. For the purpose of this study, we hence define domestic organization as the presence of forms of governance, i.e. hierarchies (like multinational enterprises or state bureaucracies), networks, or associations that could help to overcome problems of coordination among interdependent economic actors and create and implement mutually beneficial economic strategies. We differentiate among forms of sectoral governance based on the

Domestic Organization   Type of external intervention   Developmental outcome

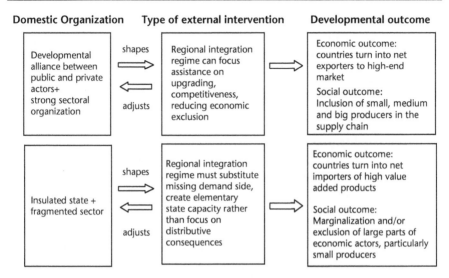

Figure 3.1 Explaining diverse developmental outcomes

complexity of economic problems that they can solve (Hollingsworth et al. 1994). If such forms of governance are absent in a particular sector we talk about a fragmented sector and/or an insulated state, while we characterize a sector as strongly organized and as being governed by a developmental alliance between state and non-state actors where these forms of governance exist (see Figure 3.1).

3.2.2 Strategies of Regulatory Integration

The literatures dealing with the link between the quality of domestic organization and developmental outcomes are blind towards the impact of regional arrangements (Bruszt and McDermott 2012). Regional arrangements differ in the way they adjust to local contexts by advancing mechanisms that allow them to monitor changes on the ground, thereby identifying not only the right incentives but also when and how to build domestic capacities to foster economic and social development. The context of EU enlargement draws attention to the limits of approaches that focus on economic and/or political incentives to explain divergent institutional outcomes (Schimmelfennig and Sedelmeier 2005; Vachudova 2005). Market incentives based on the principle of "swim or sink" will not help actors who have no capacity to swim. For example, in highly fragmented sectors, atomized actors have no capacity to establish and enforce the complex public-private governance arrangements needed in most regulatory fields. Instead of the fittest, the most organized actors with the highest capacity to coordinate will be able to meet the requirements of transnational norms and increase their potential to survive the competitive pressures in a highly regulated transnational market (Parsons 1960; Weber 1978). For similar reasons, political conditionality, i.e. the linking of "sticks and carrots" to the fulfillment of specific criteria, does not suffice to bring about and empower domestic reform coalitions in countries that have weak private actors and ineffective states (see also Langbein 2011). As argued in the Introduction, the EU integration strategies did not merely focus on facilitating compliance with the *acquis communautaire*.[1] The EU also aimed at mitigating competitive asymmetries and increasing the capacity of domestic economic actors to benefit from an enlarged market (EU Council 1993).[2]

Understanding the variation in economic and social developmental outcomes, we argue, requires a better understanding of how pre-existing qualities of domestic organizing constrain and shape strategies of regional regulatory integration to the local context in order to improve developmental outcomes. Figure 3.1 summarizes our line of argumentation.

3.3 The Cases: Why Dairy in Poland and Romania?

The Polish and Romanian dairy industries display diverging economic and social developmental outcomes. Upon EU accession in 2004, Poland had managed to build a food safety system according to EU standards and to trade high-value dairy products within the EU Single Market, turning Poland into a net exporter of dairy products (Wilkin et al. 2006; Szajner 2009). Today, all Polish dairy farms comply with EU quality and safety regulations (Szajner 2009). At the same time, the modernization has not resulted in the marginalization of small farms. While the number of dairy farms declined by 550,000 from 1990 till 2007, the majority of farms were still in the market after EU accession. The average number of dairy cows per farm was only 16 in Poland in 2007, while the average herd size in the EU-15 was 51 (European Commission 2010). Three years after Poland's EU accession, 88 percent of Poland's milk-producing farms owned one to nine cows and accounted for 44 percent of total dairy cows, while medium-sized farms (10 to 29 cows) account for 37 percent of dairy cows and large Polish farms account for 19 percent of dairy cows (Szajner 2009;

---

[1] The *acquis communautaire* is the accumulated body of European Union (EU) law and obligations. It comprises all the EU's treaties and laws, declarations and resolutions, international agreements and the judgments of the Court of Justice. It also includes all EU measures relating to Justice and Home Affairs as well as to the Common Foreign and Security Policy.

[2] Authors' interviews with an official from DG Enlargement, Brussels, 16 May 2011.

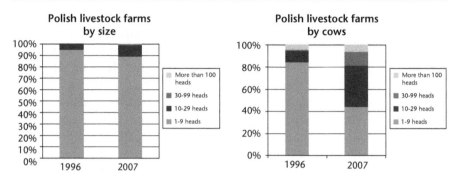

Figure 3.2 Polish livestock farms by size and dairy cows
Source: Szajner 2009: 7.

Figure 3.2). The Polish case suggests that integration in international food supply chains does not necessarily happen at the cost of excluding small farmers from national and transnational markets (see also Dries and Swinnen 2004).

By contrast, the quality of most Romanian milk is below EU standards, turning the country into a net-importer of high-quality milk (Istvan et al. 2009). In early 2009, half of the dairies and 70 percent of the collecting points were still in the transition period (Pieniadz et al. 2010: 4). Only a small share of farmers possessed appropriate health certificates required by Romanian law, which indicates high quality risks at the procurement stage. Recent reports by Romania's National Sanitary Veterinary and Food Safety Authority (NSVFSA), suggest that by December 2011, still about 19 percent of the raw milk provided to processing units did not meet the European quality requirements. Therefore, the Romanian government negotiated a transition period with the EU until December 2013. The average herd size of Romanian dairy farms in 2008 was six (European Commission 2011) with 97 percent of the population still holding five or fewer cows in 2009 (Luca et al. 2010). Only some larger Romanian dairy farms have successfully managed to create distinct brands and sell their products in almost all large, modern retailers in the urban areas (Pieniadz et al. 2010: 25). This suggests that the Romanian dairy market is bifurcated. In more developed Southern Romania (the Bucharest region) the procurement system changed from store-by-store procurement to centralized, large, and modern distribution centers. In that region, 90 percent of the dairy producers (e.g. Danone) procure raw milk directly from the (relatively larger) farms to reduce transaction costs. By contrast, in Transylvania, where small farmers produce 60 percent of Romanian's raw milk, the majority of farms cannot keep up with the quality demanded (Pieniadz et al. 2010).

The diverse outcomes in the Polish and Romanian dairy industries are puzzling. On the one hand, the two cases share similar starting characteristics. The agricultural sector in the two countries shared similar features of rural backwardness in the early 1990s. In the late 1980s, less than 30 percent of Polish villages had waterworks and only 8 percent had telephones. Similar conditions existed in Romania (Hunek 1994). Further, both dairy sectors experienced a sharp decline in milk production after 1990. From 1998/9 onwards Polish dairy production had a share of 13.6 percent in agricultural output, while the share of dairy in Romania amounted to 14.5 percent (van Berkum 2004). Dairy became a strategic subsector in both agricultural markets. By 2002, Poland and Romania were the largest dairy producers among the CEE countries: 42 percent of total milk production in EU candidate countries came from Poland and 18 percent was produced in Romania. In view of this initial rural backwardness and strategic significance of the dairy sector in both countries, we would have expected similar rather than diverging outcomes.

On the other hand, the particular outcomes are counterintuitive in view of the initial industry structure of the two sectors in the early transition years. In Poland, roughly 95 percent of Polish agricultural holdings owned one to nine cows and accounted for nearly 90 percent of the total number of dairy cows, while somewhat larger Polish farms with 10 to 29 cows accounted for the remaining 10 percent of the total number of dairy cows. The Romanian dairy industry was slightly more concentrated, since 56 percent of total production came from small private family farms, while state farms accounted for 18 percent of the production and larger farms for 28 percent (van Berkum 2004). According to conventional wisdom, a more concentrated industry structure facilitates modernization and convergence on international standards since larger farms benefit from economies of scale (Reardon and Barrett 2000; Weatherspoon and Reardon 2003; Humphrey et al. 2004). Hence, the Romanian dairy sector should have managed to converge to EU food safety standards more successfully than its Polish counterpart. As we will argue, these differences originate in the diverging ways domestic actors have reorganized these sectors after 1989.

3.4 The Polish Dairy Sector: Reorganized State and Organized Sectoral Interests

In the Polish dairy sector, and in Poland's agricultural sector in general, rural cooperatives have a long tradition. Cooperatives can be defined as bottom-up, voluntary organizations whose main purpose is to jointly sell their members' output (Małysz 1996: 13–14). Their first establishment dates back to the nineteenth century. As we will show, the somewhat unexpected survival of this form of sectoral organization has significantly contributed to the inclusive institutional change in the Polish dairy industry and prevented the marginalization of small milk producers during the preparation for Poland's EU accession. If members can produce according to the same jointly defined standards, their market position is likely to improve and prices will likely increase. In turn, the cooperatives can function as an organizational solution to collective action problems linked to meeting externally defined quality standards.

By 1988, 95 percent of the processed milk was produced by the 323 dairy cooperatives that existed in Poland at that time. After the changes in 1989, the organizational form of cooperatives did not fit the liberal agenda of the post-communist government. The Polish state stopped paying any subsidies and liberalized the prices for consumer goods, including dairy products. In the neo-liberal political atmosphere, the Polish government abolished the Central Union of Dairy Cooperatives (CUDC), leaving the dairy sector without an organization that could defend the interests of milk producers and dairy processors.

As a result of these policies, the Polish dairy sector witnessed a drastic decline. Between 1990 and 2005 the number of Polish dairy farms declined by more than 1 million, from 1.8 million to roughly 700,000 (Falkowski 2012). To address the resulting political problems the Ministry of Agriculture and Development (MARD) sought to stabilize the situation by appointing a "dairy plenipotentiary" with the task of "saving the dairy sector."[3] Thus not long after the first neo-liberal reforms, the Polish state set up an organizational structure to enact policy to revive the Polish agricultural sector in general. Drawing also on the ideational and financial support of the World Bank, the Foundation of Assistance Programs for Agriculture (FAPA) was established as early as 1992. FAPA was set up to implement development projects for the agricultural sector, to conduct research, and to prepare and publish analyses on rural development in Poland. In 1994, the Polish government founded another supporting institution for the development of the agricultural sectors. The Agency for Restructuring and Modernization of Agriculture (ARMA) was established with the aim of facilitating the upgrading of the country's farms and processing plants to meet EU food safety standards and to make Poland's agricultural sector competitive on the EU market. ARMA offered credit for construction of new buildings, food processing plants, and related activities at half the commercial lending rate. For example, loans with a 5 percent interest rate were offered to new farmers less

---

[3] Authors' interview with Ewa Domanska, Dairy Unit, Ministry of Agriculture and Rural Development, Warsaw, 17 Jan. 2011.

than 40 years of age and to existing farmers for purchase of additional farm land (Jesse et al. 2005).

At the same, the Polish dairy cooperatives managed to reinvent themselves. After the abolishment of the CUDC, former staff members and managers of dairy cooperatives occupied the CUDC's headquarters. Despite being dissolved on paper, the organization continued to work in practice. In June 1992, the National Union of Dairy Cooperatives (NUDC) was established. One of the central figures during these years was Marcin Strzelecki, then manager of the Regional Dairy Cooperative in Lowicz, which has subsequently become one of Poland's four biggest dairy producers.[4] Apart from these private initiatives geared towards the survival of dairy cooperatives and the sector's development, another factor saved the Polish dairy cooperatives. When thinking about the legal future of the cooperatives after 1989, the Polish government was uncertain whether to treat cooperatives as state-owned or private entities. The World Bank advised the Polish government to treat cooperatives as private entities, thus preventing the reprivatization of Polish cooperatives and their conversion into companies with limited liabilities or other forms of private ownership.[5]

Thanks to the survival of the cooperative movement, NUDC employees were able to join forces with the "dairy plenipotentiary" working within the MARD.[6] From early stages onwards, this new alliance closely cooperated with FAPA and ARMA in the framework of a dairy task force. As early as 1994, the FAPA steering committee, which included representatives of the dairy task force, began to translate and discuss the contents of internationally recognized food safety standards like ISO 22000 and HACCP[7] that are also applied on the EU market. Interestingly, HACCP was not even mandatory on the EU single market at that point. In fact, Polish food safety experts and officials proactively got acquainted with these food standards before the EU made them mandatory. In the framework of the FAPA steering committee, the dairy task force also developed an "Instrument for the Restructuring of the Dairy Sector" in order to "help, preserve and protect the sector."[8] More precisely, the task force sought to increase the efficiency of Polish dairy farms by upgrading production facilities. Policy-makers and producers alike understood the necessity to improve milk quality and diversify milk production in line with Poland's integration with the EU single market. Following the pressure from

---

[4] Authors' interview with Marek Murawski, National Union of Dairy Cooperatives, Warsaw, 18 Jan. 2011.

[5] Authors' interview with Jan Dabrowski, Chairman of the Regional Dairy Cooperative in Lowicz, Lowicz, 18 Jan. 2011.

[6] Authors' interview with Ewa Domanska, Warsaw, 17 Jan. 2011.

[7] Both ISO 22000 and HACCP concern quality management systems for food processors.

[8] Authors' interview with Ewa Domanska, Warsaw, 17 Jan. 2011.

the NUDC, the government put special emphasis on the support of small farms, since they were the "backbone of the Polish dairy sector,"[9] producing 85 percent of Polish raw milk in the 1990s. By 1994, Polish GDP was growing after the shock of the Balcerowicz reforms, and the Polish government introduced a system of preferential credits for the dairy sector. Funds from that source were extremely important for restructuring the processing segment in the 1990s. Expenditures under this measure more than doubled after 1995, from €6.1 million to €14.8 million in 2003 (Szajner 2009).

Despite these joint attempts to save and modernize the Polish dairy sector, the EU imposed a complete ban on all exports of Polish dairy products in 1997. Until then, a few EU member states had granted some Polish dairy plants access to the EU market. In 1992, the European Commission (EC) had already begun to promote harmonization of food standards across the EU single market and developed stricter safety and hygiene requirements in general and specifically for dairy products.[10] In the beginning, the EC fully relied on member states' border controls of food imports from non-EU countries. In response to several food scandals in the EU in the mid-1990s, the EC increased its capacity to pursue inspections and also created the Food and Veterinary Office (FVO) in 1997.[11] In the same year, FVO inspectors came to Polish dairy plants for the first time to test the implementation of harmonized EU food safety standards for dairy products. According to Jan Dabrowski, chairman of the Regional Dairy Cooperative in Lowicz, it was very clear at that time that not even the most successful dairy plants, including his own, met EU safety standards, such as scanning for bacteria. While EU officials hence justified the ban by making reference to inadequate sanitary conditions in manufacturing plants, Polish officials say the ban was mostly politics since the EU wanted to protect its own dairy industry (FAO 2003).[12] As a result of the ban, the share of EU-15 in total Polish dairy exports declined from 52.0 percent to 15.7 percent. Only by 2007, had the EU-15 reached their pre-1997 share in Polish dairy exports again, making up 56.6 percent of total dairy exports.

In light of this "market shock,"[13] the Polish state and non-state actors worked in tandem to design and implement a developmental strategy for the Polish dairy sector to meet the more demanding quality criteria. The

---

[9] Authors' interview with Waldemar Guba and Wanda Chielewska, Ministry of Agriculture, Warsaw, 17 Jan. 2011.

[10] In 1992, the European Commission introduced Regulation 92/46 that foresaw the harmonization of safety requirements for milk and milk-based products.

[11] Authors' phone interview with one official from the Food and Veterinary Office of DG SANCO, 30 June 2011.

[12] Authors' interview with Waldemar Guba and Wanda Chielewska, Warsaw, 17 Jan. 2011.

[13] Term used by Wanda Chielewska to describe the closure of the EU market for Polish dairy products in 1997; authors' interview, Warsaw, 17 Jan. 2011.

developmental alliance drew both on previous governmental programs and on the more specific policy proposals worked out by the NUDC after the "market shock." By 1995, the Polish Normalization Committee (PNC) had defined the norm "Raw milk for procurement," which was binding from 1 January 1998 onwards. The norm determined mandatory conditions for admitting raw milk to be purchased and criteria for a delivery to be accepted. The norm introduced four quality classes for procured milk, including an "extra" class which conformed to the EU standards laid down in the afore-mentioned EC Directive 92/46 (Hockmann and Pieniadz 2006). Milk producers had to indicate the particular quality level of their products through certificates from 1998 onwards. This is to say that, using the device of disclosure requirements, the Ministry enabled the improvement of the quality of dairy products and created incentives to apply EU quality standards even before EU accession. In January 2000, the Polish government imposed a procurement ban on class III milk, which was followed by a ban for class II milk in January 2003, and on class I milk in January 2007.

After the "market shock" the ministry asked the NUDC to work out a developmental strategy for the Polish dairy sector. In view of the newly introduced milk norms, the NUDC underlined that market pressure alone would not suffice to ensure the survival of the Polish dairy sector, especially with regard to small farmers.[14] The cooperatives pressed for the introduction of a special direct payment for "extra" quality milk production as financial support for dairy producers, which were introduced by the Polish government in 2002. The measure aimed at improving milk quality in the pre-accession period. During the first year of its implementation, the purchases of "extra" milk increased by 33 percent. According to several scholars, the measure made a significant contribution to the development of milk quality (Wilkin et al. 2006; Szajner 2009).

Further, the NUDC played an important role in the definition of priority measures and eligibility criteria for the EU pre-accession assistance in the form of the SAPARD program.[15] The program supported the Polish dairy sector with €120 million to build up the institutional framework of food safety control and support the Polish dairy industry in meeting EU standards. About 83 percent of the funds were assigned to the restructuring of dairy processing and improvement in the marketing of dairy products, while

[14] Authors' interview with Marek Murawski, Warsaw, 18 Jan. 2011.
[15] SAPARD: Special Accession Program for Agriculture and Rural Development. In June 1999, the EU passed Council Regulation (EC) No. 1268/99 on Community support for pre-accession measures for agriculture and rural development in the applicant countries of Central and Eastern Europe to prepare the candidate to take on EU *acquis* for agriculture and food safety.

17 percent were assigned to investments in the farms that produce milk (Agripolicy 2006: 6).[16]

Following the proposals of the NUDC, the Polish authorities also negotiated eligibility criteria with the EU that allowed smaller farms to apply for SAPARD funding. Both economic and political considerations were behind the insistence of the Polish authorities to extend the benefits of regulatory compliance to the smaller farms. By the early 2000s, the roughly one million small dairy farmers were the backbone of the Polish dairy industry, producing more than half of the Polish raw milk. In addition, Polish peasants constituted an important constituency. Considering their pronounced EU scepticism (Epstein and Sedelmeier 2008; Jacoby 2004), the Polish government was highly interested in negotiating favourable EU assistance programs in order to eradicate potential stumbling blocks to Poland's EU accession. Consequently, small farms with about six cows were eligible for SAPARD assistance (MARD 2000: 74).[17] In this respect, Falkowski (2012) notes that the assistance provided to small producers in Poland stands in sharp contrast to what researchers have found for the impact of vertical coordination on small farmers in Latin America. There, several studies have shown that small farmers were marginalized during the process of modernization (see e.g. Key and Runsten 1999; Weatherspoon and Reardon 2003).

Interestingly, the share of foreign investors has been relatively small in the Polish dairy sector (around 10 percent in 2003) when compared to other CEEC. Notwithstanding, investments of American and West European dairy processors in Poland from the mid-1990s onwards played a non-negligible role in the Polish milk sector. Upon their market entrance, foreign investors helped small Polish milk producers to adjust their production processes to EU standards. Interestingly, these foreign investors did not buy Polish milk-producing farms but rather provided inputs as well as financial and consultancy assistance. They set up cooling tanks at collection points, introduced free laboratory testing of antibiotics, and provided credits for Polish milk producers who became part of integrated supply chains (Dries and Swinnen 2004). Furthermore, foreign dairy processors invested in training programs to raise farmers' awareness of the importance of milk quality and

---

[16] According to Bryla (2004) the structure of the value of investments for milk producers applying for SAPARD was the following: 22.4 percent for buying machines to produce and store fodder, 20.9 percent for animal waste management equipment, only 2.2 percent for machines to freeze milk, 21.7 percent for the extension of buildings, 9.7 percent for the modernization of buildings, 12.5 percent for purchasing animals, and for 10.5 percent of the investment value the data were incomplete.

[17] The specific number of cows was not defined in the SAPARD Operational Program for Poland. However, it was mentioned that dairy farms needed to have minimum milk production of 20,000 l/year. Considering that the average milk yield in Poland was 3,778 litres per cow in 2000, farms with about six cows were eligible to apply for funding.

to improve quality through basic hygienic rules for farmers handling the milk in accordance with EU standards. MARD officials noted that by "watching the foreign investors" local dairy producers learned how to upgrade their production facilities and modernize the supply chains. Soon after foreign investors set up quality improvement programs, local dairies started to emulate these practices and by doing so created an important spillover effect, as shown by the dramatic milk quality improvement throughout the region after 1995 (Dries 2004).

Summing up, the survival of diary cooperatives provided the organizational basis for the intra-sectoral integration of hundreds of thousands of fragmented producers. At the same time, the developmental alliance between Polish state authorities and dairy cooperatives helped to modernize the Polish dairy sector and to foster its integration in the EU market without marginalizing small farmers. The organized Polish dairy sector was able to utilize the EU assistance programs in a proactive way by negotiating eligibility criteria for EU assistance that would not exclude small farms while also using a large part of the funds to upgrade production facilities and improve competitiveness. Preferential credit schemes, direct payments for extra class milk, as well as SAPARD assistance allowed dairy processors to make necessary investments.[18] Between 1994 and 2006, over PLN 1.13 billion of support was invested in the dairy industry, 65 percent of which were EU funds (Szajner 2009). Despite the fact that the share of foreign investment never exceeded 10 percent of the Polish dairy market, foreign investors also played a role in the process of institutional development by serving as a model for domestic dairy producers on how to upgrade production facilities and create vertical supply chains.

The share of Polish milk that was produced according to EU standards increased from 27 percent in 1998 to 85.1 percent in 2003 (Dries and Swinnen 2004). In a survey conducted with Polish as well as foreign dairy producers operating in Poland, the respondents noted that the EU export license had a significant impact on their milk quality policy (Dries 2004: 8). Membership conditionality played the least important role in the convergence of this sector to EU norms. Market access to the EU was the key factor in mobilizing the organized domestic actors to alter their institutions and upgrade their capacities. Carefully adjusting the EU assistance programs to their diverse needs helped both sectoral upgrading and broad-based distribution of its benefits.

---

[18] Authors' interview with Jan Dabrowski, 18 Jan. 2011.

3.5 The Romanian Dairy Sector: Insulated State and Fragmented Sector

In contrast to the Polish case, the Romanian dairy sector is still character-ized by a fragmented sectoral organization. Unlike in Poland, the imposi-tion of the state-controlled cooperatives in Romania under Communism has left behind a culture of distrust in cooperatives, preventing large-scale bottom-up organizing (Pieniadz et al. 2010: 32). As stressed by various inter-view partners, farmers were eager to possess their own piece of land after the fall of the communist regime and were not willing to combine forces to cre-ate producers' cooperatives.[19]

The lack of dairy cooperatives in a sector dominated by two-cow farms had significant effects on the integration of Romania's small milk-producing farms into modern supply chains as well as the inclusive allocation of assis-tance to small farmers. Although MNEs and the state both played a role in each country, alliance with the state was most important in Poland, while transnational value chains played the major role in selectively integrating farmers in Romania where the role of the state has been negligible until lately. Since 2000, in particular, there have been major changes in the Romanian dairy sector as a consequence of growing FDI. In fact, vertical coordination and contracting combined with assistance to producers devel-oped rapidly with FDI. Assistance programs include support to farmers from making feeding plans for their herd, how to increase milk quality, cleaning practices, and also full business plans. For instance, as early as 2000, Danone Romania, one of the largest multinational companies in the sector, began to negotiate special conditions for their contracted milk producers with suppliers of veterinary drugs, detergents, or machinery.[20] In 2005, Danone launched the program "Reaching West" aimed at providing their contracted milk-producing farms with favourable credit terms for investments needed to meet European standards. As a result, 90 percent of Danone's raw milk supply met European standards by mid-2010.[21] This quality allows Danone to sell its products all over Romania, mainly through large international retail markets, which demand the implementation of EU quality stand-ards (van Berkum 2004). However, leading Romanian dairy plants includ-ing Danone offer their assistance mainly to larger farms owning at least 20 cows. Considering that two-cow farms dominate Romania's dairy sector, this

---

[19] Authors' interviews with state officials, dairy producers, and processors, Bucharest, 4–6 July 2011.

[20] Authors' interview with a representative from Danone Romania, Bucharest, 6 July 2011.

[21] Authors' interview with a representative from Danone Romania, Bucharest, 6 July 2011.

strategy of foreign investors severely reduces the developmental impact of assistance (van Berkum 2004).

There were exceptions to this rule: some dairy processors including Friesland Romania, a subsidiary of the Dutch FCDF group, seemed to be more inclined to work with small farms than Danone. They assisted small suppliers and invested in overcoming transaction costs. Friesland Romania entered the market in 2000. Only three years later the company processed approximately 200–250 tons of milk per day across five factories. The company has simple contracts with approximately 40,000 small farmers from whom it purchases milk through 1,050 collecting points and from some 600 larger farms (van Berkum 2009). Friesland owns the collection points and has upgraded them by investing in cooling and inspection facilities. At the same time it is important to note that Friesland's collection points have largely not complied with EU safety and quality requirements as of 2009 (Pieniadz et al., 2010). This suggests that Friesland invested less in increasing the quality of milk than in increasing the quantity of milk supply.

Finally, larger domestic dairy companies, such as Promilch and Albalact (formerly Raraul), take care of the collection and transport themselves, which makes it easier for small farmers to deliver milk to these dairy processors (see Falkowski 2012, for a similar argument). Raraul was a former state-owned company in Romania that was privatized. In 2009, the company merged with Romanian Albalact to increase its competitive advantage vis-à-vis Danone and others through economies of scale. Some of Albalact/Raraul's dairy plants comply with EU standards; others, particularly those contracting smaller milk-producing farms, exclusively focus on the Romanian market. Promilch was started as a private company. In 1999, the ISPA dairy association with 2,000 members, most of which were small-scale farmers, invested in Promilch. ISPA's investment was made possible through the Dutch PSO support program (2004, 2009).[22] Promilch/IPSA sells mainly to small local shops and local supermarkets. IPSA has taken initiatives to provide its members with a secure market outlet and basic farm-level support on matters of key importance (feeding, milk quality, and hygiene). Still, most dairy farms owned by IPSA did not manage to comply with EU food safety standards.

The previous discussion reveals that foreign investors integrated domestic producers in their supply chains in a highly selective manner, focusing mainly on integrating larger farms. Large domestic dairies that did integrate smaller farms simply focused on the domestic market rather than upgrading. The Romanian government also did not initiate support programs for

---

[22] PSO is an association that consists of 60 Dutch development organisations. The association focuses on capacity development at civil society organizations in developing countries and gets funding from the Dutch government.

the dairy sector to the same extent as its Polish counterpart. Support programs started much later and were much more limited in their scope. The major measures that the government applied to the sector aimed at increasing the quantity of milk, while the improvement in milk quality was only expected to happen as a side effect. Moreover, the support was only available on the condition that producers hold 15 or more milk animals, or that they belonged to an association meeting this criterion (Istvan et al. 2009). These eligibility criteria excluded the majority of Romanian farms, given the average herd size of two to four cows.

Romanian authorities began to think about a development strategy for the agricultural sector only when the country started EU accession negotiations in 1999. As mentioned earlier, the EC passed its Regulation on SAPARD that same year and Romanian authorities were interested in getting access to the funds as soon as possible. However, the Romanian state was rather insulated from the sector. Back then Romania lacked a business organization that represented the interests of milk producers, as the Association of Romanian Dairy Processors (APRIL) was only established in 2000. Officials from Romania's Ministry of Agriculture and Rural Development came up with a National Plan for Agriculture and Rural Development in that year without prior consultation of stakeholders. As one official participating in the writing of this plan admitted, "We were not good in thinking strategically." Membership conditionality was the key factor in making the government act rather than the pull of EU markets and the push of organized local producers from below. High-ranking politicians were interested in legislative harmonization in order to close negotiating chapters. Unlike in Poland, considerations of economic upgrading or social inclusion did not play a central role in this program. The representatives of the government were led by the belief that the biggest processors and producers would most likely be able to meet the standards quickly and become competitive.[23]

Therefore, Romanian authorities did advantage processors and bigger milk producers vis-à-vis smaller processors and producers in terms of allocation of the SAPARD funds. To be eligible for SAPARD funding for new or modernized collecting, reception, cooling, and storage centers of milk, the farm must produce a minimum of 200,000 litres per year. Considering that the average milk yields in Romania were 2,525 litres per cow in 2000 (Adamov and Iancu 2009), a farm would have to own roughly 80 cows in order to be considered eligible for SAPARD funds in Romania. In a similar vein, Pieniadz et al. (2010) found that most of the SAPARD funds (22 percent) were allocated to

---

[23] Authors' interviews with Constantin Leonte, former Head of Selection and Contracting Unit at Romania's SAPARD Agency, Bucharest, 4 July 2011, and Dan Ghergelas, former Deputy Director of Romania's SAPARD Agency, Bucharest, 5 July 2011.

agricultural holdings and food-processing firms to facilitate the adoption of EU standards, and to actors in agri-business to improve vocational training. Only a small part of the resources were allocated to foster ties and sustainable partnerships between producers and downstream businesses (Pieniadz et al. 2010: 28). The Romanian SAPARD Plan only foresaw spending 2 percent of the funds on the creation of producer groups in support of small milk farms to modernize their facilities (MARD 2006). Also, Luca (2007) notes that mostly large units (farmers, processors) benefited from SAPARD measures, while small and medium-sized farms lacked the capacity to co-finance the investment. As Constantin Leonte, who used to work as a high-ranking official at Romania's SAPARD Agency, notes: "You will not find a single measure in Romania's National Plan for Agriculture and Rural Development that was targeted at small milk producers with four cows."[24]

Even though the European Commission was keen to ensure economic viability with regard to the spending and allocation of SAPARD funds, the Commission left it largely to the governments of the accession countries to define the boundaries of "economic viability."[25] Freedom to localize the mechanisms for development was not complemented by inclusive development. Due to the weakness of cooperatives in Romania, small dairy farmers had no voice in the policy-making process. As a result, the Romanian government could use the EU assistance in a much more exclusionary way.

Instead of the government, the EU had to build basic structures of sectoral organization in Romania. The developmental alliance between the business association of cooperatives and the state administration in Poland smoothly cooperated to meet the EU quality criteria long before the starting of the accession negotiations. In contrast, the EU progress report still complained about the "very limited management and administrative capacity" of the Romanian food safety regulators in 2003 (European Commission 2003c: 67). After several years of complaining about limited progress in the implementation of EU regulations, the EU changed strategy in 2004. In order to enhance capacity building from within, it created the National Sanitary Veterinary and Food Safety Authority (NSVFSA), the core institutions designed to coordinate *acquis* enforcement, monitor, administer, and design better policies in the area of food safety. In the 2005 Comprehensive Monitoring Report the elementary aspects of implementation are still at the forefront, specifically mentioning the need for strengthening staffing, office, and logistic facilities at NSVFSA (European Commission 2005: 43).

---

[24] Authors' interviews with Constantin Leonte, Bucharest, 4 July 2011, and Dan Ghergelas, Bucharest, 5 July 2011.

[25] Authors' interview with EU officials from DG Agriculture and DG SANCO, Brussels, 16 May 2011, and with Dan Ghergelas, Bucharest, 5 July 2011.

Even prior to the creation of the special state agency for coordinating and overseeing the implementation of EU food safety, the EU interventions in the Romanian food sector played a role that can be best described as an attempt to substitute the missing domestic demand side for state upgrading. In the various EU reports one can find long lists of demands for strengthening basic sectoral administrative capacities. The demand to reinforce the administrative capacity to implement and enforce the *acquis*, in particular in the veterinary and phytosanitary fields, was just one of the demands in a much longer list that aimed at creating basic state capacities to help the embedding of Romanian agriculture in the regional market integration. Moreover, already in the early 2000s, the EU demanded the reinforcement of the administrative structures for monitoring agricultural markets, the implementation of structural and rural development measures, the establishment of bodies and control mechanisms for such policies, the reinforcement of food control administration, and the implementation of the five-year strategy for the National Authority for Consumer Protection. Furthermore, the EU demanded the reinforcement of administrative structure in order to ensure more efficient implementation and management of SAPARD measures as well as the creation of a new state support policy targeted at the development of a market-oriented agricultural policy (European Commission 2001, 2002).

In this process of EU interventions that focused on creating and strengthening administrative state capacities, both the EU and the Romanian state realized that the process of upgrading the system of food safety would be very difficult, given the property fragmentation of Romanian agriculture. While trying to substitute for the missing domestic demand side for upgrading state capacities, the EU could not substitute for the role played by the Polish cooperatives in integrating and organizing small farmers. Given the existence of an incipient two-tier system with a few big players and hundreds of thousands of unorganized and politically under-represented small players, the EU assistance programs focused on upgrading the big producers and excluding the small ones. In Poland the small producers were represented both by the association of cooperatives and the state at the negotiations on the use of EU assistance programs. Small Romanian farmers, however, simply lacked representation when the Romanian authorities negotiated the eligibility criteria with the EU for pre-accession assistance. Neither did Romanian authorities allow small farmers to access the funds, nor did they think about ways to strengthen the role of cooperatives in order to allow for more inclusive change (Istvan et al. 2009). Their attempt at strengthening cooperatives by enabling small producers to access support when connected to larger associations only exacerbated the collective action problems rather than empowering the smaller producers.

3.6 Conclusion

This chapter has aimed to complement the studies of strategies of regional regulatory integration by investigating the factors that shape the divergence of developmental outcomes within the same integration regime. We have shown that strategies of regulatory integration had to adjust to extreme variation in domestic conditions. We also demonstrated that the effects of localized strategies were mediated by the quality of the sectoral organization of private and public actors in combination with the characteristics of the relationship between state and non-state actors.

While our study calls attention to the limitations of the learning capacities of regional organizations, it also goes beyond the assumption that mechanisms used by them to further their integration goals would work the same way across the various member states. Our findings also challenge the assumption that the relevance of these mechanisms would remain constant in the process of converging to transnational regulations. Membership conditionality was the most important factor in inducing departure from institutional status quo in Romania, complemented with direct interventions and assistance by the EU. The EU programs have largely substituted for the missing domestic demand side for upgrading administrative state capacities. The assistance programs helped to move the sector away from a low equilibrium trap by creating the elementary sectoral state capacities to monitor and sanction EU rules and to create and implement sectoral developmental policies. The emerging political organization of the sector gave a highly distorted representation to the economic actors by over-representing larger producers. In contrast, economic incentives linked to the large EU markets have played the key role in institutional change in Poland while EU assistance complemented already ongoing inclusive developmental programs.

By focusing on differences in the developmental strategies and effects of the EU, we address an under-studied aspect of the regulatory integration of the CEE countries. An international relations (IR) perspective largely dominates the field with a focus on the mechanisms linked to asymmetrical power relations and the robust political leverage of denying or giving membership in the EU (Kelley 2004; Schimmelfennig and Sedelmeier 2005; Vachudova 2005). If looking at regulatory integration from only the perspective of the IR approach, one would miss key factors of post-accession compliance to EU rules. Studies written from that perspective largely underestimated the role played by economic incentives. They also homogenized the role EU interventions and assistance programs have played in changing the preferences of domestic actors and altering their capacities to benefit from compliance. The diverse EU assistance programs have increased domestic capacities for rule compliance as the management approach suggests (Tallberg 2002). However, we have shown that EU assistance programs have also addressed, to widely differing degrees, the issue of inclusive economic development in the CEE economies. These interventions had the primary goal of reducing the need for massive post-accession transfers to compensate for large-scale loss in the economic viability of large parts of the CEE economies. But, by combining issues of compliance and development, these assistance programs have also contributed to the increased post-accession sustainability of EU regulations, increasing the incentives and capacities of CEE economic actors to profit from playing by the regional rules.

Finally, the lessons of the IR approach, linked to perfected EU membership conditionality, have limited use for attempts at regulatory integration outside the EU. Some, such as regional integration projects in South America, lack a committed regional hegemon. Others, such as the North American Free Trade Area (NAFTA), have one, but lack an equally robust reward like EU membership. The close coupling between factors of compliance and developmental opportunities discussed in this chapter provide lessons that can travel across regions. The more obvious one is that strategies that upgrade domestic institutions and allow for broad-based inclusion can also increase the chances of the sustainability of transnational regulations. The other message is that regulatory integration strategies that care about the developmental effects might face nontrivial challenges due to significant variation in the organization of domestic state and non-state actors.

4

Transnational Integration and Labor Market Regulation in Mexico and Beyond

Michael J. Piore and Andrew M. Schrank

4.1 Introduction

The arrival of the North American Free Trade Agreement (NAFTA) in 1994 represented the culmination of an almost two-decade-long movement toward the integration of the Canadian, Mexican, and United States economies. It also signaled the abandonment of the import-substituting industrial development model pioneered by Mexico's Institutional Revolutionary Party (Partido Revolucionario Institucional) and the dawn of a new model inspired by neo-classical economic theory and neo-liberal ideology. While US legislators conditioned their support for NAFTA on the adoption of a "side agreement" designed to "protect, enhance and enforce basic workers' rights" in all three countries (NAALC 1993: 1), their efforts would ultimately prove futile, for the agreement thereby produced has had a negligible impact on workplace regulation in Mexico in particular (LaSala 2001; Russo 2002; Caulfield 2010).

To understand not only *why* this is the case but the broader implications for the relationship between economic integration and workplace regulation, one needs an understanding of the two contradictory models that have guided Mexican economic policy in recent decades—import substitution and export promotion—and their interactions with two equally contradictory models of worker protection: a broadly North American model that assigns different labor and employment laws to distinct government agencies; and a Franco-Iberian alternative that gives skilled inspectors with enormous discretion responsibility for the entire body of workplace regulation. While Mexican officials could have facilitated and humanized the move from import substitution to export promotion by taking full advantage of the Franco-Iberian model in the wake of NAFTA's approval, they for the most part squandered the opportunity and were thus left to reconsider the role of labor law—and workplace inspection—in a less auspicious atmosphere of social and economic crisis in the early twenty-first century.

What are the likely results? We address the question by placing the recent reform of the Ley Federal del Trabajo (i.e. the LFT or Federal Labor Law) in regional and historical context in five principal sections. First, we discuss the Mexican economy's disappointing performance in the post-NAFTA years and offer two competing interpretations: an orthodox account that blames the allegedly inflexible Mexican labor market for impeding the adjustment of the economy and provides the intellectual rationale for the reform of the LFT; and a critical alternative that considers the labor market *too* flexible in practice and calls for government efforts to drive employers out of low-cost, low-wage activities and into more productive and profitable alternatives. Second, we discuss NAFTA's impact on the labor market and Mexican workers in particular. While NAFTA itself had a dramatic impact on the structure, composition, and location of the Mexican workforce, the labor side agreement had almost no effect at all, and Mexican workers therefore find themselves no more—and in all likelihood less—protected today than they were at the height of authoritarian rule. Third, we discuss the role of informality in the Mexican labor market, noting that it constitutes a threat to the well being of employers as well as workers. When employers have access to large pools of low-cost, unprotected workers, after all, they have neither the will nor, in many cases, the ability to engage in productive upgrading and skill formation that would ultimately redound to their own benefit as well as that of their workers. Fourth, we discuss the potential, but by no means inevitable, advantages of the Franco-Iberian model of labor inspection. While skilled inspectors in France, the Iberian countries, and a number of their colonial offshoots have used their discretion to reconcile compliance with competitiveness, their Mexican counterparts have for the most part been unwilling or unable to do so, and have thus paid a price in terms of productive upgrading and worker protection. And, finally, we discuss the prospects for a regulatory renaissance in wake of the reform of the LFT. The reforms themselves are orthodox in origin and orientation, and are thus designed to add flexibility to the Mexican labor market, but they have been accompanied by added enforcement resources that, if managed wisely, could go a long way toward reconciling protection with productive upgrading in the decades to come.

4.2 The Strategy of Economic Integration

The results of the neo-liberal turn epitomized by NAFTA have been disappointing by any measure. Privatization, deregulation, and the liberalization

Table 4.1 Mexican economic performance, 1989–2012

Variable	1989–93	1994–8	1999–2003	2004–8	2009–12
GDP growth (annual %)	3.81	3.01	2.50	3.37	1.78
GDP per capita growth (annual %)	1.69	1.10	1.06	2.10	0.52
Export growth (annual %)	5.82	17.82	5.83	7.11	5.07
Manufactures in merchandise exports (%)	57.00	79.88	83.88	75.76	74.67
High-tech exports in manufactured exports (%)	10.01	16.34	21.62	18.56	17.21
GDP per worker (constant 1990 PPP $)	17277	17483	18846	19748	19566

Note: Data are from the World Bank (2013) and represent period averages for all periods and variables with the exception of high technology exports in the final period, which constitutes the three-year average for 2009–2011.

of trade and investment have animated decidedly less growth than anticipated and have instead been associated with crisis, insecurity, and the persistence of informal employment (Zepeda et al. 2009; Arias et al. 2010; Baz et al. 2010; Hanson 2010). Table 4.1 includes data on output, exports, and productivity in the years before and after the passage of NAFTA and paints a decidedly disappointing tale.

While aggregate output, exports, and productivity have grown over the past two decades, and have diversified to some degree as well, they have done so inconsistently, and have done little for workers who find themselves trapped in "one of the largest underground economies in Latin America" (Kandell 2012: 19) in particular. In fact, the already outsized problem of informality has intensified in the era of the Great Recession "due to the decline in export demand and a sharp increase in the share of the working-age population in informal employment (up to 63 percent of total employment) during the last phase of the downturn and the initial phase of the recovery" (OECD 2011: 1; see also Arias et al. 2010: 37).

A debate has ensued as to why this is the case. One strand in that debate blames the incomplete liberalization of the economy, in general, and the maintenance of "excessive" workplace regulation, in particular (Arias et al. 2010: 32; see also Baz et al. 2010), and portrays the recent effort to reform the country's labor laws as a potential solution (see e.g. Cruz Vargas 2012; *El Universal* 2013). But the regulations in question have gone all but unenforced in practice and the notion of an inflexible Mexican labor market is arguably gainsaid by the very informality the neo-liberals decry.

An alternative perspective—to which we subscribe—holds that Mexican policy-makers and businesspeople exaggerated the stability of their country's role as a source of low-wage labor for the North American market and were thus caught flatfooted when the United States began to negotiate free trade agreements with rival countries, extend trade preferences to low-wage economies in Africa and Asia, and welcome China into the World Trade Organization in the early twenty first century (Dussel Peters 2009; Zepeda et al. 2009). If they are to survive and prosper in the years ahead, therefore, Mexican firms and workers must move upmarket into more capital- and skill-intensive activities.

The Mexican system of labor and employment regulation need not constitute a drag on the development process but could, if it were reinvigorated, contribute to the growth of the "high road" alternative we have in mind. The Mexican system derives from a model of workplace regulation developed in France and Spain and stands in sharp contrast to the North American model in at least two respects: first, it is a "general" system that assigns responsibility for the entire body of labor law (e.g. wages and hours, safety and health, child labor, etc.) to a single agency; and, second, it is "compliance" oriented and thus gives enforcement officials a wider array of tools than the sanctions that are the default option in more adversarial systems—not to mention the discretion they need to use those tools effectively. In a number of Latin American countries, in fact, that discretion has been combined with efforts to promote industrial and employment upgrading by linking noncompliant enterprises to agencies responsible for worker training, manufacturing extension, and low-cost finance through a kind of carrot and stick approach that turns workplace inspectors into the "foot soldiers of the campaign for decent work" (Piore and Schrank 2008: 21; see also e.g. Pires 2008; Schrank 2013a).

Until recently, Mexico has shown virtually no inclination to "block the low road" and "pave the high road" (Piore and Schrank 2006) in this way. But a new director assumed control over the federal workplace inspectorate (Inspección de Trabajo) in the aftermath of the Pasta de Conchos mining disaster in 2006 (Noriega 2011; Flores 2012), and was soon promoted to Undersecretary of Labor and Social Welfare, where he reports directly to the minister. He introduced managerial reforms that could in theory give him (or his successors) the ability to turn workplace inspection into a tool of development policy, and the recent labor law reform arguably gives him an incentive—and potentially the resources—to do so. After all, the new regime is designed to make compliance less costly and more common by allowing hourly wages, apprenticeships, and subcontracting arrangements that had previously been illegal in Mexico, on the one hand, and increasing the number, quality, and disciplinary authority of Mexican labor inspectors, on the other (El Informador 2013; El Universal 2013; Flores 2013; STPS 2013).

In order to take advantage of the opportunity, however, the Undersecretary and his allies at the labor ministry would not only have to encourage and motivate their own personnel to pursue a more audacious goal than mere accident (or scandal) prevention but would simultaneously have to forge links to cognate state agencies—e.g. vocational education and training, small business support, and development banks—that have themselves been debilitated by years of neo-liberal neglect. We are by no means sanguine about such an outcome, especially in light of the neo-liberal rhetoric emanating from the administration in the run-up to the reform and the persistent focus on accident prevention after the fact (*El Informador* 2012; Valadez 2012; STPS 2013).

Overall this suggests that transnational integration has had very little direct effect on the regulation of the workplace in Mexico but has instead been used by domestic political forces and technocrats to pursue their own ends for their own reasons. If the international environment has played a role, moreover, it has basically been to provide an intellectual framework in which domestic policy was developed and its impact understood. In the case of labor and employment regulation, we believe, that framework has led to a narrow understanding of Mexico's institutional heritage and a correspondingly limited view of the country's policy options today. Our goal, therefore, is to reconsider those options in light of both the history of workplace regulation in Mexico and the experiences of nearby countries that have pursued more aggressive efforts to reconcile the ostensibly competing goals of worker protection and economic efficiency in the course of late development.

4.3 Two Strategies of Economic Development: From Import Substitution to Export Promotion

In order to appreciate the importance of this understanding (and misunderstanding) of the nature of workplace regulation in Mexico, one needs to place it in the context of the evolution of Mexican economic performance in the postwar period and, with it, the evolution of the country's approach to economic development. In the early postwar period, Mexico was—like the rest of Latin America—committed to a strategy of import substitution. The federal government played an active role in fostering key industries, and the domestic economy was heavily protected against foreign competition. By almost any measure, this strategy was very successful. Between 1940 and 1970, for example, the economy as a whole grew at an average annual rate of more than 6 percent and per capita incomes grew at approximately 3 percent per year (Moreno-Brid and Ros 2009). In the 1970s, however, the Mexican economy entered a volatile era of inflation, capital flight, and devaluation, and with the dawn of the debt crisis in the early 1980s growth came to a virtual standstill.

The government reacted to these developments by abandoning import substitution for a neo-liberal alternative that involved the deregulation of economic activity, privatization of state-owned enterprises, and liberaliza-tion of trade and foreign investment. The capstone of this policy shift was the negotiation of the North American Free Trade Agreement, a move toward regional integration in which Mexico received what was then preferential access to the US and Canadian markets in exchange for concessions to north-ern investors on a range of issues including not only market access but inves-tor protection, financial regulation, and intellectual property rights (Shadlen 2005). Labor standards were a topic of discussion during the negotiations that led to NAFTA, and they found considerable support among union-backed politicians in the US and Canada, but they were ultimately relegated to a side agreement—the North American Agreement on Labor Cooperation—that obliged the three member countries not only to enforce their own labor laws but to establish National Administrative Offices (NAOs) that would review complaints about "labor law matters in the other two countries" (US Department of Labor 2005) and take appropriate action ranging from minis-terial consultations—when collective bargaining issues were at stake—to the establishment of expert committees, arbitral panels, or the eventual imposi-tion of sanctions, when technical labor standards (e.g. child and forced labor, minimum wage, and safety and health laws) were violated. While Tamara Kay traces the growth of "transnational relationships" among unions to the requirement that they "file complaints outside of their home countries" (Kay 2011: 10), and portrays the alliance thereby engendered between the United Electrical, Radio and Machine Workers (UE) in the US and the Authentic Labor Front (Frente Auténtico del Trabajo, or FAT) in Mexico as a model to be emulated, she arguably exaggerates their potential impact, for the UE and the FAT are decidedly dissident unions in their home countries and their admittedly "unique vision" (Kay 2011: 172) would therefore seem to con-firm—rather than to gainsay—Kenneth Shadlen's sense that nongovernmen-tal organizations forge transnational ties less to exploit their strength and influence than to compensate for their "weakness and isolation" (Shadlen 2004: 126; see also Keck 1995: 420)—with all that entails for the likelihood of their success. Nor are the UE and the FAT alone. On the contrary, peti-tions to the respective National Administrative Offices came from a verita-ble who's who of dissident unions including the Telephone Workers' Union (Sindicato de Telefonistas de la Republica Mexicana), October 6th Industrial and Commercial Workers' Union (Sindicato de Trabajadores de la Industria y Comercio 6 de Octubre), and the National Workers' Union (Union Nacional de Trabajadores) in Mexico, the Teamsters under dissident leader Ron Carey in the US, and the Canadian Union of Postal Workers, to name but a few. In no case did they pass beyond ministerial consultations to an expert commit-tee or arbitral panel, let alone issue in the imposition of trade sanctions (Kay 2011: 115).

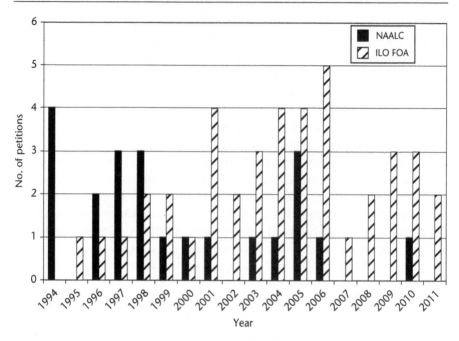

Figure 4.1 Petitions to the NAALC and the ILO CFA (1994–2011)

Data: US DOL, ILAB, 2010, and ILO, CFA, 2012; cases that were filed in both the US and Canadian NAOs are counted only once.

Not surprisingly, therefore, activists—including dissident as well as mainstream unions—have all but abandoned the NAALC process. Figure 4.1 includes data on the number of petitions submitted to the US and Canadian NAOs, on the one hand, and the International Labour Organization's Committee on Freedom of Association (CFA), on the other, on behalf of Mexican workers between 1994, when the NAALC came into effect, and 2011, when the most recent petitions were filed. Petitions to both the NAOs and the ILO tend to address freedom of association and collective bargaining practices in Mexico (Nolan 2011: 53), and the data therefore reveal three things.

First, the number of complaints is relatively stable. The two organizations received 29 complaints in the nine years between 1994 and 2002 and 34 complaints in the nine-year period since 2002, and to the extent that complaints are a valid indicator of the underlying distribution of violations—an admittedly generous assumption—it would seem that the collective bargaining situation in Mexico continues to leave much to be desired. Second, the NAALC has lost ground to the ILO over time. While the US and Canadian NAOs received slightly more complaints than the CFA between 1994 and 2002, the subsequent ratio is almost 4:1 in the opposite direction, and the

NAFTA institutions therefore appear to be losing legitimacy among the very activists who are indispensable to their success. And, finally, the NAALC has fallen into virtual disuse. In the past five years, only one new petition has been filed on behalf of Mexican workers through the NAALC process.

The NAALC's impotence is less an accident than a predictable consequence of the fact that not only the Mexican government but certain factions in the US and Canada viewed NAFTA as part of an approach to economic management that demanded the elimination, rather than the imposition, of labor regulations, and Norman Caulfield therefore worries that by mandating the enforcement—rather than the adequacy—of domestic labor law, the side agreement gives member countries an "incentive to attract investment through the deregulation of their respective labor law regimes" (Caulfield 2010: 67). For all of its obvious importance, therefore, NAFTA is less an independent factor in the evolution of the North American labor market than a reflection of economic policy-making *within* Mexico and the United States.

The new strategy has nonetheless had an enormous impact on the Mexican economy and society. In fact, the structure of the economy has been completely transformed in the NAFTA era. Mexico almost immediately displaced Japan as the second largest market for US exports and by 1999 had eclipsed Japan to become the second largest US trading partner overall (Vargas 1999). In Mexico itself, moreover, the main axis of development shifted from the Federal District of Mexico City, where it had been centered during the era of import substitution, to border and coastal cities with easy access to the US market (Sánchez-Reaza and Rodríguez-Pose 2002). Aggregate growth rates have accelerated at times, but they have apparently been accompanied by industrial abuses and accidents (cf. Takala 1999: 644; Hämäläinen et al. 2009: 135) and they nonetheless pale in comparison to both the "miracle" years of the postwar era and the growth rates found in more dynamic Latin American economies like Chile, the Dominican Republic, and Peru today, let alone Brazil, Russia, India, and China—the so-called BRICs.[1]

4.4 Labor Market Regulation and Mexico's Malaise: Cause or Potential Cure?

The failure to achieve higher growth rates has engendered a renewed debate about Mexican economic policy, and debate that has gained force in the wake of the return of the PRI under President Enrique Peña Nieto in late

---

[1] By way of illustration, productivity—measured by GDP per worker employed (World Bank 2013)—has grown by a mere 11 percent in Mexico since the implementation of NAFTA and by 21 percent in Brazil, 75 percent in Russia, 130 percent in India, and 311 percent in China over the same period.

2012. From a neo-liberal perspective, the obvious explanation is that the market-oriented reforms are incomplete; they have not gone far enough and the solution includes the modification or elimination of a long list of demands that have traditionally been placed upon employers. These demands include not only regulations governing wages, hours, working conditions, and collective bargaining but legal requirements for severance payments, low cost housing loans, health insurance, disability and retirement pensions, training, and profit sharing (see, e.g., Levy 2007; Arias et al. 2010). Most of these provisions date from the Mexican Revolution itself and are enshrined in the Constitution or the Federal Labor Law. In the neo-liberal literature, they are viewed as anachronistic products of an ill-advised effort to impose institutions copied from the advanced industrial countries on the less developed economy of Mexico. Thus, Javier Arias and his colleagues asserted that Mexico has "the highest labor rigidity among similar less developed countries" (Arias et al. 2010) in 2010 and blamed the country's labor laws for the inefficiency, informality, and stagnation of the Mexican economy.[2]

The alleged rigidities of the Mexican labor market are nonetheless gainsaid by the very informality they are said to produce (UNECLAC 2009: 62; Burgess 2010: 219). While the country's labor and employment laws are burdensome in theory, they are flexible in practice, for their enforcement is at best sporadic and at worst imaginary (see Bensusán 2008; Ruiz Durán 2009; Santos 2009). Mexico has one of the highest ratios of workers to labor inspectors in Latin America—and perhaps the world (ILO 2006a: 15). And the country's labor courts are notoriously hostile to workers as well. In fact, David Kaplan and Joyce Sadka have demonstrated not only that Mexican "labor law is unlikely to be enforced even after the worker wins a case in a labor court" but that "the court's inability to enforce judgments has an important impact on the entire bargaining process, tilting the de facto regulatory environment towards the interests of the firm" (Kaplan and Sadka 2008: 3).

The alternative interpretation to which we subscribe is that NAFTA turned out to be the first of a series of free trade agreements forged by the United

---

[2] Santiago Levy provides a more sophisticated variant of the neo-liberal interpretation. He not only blames the regulation and taxation of salaried employment for the initial growth of the informal sector but portrays compensatory programs designed to offer non-salaried workers access to an à la carte menu of "health, housing, day care and more recently pension benefits" (Levy 2007: 4) as a greater inducement to informality. His reasoning is straightforward. While the benefits that accrue to salaried workers are paid for by payroll taxes, and are therefore a *substitute* for cash wages, the benefits that are available to non-salaried workers are paid for by the government (subject to a nominal contribution from the recipient), and are therefore a *complement* to cash wages. A rational worker will therefore maximize his or her wage and benefit portfolio by defecting from the high-productivity formal sector into the low-productivity informal sector—and in so doing hive the costs of social protection onto the already overburdened Mexican state. Nevertheless, Levy provides little evidence that workers defect from the formal sector in order to take advantage of compensatory social programs, and the bulk of the empirical evidence appears to gainsay his argument (see e.g. Arias et al. 2010: 44, for a brief review).

States and was followed by the expansion of unilateral preference schemes (e.g. the African Growth and Opportunity Act) and China's incorporation into the WTO. Mexico's privileged access to the US market therefore turned out to be short-lived. Some of the plants that had already (or might otherwise have) moved to Mexico instead moved to lower wage countries in other parts of the world. And Mexican producers of labor-intensive manufactures suddenly found themselves in a life-or-death struggle not only for the US market but for their home market as well (Dussel Peters 2009; Zepeda et al. 2009).

The impact of the opening of China has been particularly hard on Mexico, especially during the volatile years at the turn of the century when labor-intensive manufacturers responded to the initial decline in US demand by laying off workers in Mexico and to the subsequent revival of US demand by expanding operations in China. Mexican officials might have used the advantages afforded by NAFTA to lay the groundwork for an effort to move upmarket through the dissemination of education and training, more sophisticated production technologies, and managerial skills. But they failed to do so, in no small part because of their commitment to a neo-liberal ideology that eschewed the kinds of programs that would have been needed to facilitate such an outcome.

Mexico's adjustment to the pressures of foreign competition turned out to be incomplete as well, and the country was therefore unable to take full advantage of the opportunities afforded by regional integration. A number of the "national champions" that had grown up under the umbrella of import-substituting industrialization moved into foreign markets with a vengeance and thrived in the open economy (see e.g. Schrank 2005). But most of the adjustment took place through foreign direct investment and decentralized production networks that linked global buyers to contract manufacturers in Mexico's *maquiladoras* (Dussel Peters et al. 2002). Small firms in traditional industries like apparel, footwear, and furniture manufacturing floundered, and the government—again guided by neo-liberal strictures—offered them neither the financial nor the technical support they would need to take advantage of market opening (Dussel Peters 2001; Shadlen 2004). While labor standards would almost certainly have provided an incentive to move upmarket, and in so doing served as a "beneficial constraint" (Streeck 1997) on Mexican firms, they were rendered all but impotent by their relegation to an ineffectual side agreement—itself a product of the same neo-liberal ideology that was responsible for the character of NAFTA in the first place.

In a final irony, NAFTA was the last major US trade agreement to ignore or downgrade the importance of the labor question. The US Congress reacted to the outcry engendered by NAFTA by conditioning the approval of future trade accords—including those with Chile, Colombia, the

Dominican Republic, Panama, Peru, and the Central American countries—on the inclusion of more exacting, if by no means foolproof, labor standards in the bodies of the agreements themselves (Bolle 2007). The political underpinnings of the post-NAFTA labor standards are complicated, and there is a separate story to be told in each country, but their universal acceptance appears to be the joint product of domestic political forces, on the one hand, and the "competitive liberalization" (Shadlen 2005: 751) engendered by NAFTA itself, on the other. While developing country labor unions and their allies have always advocated more aggressive workplace regulation, after all, their influence grew in the wake of NAFTA's approval—since public officials and their private interlocutors began to fear their exclusion from similar preferential schemes (Andriamananjara 2003: 2).

The results are by now obvious. Figure 4.2 includes data on a variant of the ILO's standard measure of the labor law enforcement effort—i.e. the ratio of labor inspectors to workers (ILO 2004: 13)—for 18 Latin American countries in 2010 and 2011 and reveals not only Mexico's lackluster performance but the enviable records of countries that have signed free trade agreements with the US *since* NAFTA—including eight of the top ten

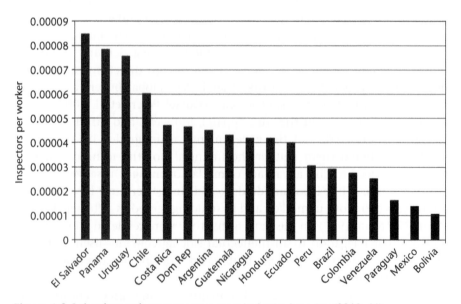

Figure 4.2 Labor law enforcement resources in Latin America (2010–11)

Data: Author's calculations based on USDOS (2010); Vergara et al. 2011; Giuzzio and Colotuzzo (2011); Monroy Gallego (2011); MRL (2011); MTEPS (2012); Navarro (2011); Oberto et al. (2011); OIT (2011); Romero Gudiño (2008); STPS (2011); Zangrando (2011); World Bank (2012).

performers. Nor is the relationship likely to be spurious. While enforcement efforts have been enviable for some time in Chile and Costa Rica, they have almost certainly been multiplied in direct response to FTAs and related trade pressures elsewhere in the region (see e.g. Murillo et al. 2011).[3]

Other Latin American firms have therefore been under precisely the kinds of pressures that Mexican firms have, to their detriment, escaped, and to the extent that production practices and standards evolve in response to these kinds of pressures, Mexican industry will in all likelihood find itself isolated from international "best practices" and will therefore find it harder to share in the international pool of innovations or even to sell in international markets that are attuned to prevailing standards. The problems faced by Mexican firms in the future are in that sense likely to mimic the problems confronted by Mexican firms in the past, when they were unable to understand—let alone to meet—the quality standards imposed by global buyers like Wal-Mart at the dawn of the neo-liberal era.

By way of summation, we have attributed Mexico's post-NAFTA malaise, in general, and affinity for informality, in particular, less to a surfeit than to a shortage of regulation. Labor and employment laws that might otherwise have driven Mexican producers off of the proverbial low road of union-busting, sweatshops, and child labor and onto a potentially higher road marked by human and physical capital formation have gone all but unenforced, and in so doing have tempted Mexican employers to compete on the basis of an unsustainable competitive advantage in low-cost labor. Only by undertaking a concerted effort to enforce their labor laws, therefore, can Mexican policy-makers ensure both a decline in the prevalence of informality and an increase in the rate of growth in the years to come.

A skeptic might respond by noting that most Mexican firms are paralyzed by the aforementioned skill and capital shortages and would thus respond to more aggressive enforcement efforts not by moving upmarket but by declaring bankruptcy and, in the process, destroying the very jobs the enforcement agents were trying to improve, and the skeptical view appears to underpin recent effort to reform Mexico's labor law (Camarena 2012). But the skeptical view is based upon a fundamental misunderstanding of the approach to labor law enforcement available to Mexican officials, an approach to which we turn in the following section.

---

[3] Parties to post-NAFTA FTAs include Chile, the Dominican Republic, El Salvador, Guatemala, Honduras, Nicaragua, and Peru. Colombia and Panama have signed FTAs with the US but they have yet to be ratified by the US Senate. The differences between signatories and non-signatories are significant at $p = .06$ under a variety of simple nonparametric tests and more so when controls for per capital income are added.

4.5 Beyond Beneficial Constraints: Two Models of Labor Law Enforcement

The debate about workplace regulation in Mexico follows the broad contours of the international debate as it has been structured by the World Bank and the International Monetary Fund. The image of regulation that is implicit in that debate is the regulatory system in the United States, a system that is both specialized and adversarial. The US system is specialized in the sense that regulatory responsibility is divided among a host of different agencies, each with a narrow jurisdiction that is defined by a particular body of law (e.g. the Wage and Hour Division of the Department of Labor administers the Fair Labor Standards Act; the Occupational Safety and Health Administration addresses the question of workplace safety and health; Immigration and Customs Enforcement agents are responsible for laws against the employment of undocumented immigrants; the National Labor Relations Board protects collective bargaining rights; the Office of Labor-Management Standards roots out union corruption; the Federal Mediation Service addresses labor-management conflict; the Equal Employment Opportunity Commission fights employment discrimination; and a host of analogous state-level agencies provide complementary—and at times redundant—protections). Furthermore, the US system is adversarial in the sense that violations, when they are revealed, are sanctioned with a penalty, almost always a fine of some kind, and payment of the fine discharges the obligation of the offending enterprise.

The US approach is premised upon deterrence. It assumes that employers make a simple comparison of the cost of compliance and the cost of non-compliance—i.e. the cost of the potential sanctions discounted by the probability of being sanctioned in the first place—and that compliance is therefore best assured by increasing either the size of the sanctions themselves or the probability of discovery and prosecution, perhaps by taking advantage of the division of regulatory labor and/or increasing the number of inspectors.

The US approach stands in sharp contrast, however, to the enforcement model that Mexico—and the rest of Latin America—imported from France by way of Spain in the early twentieth century. After all, the Franco-Iberian model is *general*, in the sense that the whole labor code is administered by a single agency, and *compliance-oriented*, in the sense that the employer's legal obligations are not discharged by the mere payment of a fine. On the contrary, the employer is expected to come into conformity with the law and inspector's role is to help him or her do so. Sanctions may help the inspectors achieve their goals, but they are by no means their first resort—let alone the only instrument available to them.

The line inspectors in the Franco-Iberian system are what the literature on public sector management refers to as "street level bureaucrats" (Lipsky 1980; Piore 2011; Silbey 2011). Like police officers, teachers, and welfare investigators, they operate beyond the physical reach of their supervisors and thus have enormous autonomy and discretion as they go about their daily routines. The discretion available to street-level bureaucrats frequently derives from an imbalance between their resources and their responsibilities, an imbalance that is itself the product of either mission creep or budgetary shortfalls. But the labor administrators who pioneered the Franco-Iberian model in Belle Époque France self-consciously imbued their inspectors with autonomy in the hope that they would use their discretion not only to compensate for their limited resources but to reconcile potentially competing values in a context-sensitive manner. French labor inspectors therefore began to pursue a number of "extra-regulatory modes of action" (Reid 1986: 76) including the dissemination of modern production techniques from profitable firms that were in compliance with the law to their less profitable and non-compliant counterparts. "Inspectors became proponents of cooperation among businesses and the possibilities inherent in technological progress," explains historian Donald Reid. "They took these ideas, mainstays of the Second Industrial Revolution which big business in France was undergoing at the time, and spread them among smaller firms" (Reid 1986: 78).

In other words, French labor inspectors not only blocked the low road by imposing potentially beneficial constraints on private actors but simultaneously paved a higher road by means of extra-regulatory actions designed to help their *administrés* meet their legal obligations. Nor were they exceptional. Practitioners of extra-regulatory action can be found in Latin America today and include Dominican inspectors who built relationships "between employers in the private sector and training agencies in the public sector" (Schrank 2009: 101) in an effort to facilitate the business community's adjustment to the country's new—and more demanding—labor code in the 1990s; Brazilian inspectors who learned enough about dangerous industries like fireworks manufacturing "to propose concrete and specific changes in the production process" (Pires 2008: 212) that issued in improved safety and product quality a few years later; and Chilean inspectors who have recently been told to build human capital by means of enforcement actions by former labor minister Evelyn Matthei (Gobierno de Chile 2011).

Efforts to reconcile compliance with competitiveness in this way are simultaneously *motivated* by the inspector's obligation to bring the firm into compliance with the law and *facilitated* by his or her autonomy, and they are therefore a common by-product of the Franco-Iberian enforcement model; hence their presence in contexts as disparate as the French Third Republic and the contemporary Dominican Republic—where the labor ministry not

only utilizes the services of small business support agencies but actively lob-
bies on their behalf (Nivar 2010)—and their corresponding absence from
the US. While North American inspectors operate at the street level as well,
and thus have a degree of autonomy, their discretion is limited—if by no
means eliminated—by their narrow jurisdictions, on the one hand, and their
commitment to "first instance sanctions" (Kelman 1981), on the other. The
former ensure that individual regulations are considered in isolation from
each other and that the system as a whole lacks an Archimedean point from
which the total regulatory burden can be weighed. The latter militate against
the use of extra-regulatory enforcement measures like efforts to ensure that
"compliance is good business" (Reid 1986: 77). And the result is an inflexible
regulatory system that tends to live up (or perhaps down) to the neo-liberal
critique. By simultaneously forcing and facilitating the inspector's efforts to
bring the firm into compliance, however, the Franco-Iberian model gains a
degree of flexibility that is inconceivable in the US and all but unacknowl-
edged in Mexico, where an almost pathological focus on the alleged costs
of de jure protection has until now left neither the time nor the space for a
discussion of de facto enforcement practices.

4.6 Mexican Labor Inspection in Practice: Potential and Reality

Labor inspectors in the Latin world can not only tailor their enforcement efforts
to the distinct needs of particular firms and workers but can take the viability
of the enterprise and the value of the jobs it generates into account when making their enforcement decisions—all the while looking for ways to reconcile
compliance with competitiveness. Whether this flexibility is realized in practice depends on how well the inspectors are funded and whether and how
their discretion is managed. Efforts to manage—rather than curtail—discretion have been all but absent from the debate over workplace regulation, where
the emphasis has instead been on the use of simulated market mechanisms
in line with the so-called new public management (Coolidge 2006). But an
older literature, as well as our own interviews and interviews conducted by our
students, suggests that street-level bureaucrats operate with an implicit code
that is passed from one generation to the next (Kaufman 1960). The code is
adjusted to take account of changing technology and organization and evolves
through discussion and debate among colleagues who seek each other's advice
as they confront new experiences and challenges. Managers can influence
the evolution of the code not only by recruiting, screening, and training new
bureaucrats in a self-conscious manner but by entering into and directing the
discussion and debate among the bureaucrats themselves (Piore 2011).

Unfortunately, Mexico is nowhere near realizing the full potential of the Franco-Iberian model of workplace regulation. The gold standard for labor standards administration is the Inspection du Travail in France, where the model originated. Inspectors in France are civil servants who have a social status and salary comparable to that of a court magistrate. They are recruited through a competitive examination, have the equivalent of a four-year college degree, and attend two-year specialized school before actually entering the service. Every inspector has a private office and a laptop computer, and the local administration maintains a fleet of cars which the inspectors can use for site visits.

By way of contrast, Mexican inspectors were until recently paid approximately 7,000 pesos a month, which placed them in the lower ranks of government officials. They faced no degree requirements, were hired without resort to an examination, and were trained on the job by accompanying their more experienced counterparts on site visits. They operated out of cramped offices that not only signaled their relatively weak status to any and all visitors but also inhibited their ability to coax meaningful testimony out of aggrieved workers, who tended to feel exposed when they came to level complaints. And, finally, they had no special equipment and used their own cars or public transportation when they visited enterprises.

The woeful state of Mexican labor inspection reflected not only the malign neglect of recent administrations but the broader shift in development strategies—and arguably in the economic regime itself—from import-substituting industrialization guided by a proactive state to a neo-liberal alternative that exalts free trade and unfettered market competition. Mexican regulatory institutions have always involved a complex division of responsibility between the federal and state governments. While federal officials retain nominal jurisdiction over the country as a whole, they can and do delegate responsibility for certain types of industries and enterprises to the states through specific conventions. In essence, the heavy and strategic industries that have until recently been state-owned fall under the exclusive jurisdiction of the federal government, and light industries, services, and commerce were relegated to the states. But state and local officials are not necessarily better equipped to administer work and employment regulations than their federal counterparts; if anything, they are less equipped to do so. In a study carried out several years ago, for instance, we visited a number of cities in different states and found an enormous range of variation in their regulatory capacities. Major cities like Guadalajara and Monterrey had relatively serious inspection services—albeit nothing like the services found in Brazil, Chile, or the Dominican Republic. And less developed states in the south simply lacked departments of labor and thus abdicated their responsibilities to their already overburdened federal counterparts.

Under the old development strategy, the economy was moving gradually toward the sectors and geographic regions where inspection was the strongest, and one could argue that the society would gradually come into compliance with the law as it developed economically. But under the neo-liberal model the economy is actually moving away from heavy industry, where standards are most heavily policed, toward light industry and services, where they are less so, and simultaneously moving away from parts of the country that have the most effective state-level inspectorates for peripheral areas that are devoid of administrative capacity.

Of course, Mexico is not alone in falling short of the standards set by France. One finds similar regulatory deficits in parts of the Andes and perhaps Central America (although Mexico does not usually think that this is the relevant standard in judging its public services). But a number of Latin American countries have made tremendous strides of late, and have thereby gainsaid the idea that deregulation is the only option. For instance, the Dominicans recently responded to "the most successful application of trade-based labor sanctions" (Frundt 1998) on record by tripling the size and improving the quality of their labor inspectorate. New inspectors are recruited by exam, required to have a law degree, paid a solidly middle-class salary, given secure tenure, and subject to monthly training and team-building exercises designed to help manage their discretion (Schrank 2009: 96). The Dominicans simultaneously established a dedicated system of labor courts and a corps of legal aid lawyers who defend workers who fail to achieve redress through the inspection process but are unable to afford an attorney of their own (Schrank 2009: 98).

Nor is the DR unique. Brazilian inspectors have been recruited and remunerated on the basis of meritocratic principles since the democratic transition in the 1980s (Pires 2008: 203) and work in tandem with prosecutors who are no less competent and creative (Coslovsky 2009). Chilean officials have recently doubled the size of their own labor inspectorate and have radically reformed their labor courts as well (Rosado 2010). And a number of countries have undertaken similar reforms in an effort to meet the labor standards that are associated with post-NAFTA trade agreements.

It is perhaps worth noting that the growing commitment to workplace regulation in parts of Latin America has gone hand-in-hand with a growing commitment to the development of small and medium-sized enterprises (SMEs). Labor administrators not only create demand for the services provided by small business support agencies like SEBRAE (i.e. Serviço Brasileiro de Apoio às Micro e Pequenas Empresas) in Brazil and PROMIPYME (i.e. Programa de Promoción y Apoyo a la Micro-, Pequeña, y Mediana Empresa) in the Dominican Republic but encourage the payment of the payroll taxes that underwrite their budgets and lobby on their behalf as well (see e.g. Batista 2007; Coslovsky 2009; Puig 2010).

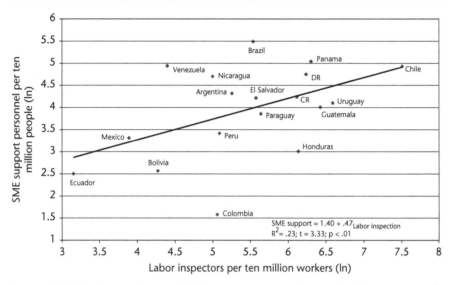

Figure 4.3 Labor inspection and SME support in Latin America (*c*.2005)

Note: SME support personnel from Angelelli et al. (2006); labor inspectors from Murillo et al. (2011); and population and labor force in tens of millions (for ease of exposition) from World Bank (2011).

The affinity between labor law enforcement and small business support is a two-way street, however, for agencies like SEBRAE and PROMIPYME tend to condition their financial and technical services on compliance with tax and labor regulations and in so doing encourage formalization and upgrading at the same time (Almeida 2007; Severino 2010). Figure 4.3 plots the number of small business support personnel by the number of labor inspectors on a relative basis for 18 Latin American countries in the year 2005 and underscores not only the striking association between the two variables but Mexico's underperformance on both.

The results are perhaps unsurprising, for neo-liberals who abjure government regulation of the labor market are unlikely to embrace government support for small business, but they are nonetheless disconcerting, for informality is much more prevalent in countries like Mexico that starve their labor inspectorates and small business support agencies than in countries that give regulatory and development agencies the resources and authority they need to reconcile compliance with competitiveness.[4]

In the last few years, however, an opening has appeared due to an accident that killed dozens of coalminers in the northern state of Coahuila, on the

---

[4] The rank correlations between the labor inspection and SME support variables, on the one hand, and the level of informality, on the other, are -.5 and -.6 respectively (*p* <.05). Informality data come from the ILO (2006b).

one hand, and the reform of the federal labor law, on the other. The director who assumed control over the federal labor inspectorate in the wake of the accident had no experience in work and employment regulation per se, but he had worked in a number of different regulatory agencies and brought with him both a reputation for probity and a team of experienced assistants who set out to recruit 158 new inspectors—a 72 percent increase (STPS 2010)—and adopt new managerial practices as well. While he was unable to raise their salaries, he was able to give the inspectors access to computers and vehicles, and he began to develop protocols for particular industries through discussion and debate in industry committees before being promoted to Undersecretary of Labor and Social Welfare.

The protocol development process he described in January 2011 is exactly the kind of exercise required to manage and direct the discretion of a street-level bureaucracy (Piore 2011: 159). He also described a self-conscious effort to promote inter-institutional coordination, including joint inspections of oil platforms with environmental inspectors, banana plantations with educational and public health officials, and coal mines with investigators assigned to the Office of the Federal Attorney for the Defense of Labor (i.e. Procuraduría Federal de la Defensa del Trabajo). He did not, however, discuss concerted efforts to link workplace regulation to productive upgrading, and it remains to be seen whether such efforts will be motivated by the recent labor law reform. While the STPS has in fact recruited almost 200 new inspectors over the course of the last year alone (STPS 2013), neither their aptitude nor their approach to enforcement can be taken for granted. After all, the new law stipulates that inspectors need have nothing more than a high school diploma—itself an improvement over the previous law, which imposed no academic credentials at all—and gives inspectors added sanctioning authority that would seem more compatible with a deterrence than a compliance-based approach (*El Economista* 2013; *El Informador* 2013).

Nor has the admittedly ambiguous level of federal activity been matched by comparable activity at the state level. Enforcement varies widely geographically and by industry. It is most effective in heavy industry, which comes under the jurisdiction of the national government, and in the more industrialized states, especially Nuevo Leon, the State of Mexico, and the Federal District, where investment and population were drawn in the mid-twentieth century; and it is least effective in peripheral areas with better access to the US market and labor-intensive manufacturing, where economic and demographic activity have shifted in the NAFTA era. A recent study of state-level labor policy nonetheless found virtually no innovation at all in terms of inspection within the states (Ruiz Durán 2012). This is particularly striking in light of both the structural shifts occasioned by NAFTA—and the concomitant growth of state responsibility for the enforcement of workplace regulation—and the fact that political decentralization and the emergence of party competition have led a number of states to pursue the kinds of industrial policies that workplace inspections could in theory serve to complement (Samford and Ortega Gómez 2012).

The managerial reforms that are underway in Mexico thus appear to constitute a domestic political reaction to a catastrophic workplace accident rather than a product of regional integration per se, let alone a symptom of neo-liberalism's demise. They could certainly evolve into a more thorough-going campaign to link compliance to competitiveness over time, and the adoption of a new labor law may encourage them to do so, but the road from here to there is filled with potholes—not least of all the persistent legacy of neo-liberalism, the corresponding lack of supporting institutions (e.g. vocational education and training programs, manufacturing extension services, providers of low cost finance, etc.) elsewhere in the Mexican state, and the possibility—if by no means inevitability—that the new labor law will reinforce, rather than impede—the country's neo-liberal tendencies (Alcalde 2012; Camarena 2012; Cruz Vargas 2012).

4.7 Conclusion

By way of conclusion, we would simply like to reiterate five points that flow out of our analysis. First, the Mexican malaise is a product of insufficient rather than excessive labor protection. The de facto labor market flexibility afforded by the non-enforcement of labor law tempts Mexican producers to pursue low-road strategies that are inevitably self-defeating and militates against the abandonment of neo-liberalism for more promising development models. Second, the most dynamic countries in Latin America have already abandoned neo-liberalism for heterodox approaches that combine labor protections designed to block the low road with industrial policies designed to help their firms, and their SMEs in particular, move onto a higher road. The shift has been animated in part by the labor standards incorporated into post-NAFTA free trade agreements, in part by domestic politics, and in part by the realization that low-road competition is no longer viable in the face of Asian competition. Third, the Franco-Iberian approach to labor law enforcement is particularly conducive to the high-road strategy. Labor inspectors in the Latin world have both the discretion and the authority they need to link firms, farms, and families, on the one hand, to training and financial institutions, on the other. Fourth, the new labor law gives Mexican policy-makers a unique opportunity to make use of the Franco-Iberian approach. By augmenting the number, quality, and tools available to their inspectors, even at the margin, Mexican officials have opened the door to a fundamental rethinking of the relationship between compliance and competitiveness. And, finally, the costs of foregoing this opportunity are likely to be enormous. Left to their own devices, Mexican employers and—through no fault of their own—workers are likely to wind up squeezed between lower cost competitors in the East and more productive challengers in the West, with pernicious consequences for all involved.

5

The NAFTA Side Agreements and Governance in Mexico

Mark Aspinwall

5.1 Introduction

In this chapter I examine the NAFTA Transnational Integration Regime (TIR). NAFTA's developmental purpose was to create a regime in which both trade and investment were encouraged above all else, under the assumption that new economic opportunities would stimulate development and jobs in Mexico. This limited scope was widened by the conclusion of talks leading to two "side agreements," in which environment and labor domains were included within the NAFTA TIR. But while this broadening was not accompanied by a deepening of the goals, there are key differences between the side agreements in terms of their means.

Formally known as the North American Agreement on Environmental Cooperation (NAAEC) and the North American Agreement on Labor Cooperation (NAALC), their principal purpose was to address compliance weaknesses by creating mechanisms of oversight and complaint, and by creating opportunities to build capacity. They were formed because of the fear that increased trade and investment opportunities in Mexico would give firms there an unfair advantage against US-based firms unless Mexico enforced its own rules. Thus, the "rules" embodied in the side agreements did not supplant domestic regulations, norms, laws, or other rules, but rather required the three NAFTA member states to *enforce the rules they already had in place*.

While NAAEC and NAALC differed in their structure and powers, they both provided venues whereby domestic non-state actors were given the opportunity to complain about non-compliance; and they simultaneously made resources available to upgrade capacity, especially on the environmental side. However, the resources dedicated to these tasks were so scant that virtually no one ever considered that they may have had developmental outcomes of their own, much less that the differences between the side agreement structures and between the domestic institutional legacies might hold some lessons about what works and what doesn't work in terms of how regional integrative rules can encourage development.

Indeed the start was inauspicious, as Mexican regulators in both the environmental and labor agencies initially saw the proposed side agreements as an unwarranted, unwelcome interference and an invasion of Mexican sovereignty by the regional hegemon, the United States. They also rejected independent and critical non-state actors, and they rejected the idea that information about their activities should be openly available. But NAALC and more especially NAAEC *did* have important developmental consequences, and at a surprising bargain—only about $9 million per year for the NAAEC and $2.1 million per year for the NAALC.

Small but important steps were taken to improve the culture of rule of law and build capacity. The scrutiny and oversight institutionalized through the side agreements reinforced capacity building among civil servants and civil society in Mexico as individuals engaged in the complaint process and in the agenda-setting and work programs of the side agreement institutions. A dense web of cross-border communication was created by the side agreements, and social views were facilitated through it. Moreover, domestic democratic reforms in Mexico, including strengthened regulatory and judicial institutions, policy reforms, and others, were buttressed by the external pressures of the NAAEC and NAALC. In particular, specific mechanisms within the NAAEC promoted the mechanisms of multiplexity and joint problem-solving, which in turn empowered key environmental NGOs and state actors in Mexico.

5.2 Institutional Characteristics and Regulatory Change

The historical legacies and domestic capacities of Mexico's environment and labor regulatory authorities varied in terms of the receptiveness and openness of agency officials to outside influence and the ability of non-state actors to argue for normative change. The environment agencies were newer, expanding, more dynamic, and drawing on a cadre of young professionals. Labor agencies were older, more balkanized and corrupted, and led (in the official, government-sponsored unions) by old men often lacking formal education. In both domains, it was the independent NGOs who mobilized to change the status quo—but with very different results because of the different profiles and characteristics of the groups within the domain, and also because of differences within NAAEC and NAALC, specifically in their level of independence from state control and the access and standing that they provide for non-state actors. These differences are critical to development of domestic capacities because of the very different incentives and opportunities for state and non-state actors.

Meanwhile, the process of democratization brought more independent courts (beginning in the 1990s) and a new freedom of information agency (IFAI), in 2002. These domestic institutions—which often linked their arguments to and based their demands on external obligations, including NAAEC and NAALC—meant that the pressures on the domestic environmental and labor agencies grew from inside as well as outside.

The difference in the capacity of domestic state and non-state actors means that governance in the environmental regime has moved from one in which officials rejected participation, criticism, and scrutiny, to one in which these were far more welcomed (i.e. from the lower left toward the upper left quadrant of Figure 5.1). In brief, this occurred because the NAAEC included capacity-building resources to develop environmental programs, a permanent agency through which non-state actors helped set the agenda and govern the regime, and a neutral complaint mechanism which, unlike the complaint mechanism in the labor regime, was not tainted by association with one particular member state, nor by waxing and waning priorities depending on the ideological makeup of the governments.

In terms of how the NAAEC and NAALC provided assistance and monitoring, several crucial differences emerge. While both feature "multiplex" interactions, not all relevant labor actors participated. State-connected corporatist unions affiliated with the main umbrella organization Confederation of Mexican Workers (CTM) remained outside the process of interaction with the NAALC, and the federal labor ministry STPS often refused to accept the findings of cases brought before the relevant investigating body. The levels of "symmetry" between external and internal actors also differed. NAAEC provided a more neutral multinational investigating body, while NAALC investigations relied on one member state (usually the US Department of Labor) conducting them, making them subject to nationalist antipathies, and flagging interest from conservative anti-labor administrations. Environmental politics was also subject to greater levels of "joint problem-solving," in which resources were made available to build capacity. Such activity was far less evident in labor politics.

In a nutshell, improvements to governance include stronger domestic institutions, better capacity in these institutions and among agency officials, and healthier NGOs. Greater communication, professionalization, transparency, and information have led to improvements in expectations and attitudes regarding rule of law. NAAEC is more independent of member state control, provides institutionalized access for civil society, and built capacity in civil servants and civil society. Environmental officials moving between NGOs, federal agencies, and the NAAEC institutions facilitated communication and normative transfer. Domestic environmental institutions were expanding and more permeable to new norms.

Environmental activists and civil servants have become more capable of using scientific and legal rationales, whereas this capability is rarer among labor unions and civil servants. Thickening cross-border communication among technocratic agency officials and civil society groups (lawyers, NGOs, and others) built capacity among the actors themselves. That is, transnational institutions which were structured in such a way as to encourage cross-border dialogue also led to higher levels of professionalization among civil society actors and bureaucrats in Mexico. Engagement in the side agreement institutions helped upgrade skills. The environmental side agreement provided for NGOs to make complaints and engage in agenda-setting within the institution, and allowed for independent factual reports to be published by the side agreement agency (the Commission for Environmental Cooperation). Labor activists could complain too, but only to the labor ministry of another member state, whose subsequent investigations were tainted by accusations of violation of sovereignty and ideological bias (under the Bush administration).

Thus, variation in the structure and powers of the transnational regime provide part of the answer as to why rule of law improved far more in the environmental domain than the labor domain. In addition, certain differences in domestic institutions (their historical legacies, growth, and permeability) and in domestic state and non-state actors (levels of professional training and mobility) made a difference to how these domains adapted to pressures from external and internal sources. Legally trained NGOs hungry for change seized the opportunity to link up with NGOs in other member states, and bring complaints to the transnational institutions.

Certain of these factors existed or emerged independently of the NAFTA institutions. For example, the levels of professionalization and mobility of actors in NGOs and state agencies occurred independently of the effect of NAAEC and NAALC, but combined with the growing pressures from the external NAFTA institutions and from the newly empowered domestic institutions (the courts and IFAI), their profiles enabled them to leverage pro-rule of law pressures more effectively. On the other hand, some factors *were* affected by the NAAEC and NAALC institutions. They include the rapid growth of environmental institutions (which occurred as Mexico sought to show its commitment to environmental governance).

5.3 External Pressures, Institutional Design, and Domestic Capacities

The side agreements are narrow in scope and shallow in depth compared to the EU, and they are also more static. There are no institutional processes outside intergovernmental negotiations in which new policy areas may be subject to rule-governing cooperation or old policy areas subject to deeper forms of governance. Everything was negotiated at the outset. NAFTA operates according to a "Cassis de Dijon model" of regulatory integration, whereby the regulations of each member state are recognized as valid by other member states. Convergence, harmonization, and standardization of regulations are not the objective, and little of it occurs. The objective is to ensure consistent application of the rule of law in each of the member states, alongside a liberalized trade and investment regime. The norm of rule of law had a strong countervailing norm though, namely a developmental pro-jobs norm that tolerated rule-bending and breaking to facilitate investment, development, and employment (see Figure 5.1).

International institutions (such as TIRs) provide an opportunity structure in which domestic NGOs can pressure states (Keck and Sikkink 1998; Risse and Sikkink 1999; Keohane et al. 2000; Kay 2011; Graubart 2005). When NGOs are taken seriously by an international institution, it increases their legitimacy and credibility back home (Reimann 2006; Kay 2011). It becomes harder for states to backtrack on commitments. Moreover, when TIR institutions have the power to accept petitions by NGOs, it has an important signaling effect in the home polity: it indicates that the complaint has merit, and it initiates a discussion over legal principles. The accused member state must justify its practices before an international tribunal. It can also serve as a benchmark for future review (Graubart 2005: 104).

Table 5.1 Jobs or rule of law? Two logics of action

	Jobs	Rule of law
Environment	Permitting process for development projects does not respect environmental impact assessment requirements. Aim is to promote investment and create employment.	Permitting process for development projects respects impact assessment and other legal requirements; results are fully open and transparent; a forum exists to challenge results.
Labor	Anti-labor practices such "phantom" trade unions, open balloting for union leaders, failure to report openly are tolerated to keep the labor peace and prevent labor costs rising. Aim is to provide employment, attract investment.	Trade unions and firms are required to respect legal requirements in their labor practices. Their behavior is open to scrutiny and shortcomings may be identified and challenged through legal channels.

However, these external pressures vary according to (1) whether the TIR institutions provide formal roles for civil society groups, and (2) whether they are independent from member state control (Aspinwall 2013). Giving NGOs formal roles refers to permanent institutional participation within committees or other structures, as well as to ad hoc opportunities to make complaints. This standing increases the effectiveness of transnational activism because NGOs become more committed to the process. They serve in specific, ongoing capacities within the TIR institution, they influence the work agenda, help with identification of priority issues and problem-solving, and communicate with the permanent Secretariat and with member state principals over priorities. Permanent standing commits NGOs to the institution, so that *even if they lose individual cases* it is more likely that they remain engaged with the institution and its work on oversight, investigation, and capacity-building.

Moreover, TIR institutions with relative independence from member state control are more likely to promote continuity and depoliticize regulatory integration (Pevehouse 2002). Their continuity is visible in agenda-setting, work plans, strategies, and other tasks, which are not tied to political cycles such as elections, or dependent on good will. They depoliticize norm diffusion because they separate regulatory pressures from sovereignty concerns or changes in government ideology. Both can cause variation in propensity among member state principals to pursue investigations. Thus, it is likely that the impact of fact-finding and reporting will be greater if the institution has independence from member state principals, because it is more likely to be treated as authoritative and untainted by power politics (for related arguments see Goldstein et al. 2000; Keohane et al. 2000).

While TIRs establish principles and rules to regulate behavior, their effect on developing economies depends on certain features of the domestic institutions and also on domestic capacities. The domestic factors that affect regulative institutions and the quality of governance more widely are (1) the "vestedness" of civil society groups and their propensity to engage in rent-seeking behavior; (2) the existence and functioning of domestic oversight/ombudsman institutions which provide scrutiny of domestic regulatory institutions; (3) the level of transparency and availability of information; (4) the level of professionalization/technical capacity of both civil servants and civil society groups; (5) the permeability/newness of domestic regulatory institutions and the opportunities for job mobility; (6) the extent to which federal/national governments are the primary TIR partners as opposed to sharing the role with subnational authorities.

Accordingly, we should see more rule-consistent behavior and more agile regulatory adaptability where: (1) civil servants and civil society groups do not engage in rent-seeking behavior (but rather pursue a more general interest); (2) in policy sectors which are open to scrutiny and where information is readily available; (3) individual civil servants and members of relevant civil society groups are well-trained in sciences, law, or other professions; (4) agencies are open to outside influence; (5) the federal or national government is the primary conduit to TIR institutions. The reason is that these policy sectors are likely to be dominated by trained technocrats with experience in different regulatory systems, and with access to information on best practice.

5.4 External Monitoring and Complaints

Mexico's key environmental institutions are SEMARNAT (the federal environmental ministry[1]) and Profepa (the environmental attorney general's office). In addition there are a number of specialized agencies. The relevant labor institutions are the federal labor ministry (STPS) and the federal and state Conciliation and Arbitration Boards (CABs). At state level, the CABs register unions and serve as tribunals, addressing disputes between workers and employers. At the federal level, unions are registered with the STPS but disputes are resolved in the federal CABs.

NAFTA's side agreement institutions have issued highly embarrassing public reports regarding law enforcement weaknesses by these institutions. At the same time, a dense web of technical contacts has developed between ministries in the three member states. Bureaucrats have become enmeshed in de-politicized, non-confrontational discussions, insulated from public scrutiny, even as the trilateral institution reports politicized their failings. But Mexican bureaucrats reacted in very different ways when confronted with these findings. Environmental officials acknowledged problems and explained their plans to rectify them. Labor officials denied problems and criticized the behavior of the United States, who they believed had misused the side agreement.

The difference is due in part to the side agreement monitoring mechanisms. There are two that merit attention and that are consistent with my claim that independent mechanisms with civil society input can be more effective. One is the relative independence of the NAAEC Secretariat in terms of the fact-finding and reporting it does in response to civil society concerns. NAAEC established a Commission on Environmental Cooperation (CEC), whose Secretariat provides support for the Council of Ministers (the environment ministers from the three member states). The second is the Joint Public

---

[1] SEMARNAT was known as SEMARNAP until 2000, at which point its name was changed to reflect the move of competence over fisheries to another ministry.

Advisory Committee (JPAC), a permanent institutionalized citizen advisory body of five civil society representatives from each member state. Its role is to advise and provide information to both the Council and the Secretariat (see GAO 1997). It does not act on behalf of governments, but sets its agenda in response to public input, through its own ideas, and in response to Council requests. In its first 10 years it had held nearly 100 meetings and made some 79 recommendations, as well as issuing a number of reports (Bourget 2004).

The CEC has two mechanisms to respond to civil society concerns.[2] The first is article 13 public reports, which the Secretariat may prepare in response to public concerns.[3] Article 13 reports can be done by the Secretariat without Council approval, thus representing an independent source of power for the former. The second mechanism is the article 14/15 procedure. Individuals or groups are entitled to petition the CEC Secretariat if they believe national environmental laws are not being enforced, a process which is known informally as "citizen submissions." The Secretariat may recommend to the Council that a factual record be created, including information on the history of the case, pertinent facts, the obligations of the relevant member state, and their actions in the case (CEC 2002). In preparing the factual record, the Secretariat has the power to consider not simply information provided by the member states, but also publicly available information that is submitted by interested parties or generated by the Secretariat itself or by independent experts (NAAEC Treaty, article 15).

Of the 72 citizen submissions made under NAAEC, 37 have been against Mexico, resulting in seven completed factual records and one unfinished factual record. Complainants accused the government of failing to effectively enforce environmental rules by overlooking permitting procedures, inadequate impact assessments, and similar shortcomings. The involvement of the CEC raised the profile of the cases, and the ensuing media attention on processes that were incomplete and slanted toward development caused embarrassment to the government. The citizen submission process permitted groups to challenge observance of the law and marked a significant strengthening of the legal process (Martin interview 2008).

The Mexican government reacted strategically to some CEC investigations. It took anticipatory or after-the-fact actions. It delayed approving requests for some factual records, or sought to limit their scope. It failed to respond to

---

[2] Under part V, sanctions for persistent failure to enforce environmental law may be imposed, including monetary penalties or withdrawal of NAFTA benefits (article 22). However, to date it has not been employed.

[3] According to a media report, the first investigation in Mexico—the Silva Reservoir case—was welcomed by the Mexican government, and was a sign of its increasing openness to international scrutiny. *New York Times*, 1 Aug. 1995, <www.nytimes.com/1995/08/01/science/treaty-partners-study-fate-of-birds-at-polluted-mexican-lake.html?sec=&spon=&pagewanted=all> accessed Apr. 2009.

some requests for information from the CEC, and complained that the CEC exceeded its authority (CEC 2007). At the same time, the Mexican government acknowledged shortcomings in enforcement, and took pains to explain itself (SEMARNAT 2007: 99–100; Garver 2001). The frequent public admissions of enforcement shortcomings and explanations of planned improvements were brought about in large part because of these cases. SEMARNAT's head of Social Participation and Transparency states that the cases represented an important turning point for transparency, law enforcement, institutional infrastructure, and strengthening of rules (Castillo interview, 2008). Environmental NGOs have often been disappointed that results did not go further, but they have remained engaged in the process.

On the labor side, NGOs faced a different external monitoring structure, and it affected their commitment to the side agreement complaint process. NAALC comprises a Commission on Labor Cooperation (CLC), with a different organizational structure to CEC. In addition to a Council, made up of the heads of the labor ministries in each government, and a Secretariat (closed since 2010), there is also a National Administrative Office (NAO) in the labor ministry of each country. There is no counterpart to JPAC, through which civil society gains standing. Unlike the NAAEC, a complaint must go to the NAO (i.e. the labor ministry) in a different member state from where the violation allegedly occurred, and not to the CLC. That NAO may then conduct an investigation of the case if it so decides. The CLC was never part of the public communication process and was not involved in findings of fact or reporting. Its impact was virtually negligible.

By 2009, a total of 35 complaints had been made against the three member states, 24 of them against Mexico. The complaints were made to the US NAO in virtually all cases. They mainly concerned violations of the rights to strike and bargain collectively. In 11 of the cases (nine of them during the Clinton administration and two during the Bush administration), the US government took some kind of action, including ministerial consultations, public hearings, and follow-up information dissemination events. In some cases Mexico refused to permit information to be gathered, or the partner country yielded to political pressure to reject or downplay the investigation.

The cases made clear that labor authorities were complicit in abuses against workers and independent pro-worker unions seeking to represent them (Nolan 2011; Alcalde 2006: 168). Some of the worst offenses occurred at the state level, where officials contrived spurious reasons to reject union registration applications, and where workers were intimidated in voting procedures, often with government officials present. Two NAALC cases resulted in a declaration in May 2000, whereby the governments of the three member states committed themselves to ensuring secret votes and open information regarding collective contracts. However, Mexico did not comply with this until later (Alcalde 2006: 170–1). Details of collective contracts were guarded until a 2007 policy change at the federal level, the main argument being that the documents contained private information which should not be made public (Giménez 2007). The government has been reluctant to provide transparent systems whereby workers can identify their union leaders, much less require that union accounts be open or that elections be held fairly and without intimidation (Bouzas 2006).

Mexico responded to NAALC allegations by putting pressure on individual firms and CABs, and through a (reluctant) process of strengthening its policies and procedures (Nolan 2011; Graubart 2005: 134–5; Teague 2002). The federal ministry STPS sometimes claimed it had no authority to intervene, and other times (because it had the primary responsibility for relations with other NAFTA labor ministries), it pressured state authorities through informal political channels. It agreed to hold consultations following the Itapsa case (filed in 1997) to address issues of freedom of association and collective bargaining, registration of collective bargaining contracts, and public registration of unions (see also Aspinwall 2013; Nolan 2011; Graubart 2005: 126; Alcalde, interview 2010).

Following a case on pregnancy testing, the Mexican government created special offices to look into several related issues, including women in the workplace, child labor, and disabled workers. It organized an education campaign in the maquiladora zone to educate female workers on their rights regarding pregnancy testing. An office for equality and gender issues was created in 1999. The federal government continued to press for reform in company practices even after the NAALC case was finished, signing agreements with a number of states to eliminate workplace discrimination based on pregnancy testing. The Federal Prevention and Elimination of Discrimination Act came into effect in 2003 as well, which prohibits discrimination on the basis of pregnancy (US NAO 2007: 50).

Union registration was a further case of reaction to criticism. Following the Sony case (filed in 1994) and subsequent ministerial consultations, the federal government established a panel of labor experts who recommended that the union registration process be depoliticized and made more consistent. Mexico agreed to promote secret ballots in voting procedures as well as publicly available information on collective contracts, so that workers could learn whether they were represented by a union (Alcalde interview, 2010). They also led to secret votes being used in federal votes, although the federal government did not make secret ballots part of labor law reform because it argued that federal law did not prohibit open voting.

Notwithstanding these changes, many of which were reactive, late, and half-hearted, little progress was made in changing the culture of labor administration and justice. Labor authorities continued to permit routine flouting of the law, and the US NAO, which conducted the investigations, made repeated calls for professionalism and capacity to be strengthened.

5.4.1 *Small Differences in TIR Monitoring Explain a Lot*

Evidence indicates that variation in the way the NAAEC and NAALC institutions are structured affects the monitoring process. The NAAEC's Secretariat has more operational independence than the NAALC's Secretariat. Its factual records do not come from another member state but from the trinational institution. In addition, because provisions were made for institutionalized civil society participation, environmental NGOs have become more committed to NAAEC. Through JPAC they participate in agenda-setting, gaining recognition and standing, increasing the legitimacy of public participation in Mexican environmental politics and strengthening capacity. This commits civil society groups to the process and to the institution (GAO 1997; Silvan, 2004; Torres 2002). In fact, one of Mexico's most influential environmental lawyers, Gustavo Alanís, was convinced to join the JPAC as one of the 15 members for a third time in 2012, despite his criticism of the CEC and JPAC for their inability to overcome national interests and create a more transnational pro-environmental approach.

Some public participation in environmental governance is mandatory—border projects funded by the NADB are required to have local community group participation. This provides forums for debate, transparency, access to information, and inclusion in decision-making. It has increased legitimacy and support for projects, and often spills over into other forms of local governance, increasing awareness of rights and access to information (see Abel and Sayoc 2006; Cabrera interview 2008).

On the labor side, NGO commitment to the NAALC complaint process varied according to their success. As investigations increased in the mid-1990s and as the results became more favorable, labor groups devoted greater resources to complaints (Nolan 2011). When the Bush administration lost interest and reviewed fewer cases, labor groups turned away (Alcalde 2006: 175). The lack of an independent trilateral agency with powers similar to the NAAEC robbed them of a sense of neutrality and politicized them in two ways. First, there was a strong nationalistic reaction (STPS interviews, 2007, 2009, 2010). In its report on NAALC's first four years, the Mexican NAO complained bitterly about the US NAO.

> We are concerned that declarations made by Party officials have given rise to the assumption that the mechanisms set down in the NAALC effectively circumvent internal policy or serve for the *exertion of pressure between the Parties*. [The Mexican NAO] does not believe it should participate in hearings staged by its

United States counterpart, since *even its observer status would necessarily jeopardize national sovereignty.*[4]

Second, the Bush administration accepted many fewer NAALC cases than the Clinton administration. Ten cases were accepted for review in the seven years of overlap between the NAALC and the Clinton administration (out of 15 submissions). Only two cases were accepted in the eight years of the Bush administration (out of four submissions).[5] It was widely believed that the Bush administration would be unsympathetic to complaints against labor violations (de la Calle interview, 2009; Graubart 2005: 139). In fact, by 2004, the Mexican NAO was taking less seriously the requests for information from the US NAO, playing the weaknesses in the NAALC to its advantage (Davis interview, 2009).

Politicization had an impact on the commitment of NGOs to bring cases. Even with the assistance of North American partners, Mexican labor groups found the process to be inconsistent, uncertain, and ineffective (Polaski 2006: 35). NAALC lost legitimacy in the eyes of civil society stakeholders (Polaski 2006: 50–1). The loss of commitment had considerable consequences, because although NAALC strengthened civil society groups when it worked, it only worked on an ad hoc basis.

5.5 External Capacity-Building

The environmental and labor side agreements also differed in their direct capacity-building assistance for Mexico (see Figure 5.2). Mexico's environmental regulatory structures and processes have been assisted more fully—both directly through funded capacity-building measures, and indirectly through learning processes as NGOs and civil servants take part in trilateral activities. There is a widespread consensus that NAAEC was critical to upgrading Mexico's environmental institutional capacity.[6] According to one early report, the NAAEC "has been an important catalyst for developing a more transparent regulatory process and ensuring a more consistent application of environmental laws in Mexico" (GAO 1997: 22). The citizen submission process helped improve environmental impact assessments in Mexico, due

---

[4] Cited at <www.naalc.org/english/review_annex2.shtml> accessed Apr. 2010. Emphasis added.

[5] Data from the NAALC website, <http://new.naalc.org/index.cfm?page=229> accessed Nov. 2009.

[6] I base this assertion on reviews of academic and agency publications, first-hand accounts, and dozens of interviews with high-ranking policy-makers and NGO officials—including the number two at SEMARNAT during the Calderon administration, the former head of SEMARNAT, the former heads of two other environmental agencies, the head of CEMDA, the number two at the CEC secretariat.

Table 5.2 TIR institutions in NAFTA's environmental and labor side agreements

	Environment	Labor
Monitoring	• (Relatively) independent fact-finding, reporting, and agenda-setting powers in the CEC • Permanent institutional access for NGOs	• State-led oversight of other member states (sovereignty concerns and ideological variations) • Ad hoc access to complaint mechanisms by NGOs.
Assistance	• Training programs through CEC and border institutions. • Information-gathering and reporting activities.	• Some limited information-gathering activities but CLC now closed.

to greater pressure being exerted by NGOs (Gallagher 2004: 77; also Vaughan 2003: 66; Blanca Torres, cited in Fox 2004: 267). Block (2003: 516) found that the CEC had improved transparency and access to information in Mexico, and that public expectations had been affected in a positive way because of its policies and processes.

In terms of direct capacity-building measures, the CEC's 2005–10 strategy sought to strengthen capacities to improve compliance with wildlife laws; improve private sector compliance; strengthen capacities to conserve species and habitats by building planning, tracking, and enforcement capacities; and strengthen capacities to assess and control chemicals of interest. The CEC stated in an undated document that its capacity building was targeted at "systemic" issues, namely the "abilities and efficiency of institutions and their instruments," including policy formulation, institutional arrangements, science and technology, infrastructure, funding mechanisms, and public participation. This was to be achieved through workshops, informational publications, and educational guides, among others.

The CEC's annual work program seeks to strengthen domestic laws and programs; improve transparency and public participation; increase the flow of information; improve the availability of funding; provide training; work toward common views on environmental management goals; and help standardize data collection. The CEC also helped establish guidance on risk assessment, disseminated techniques for collecting information on emissions and baseline data, helped foster technical standards, and helped in testing samples of air and water quality, among others (Gilbreath 2003: 54–5). It developed a strategy for including stakeholders, such as Profepa (enforcement) inspectors, who help set the agenda on the wildlife program. A new course was created leading to a certificate from the Mexican National Institute for Penal Sciences, which qualifies the inspectors as forensic environmental scientists.

Sectoral capacity-building programs include a Pollutant Release and Transfer Registry (PRTR) and action plans to decrease or eliminate emission and use of toxic substances, among other initiatives (SEMARNAT 2000: 358–9). The PRTR is a program in which firms report emissions and movements of specified chemical substances. The resulting database is made available to the public.[7] The Mexican government and the CEC are also developing a chemicals inventory as part of the Sound Management of Chemicals initiative. The purpose is to make information available among ministries and between member states; facilitate trade, information, and knowledge on the location and levels of hazardous substances in member states; harmonize standards; and facilitate adoption of other international agreements on chemical substances.

The chemical inventory program required development of a technical report and a legal framework. SEMARNAT and representatives from the Mexican Chamber of Chemical Companies visited the US and Canada to review the way they manage their inventory systems. The Mexican Chamber was responsible for providing much of the information necessary to complete the technical report, but SEMARNAT was also involved. The CEC acted as project manager—as coordinator and catalyst—leading, organizing, and managing the program. A revised legal framework was necessary to require firms to provide data, and the CEC worked with a SEMARNAT nominee to develop terms of reference and put out a call for Mexican legal advisors. The CEC's role was to provide funds and manage the contractor, as well as bring together other Mexican ministries (Garcia interview, 2008).

Indirect capacity building occurs through JPAC's activities. Information diffusion, access, and funding for participation in the advisory process help civil society upgrade capacity. The North American Fund for Environmental Cooperation (NAFEC), discontinued in 2003, enabled local groups to exchange information, create networks, and participate in the public advocacy process (Silvan 2004; see also Gallagher 2004). Between 1995 and 2003, 196 grants were made (79 of them binational or trinational) (TRAC 2004: 41). A total of 109 Mexican environmental interest groups were funded during the lifetime of NAFEC. The result was that "practitioners are in closer contact with their counterparts, not only in governments but also in NGOs and academia" (TRAC 2004: 15; Dannenmaier 2005: 3).

The US and Mexico created two additional institutions, the Border Environmental Cooperation Commission (BECC) and the North American Development Bank (NADB), to respond to environmental stress along the border. BECC provides technical assistance to border communities and certifies proposed projects for funding by the NADB. Initial priorities were in the areas of wastewater treatment, drinking water, and municipal solid waste

---

[7] See the SEMARNAT website, <http://app1.semarnat.gob.mx/retc/tema/anteced.html> accessed Jan. 2009. Translation mine.

projects. The intent was to assist local communities in project development and environmental assessment, as well as to build institutional capacity.[8] Project sponsors may call on funding programs to enable preliminary engineering work, designs, planning studies, and environmental impact statements to be carried out.

Up to 2008, the BECC had provided $34.9 million in grants (some of this money coming from the EPA) to 147 communities (BECC and NADB 2008: 5). In addition to the funding, the BECC provides advice and guidance on sustainable development plans, public participation, coordination among the different projects, and it also works with EPA and SEMARNAT on long-term border plans. In making funding decisions, the BECC requires that environmental impact assessments provide a higher level of reporting than the Mexican government has traditionally required—it asks for analysis of environmental data in addition to reporting of it, thus allowing interested parties to challenge the impact assessments of the government (Abel and Sayoc 2006).

NADB provides financial and managerial guidance, loans on its own account, help in structuring financial packages (including loans or grants from other sources), guarantees to secure outside financing, and administers US EPA grant funds (BECC and NADB 2008: 3). In its first 15 years, the BECC certified 138 projects, mainly in water and wastewater infrastructure. Of the 138, 75 were in the US and 63 in Mexico. At the same point in time, the NADB had approved financing for 119 projects, with a total cost of $2.8 billion. More of these projects are located in the US (64) than in Mexico (55), but the funding level is higher for Mexico ($1.8 billion as opposed to $1 billion for the US) (BECC and NADB 2008: 14). While NADB was responsible for roughly 21 percent of US project costs, it provided 50 percent of Mexican project costs. Mexican projects were far more heavily dependent on NADB-administered funding and without it many would not have been pursued. Moreover, projects funded by the NADB are required to have local community groups participating in various stages of the projects. Public participation has increased legitimacy and support for projects, and often spills over into other forms of local governance, increasing awareness of rights and access to information (see Abel and Sayoc 2006).

Capacity has been built because projects need to meet technical, economic, and financial viability criteria, consideration of social aspects, and community participation (GAO 2000; Lehman 2001). For example, the Utility Management Institute (created within the NADB as part of its Institutional Development Cooperation Program) trains officials in financial

---

[8] BECC and NADB 2008: 3; see also GAO 2000, for a more complete description of BECC activities.

administration and utilities planning. The public process by which the rules and procedures of projects are defined and applied in the public sphere has been opened, according to the BECC's Head of Communications and Community Management (Bravo 2008). Public participation is mandatory, and information is made available to local communities.

The consultation process has brought together SEMARNAT, Conagua, EPA, the Boundary and Water Commission, NADB, state and municipal governments, and communities on both sides of the border. In the planning stages, citizen committees must be formed, with information provided through public campaigns, media outlets, public meetings, and education (Bravo 2008: 43). Moreover, a plan has to be developed specifying how community participation will continue in the operation and maintenance phases later. As of late 2008, 337 public meetings had been held, 115 citizen committees established, and more than 1,000 local organizations had received information regarding projects and certification (Bravo 2008: 45). The strengths of this process are that the process of planning and continuity are improved, consensus is built, legitimacy raised, and democratic processes built through social participation.

Labor politics has benefited from far less capacity building, because it was already more firmly entrenched, and because the resources of the CLC did not extend to capacity-building measures. The few initiatives that did occur were bilateral US–Mexico programs. However, it is worth mentioning that communication and technical cooperation between STPS and its US and Canadian counterparts increased as a result of the NAALC (Karesh interview, 2005; STPS interviews, 2007, 2009). The establishment of offices (the NAOs and the CLC) created structures which institutionalized cooperation, including information-sharing, expertise-building, and outreach. A number of technical cooperation initiatives were established, often as a result of NAALC cases. At the end of the 1990s, the three member states convened a group on occupational safety and health issues (training, webpages, hazardous materials, and voluntary protection programs) to resolve a NAALC complaint against Mexico (STPS interview, 2009). Experts worked on exchange of best practices for four years. US labor bureaucrats have also worked at the technical level with counterparts in Mexico to improve their electronic job banks and employment service centers (Karesh interview, 2005).

5.6 Domestic Constraints to Regulatory Integration

Not only was the range of direct capacity-building assistance for labor lower than for the environment, but there are important domestic legacies affecting the impact of monitoring and assistance activities, as I argued earlier.

They are broadly centered around the professional qualities of individuals and their partiality; the permeability of domestic institutions to outside influences; and the levels of transparency and information. In this section I review how these varied between the two sectors and how they affected regulatory integration. These qualities affected the interaction between the transnational regulatory institutions of NAAEC and NAALC, and the domestic state and non-state actors involved in the domain.

5.6.1 *Professionalization and Leadership*

Professionalization and leadership qualities are far more evident among environmental actors than labor actors. Professionalization improved compliance with the law because agency officials were better equipped to apply the law and civil society officials were more capable of holding them to account. In some cases, professionalization was clearly expedited by agency leaders. Environmental agencies sought to professionalize their work as they expanded in the post-NAFTA years. Sometimes they worked with the CEC's outreach, training, and technical assistance programs. Other times they responded directly to domestic initiatives. For example, as the PRTR data monitoring program was being rolled out, the Mexican environmental agency INE created a manual for firms on how to complete the database, and along with SEMARNAT, academics, industrial groups, and associations, it began to offer training courses (CEC 2001). By 2002, following consultations with industry groups, Mexico had passed a new law requiring mandatory reporting of emissions at federal, state, and municipal levels. Evan Lloyd (the number two official at the CEC) explained that the development of the mandatory PRTR registry "clearly would not have happened without NAFTA. There has been a raising of the bar in terms of environmental standards in Mexico" (interview, 2008). Equally, SEMARNAT responded to the 2002 Transparency Law by upgrading its information processing, using resources from the federal transparency and information agency to improve cataloguing and filing so that it knew what information it possessed.

Leaders of the environmental agencies encouraged the president to modernize environmental politics as NAFTA was being negotiated, partly to signal its modernization (Rabasa interview, 2008; Carabias interview, 2010; Lendo interview, 2008). They appointed key staff who helped shift agencies in new directions. Environmental NGOs have also professionalized. Staff have acquired law or advanced science degrees, learned to communicate in sophisticated ways, and improved their leadership, management, fund-raising, and personnel resources (Puentes interview, 2008). The major environmental groups, such as CEMDA and FMCN are led by individuals with master's degrees, law degrees, or Ph.D.s. This makes them capable of communicating with civil servants, and candidates to take professional positions in the CEC and SEMARNAT.

CEMDA, which formed in 1993 as a result of NAFTA, marked a change in the NGO world in that it was the first organization to use litigation consistently to bring about policy change (Puentes interview, 2008). CEMDA's director noted that "the law is being used more and more by NGOs in Mexico, and this strengthens NGOs in front of institutions. Technical, scientific and legal arguments are replacing direct action" (Alanís interview, 2008). The NGOs are often disruptive and annoying to environmental authorities, but they are welcomed nonetheless. "Thank god we have NGOs with the technical capacity to discuss issues. Capacity-building for Mexican society was very important," said the Chief Advisor to the Secretary of SEMARNAT (Guerrero interview, 2007). CEMDA is also involved in capacity-building work, giving training workshops and creating manuals on environmental law, which explain legislation, rights, and responsibilities. In addition, the conservation group Pronatura has trained and educated more than 6,000 rural farm workers, civil society representatives, and local and state officials on private conservation tools, water conservation, private and *ejidal* (communal) land management, and technologies such as GIS (Salazar interview, 2008; Pronatura 2007).

Although infrastructure development along the border has not yet met Mexico's needs, the BECC and NADB have also helped professionalize civil servants and civil society groups. The BECC, for example, forced Mexico to engage local social groups (SEMARNAT 2001: 104). Javier Cabrera, the head of BECC from 1997 to 2005, explained that "with time the Mexican authorities saw that public participation wasn't dangerous, they could cope with the criticism. Things could no longer be done in the traditional way, and it took them time to understand. This is the big contribution of BECC. We have taught local governments and communities that things could be better. And it is a lasting change" (Cabrera interview, 2008). Border projects are more coherent because the EPA (the source of much of the funding through the BEIF) insisted on overall strategic plans. Communities were required to think strategically and develop long-term integrated programs. Continuity was improved through the public consultation process too. Governments understood that, because they were getting the support of the public, it had become more difficult to cancel projects with a change in government.

Professionalization is rare in the labor sector because leaders of traditional union confederations benefit from the cozy relationships they have with regulators. They have a vested interest in the status quo, and this impedes improvements to governance. They fear that privileges would be overturned if regulatory activity was more open to monitoring. For those non-traditional labor interests (independent trade unions, labor lawyers, research organizations, and networks of activists) who fall outside the coopted union-government structure, the most important results of the NAALC have been strengthened cross-border cooperation with US and Canadian counterparts. The requirement that a complaint be filed with the NAO of a country *different* from the one in which the infraction allegedly occurred meant that Mexican labor groups needed to locate and work with partners outside Mexico. With support from American and Canadian sources, they gained experience and knowledge as a result (Bensusán 2006a: 262; de Buen Unna 1999: 2; also Compa 1999, 2001; Díaz 2004; Fox 2004). The cases required that the partners coordinate their positions in order to bring them forward (Compa 1999: 95; Kay 2011; Graubart 2005). Unions jointly develop work strategies, write complaints and testimony, create press releases, organize demonstrations, and participate in capacity-building activities (Davis interview, 2009).

Cross-border capacity building that occurred through civil society interaction was very important. Yet this capacity-building and professionalization did not extend to all labor interests—those most in need of it, the powerful confederations, remained committed rent-seekers. There is little sign they have made any efforts to increase technical training or professionalization. Few leaders have undergraduate university degrees, much less graduate or professional degrees (see Figure 5.3). In a report on foreign labor trends, the US Department of Labor and US Embassy in Mexico showed that of the 15 national labor confederations and unions they studied, four of the leaders had achieved a BA-level university degree. Of the 14 major unions affiliated with the CTM, none of the leaders had a BA degree. Of the 11 major unions affiliated with the CROC, one leader had a BA degree. Of the five associated with the public sector confederation FSTSE, two had BA-level degrees. Among 12 independent federations and unions, one leader had a BA degree

Table 5.3 Education of environmental and labor leaders

ORG	Leader	Dates	University education
Labor leaders			
CTM	Fidel Velázquez	1941–97	None
	Blas Chumacero Sánchez	1997	None
	Leonardo Rodríguez Alcaine	1997–2005	None
	Joaquín Gamboa Pascoe	2005–	BA
Environmental leaders			
CEMDA	Gustavo Alanís	1993–	MA
FMCN	Lorenzo Rosenzweig	?	MS
Pronatura	Roberto Zambrano Villareal	2002–5	BA
	Guillermo Barroso Montull	2006–	BA plus Alta Dirección degree

and one had a professional degree. Among the 13 major CTM state federations, two leaders had BA degrees. Of the seven major CROC state federations, one leader had a BA degree (US Department of Labor Bureau of International Labor Affairs and US Embassy 2002).

The result is that norms of nationalism and clientelism have not been supplanted by international norms and standards such as respect for rule of law and regulatory strengthening. Reviews of NAALC cases by the US NAO *repeatedly* found that the labor authorities were unprofessional and highly politicized, making decisions that favored their own interests at the expense of impartiality. They also made procedural errors which delayed resolution of issues and caused confusion. The investigating NAOs made numerous requests that improvements be made to transparency, communication, information, levels of training, and education among local CABs. As late as 2007, a US NAO report stated that pregnancy testing had continued at the plant it was investigating at least until July 2005, despite earlier commitments by Mexico that it would eliminate the practice (US NAO 2007: p. iii). The report makes clear the frustration felt by the US NAO at the continuing failures to ensure justice.

> The use of administrative formalities to deny union registration has been raised as a concern in prior reports... the OTLA reiterates its recommendation that the Mexican government commit to making up-to-date information on unions and collective bargaining agreements available to interested parties through the establishment of a public registry. (US NAO 2007: 30, 33)

5.6.2 Permeability and Mobility

One of the most important differences between the two sectors is that environment agencies were in a process of expansion, and labor was more static. Mexico began to reform and expand its environmental laws and institutions in 1988, when LGEEPA (a comprehensive environmental law) was passed. From that point through the early 2000s, a number of new institutions were created and its legal code overhauled (Gil 2007; Gilbreath 2003). These reforms created opportunities for new entrants. NGO officials, national and international civil servants moved between ministerial agencies, the CEC, and NGOs. Moreover, connections were made between the trilateral JPAC and the Mexican regional environmental councils because many personnel serve in both organizations simultaneously.

Examples of personnel movement are abundant, and in striking contrast to the labor sector. The central offices of Pronatura had one director (Dr Flavio Cházaro) who moved to the National Commission for Natural Protected Areas (CONANP) as Director General (second in command, beneath the

Commissioner). Another Pronatura director (Hans Herrman) worked at the CEC as Director of Biodiversity Conservation. A Director of Environmental Policy at Pronatura (José Carlos Fernández Ugalde) worked afterwards at the Instituto Nacional de Ecología (INE, a government environmental research agency), and later as one of the Directors for the Environment and Trade Program of the CEC. CONABIO personnel have moved into NGOs. Examples include Gael Almeida who went on to work for the Fondo Mexicano para la Conservación de la Naturaleza (FMCN), and Eglé Flores, who worked for the Environment Secretary in the State of Puebla and then moved to FMCN. Other examples are Regina Barba Pirez (from SEMARNAT and later a private environmental consultant and part of Pronatura's board). Gabriel Quadri (former director of INE) is also part of Pronatura's Board, and Eduardo Vega (academic, UNAM-Economy Faculty) was formerly the Secretary of the Environment in Mexico City (Alejandra Salazar, personal communication 2010).

Environmental interests not only receive government information—and serve as a conduit for this information—but communicate with each other to work out problems. The consensus logic means that environmental interests have become sensitive to the positions of other interests, and better informed about the limits of government capabilities. Through the process of meeting and discussion, NGOs changed the way they conducted themselves, negotiating and presenting policy alternatives that actually solved problems, rather than simply making demands (de Buen interview, 2008; Martin interview, 2008). Communication between NGOs and public officials in environmental agencies is informal—the individuals involved know each other well, have become friends, speak on the phone frequently, and are part of a fluid, informal network (Guerrero interview, 2007).

In contrast, labor interests—notably the CTM and local CABs—are entrenched in historically rooted institutions of governance. Independent unions promoting workers' rights and the rule of law do exist, but the "official unions" connected with the CTM and similar confederations ensure that conflict of interest, abuse of power, corruption, and discretionary application of laws are rampant (Giménez 2007: 22; Bensusán 2006b: 330ff.). Even though there is a transnational network of trained labor activists which includes Mexicans, they do not interact at the domestic level with a similarly trained set of labor technocrats, especially within the local CABs (Martínez interview, 2010). This undermines the formation of common views, and retards the process of regulative integration in most labor agencies.

Thus, path-dependent relationships and practices hindered inward mobility of actors with new values. In the environment, the relative youth of the agencies and their rapid expansion made them more open to normative influence from external ideas, including those imported by new employees. At the outset of the NAAEC, SEMARNAT was a new agency, while the labor ministry STPS was stable and established. Federal environmental authority evolved from an under-secretariat with roughly 1,000 environmental employees in 1990, to a full cabinet agency in 1994. By the late 2000s it had about 30,000 employees. STPS was stable in size. Long-standing labor agencies with well-established and fixed practices guaranteed institutionalized privileges for narrow economic interests, and proved impermeable to influence from outside. While independent labor interests *did* emerge, and *did* build capacity, often in partnership with American and Canadian unions, they did not overcome the protected and privileged position of the coopted union confederations.

In terms of the final two domestic variables, their effects were felt equally between the labor and environment sectors or were not consistent. Domestic oversight institutions such as courts and the public information agency IFAI were cross-sectoral and therefore applied to the environment and labor agencies equally (although predictably the environment agencies were far more enthusiastic promoters of information access). SEMARNAT stated that access to information is important: (1) for purposes of scrutiny and oversight by the public, including reducing corruption, strengthening the rule of law, and improving accountability; (2) to help change the culture of secrecy and bring greater democratic maturity, which would increase public confidence in institutions, and strengthen freedom of expression; and (3) limit the arbitrariness and discretion of authorities, in turn improving the decision-making environment (SEMARNAT 2004: 13–14). Local issues are accessible to citizens, who can watch to see if permitting, regulatory enforcement, authorizations, and other processes are done correctly, explained Oscar Callejo, Adjunct Director General for Studies at the ministry (interview, 2008).

The difference between federal and state enforcement was as predicted in the environment sector, because federal officials were the ones who had to answer questions about regulatory anomalies and were less susceptible to local corruption. But in labor, it was a local board (in Mexico City) where the most pro-rule of law progress was made, and this can be traced back to commitment by political leaders to allow technocratic officials to prioritize rule of law. Committed leadership and importation of technocrats began to change the culture within this agency.[9] A number of trained lawyers were imported from the National Association of Democratic Lawyers at the behest of the CAB's new leader, Jesus Campos.[10] Autonomy was granted by the Mexico City government, which (unlike many labor authorities) allowed the

[9] The former head of the CAB, Jesus Campos, believes this is very tentative and much remains to be done (interview 2010). Outsiders representing independent unions agree with this, but confirm that it has made progress.
[10] Campos was a founding member of ANAD and president of it 1993–5. ANAD is active in promoting workers' rights.

professionals to make decisions according to the rules rather than to satisfy particular interests (Campos 2009). It became more technocratic and less political. Innovations included a diploma in law and a morning school in law within the CAB, in order to train and professionalize the legal staff, and more openness in information about union contracts.

5.7 Conclusion

Domestic institutions are more robust as a result of a transnational governance mechanism in environmental regulation, which includes federal/national environmental agencies from the three member states, the trinational Commission on Environmental Cooperation, and a dense network of environmental NGOs. On the labor side, domestic NGOs are better connected and more capable of making legal arguments, but they have not succeeded in denting an iron triangle comprised of traditional "official" union confederations, federal and state labor agencies, and domestic firms. The quality of environmental regulation (and the process of regulating) has improved. There is more transparency and public participation, more information, more professional civil servants and NGOs, higher levels of training, and depoliticized communication among the bureaucracies of the member states.

Mexican environmental officials came to accept that application of the rule of law was part of the process of modernization. In the words of a former BECC head, NAFTA was Mexico's "school of democracy" (Cabrera interview, 2008). SEMARNAT originally resisted the NAAEC and was unhappy that the Clinton administration forced it on its NAFTA partners. It later stated that it "has contributed to the environmental regulatory framework, compliance on the part of producers, and has also encouraged social participation in decision-making" (SEMARNAT 2007: 135; also SEMARNAT 2000: 359). The chief advisor to the Secretary of SEMARNAT called NAAEC "a catalyst of better behavior in Mexico" (Guerrero interview, 2007). A legal officer in the CEC explained that the quality of application of environmental law has improved, that environmental impact assessments are taken more seriously, and that NAAEC is responsible for these changes (Solano interview, 2008). The environment agencies are more relaxed about criticism from NGOs, and no longer hand-pick friendly participants to take part in CEC meetings.

> The CEC's access to information policies, decision making records, citizen submission process, and public Council sessions have helped shape Mexican citizens' expectations for the conduct of government business for national agencies and public institutions. That [SEMARNAT] is regarded as one of the more open

and transparent Mexican government agencies is in a small, but not inconse-
quential way, due to its intense interaction with the CEC and civil society. (Block
2003: 516; see also Herrera 2008)

An important interaction effect occurred between the transnational institutions (CEC and JPAC) and domestic officials in environmental agencies
and NGOs. Relatively independent NAAEC institutions generated pressures
on the Mexican government to account for its practices. As complaints succeeded, NGOs became more firmly committed to the NAAEC process, even if
their wishes were not always granted. Meanwhile, JPAC also locked in participation, and agenda-setting, funding programs, and other capacity-building
activities kept Mexican bureaucrats and NGOs committed to the NAAEC
and learning from it. Legal proficiency grew among environmental NGOs,
through their experience in the NAAEC and through interaction with foreign foundations. This had important feedback effects on domestic environmental governance, as a community of trained officials were capable of
moving from positions in domestic NGOs to federal agencies and to the CEC
Secretariat in Montreal.

In comparison with the environment, labor politics has been more resist-
ant to regulatory integration, despite a high level of technocratic interaction,
periodic shaming, and some strategic responses to investigations (Gambrill
interview, 2009). Officials in the Mexican NAO are adamant that the NAALC
has resulted in no change to Mexican labor administration. The role of that
office is to "explain" Mexican labor law and practice. Labor law is advanced
and there is no need for intrusive action by the CLC or other member states
(STPS interviews, 2007, 2009). When NGOs received favorable decisions on
their complaints to the US NAO they increased their efforts, but the process
of accepting complaints was arbitrary and they had no permanent role in
NAALC. They remain at the mercy of both entrenched economic interests in
the CABs (which continue to make decisions in contravention of the law) and
also of fluctuating commitment by partner states when they do make complaints. The spotlight of NAALC was not bright enough or sustained enough
to shame Mexican authorities into full compliance with labor law.

Moreover, the training of labor NGOs and labor civil servants is highly
variable. The CLC Secretariat did not have institutionalized public access or
capacity-building resources. CABs were criticized repeatedly for their lack of
professionalism and knowledge of the law. The one partial exception is the
Mexico City CAB, which gained a reputation as being relatively open and
honest. The courts and IFAI added to the pressure. The courts were especially influential in labor. NAALC rulings were "part of the context" for their
decisions in favor of workers' rights (Herzenberg 1996: 18; Bouzas interview,
2010; Suprema Corte 2008). Furthermore, IFAI has forced labor authorities to

justify negative decisions, making it harder to shield corrupt, arbitrary practices from scrutiny (Giménez 2007: 32; interview with Mexico NAO, 2010).

Finally, this study shows how the monitoring and assistance processes are linked when TIRs allow civil society participation, because groups who participate in monitoring processes learn to use the legal process, engage with norms of law, work with other NGOs to file complaints, compile information, and request investigations. Expectations are changed through this process, but equally important, capacity is built.

6

Greener Together? Multi-Level Integration and Environmental Protection in the Enlarged EU

Liliana B. Andonova and Ioana A. Tuta

6.1 Introduction

European enlargement has aligned the environmental policies of the new member states in Central and Eastern Europe (CEE)[1] to the complex regulations of the European Union (EU). As a condition for their membership and in a first step towards regulatory harmonization, the CEE states passed the hurdle of adopting a body of over 500 EU environmental regulations and directives. These countries were thus largely rule-takers in the accession process, which brought about both substantial costs of regulatory adjustment as well as opportunities for market, policy, and democracy development. In the post-accession period, the sustainability of regulatory integration depends on the domestic capacity and political alignment of interests to operate within the institutional and normative conditions of the transnational regulative regime.

This chapter focuses on transnational networks as an important dimension of the strategy of European regulative integration, and inquires to what extent and through what mechanisms networks impact the effectiveness of environmental regulatory integration in the new member states. Our research is informed by the observation that CEE countries, as a consequence of EU enlargement, have become part of a regional integration regime characterized both by a substantial supranational regulatory structure and significant

---

[1] Bulgaria, Hungary, the Czech Republic, Latvia, Lithuania, Estonia, Poland, Romania, Slovakia, Slovenia.

density of transnational networks involving joint and "multiplex" forms of problem-solving, monitoring, coordination, and capacity-building across public and private actors (Bruszt and McDermott 2012: 3). Yet the literature, which initially focused strongly on accession conditionality, has paid limited attention to the interplay between the network, institutional, and regulatory parts of the regime and the way it may shape the integration project after conditionality.

Theoretically, the research is informed by the broader conjecture in the European studies literature whereby the transnational organization of sub-national actors facilitates the project of regional integration (Haas 1958; Alter 2007; Burley and Mattli 1993; Hooghe and Marks 2001; Pollack and Schaffer 2001; Bruszt and McDermott in this volume). Transnational networks are a mode of organization involving actors across levels of jurisdictions and governance in a horizontal, voluntary, and reciprocal pattern of interaction and communication.[2] Such networks span a variety of actors and political spaces and constitute an important element of the transnational integration regime in Europe and its multi-level governance structure (Bruszt and McDermott 2011; Hooghe and Marks 2001).

Our argument stipulates that transnational networks, on balance, can strengthen domestic capacities and interests or the "domestic developmental agency" (Bruszt and McDermott in this volume). They thus impact both the demand and supply side of domestic institution building to sustain the environmental regulatory integration of rule-takers. The potential for such enabling influence is likely to be greater in the presence of institutional points of access that enable opportunities and channels of interplay between formal regulatory institutions and network activities. Under such conditions networks constitute a vehicle of transnational agency in the context of the EU integration, supporting a dynamic view of regional integration (Bruszt and McDermott in this volume).

The chapter develops the argument as follows. We first review the literature on the role of transnational networks in multi-level integration regimes such as the EU and environmental governance. Our theoretical framework extends that literature by specifying the mechanisms through which transnational networks can influence the societal demand for and public supply of regulatory integration, and the conditions underlying such effects. The impact of transnational environmental networks is assessed empirically in two recent member states of the EU, Romania and Bulgaria, with respect to their adaptation to two domains of EU environmental regulation: chemicals

---

[2] This definition follows the conceptualization of networks as a horizontal mode of organization and its application in studies on transnational advocacy and governance networks in international relations (Keck and Sikkink 1998; Risse et al. 1999; Andonova et al. 2009).

safety and biodiversity conservation. The conclusion discusses the broader implications of the study for understanding the variable roles of networks in complex governance systems (see also Jordana and Levi-Faur in this volume).

6.2 Networks in Multi-Level Integration Regimes

In multi-level governance structures such as the EU, rule-making involves a supranational level where rules are drafted and formally adopted, a domestic level where national authorities implement these rules, and an increasingly active transnational layer where public and private actors mobilize across borders and engage in the design and implementation of rules according to their particular interests. Our research focuses on this transnational layer and identifies one type of transnational arrangement—transnational environmental networks—as likely to facilitate the process of regional environmental integration.

The emphasis on networks as horizontal and flexible forms of transnational political organization has been informed theoretically by the neofunctionalist and multi-level governance arguments about the nature of the European polity. This literature stipulates that the process of integration is sustained and deepened by the emergence of a transnational class of actors with interests and identities loyal to the European project. Ernst Haas (1958), in his seminal book *The Uniting of Europe*, anticipated transnational interest and community formation as the political belt that propels economic integration and its functional spillover. While Haas's neofunctionalist perspective drew criticisms for underplaying the significance of intergovernmental politics and power in shaping the course of European integration, its insights on the nexus between market integration and the political role of transnational interests, elites, and their professional networks was later revived.

Studies of peak associations have uncovered the dynamics of trans-European aggregation and organization of industrial interests (Schmitter and Streeck 1999). Research on legal integration in turn has emphasized the role of the European Court of Justice and transnational networks of judges in advancing the European project domestically and at the supranational level (Burley and Mattli 1993; Alter 2007). The literature on EU policy development has captured the relevance of transnational coalitions that span domestic, national, and supranational actors in shaping agendas and the menu of policy choices (Majone 1996). Several analyses of the EU accession process have opened the box of EU institutions to highlight the role of trans-European coalitions and associations (Andonova 2004) and transgovernmental networks (Dimitrova 2002; Sissenich 2008) in shaping institutional and policy outcomes.

Subsequently, the study of EU governance found a strong expression in the conceptualization of Europe as a sphere of multi-level politics (Pollack and Schaffer 2001) and "multi-level governance" (Hooghe and Marks 2001 and 2003), which involves interplays across jurisdictions alongside with horizontally organized actors and functionally structured jurisdictional spaces. Transnational networks are thus strongly present in the conception of Europe as a multi-level integration regime (Bruszt and McDermott 2011; Falkner 2000; Knill and Tosun 2009).

The agency of transnational networks is similarly visible in the study of international environmental politics (Haas 1989; Keck and Sikkink 1998; Jordan 2005; Wapner 1995). Increasingly, transnational networks form the organizational basis of voluntary environmental regulations and governance of issues such as forestry, chemicals, sustainable fisheries, climate change, and ecologically defined regions (Cashore et al. 2004; Garcia-Johnson 2000; Prakash and Potoski 2006; Andonova et al. 2009; Andonova 2010). Studies of the development of environmental non-governmental organizations (NGOs) in CEE underscore the substantial transnational influence of donor organizations, including the EU as well as other state and non-state organizations (Börzel and Buzogàny 2010a; Carmin et al. 2003; Carmin and Fagan 2010; Fagan 2006). External assistance is reported to produce somewhat contradictory effects on environmental advocacy organizations in CEE. While augmenting the resources and skills of the sector, it has also contributed to their increasing professionalization toward consultancy-type services and detachment from their grassroots base and membership (Carmin and Fagan 2010; Fagan 2006). As a consequence, while some analyses maintain the assumption of weak societies in the new member states of the EU,[3] others have argued that looking at state–society interaction in isolation of the transnational networks might result in underestimation of the influence of non-state actors on domestic politics and regional integration (Parau 2009; Petrova and Tarrow 2007; Carmin et al. 2003).

Theories of European integration and environmental governance thus imply an important role for transnational environmental networks in the post-accession regulatory politics of the new member states. Several analyses have noted the relevance of transnational interests and EU-centered networks in the conditionality-dominated accession process of the CEE states (Andonova 2004; Sissenich 2010). However, there has been limited exploration on whether and how transnational networks may impact the development agency and capacity of these states for long-term regulatory integration within the European regime. This issue becomes even more salient in the context of several studies raising concerns about the sustainability

---

[3] See the special issue of *Acta Politica*, "Civil Society on the Rise? EU Enlargement and Societal Mobilization in Central and Eastern Europe" (2010) for more on the impact of EU enlargement on the civil society in CEE.

of regulatory integration after accession due to limited domestic capacity and mobilization of state and society alike (Sissenich 2010; Goetz 2005; Börzel and Buzogàny 2010b). As the literature on multi-level governance in Europe implies, it would be important to examine the interplay between transnational environmental networks and processes of integration centered on national and subnational administrations and their ability to incorporate the requirements of EU environmental regulations (Hooghe and Marks 2001 and 2003; Bruszt and Vedres 2013). This chapter therefore advances the line of research that examines the role of transnational networks in multi-layered systems of governance and regional integration regimes (see also Jordana and Levi-Faur in this volume). The next section elaborates our theoretical framework by specifying how and under what conditions transnational networks can influence regional environmental integration by linking regional and domestic constituencies and institutional capacities.

6.3 Network Influence across Regional and Domestic Regulatory Planes

The process of transnational regulatory integration in a rule-taking country is a multi-layered process of domestic change, reshaping its legislative and normative framework with consequences for the behavior of state and non-state actors. It involves a reconfiguration of domestic interests and institutions. There are two important interrelated elements that characterize regulatory integration. First, there is the dimension of convergence of policies, legislation, regulations, or norms. Secondly, there is the dimension of actor behavior and the extent to which actors reinterpret their role and interests in light of regulatory changes and "use their resources and seek alliances to influence policies and rules within TIRs" (Bruszt and McDermott 2012: 7). We hypothesize that, along these two dimensions, transnational networks produce changes and empower their members to strengthen the domestic capacities for regulatory integration. Our analysis therefore exemplifies how networks can "alter domestic socio-economic and institutional conditions in rule taking countries" and thus act as transnational agents of change in both the domestic and international planes of regulatory regimes (Bruszt and McDermott in this volume).

More specifically, we stipulate that networks influence integration by impacting the continuum depicting variation in organizational capacities of public and private actors, identified as one of the two factors shaping the outcome of regulatory integration (see the Y axis of Figure 1.1 in Bruszt and McDermott's chapter). They do so by bringing new sources of influence to their members. Networks can thus help to activate additional mechanisms of societal mobilization and public capacity for regulatory reform and implementation. In the following sections, we build on the insights of the literature on transnational networks to specify how networks can affect the demand and supply of regulatory integration across domestic and regional jurisdictions via the diffusion of information (Haas 1989; Parau 2009; Slaughter 2004; VanDeveer 2011), resources (Carmin 2010; Marks and McAdam 1996; Börzel and Buzogàny 2010b), and political leverage (Andonova 2004; Keck and Sikkink 1998; Parau 2009). We furthermore stipulate the scope conditions for the potential realization of positive synergies between networked and hierarchical governance in integration regimes.

6.3.1 *The Societal Demand Side of Regulatory Integration*

Transnational networks can enhance the capacity of their members to develop or reshape their agenda in the context of the regulatory changes, and effectively influence policy and institutional priorities related to regional regulatory regimes. One important comparative advantage of networked organization is the diffusion of information and organizational resources across governance jurisdictions and scales. Information is particularly important in environmental governance that often entails technical and knowledge-specific regulation and in the process of translation of regional regulation to domestic circumstances (Keck and Sikkink 1998; Haas 1989; Slaughter 2004). It enhances the knowledge of network members of institutional structures and rules and thus supports better adjustment of private or public governance practices to supranational norms. Transnational business networks can, for instance, help to clarify the implications of European regulations for domestic entities and increase their capacity for compliance and accountability through informal monitoring, which promotes the leveling of the regulatory playing field (Garcia-Johnson 2000; Andonova 2004). Transnational advocacy networks have perhaps the most substantial potential to increase the capacity of environmental advocates to demand better implementation of EU rules and activate decentralized "fire alarm" type of monitoring.

Another source of network influence lies in the increased political leverage of domestic members, as they have better access to international and regional institutions (Petrova and Tarrow 2007; Slaughter 2004; Sikkink 2005). In view of their capacity to mobilize membership across jurisdictions and harness expertise on specific issues, transnational networks are better positioned to undertake international advocacy and build contacts with international or regional intergovernmental organizations. Network members can capitalize on such opportunities to present their domestic concerns to international policy-makers and achieve better access to formal channels of international reporting to expose instances of domestic non-compliance. By linking domestic priorities with international platforms and mechanisms of monitoring (Keck and Sikkink 1998; Carmin and Hicks 2002), networks can amplify the pressure for implementation on national governments via powerful actors such as the European Commission. Studies on the engagement of NGOs in transnational networks, for example, demonstrate a substantial lift in the capacity and leverage of participating organizations in CEE to link domestic and regional institutional planes and causes (Parau 2009; Petrova and Tarrow 2007; Carmin et al. 2003). The possibility to engage in symbolic politics across jurisdictions (Wapner 1995; Parau 2009) furthermore strengthens network members' legitimacy and their efforts to mobilize popular support around their advocacy agenda.

Networks can also improve the relative position of domestic proponents of environmental regulation over that of veto-players and advance the domestic implementation process via preemptive framing and issue-linkage between specific regulatory reforms and broader political benefits of EU integration project (Andonova 2004). They thus help create and sustain broader constituencies for regional integration by linking market access to regulatory integration and diffusing resources and benefits across domestic layers of governance. Overall, networks consolidate and mobilize domestic actors to engage in and develop stakes in the process of regulatory integration, which shapes the general dynamics of state–society relations.

6.3.2 The Public Supply Side of Regulatory Integration

Transnational networks, through the provision of resources and knowledge, affect domestic capacities to supply regulatory change toward a more coherent regional integration regime. They can empower their domestic members to provide support to the administrative structures to define, implement, and enforce rules. Resources such as financial support, training schemes, organizational and management strategies (Carmin 2010; Marks and McAdam 1996; Börzel and Buzogàny 2010b) strengthen network members' capacities, while the diffusion of knowledge and expertise enables interpretation and consensus building around regulations (Haas 1989; VanDeveer 2011). Transgovernmental and expert networks, for example, have been important participants in the work of public administrations to adopt, adjust, and cope with the challenges of implementation of supranational EU rules and norms (Alter 2007; Sissenich 2008; Slaughter 2004). They may therefore contribute to the reduction of involuntary non-compliance with EU regulations or the time within which unintended non-compliance is resolved. Sub-regional networks, particularly in the multi-level sphere of EU governance, have in turn provided a channel for a more direct influence over legal and governance conformity at the municipal levels through functional and multi-stakeholder collaborations (Bruszt and Vedres 2013; Hooghe and Marks 2001).

Transnational networks of non-state or hybrid membership, such as industry networks or professional associations, work in a number of issue areas to improve the understanding and application of international market-related standards within specific sectors and to alleviate implementation or capacity concerns of non-state actors (Andonova 2004; Garcia-Johnson 2000; Koutalakis 2010; Vogel 2008). Such activities often contribute indirectly to the capacity of domestic institutions to cope with regulatory adjustment implied by regional integration regimes. Increasingly, networks of international and local NGOs engage in direct governance by strengthening the capacity of local communities to manage environmental resources and development priorities, which has an impact on the societal ability to adopt international rules and alleviates capacity concerns in transition states (Andonova 2014; Carmin 2010; Bruszt and Vedres 2013). In sum, by pooling resources and information across sectors of society and scales of governance, transnational networks provide new cross-scalar mechanisms for supporting implementation capacity, rule interpretation, and institutional consensus building. Through such processes they affect institutional resources and state–society interactions with respect to regional integration and its market and regulatory implications.

6.3.3 Traction with Regional, Transnational, and Domestic Institutions

Our argument suggests that transnational networks have the potential to contribute to more cohesive regional integration by altering the domestic status quo via non-hierarchical mechanisms. We do not assume, however, that the activation of transnational mechanisms or their hypothesized positive impact on regulatory integration will automatically or necessarily materialize. The chapter by Jordana and Levi-Faur in this volume finds, for instance, high degree of fragmentation in the network governance of the telecommunications sector in Latin America. Studies of global environmental governance similarly mention the fragmentation and growing complexity of international regimes in part as a consequence of the proliferation of transnational network-based governance (Betsill and Bulkeley 2004; Keohane and Victor 2010), with as yet uncertain implications for the regulatory and domestic uptakes of integration regimes.

The broader literature on transnational networks leads us to stipulate that the potential for a positive impact of transnational networks on regional integration regimes is likely to be conditional on some degree of traction between the transnational networks and supranational and domestic institutions. Traction between informal networks and formal institutions is understood to include some institutional access points and at least a minimal coordination of governance purposes. Neofunctionalist and multi-level governance perspectives on European integration argue precisely that the regional integration regime itself has motivated and supported the emergence of networks with some congruence in governance purpose, which creates positive reinforcement across levels of integration (Haas 1958; Hooghe and Marks 2001; Burley and Mattli 1993). Scholars of transnational advocacy networks have also found that, as access to domestic and international institutions improved over time due to processes of democratization and institutional reforms, the impact of networks has increased and the opportunity structure for such influence has expanded (Sikkink 2005; Haas 1989). Conversely, it is possible that transnational governance or advocacy networks, as a consequence of a narrow or specific focus, operate in parallel to, rather than in interaction with, formal institutions for regional integration. In the arena of environmental governance, multiple transnational networks are organized around the governance of specific eco-regions, but their activities may remain rather disconnected from EU regulatory harmonization, for example. The proliferation of transnational governance activities in the form of public-private partnerships, market-based certification governance, or other network-based governance has indeed raised concerns about the possible negative effects of the fragmentation of environmental governance more broadly and the undermining of formal intergovernmental instruments of regulation.

Generally, the EU integration regime has high potential for traction between hierarchical and horizontal governance mechanisms. Its relatively strong supranational specialization involves interplay with and often support for transnational professional communities, as well as the creation of access points in response to concerns about democratic deficit. Even within the multiplex system of the EU, however, the potential for synergies between supranational, transnational, and domestic mechanisms of environmental integration remains variable and in need of further examination. Moreover, while the conditions for a minimal degree of traction might be met, the overall impact of networks on regulatory integration might play out differently depending on the particularities of the state–society relations in each domestic context. Important for the inquiry of this volume, differential domestic institutional structures and politics may condition differential initial levels of network mobilization and access. In their chapter, Bruszt and Langbein persuasively explain how the level of organization of domestic actors and the quality of the cooperation between state and non-state actors can shape the development effects of EU regulatory integration. Such considerations prompt the following comparative analysis on the extent to which the hypothesized impact of transnational networks might depend on historically shaped domestic structures, and on the extent to which such networks could compensate over time for institutional deficiencies and contribute to greater regulatory cohesion.

6.4 Empirical Approach

The empirical part of the chapter analyzes the impact of transnational networks on environmental regulatory integration in two of the recent members of the EU, Bulgaria and Romania, both in the pre- and post-accession periods. We selected these countries since their national administrations are generally assessed to have a lower capacity to implement EU laws and cope with their distributional consequences (Börzel 2010). In such cases the hypothesized lift in domestic capacity attributed to transnational networks should be clearly observable and should go against conventional expectations of regulatory backsliding once accession conditionality is removed.

The empirical analysis is structured around the two supranational regulatory areas: chemicals safety and biodiversity protection. In these two areas of EU environmental regulation there is a relatively high number of transnational organizations (Andonova 2004; Carmin et al. 2003; Börzel and Buzogàny 2010a). Their selection allows us to trace the influence of networks that differ in terms of their membership (non-governmental organizations, employers' associations) and their organizational structure (Brussels-centered, regional networks, international networks) and understand the policy variation they facilitate. We rely on the comparative case study method to analyze the resources, information, and leverage that different types of networks bring to their members, and the extent to which they produce variable influence on the domestic demand and supply of regulatory integration. The cross-country comparison allows us to investigate how initial domestic institutional conditions mediate the anticipated influence of transnational networks and under what circumstances transnational networks might compensate for such differences. The evidence is collected from primary documents, text analysis, and interviews.

6.5 Networking from Above: The Case of Chemicals Legislation

6.5.1 Networks and Regulation

The regulation of chemicals is one of the oldest and expanding areas of EU legislation. The EU regime for chemical safety exemplifies the multiplex intergovernmental and transnational dimensions of European integration. Since the late 1960s, the supranational regulation of chemical substances responded to pressures from environmental movements and the chemical industry to level the regulatory playing field across the highly integrated West European and US markets (Vogel 1995). Since the Treaty of Rome (1957) establishing the European Economic Community did not include environmental protection among its objectives, chemical safety standards were initially based on Article 100 of the Treaty, which stipulates the harmonization of regulations directly related to the functioning of the Common Market.

The European Community adopted its first directive for the protection of human health and the environment from harmful chemicals in 1967, regulating the classification, packaging, and labeling of more than 1,000 substances. At present, the EU legislation on chemicals includes directives related to classification and labeling, accidents, trade, exposure, and effects of specific toxic substances. The 2007 Regulation on Registration, Evaluation, Authorization and Restriction of Chemical substances (REACH) further expands the requirements for testing, registration, and provision of information on certain classes of chemicals.

Prior to EU accession, there was low compatibility between the chemical regulations of CEE countries and those of the EU (Andonova 2004; CEFIC 1998). The chemical industry had the reputation of one of the most polluting sectors in post-communist Europe. The regulatory misfit and substantial adjustment requirements in the regulation of chemicals echoed broader concerns about difficult regulatory integration.

EU integration brought CEE countries not only into a highly regulated supranational regime on chemical substances, but also into a domain of established transnational activity. The European Chemical Industry Council (CEFIC), a Brussels-centered industrial network, has had the most direct access to the EU integration process of CEE states and regulatory harmonization in the area of chemical safety. Founded in 1972, precisely around the time of heightened regulatory pressure, CEFIC's membership includes national chemical industry associations, corporate members, associated companies, and affiliated sector associations and partners. Described by environmental organizations as one of the most powerful industrial lobby groups in Brussels (Contiero 2006), CEFIC steers a network of over 40,000 large, medium, and small chemical companies, eleven of which are also members of the influential European Roundtable of Industrialists. Linking to the global level, CEFIC is a member of the International Council of Chemical Associations (ICCA), and coordinates on behalf of ICCA the promotion and implementation of the Responsible Care program in Europe. CEFIC's network is active in both lobbying, as evidenced by its massive efforts to limit the scope of environmental regulations such as REACH (Selin 2007; Contiero 2006), and in governance activities by supporting the adoption of voluntary standards for chemical safety and the implementation of EU regulations.

CEFIC actively extended its transnational network to the East, informed by the interests of its West European members to assure regulatory stability and safeguard the image of the chemical industry in an expanded European market (De Bree 1995; Andonova 2004). Moreover, the European Commission (EC or the Commission) and CEFIC worked together during the pre-accession process to expand the industrial network to chemical industry associations in CEE and engage them through a series of jointly managed projects in the interpretation and understanding of EU chemical standards (see Table 6.1). The Commission and CEFIC's membership thus had a specific congruence of purpose in supporting the transposition and implementation of EU chemicals regulations to level the regulatory playing field. This congruence of purpose underpinned both the expansion of the CEFIC network and its access to the pre-accession harmonization process.

In addition to CEFIC, several trans-European NGO networks are also active in issues concerning the regulation of chemicals. Most prominently, these include the Brussels-based Health and Environment Alliance (HEAL), which has a membership of 14 European or international networks and 53 member organizations across 26 different countries including Bulgaria and Romania,[4] and the European Environmental Bureau (EEB),[5] which together with Greenpeace, WWF, and Friends of the Earth mobilized significant transnational advocacy for the adoption of REACH (Mazey and Richardson 2005; Selin 2007). While these networks had an important impact on deepening regulation at the supranational level, they were weakly involved in building domestic capacity to support and push for regulatory integration in the new member states. They have supported primarily advocacy activities related to education on chemical substances and access to information. In this context, the dominant position of the industry network has had important implications, as we shall see, for the types of domestic capacities developed to advance regulatory harmonization.

6.5.2 *Network Influence and Industry Demand for Regulatory Integration*

Two main mechanisms of network influence underpinned the domestic industrial politics of regulatory harmonization and application. First, the

---

[4] Bulgaria members are: My Right to Know Foundation; Women and Mothers against Violence; Earth Forever Foundation; Institute for Ecological Modernisation; Sustainable World Foundation; Romanian members: Eco Counselling Centre Galati, Romania.
[5] The EEB has one member organization in Bulgaria and three in Romania.

CEFIC network channeled substantial organizational resources to support the capacity of industry associations as well as their industrial members to engage in the pre-accession regulatory harmonization process. Secondly, and as anticipated by the theoretical framework, the network diffused information and built domestic expertise to influence the understanding of EU chemical laws and promote their interpretation in line with the interests of export-oriented market actors (Andonova 2004). The diffusion of organizational resources and information to support the development and capacity of domestic constituencies for regional integration materialized primarily through the series of joint projects and twinning activities coordinated by CEFIC and supported by the Commission. Table 6.1 lists in chronological order the projects supported by the EC and managed by CEFIC, including their objectives, activities, and main participating organizations.

As a consequence of CEFIC activities, in the span of five to ten years, a trans-European network of experts from industry, governments, and the Commission emerged and thickened. A 2002 presentation by Frantisek Doktor, former Director for Central Europe and Regulatory Affairs of CEFIC, highlights that projects such as the ChemFed and ChemLeg have facilitated the establishment of "60 local networks and working groups involving over 1000 experts" across CEE (Doktor 2002). The creation of an influential regional network of the chemical industry in CEE with "active involvement in European advocacy" was considered one of the main achievements of such programs (Doktor 2002: 38).

Text analysis of documents of the projects listed in Table 6.1 and of recent documents of the Bulgarian Chamber of Chemical Industry (BCCI)[6] and the Romanian Employers' Federation of Chemical and Petrochemical Industry (FEPACHIM)[7] reveals that considerable organizational and technical resources were channeled through the CEFIC network into several strategic directions: the strengthening of national chemical industry associations; establishment of close working relations between these associations, CEFIC, and government authorities; and technical support for the interpretation, transposition, and implementation of chemical safety policies.

The influence is particularly visible in the Bulgarian case, where the industry association BCCI became engaged with the CEFIC network shortly after its establishment in 1994 via the CEFIC/PHARE project on "The Impact

---

[6] The Bulgarian Chamber of the Chemical Industry (BCCI), established in 1994, has a membership of 48 chemical companies, which represent approximately 85 percent of chemical production in the country, and respectively 80 percent of exports and 65 percent of the employment in the sector (Pelovski 2006).

[7] The Romanian Employers' Federation of Chemical and Petrochemical Industry was legally established in 1992 and reunites 116 companies representing 54.1 percent of the employment in the chemical and petrochemical sector.

of the European Commission's White Paper on the Chemical Industry in CEE Countries" (Table 6.1). One of the main objectives of the initiative was "to train experts on legislative issues for these Federations and to have the National Coordinators as 'insiders' in the policy processes" (CEFIC 1998). The European chemical industry network strengthened the organizational

Table 6.1 Activities of CEFIC network in CEE

Year	Project	Objectives	Actors Involved
1997–1998	Impact of the Commission's White paper on the Chemical Industry in the Central and Eastern European Countries.	Twinning between industry experts in the EU and CEECs; screening of national chemical legislation; identifying the changes required for approximation with EU laws; and anticipated effect on the chemical industry in the CEECs.	EU Commission, CEFIC, national
	CEFIC/TAIEX (Technical Assistance Information Exchange Office) Programme on Technical Assistance.	Assisting the CEEC Federations with regard to the transposition of the *acquis communautaire*	CEFIC, national federations, public authorities, DG Enlargement, DG Enterprise
1999–2000	Transposition activities	Assist the Candidate Countries to align their chemicals legislation to that of the European Union, review state of transposition, seminars, workshops	
1999–2000	Industrial Forum on Enlargement	Involve representatives from the chemical industry from the EU, Bulgaria, Czech Republic, Estonia, Hungary, Malta, Latvia, Lithuania, Poland, Romania, Slovakia, and Turkey in this initiative of the EU Industry Council	EU Commission, CEFIC, Industry Council, national federations and chemical enterprises
2000–2002	ChemFed	Strengthen the capacity of CEE Chemical Industry Federations, prepare for the EU enlargement, promote Responsible Care	CEFIC, national federations of EU-15, CEE chemical federations, EU Commission (funding)
2000–2002	ChemLeg	Strengthen the capacity of CEEC Federations to provide for regulatory services to assist business operators in CEECs to cope with the requirements of the *acquis*. Provide information on requirements, training, toolkits on implementation, training of trainers.	CEFIC, national federations of EU-15, CEE chemical federations, EU Commission (funding)
2001–2005	ChemFed/ChemLeg2	Assistance with implementation and compliance with the environmental and social *acquis*; information diffusion, training, prepare conditions for collaboration on registration of chemicals for the REACH	CEFIC, national federations of EU-15, CEE chemical federations, EU Commission (funding)

Source: <http://www.cefic.be/Templates/shwStory.asp?NID=25&HID=289&PHID=288> accessed May 2008.

resources of BCCI in several ways. It provided a stream of financing, which supported the work of the association and its ability to engage member companies on issues related to chemical safety, environmental regulations, and voluntary standards. The ChemFed and ChemLeg projects and associated activities such as internships, workshops, and seminars involved substantial support for organizational development and contributed to, according to the formal assessment of project outcomes, the strengthening of the organizational position of BCCI, its expertise, strategy, recognition by public authorities, and access to international institutions (Doktor 2002). Such activities enhanced the expertise of BCCI staff and their capacity to produce information materials and training modules with respect to EU legislation on chemicals and voluntary Responsible Care program (Pelovski 2006; Dombalova 2011).

In the Romanian case, the trans-European chemical industry network has had a similar influence, but to a more limited extent, due to the less extensive and shorter involvement of FEPACHIM in the network. The Federation did not participate in the early initiatives and projects organized by CEFIC and the Commission. The document of the 1997–8 CEFIC/PHARE project, which was indeed the first major initiative familiarizing the national chemical associations with the requirements of the EU legislation on chemicals and facilitating their access to national authorities and EC, indicates that the Romanian industry association did not participate in the project and the Romanian report was based on "ad-hoc meetings with industry experts...and Romanian authorities" (CEFIC 1998: 14). FEPACHIM became engaged with the network only in 2002 when it was the last Federation to join the ChemFed/ChemLeg projects already in their final year.

The participation of FEPAHIM in the ChemFed project nonetheless produced a strategy for organizational development of the Federation. Two members of its staff were trained to promote the implementation of the Responsible Care program in Romania. With the support of experts from CEFIC, it organized two meetings on Responsible Care for Romanian companies and translated and disseminated a Manual on Responsible Care and Product Stewardship. In 2003, this initiative was followed up with a project financed by the Japan International Cooperation Agency on the implementation of voluntary standards regarding the integrated management of waste. In spite of these network activities, which remained considerably more limited compared to other CEE countries such as the Czech Republic, Poland, or Bulgaria (Andonova 2004), Responsible Care has not gained momentum in Romania, which now remains the only country in the EU where companies are not bound by such voluntary standards.

While FEPACHIM did not evolve into a fully fledged organization with permanent staff providing periodic capacity building programs and information resources, it nevertheless maintained its visibility through its participation in the Social Dialogue with labor organizations and governmental actors. Together with the Federation of the Free Trade Unions of the Chemical and Petrochemical Industries, it forms the Sectoral Committee for Chemistry and Petrochemistry that negotiates and signs the collective labor agreement within the industry. In 2006, financed by the Swiss Agency for Development and Cooperation, FEPACHIM organized seminars to improve the practices of social dialogue with a focus on the arbitration and mediation of labor conflicts. The visibility of FEPACHIM was enhanced by the special circumstance whereby its president was at the same time the president of the General Confederation of the Romanian Industrial Employers UGIR-1903, the oldest and most important employer confederation in Romania, with significant leverage in the social dialogue structures at the governmental level.

6.5.3 Network Influence and the Supply of Regulatory Integration

The activities of the CEFIC network have had a visible impact on the role of industrial actors and domestic institutional capacity to foster regulatory integration both in the pre-accession and post-accession periods. The BCCI gained considerable informational advantage and leverage that made it a central player in domestic regulatory reforms, working closely with European experts and national experts of the Ministry of Environment and Water on successful pre-accession harmonization of EU chemicals safety regulations (CEFIC 1998; Andonova 2004; Pelovski 2006). An indication of the durable impact of the transnational chemical industry network is the fact that the BCCI maintained its central position in the diffusion of information and implementation guidelines even after Bulgaria's accession when European projects were scaled down considerably. The BCCI, according to documents published on its website and interviews with its representatives, is itself actively using the network to disseminate to its members information prepared by CEFIC on the implementation of the 2007 REACH regulation. It also assists member companies with preparation for obtaining permits under the EU Integrated Prevention and Pollution Control, supporting work safety programs and promoting energy efficiency and pollution reduction practices (BCCI 2011). The association increasingly works with small and medium-sized chemical enterprises that have the lowest financial and human capacity for implementing REACH, and advocates for greater availability of public support for technical training and capacity building (Pelovski 2006). The resources and access afforded through the transnational chemical industry network have also enabled the BCCI to engage in sectoral social dialogue at the European level and subsequently to conclude a "cooperation pact" between employer and labor organizations in the Bulgarian chemical sector (Dimitrova 2007).

The activities of the network and its local branch, BCCI, contributed to the relatively smooth adoption of the EU legislation on chemicals (Andonova 2004) and the subsequent improved capacity of BCCI member companies, predominantly export-oriented large enterprises, to comply with EU standards (Pelovski 2006). By 2012, 40 chemical enterprises had qualified for participation in the voluntary Responsible Care program and all but one of the 40 large chemical enterprises had prepared for compliance with the REACH regulation,[8] which indicates further reinforcement between voluntary, network-based governance and the formal requirements of the regional integration regime.

The CEFIC network through its ChemLeg project also contributed to the engagement of the Romanian Federation in the translation of the European legislation on chemicals and the dissemination of guides explaining those directives and the REACH requirements to its membership (Coraci 2006). A network of Romanian experts within the industry furthermore benefited from trainings on European legislation. As result of these activities, FEPACHIM contributed to the timely transposition of the *acquis communautaire* for chemicals and began to cooperate with the Ministry of Environment on aspects related to the interpretation of directives and evaluation of implementation strategies.

Besides ChemFed/ChemLeg, FEPACHIM engaged with CEFIC in just a few other instances, when participating at a seminar on Responsible Care in Bulgaria in 2007 and lobbying the Romanian MPs in the European Parliament for delaying the adoption of the European Trading Scheme in 2006.[9] Despite being listed as an affiliate federation of CEFIC, FEPACHIM has been an inactive member in the post-accession period. Explaining this situation, the president of FEPACHIM mentioned the high membership fee in the context of the economic crisis and the participation in networks that better meet the needs of the organization, such as the European Chemical Employers Group.[10] The general context has also been unfavorable as the liberalization of the market and the financial crisis compelled many companies to stop or reduce their production.

A comparison of the Bulgarian and Romanian cases suggests that the length and extent of transnational network membership and involvement does have an impact on the degree to which resources and information are diffused and the ability of the network to exert substantial influence on regulatory integration. Thus domestic organizational priorities and capacity also interplay with network activity to shape the extent of traction between transnational networks and domestic constituencies. These cases also reveal

[8] Interview with Yoncho Pelovski, BCCI, Feb. 2012.
[9] Interview with Ioan Cezar Coraci, President of FEPACHIM, Bucharest, Dec. 2011.
[10] Interview with Ioan Cezar Coraci, Dec. 2011.

that the type of transnational network that becomes relevant is important for the kind of ideology, resources, and influence it will seek to exert on the domestic regulatory processes. The CEFIC network has advocated a more collaborative approach between industrial associations and public authorities and labor organizations on the one hand, and between industrial associations and member companies on the other hand, to advance the understanding of and capacity for regulatory harmonization. This type of policy network, however, has had the effect of largely leaving watchdog NGOs out of the regulatory process. In the context of a limited engagement of alternative networks, such as those of advocacy NGOs, the CEFIC network has helped to redistribute political influence to its industry constituency. The following section examines, in turn, how advocacy networks have influenced the regulatory integration of Bulgaria and Romania with respect to EU biodiversity policies.

6.6 Networking from Below: The Case of Biodiversity Conservation

6.6.1 Biodiversity Networks and Traction with EU Regulations

The European biodiversity field is characterized by a rich transnational activity dating back to the second half of the nineteenth century (Van Koppen and Markham 2007). At the same time, the EU biodiversity policy, with its core Wild Birds (1979) and Habitats (1992) Directives, comprises a series of regulations that demand considerable domestic capacity for adoption and implementation. The former requires member states to establish a network of Special Protected Areas (SPAs) to protect endangered, vulnerable, rare birds and their most important habitats across the EU. The latter creates the obligation to protect endangered animal and plant species in their habitats by creating Special Areas of Conservation (SACs) that together with SPAs are to be integrated into a pan-European ecological network known as Natura 2000. The Habitats Directive recognizes over 200 habitat types and 1,000 species of plants and animals as of "Community interest" and in need of special protection to safeguard their future. Member states are required to protect these sites by creating management structures and avoiding harmful development projects.

The regulatory integration process starts with the designation by member states of their biodiversity sites within an agreed timeframe. While in the case of the Wild Birds Directive the process takes place in one stage, for the Habitats Directive the process is more complicated and involves three steps. States first provide a list of proposed Sites of Community Importance.

Then, the Commission verifies and discusses the list within the so-called Biogeographical Seminars which involve a variety of stakeholders including states, NGO representatives and officials from the Directorate General for Environment (Papp and Toth 2007). Finally, depending on the results of these seminars, states propose updated lists that, if approved by the Commission, can be officially declared as SACs and Natura 2000 sites. These requirements put a heavy burden on state capacity. The identification of habitats presupposes the gathering of specialized knowledge, the designation must be done with the consultation of landowners, and the intense lobbying from business interests can slow the legislative process. This partly explains why nature conservation in the environmental field, together with water and waste management, reveals persistent difficulties of implementation.[11]

While the biodiversity field includes a flurry of transnational organizations, we identified two categories of transnational networks with substantial degree of congruence with Natura 2000 directives in terms of both the purpose of activities and degree of access to supranational institutions. One type of network is generated by highly visible and established international non-governmental organizations, such as WWF and Birdlife International. The activity of the WWF in CEE can be traced back to the opening of the Danube Carpathian Programme Office (DCPO) in 1998 in Vienna with the objective of the conservation, restoration, and sustainable management of the Danube River and the Carpathian Mountains. From 2006, DCPO has registered organizations in Bulgaria and Romania that are directly linked to the global strategy carried out by WWF International and are well connected to older branches in Western Europe. They thus capitalize on the visibility and legitimacy of a global network that sets the agenda of environmental advocacy.

In Romania and Bulgaria, BirdLife Europe implements its conservation and protection program through national partnerships with the ornithological organizations Romanian Ornithological Society (SOR) and Bulgarian Society for the Protection of Birds (BSPB), two of the oldest environmental NGOs in those countries. These national partners help BirdLife in implementing locally their targets and objectives, while BirdLife offers advice, expertise, and access to EU stakeholders. Moreover, since 1981 BirdLife has run the European Important Bird Areas Program (IBAs) through which it has identified and created an inventory of bird sites in need of protection. The Commission has endorsed this inventory as the reference list against which to evaluate the national lists of designated SPAs. This governance partnership between the EC and Birdlife has empowered the partner NGOs in Romania

---

[11] See <http://ec.europa.eu/environment/legal/law/statistics.htm>, Jan. 2012.

and Bulgaria, which were called upon by administrative authorities to carry out the respective designations.

In addition to the networks facilitated by large international NGOs, there are regional European networks with a federal organizational structure involving various NGOs, including grassroots and local organizations. The Central and East European Working Group for Biodiversity (CEEweb) was founded in 1994 and quickly evolved into a network of 64 nature conservation NGOs from 18 CEE countries, being one of the most active regional networks including with respect to designation of Natura 2000 sites. The network has eight members from Romania[12] and nine from Bulgaria,[13] with Milvus and the Bulgarian Biodiversity Foundation being among the most active on Natura 2000 related issues.[14] With the objective of "conserving biodiversity in CEE through the promotion of sustainable development," CEEweb has a strong policy and advocacy focus. At the EU level, its access to relevant decision-makers, such as the Natura 2000 Management Working Group of the Commission, is strengthened by its active participation in the European Habitats Forum, a group of NGO networks that provides in an institutionalized manner advice to the Directorate General (DG) for Environment. Moreover, CEEweb coordinates the input of CEE NGOs in the Biogeographic Seminars and is therefore involved in the designation of the participant NGOs. This position entails good knowledge of the national NGOs and the capacity to train and prepare them to ensure strong lobby within the Seminars. In 2003, CEEweb created a Working Group on Natura 2000 as a forum for its members to share experiences and exchange information about the requirements of the EU legislation.

6.6.2 Network Influence and the Demand for Biodiversity Integration

Environmental NGOs in Romania and Bulgaria can be considered what Bruszt and McDermott call "beneficiaries of regulatory change" (Bruszt and McDermott in this volume). For these NGOs the implementation of the Natura 2000 regulations in their countries has been an invaluable opportunity to obtain validation for their work and gain credibility vis-à-vis local and national policy-makers.

---

[12] Agora, Ecosilvex 2000 Foundation, Foundation ADEPT Transilvania, Green Echoes Association, Green Valley Association, Greentourism Ecological Association, Milvus Group, NGO Sustainable Sighisoara, UNESCO Pro Natura Ecological Club.

[13] Balkani Wildlife Society, Birds of Prey Protection Society, Bulgarian Biodiversity Foundation, Environmental Organization-Rhodope, NC Future Now, Green Balkans, Rodope-Mountain for Everyone, Sand Glass Foundation, UNEP National Committee.

[14] Communication by email with Agnes Zolyomi, Natura 2000 Working Group Coordinator, CEEweb for Biodiversity, Jan. 2012.

In Romania, the development of a domestic environmental constituency has been slow and gathered impetus once the EU accession process started and more funding opportunities were made available to NGOs (Parau 2009; Börzel and Buzogàny 2010a: 718). The environmental movement in Bulgaria has had stronger local roots as it was a core part of the anti-communist dissident movement prior to democratization and played an important role in confronting the state on environmental issues. Bulgarian NGOs, such as Green Balkans and BSPB, have expanded substantially their conservation activities since 1990 in collaboration with transnational partners, but also with local branches and experts. While this variation in domestic societal mobilization is reflected in the timing and process of domestic mobilization and policy change, NGO participation in networks contributed in both cases to regulatory integration. Several mechanisms of network influence empowered Romanian and Bulgarian NGOs to demand more effective implementation of biodiversity directives, and subsequently to monitor the extent to which the institutional and policy changes have been genuine.

To begin with, networks supported the capacity of member NGOs by providing organizational resources and by disseminating information and knowledge both in the pre-accession and post-accession periods. WWF acted as a secretariat to the Romanian Natura 2000 NGO Coalition, a network of local environmental NGOs established to monitor, advance, and contribute to the implementation of the Natura 2000 directives. WWF was elected to this position because of the need for a focal NGO with the resources to carry out coordinating functions (Statute Natura 2000 NGO Coalition). As the NGO coordinating the Coalition, WWF facilitated working meetings, implemented the communication strategy, and maintained the relationship with other stakeholders.

CEEweb also played a key role in respect to capacity building. Bulgarian and Romanian members benefited from the transfer of knowledge and information that this regional network enabled. In 2004, CEEweb organized a Train the Trainers workshop in order to empower "independent advocates for timely and effective implementation of Natura 2000 in their home countries."[15] In 2007, Romanian and Bulgarian NGOs participated in two preparatory meetings dedicated to understanding the working rules of the Biogeographic Seminars, which helped these organizations to identify how to best pool their resources and effectively contribute to the domestic implementation of the biodiversity regulations.

National NGOs have also benefited from the constant flow of information that the Secretariat of CEEweb facilitated. From the perspective of local

---

[15] Communication by email with Agnes Zolyomi, Natura 2000 Working Group Coordinator, CEEweb for Biodiversity, Jan. 2012.

member organizations, CEEweb was instrumental in enabling better access to European decision-makers and information about future actions and decisions of DG Environment, while the online communication groups it manages allowed members to share experiences and identify reliable partners for projects and campaigns.[16] The flow of information horizontally across the network and vertically across levels of governance has helped NGOs to interpret EU legislation and design effective strategies and work programs.

In 2006, CEEweb organized its Annual Academy, a yearly program of seminars and trainings, in Bulgaria with the theme of strengthening civil society participation in the implementation of EU nature directives through the experiences gained by the ten new member states. Members from both the Green Balkans and BSPB participated in these seminars and engaged in constructive dialogue about the role of NGOs in "bringing to life" the European ecological network. This included strategies for effective communication of the benefits of the Natura 2000 sites to address more effectively opposition and concerns by local stakeholders and municipalities (CEEweb 2006). Importantly, CEEweb seminars also facilitated the diffusion of information and understanding of the EU complaints procedure and making an infringement case "effective" (Barov 2006).

Another mechanism empowering domestic actors to demand regulatory integration was transnational network leverage through lobbying and watchdog activities. Since 2006, with the support of BirdLife UK, the Romanian SOR established the position of Danube Delta Casework Officer responsible of closely monitoring developments in Delta Danube, the Natura 2000 site hosting the most diverse bird species in Europe. Benefiting from the support of a BirdLife partner with experience and access to the EC, SOR has identified cases of inadequate protection of Natura 2000 sites and exerted pressure to reverse harmful developments.[17]

NGOs in Bulgaria have similarly staged street protests and launched nation-wide campaigns to first pressure the government to include all their proposals in the official designation list and later on to unmask development projects harmful to biodiversity conservation. Transnational support has been instrumental for the visibility and larger impact of such efforts. In 2006, WWF helped launch the campaign "Save Bulgaria's treasures!" in order to bring to an end illegal activities affecting protected areas. The campaign tried, through petitions and letters of concern from external actors, such as the General Director of WWF, to pressure Bulgarian authorities into putting biodiversity objectives ahead of economic and business interests (WWF DCPO 2012). WWF as well as the BSPB have been part of the "For the Nature" Coalition

---

[16] Interview with Papp Tamas, President Milvus, Tg. Mures, Nov. 2011.
[17] Royal Society for the Protection of Birds website, <http://www.rspb.org.uk/ourwork/casework/details.aspx?id=tcm:9-227894>, Jan. 2012.

that organized in 2007 and 2008 a series of protests that mobilized thousands of people around the protection of Natura 2000 sites (WWF DCPO 2008). Bulgarian NGOs along with transnational coalition partners were instrumental in submitting a number of official complaints to the EC regarding the construction of infrastructure in mountain and seafront protected areas (BirdLife 2008; Green Balkans 2008). They also launched campaigns and worked with mayors and regional authorities to emphasize the local development benefits associated with Natura 2000 and to counteract domestic contestation on the part of interest groups, such as developers, logging companies, and landowners.

6.6.3 *Strengthening the Supply of Regulatory Integration*

Networks have also had an effect on the supply side of institution building by enhancing the capacity of state authorities to meet the requirements of the directives and work more closely with civil society and epistemic communities towards those objectives.

Bulgarian NGOs supported state authorities in meeting their obligations under the Natura 2000 directives by collaborating on the identification of sites for designation. Green Balkans, one of the oldest nature conservation organizations in Bulgaria, conducted significant field work, species inventory, and site designation for the implementation of Natura 2000 (Marin 2006). With a membership of 4,500 individual members united in four regional offices and 25 correspondent centers, this NGO enjoys the support of many citizens and has built strong ties with governmental actors, including international NGOs and public institutions. As early as 2002–3, Green Balkans, in cooperation with the Ministry of Environment (MoE), conducted the first systematic study on habitats and continued this work throughout the following years, covering and proposing for designation 30 percent of the country's territory. Such close state–society collaboration was supported via a transnational pre-accession twinning project financed by the Danish Environmental Agency. It also spurred the establishment of the Natura 2000 coalition of NGOs, including Balkani Wildlife Society, WWF Bulgaria, and the Centre for Environmental Information and Education (Green Balkans 2011). In 2005, the Bulgarian MoE "delegated" to the Green Balkans coordinator the preparation of the national list of Natura 2000 sites (Marin 2006).

The BSPB played a central role in advocating the inclusion of the Important Bird Areas in the Natura 2000 network, a position that was strengthened by its participation in transnational networks linked to BirdLife International and transnational twinning projects in Bulgaria. As result of its activities in the Phare project "Increasing the readiness of Bulgaria to establish the Natura 2000 network," BSPB published the *Guide on Natura 2000*, the first book of this type written in Bulgaria (BSPB 2012). Indeed over half of all sites under the Wild Bird

Directive were proposed by BSPB. The work and advisory effort of the organization involved providing scientific data for bird numbers and distribution, maps of the sites, and all other information needed for the standard data forms. This was done in the frame of contract with the Ministry of Environment and with the mobilization of BSPB regional offices and branches in smaller towns.[18]

WWF's contribution to the implementation of the Wild Birds and Habitats directives consisted of various conservation activities within the context of the Lower Danube Green Corridor Agreement. As an extension of such activities organized around a functionally designated transnational ecological region, WWF proposed habitats and species to be protected under the Natura 2000 conservation regime. The NGO networked with and engaged local stakeholders to develop this area according to biodiversity conservation principles and supported the effort of societal consensus-building for the management plans of the Natura 2000 sites. The work of the Natura 2000 NGO Coalition, in coordination with government institutions and the Ministry of the Environment in particular, ultimately produced a proposal that included 500 potential sites for designation in Bulgaria or approximately 36 percent of its territory (Marin 2006; Stoychev and Poliyakov 2009).

In Romania where the capacity and political leverage of domestic NGOs was historically weaker compared to the Bulgarian case, WWF has been an important partner of state actors in gathering the scientific knowledge necessary for the designation of the Natura 2000 sites during the accession process. Within the framework of the EU financed project "Priority forest, sub-alpine and alpine habitats in Romania," WWF has contributed to the development of the Habitats Manual comprising all natural habitats in Romania and serving as a scientific basis for the designation of Natura 2000 sites by the Ministry of Environment (Florescu 2009). An important role in scientific research and designation was also played by the local partner of BirdLife. Based on the Important Bird Areas scientific criteria and directory developed by BirdLife Europe, SOR was contracted by state bodies to identify the Natura 2000 bird sites that should be included in the initial national designation list. Milvus, the oldest and most active Romanian member in CEEweb, also contributed to the designation process. Not only were two of its staff members elected to represent Romanian NGOs at the Biogeographic Seminar, but it also documented and proposed 90 percent of the sites that the Romanian government added to its official designation following the conclusions of the Seminar.

The influence of transnational networks on building domestic capacities for regulatory integration was consequential in Romania where the authorities were slow to designate the Natura 2000 sites and reluctant to

---

[18] Email communication with Stoycho Stoychev, Conservation Director, BSPB, Sofia, Feb. 2014.

include vast portions of land in the conservation regime. The initial deadline for the transposition of directives into national legislation was missed, and the initial designation lists were assessed as insufficient. In 2008 during the Biogeographic Seminar, Romania was asked to make significant additions to its lists. Whereas state authorities decided to commit 17 percent of the territory to conservation, the review of the designation process raised that percent to 25 percent. Through their watchdog activities and effective representation of conservation objectives defined at the supranational level, Romanian NGOs, empowered by their network membership, had an important part to play in the significantly larger part of territory covered by the Natura 2000 regulatory regime.

This influence of network members on the administrative processes and procedures entailed by the implementation of directives was possible because of the particular EU strategy of regulative integration focusing on joint forms of problem-solving, monitoring, and domestic capacity building. The Biogeographic Seminar is a relevant example of how the EC created enabling conditions for the participation of NGOs in the decision-making processes determining the effectiveness of the supranational regulatory integration. By providing NGOs with a space to publicly comment on the way in which the authorities comply with the scientific criteria and standards for the Natura 2000 protection regime, the supranational regulatory institutions "alter the parameters of domestic contexts and improve the chances that various domestic actors will benefit from the taking of the transnational rules" (Bruszt and McDermott in this volume).

The capacity-building partnership between states and NGOs as facilitated by transnational networks and within the framework of the Biogeographic Seminar should not convey the impression of a smooth cooperation between the state and non-state actors, but rather of a dual dynamic of cooperation and confrontation. In Romania, the president of Milvus observed that the direct confrontation between governments and NGOs on the percentage of territory committed to the conservation regime during the seminar left deep scars on their subsequent relationship.[19]

In Bulgaria, despite the comprehensive proposals for site designation coming from NGOs and their collaborative work with the Bulgarian Ministry of Environment, the government initially designated only 18.1 percent of the territory for protection, or approximately half of the territory initially proposed by joint NGO studies, which amounted to about 36 percent. Following public mobilization and the intervention of the EC, the Bulgaria's final list of Natura 2000 sites, which was approved by the Commission in 2008, covered 33.89 percent of the country's territory (Avramov 2010). (See Figure 6.1.)

---

[19] Interview with Papp Tamas, Nov. 2011.

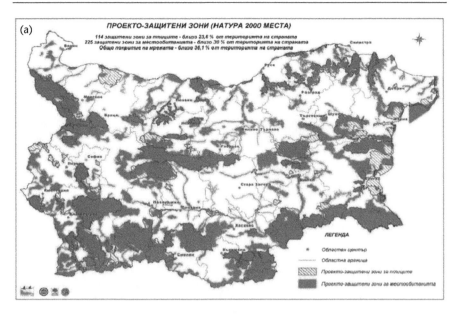

Figure 6.1 (Continued)

In the post-designation stage of domestic adjustment and with the support of networks with staff actively lobbying Brussels, Bulgarian NGOs exposed instances of non-compliance and sent complaints to the Commission which opened infringement cases based on the information they had provided. CEEweb facilitated monitoring through periodic reporting via the Natura

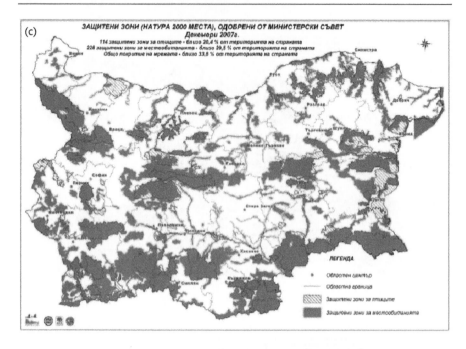

Figure 6.1 NGO influence on Designation of Natura 2000 Sites in Bulgaria

(a) Projected Natura 2000 territories (36.1% of national territory), 2006
(b) Government-proposed Natura 2000 sites to EC (18% of national territory), March 2007
(c) Adopted Natura 2000 sites in Bulgaria (33.8% of national territory), December 2007, following NGO action domestically and transnationally.

Source: Stoychev and Poliyakov 2009, Bulgarian Society for the Protection of Birds (BSPB), with permission to reproduce images by BSPB.

2000 Implementation Fact Sheet, which is shared across the network and facilitates the exposure of threats to the Natura 2000 regime (Avramov 2010). As a result of such actions, the Bulgarian government designated four additional SPAs in 2011, increasing the Natura 2000 protected areas by an additional 2.2 percent of the territory of the country.[20] The annual report of BSPB (2011: 31) summarizes eloquently the role of domestic advocacy, transnational networks, and their interaction with governance institutions across regulatory planes: "This important step on the part of the Bulgarian government results from the infringement procedure 4850 of the European Commission... started in 2008 as a result of a complaint submitted by BSPB. The success was achieved, on one hand, through the positive efforts of the BSPB and Bidlife International with the support of 'For the Nature' Coalition at national and European level..."[21]

---

[20] Email communication, Stoycho Stoychev, Conservation Director, BSPB, Sofia, Feb. 2014.
[21] Translation of quotation text from Bulgarian by the authors.

Through projects such as "We want a chance for nature in justice," "Letter from my protected areas" or "Legal ski in Romanian protected areas," WWF Romania sought to strengthen the capacity of civil society to react to illegal authorizations of constructions in Natura 2000 sites. It provided legal advice in three litigation cases and published a practical guide for preventing illegal actions, with information on the legal procedures that can be followed in cases of bad implementation of the legislation (WWF Activity Reports 2007/2008/2009).

In sum, there is considerable evidence that the activities of transnational networks enabled domestic actors to advocate the benefits of regional biodiversity management and demand for regulatory integration. They supported the integrative process by enabling a strong domestic constituency, as well as through ongoing efforts at contestation and consensus creation on the compatibility between local development and regional environmental integration. The capacity of Bulgarian NGOs for policy engagement was more substantial at the beginning of the Natura 2000 policy integration due to their stronger local base. Compared to the Romanian case, Bulgarian NGOs pushed the government to adopt relatively quickly the more ambitious blueprint for Natura 2000. The Bulgarian list of designated sites was approved by the Commission and published in February 2009 (Avramov 2010). In the Romanian case, it was only in November 2011 that the government adopted a list of complete SPAs, while in the case of SACs it was yet to adopt such a list in 2011. Despite such differences, transnational environmental networks in both countries have been instrumental in increasing the leverage of domestic constituencies of environmental integration, in many instances compensating for institutional differences or deficiencies. The relevance of domestic politics and capacity remains significant, however, as the implementation of Natura 2000 will continue to entail competing regional, economic, and environmental interests and hence contestation and ongoing societal and institutional adjustment.

6.7 Conclusion

This chapter has advanced the argument that transnational networks represent a source of transnational agency modifying the position of societies and governments on the demand and supply side of regulatory integration. Our research reveals that such interplay and its effect on integration is particularly important in the European regional context, characterized by relatively dense formal as well as transnational activity. Indeed, both theoretically and empirically, our study demonstrates that some degree of traction, defined as network access to formal institutions and some congruence of purpose, is likely to be a necessary scope condition for the anticipated reinforcement effect. In the area of chemical safety, for instance, transnational advocacy networks were preoccupied with the strengthening of supranational regulations and remained detached from and largely irrelevant to the adoption of chemicals legislation in the new member states. The chapter by Jordana and Levi-Faur in this volume similarly finds a limited impact of voluntary governance networks in the Latin American telecommunication sector, which remain largely detached from formal regulatory processes.

Where transnational networks and regional integration regimes establish traction, however, our study suggests that their interplay can have important developmental and regulatory impact, including on states with weaker domestic capacity. Contrary to the conventional wisdom of weak states and weak societies in CEE, our study reveals that transnational networks across the two different environmental issue areas have supported the agency and capacity of their societal members through resources, information, and leverage. They have also fostered policy networks with state institutions supportive of the timely adoption and ongoing implementation of European regulations. These effects are mediated by domestic institutional conditions and the degree of local actor involvement in the transnational network, as evident by the stronger domestic uptake of transnational and regime influence in Bulgaria compared to Romania. Nonetheless, transnational networks have had some compensatory effect, particularly evident in the biodiversity case, whereby the diverse networks and resources have to a large degree compensated for the more limited initial capacity, access to, and influence over government institutions of Romanian environmental NGOs.

The relevance of network activity for regional integration regimes is also evident in the differential development and regulatory effects of different types of networks. In the case of chemicals, the supranational regulations created new obligations for chemical companies in the new member states. The European chemical industry network sustained by CEFIC has promoted the interests of actors directly targeted by the legislation and built expertise and capacity among domestic industry to support its adoption. In contrast to the chemicals legislation, the biodiversity directives created burdensome obligations for state authorities at the national and local level with responsibility to designate, protect, and assess the environmental impact of development projects in Natura 2000 sites. For the networks of environmental and conservation NGOs, the supranational regulatory regime has been both an opportunity to pressure the state to commit to stronger environmental standards, as well as an exercise of advocacy and capacity building to support public capacities for their implementation. Such evidence reveals a substantial lift in the domestic development agency across the new member states, and makes the case for a broader research agenda to examine the interplay between networks and regional harmonization in other integration regimes and issue areas.

Finally, our study also produced important new evidence on the relevance of public institutions, particularly at the international level, in fostering traction and synergetic development effects of networks and regional regulatory regimes. In both regulatory arenas examined here, the European Commission facilitated the access of transnational networks to the regional integration regime and domestic institutions. In the case of biodiversity, such societal access was envisaged by the regulatory instrument itself, while the public endorsement and support of the transnational networks facilitated capacity for such access. In the area of chemicals regulations, the European Commission relied on informal mechanisms such as twinning projects to create opportunities for the expansion of the industrial network to CEE and to foster its subsequent access to the integration processes. The possibility for interplay between transnational networks and formal institutions has fostered a greener Europe despite its variable geometry. We invite further studies to bring new evidence on the broader relevance of such interplay across integration regimes.

7

Strategies for Integration in the EU's Pre-Accession Process

Reshaping Party Positions and State Institutions

Aneta Spendzharova and Milada Anna Vachudova

7.1 Introduction

The democratization of East Central Europe brought a sea change in the apparent diligence, perseverance—and success—with which transnational actors have promoted institutional and policy change in the context of advocating liberal democracy and a market-based economy. The European Union (EU) has had by far the greatest impact in shaping the course of political and economic change in credible candidate states. The EU has had an outstanding reward—membership—to offer states that establish a functioning liberal democracy and market economy. This reward has been conditional on satisfying a wide range and quantity of requirements while advancing through the EU's long pre-accession process. In comparison, other international organizations and other kinds of external actors have, individually, much less to offer—and have asked for much less in return.

Nearly 10 years have passed since the dramatic 2004 enlargement expanded the membership of the EU from 15 to 25 states; Bulgaria and Romania followed in 2007 and Croatia in 2013. In this chapter we explore how the EU has adjusted its enlargement policies in response to two factors: the successes and failures of EU policies toward earlier candidate states; and the different—and more difficult—domestic conditions present in the later candidates. Has the EU learned any lessons about the performance and limitations of its active leverage over the last decade? How have the tools of EU leverage evolved over time? Has the European Commission used past experiences to improve these tools? Has it been forced to change the tools in response to local conditions? By active leverage, we mean the deliberate conditionality exercised in the EU's pre-accession process, in contrast to passive leverage, which is simply the attraction of EU membership (Vachudova 2005). We are interested in the mechanisms that allow this supranational body to adapt its programs to improve the effectiveness and durability of domestic institutional change.

This chapter demonstrates that, compared to other transnational integration regimes (TIRs), the EU's integration strategy toward new member states and candidate countries combines the imposition of the EU legal order, the *acquis communautaire*, with proactive attempts to bolster domestic state capacity to resist corruption and deliver public goods. Reflecting the framework depicted in Figure 1.2, our analysis reveals how the EU strategy can help a country move away from the second ideal-typical outcome, where the country is a passive "regime-taker," and toward the first ideal-typical outcome, where regulation serves a common interest. Other TIRs may lack either the capacity or willingness to influence the domestic consequences of regulatory integration. In this chapter, we focus on a policy area in which the EU has learned from other experience to actively intervene to support the domestic demand side of institutional change—in this case the demand for reducing corruption and improving the rule of law.

We argue in this chapter that the EU has learned from the ongoing process of enlargement, and that it has applied some of those lessons both in the post-accession monitoring of Bulgaria and Romania, and in the pre-accession process engaging Western Balkan states still in the membership queue. We show how active leverage has been repurposed in the Cooperation and Verification Measure (CVM) to mitigate severe shortcomings in the rule of law and the fight against corruption in Bulgaria and Romania. The CVM mechanism has been useful, but not sufficiently powerful. We show how consequently the EU has become more proactive about using its active leverage vis-à-vis the Western Balkan candidates, insisting on the resolution of any national and territorial disputes, and on visible progress in the most difficult reform areas early in the pre-accession process, well before the final stages of the negotiations. The EU has become more vocal and blunt about necessary reforms, and focused more intensively on the rule of law and the quality of domestic institutions.

This chapter demonstrates that, compared to other transnational integration regimes (TIRs), the EU's regulatory policy toward new member states and candidate countries combines passive acceptance of the EU legal order, the *acquis communautaire*, with active attempts to bolster domestic state capacity. Our analysis of combating corruption shows a move away from the second ideal-typical outcome, where new member states and candidate countries are passive "regime-takers," to the first ideal-typical outcome, where regulation serves a common interest (see Bruszt and McDermott in this volume). Other TIRs may lack either capacity or willingness to influence the domestic consequences of regulatory integration. In this chapter, we focus on a policy area in which the EU has actively intervened to support domestic demand—the domestic demand to reduce corruption and improve the rule of law.

The CVM was seen only as a stop-gap measure for tackling the problems that the pre-accession process had failed to fix in Romania and Bulgaria. Croatia and the other Western Balkan candidates are to complete all necessary reforms *before* accession, obviating the need for the CVM; and indeed Croatia entered in 2013 without a CVM. We focus on two mechanisms that enable the EU to impact domestic political change over time: changes in party positions in response to EU-driven incentives, and pressure to make specific institutional reforms in order to satisfy EU requirements.

There is a general consensus that joining the EU has many benefits, promoting the development and consolidation of liberal democracy and a free market economy in different ways. Reforming the state administration in the run-up to EU membership improves how the state treats its citizens. Joining the EU's internal market benefits the economy, and there are a variety of direct benefits for ordinary citizens including opportunities for travel, study, and work abroad. However, high levels of corruption and low judicial quality obstruct many of these benefits and distort the economic gains, directing them to a small group of elites. They also increase the costs and reduce the benefits to other EU member states of having the state as a member. Even before 2004, the EU did a certain amount of updating as it learned from its interactions with the East Central European candidates—and in some areas this updating was insufficient. We know that judicial quality, for example, is low in many new members. However, the greatest changes came in response to problems with judicial quality and the rule of law in Bulgaria and Romanian after their accession in 2007. Several candidates in the Western Balkans pose a similar or even greater challenge, combining high levels of corruption and low judicial quality with strong ethnic politics and outstanding territorial disputes. When all major political parties in a candidate country embrace the EU pre-accession process, this is an important first step, but it must be followed with far-reaching institutional reform.

The rest of this chapter is divided into three parts. In the first part we look at how the EU has imposed post-accession monitoring on Bulgaria and Romania through the CVM and whether it has impacted party positions and institutional reforms. In the second part we look at recent World Bank data to see whether Bulgaria and Romania have improved their performance since accession—and how they compare to the EU's newest member, Croatia. In the third part we look at how the EU is treating the Western Balkan states, and whether leverage has triggered institutional change in Croatia and Serbia.

7.2 Corruption and Judicial Quality in Romania and Bulgaria

Since the fall of communism in 1989, 11 states have passed through the EU's demanding pre-accession process. The tremendous benefits of EU membership created political incentives to satisfy the EU's vast membership requirements. These incentives, along with certain characteristics of the pre-accession process that reward progress and publicize shortcomings, create the EU's active leverage on domestic reform. Scholars studying the relationship between the EU and East Central European states have demonstrated that transnational influence on key domestic actors, such as political parties, ruling elites, and public officials, can profoundly influence policy-making in particular policy areas (Jacoby 2004; Kelley 2004; Grabbe 2006; Schimmelfennig and Sedelmeier 2005). Under certain domestic conditions, EU leverage can even help determine regime type by pushing states from one trajectory of political change to another. EU leverage has helped compel candidates to reform the state and the economy, improving the quality of democracy and the efficiency of state institutions in various ways (Grabbe 2006; Vachudova 2005; and see Sedelmeier 2011). By 2005, the eight post-communist states that joined the EU in 2004 were, on average, indistinguishable from the EU's old member states on measures of political rights and civil liberties (Cameron 2007: 199).

However, the two post-communist states that joined in 2007, Bulgaria and Romania, have struggled to achieve the same relative success. Severe problems with corruption, judicial quality, and state capacity remain (see also Noutcheva and Bechev 2008; Trauner 2009). During the pre-accession process, strict enforcement in some areas was limited to the adoption, not the implementation, of EU rules. In other areas, especially those related to corruption, there were few specific rules to enforce. After 20 years of democratization, Bulgaria and Romania find themselves in the category of "semi-consolidated democracies"—in contrast to the other eight post-communist EU members that are considered "consolidated" (Freedom House 2010). Domestic conditions in Bulgaria and Romania at the moment of democratization were less auspicious than in neighboring states. An extensive literature on the comparative politics of post-communism has revealed the importance of communist and even pre-communist legacies in shaping political trajectories after 1989. Bulgaria and Romania suffered under oppressive and highly clientelistic communist regimes that took power in societies that had low levels of industrialization and civil society organization in the pre-communist period. The "revolutions of 1989" in these countries were instead an internal communist coup where second-tier opportunists reinvented themselves as transitional democratic leaders, and then used the power of the state to win early elections. For much of the 1990s partial economic reform enriched the elite and entrenched networks of corruption, while prolonging the economic hardships of the average citizen (see, among many, Ganev 2007; Grzymala-Busse 2007). In both countries, the communist successor parties have been implicated in the most far-reaching and systematic corruption, as years of state capture by these parties would have led one to predict.

By 2000, however, both Bulgaria and Romania were making relatively dramatic progress. The benefits of qualifying for EU membership clearly inspired some of this effort, including significant changes in party positions and important domestic institutional reform (Grabbe 2006; Schimmelfennig and Sedelmeier 2004; on limits see Haughton 2007; Dimitrova 2010). But was it enough? The scale of the problem of corruption in Bulgaria and Romania, in comparison to the "old" EU member states, depends entirely on which old member states serve as the point of reference. In Transparency International's 2011 corruption rankings (which are based on perceptions of corruption), 10 EU member states are on the list of the world's 20 least corrupt countries. Romania is ranked at no. 75 and Bulgaria at no. 86; however, they are not alone well down the list, as Italy keeps them company at no. 69 and Greece at no. 80.[1]

In the run-up to the 2004 enlargement, the EU was fairly effective in requiring candidate states to adopt and implement the *acquis communautaire* (the rules and regulations in force among EU member states). In general, greater attention was paid to those parts of the *acquis* that determine the performance of state institutions and economic actors in the internal market. On the one hand, new members must be competitive in the internal market; on the other, they must enforce EU rules in order to ensure a level playing field. Many observers were concerned about what happens when the leverage of the pre-accession process disappears at accession. After all, the adoption of legislation is generally much easier to track than the quality and durability of the institutions that implement and enforce it. Here, however, the preliminary evidence is more positive than expected: the eight post-communist states that joined the EU in 2004 have outperformed older members in many respects when it comes to enacting EU law and dealing with infringements (Sedelmeier 2008, 2011).

The fight against corruption as such, however, is not part of the *acquis*. The process of joining the EU can help combat corruption in indirect ways. Liberalization of the economy, including privatization and the promotion of new small and medium enterprises, reduces the reach of state officials in the

---

[1] For full details, see the website of Transparency International at: <http://cpi.transparency.org/cpi2011>.

economy. Also, the reform of state institutions—including greater transparency and efficiency—may at least constrain the opportunities for corruption across different levels of government. However, the experiences of Bulgaria and Romania, to be detailed here, show that these indirect measures alone are insufficient when a critical mass of high-level politicians are corrupt, when organized crime has thoroughly penetrated the economy, and when the judiciary is weak and corrupt. And they are not alone: since accession a steady stream of corruption scandals in the Czech Republic and Slovakia—some of them spectacular—have driven home the fact that state oversight institutions and the rule of law are weak, leading to a strong domestic demand for anti-corruption parties in both countries.

But it was the even more blatant problems with corruption in Bulgaria and Romania that pushed the EU into largely uncharted territory. Similar to the protection of ethnic minority rights, EU members are now in agreement that a spirited fight against corruption should be required of candidate states. However, they had never agreed to a set of EU-level anti-corruption policies, just as they have never agreed to EU-level policies to protect ethnic minority rights. Only the most blatant cases of corruption are now being addressed by the EU, just as only the most discriminatory and destabilizing policies against ethnic minorities by candidate state governments have become the subject of EU opprobrium and conditionality. In other words, in protecting ethnic minority rights, the EU could find consensus to "put out fires," but was not well equipped to do more. The scholarly debate on the success of EU leverage in improving the treatment of ethnic minorities in the candidate states is relevant here. Scholars have shown that specific changes in minority rights policies were a direct result of the EU's leverage (e.g. Kelley 2004). And most would argue that changes in legislation, institutions, agendas of political parties, and the tone of the discourse in the country have had an enduring effect. Other scholars, without disputing the initial findings, have argued that the EU's impact was limited in scope and in time. Once the fire had been put out, the EU's leverage waned—and conditions on the ground went into stasis or even regressed (Sasse 2008).

The absence of a corruption-fighting *acquis* has also meant that it has taken the European Commission more time to develop the tools to compel candidate states to work harder in addressing corruption problems. Here again there is a strong parallel to the provision of ethnic minority rights. The wars in the disintegrating Yugoslavia put encouraging peaceful coexistence among ethnic majorities and minorities in East Central Europe squarely on the EU's agenda as early as 1994 with the Balladur Plan. Over the next four years, the Commission became more specific and more insistent in its requirements in this area, culminating in its detailed requirements to the Slovak government in 1998, and later its direct involvement in rewriting the constitution of Macedonia to expand the rights of the Albanian minority.

While the first eight post-communist countries prepared to join the EU between 1997 and 2002, and were subject to the full force of the EU's conditionality, the fight against corruption played a minor role. The problems were not so stark as in Romania and Bulgaria. Moreover, many EU governments that have substantial corruption problems at home were reluctant to see corruption take a prominent place on the EU's agenda vis-à-vis the candidate states. As a result, the Commission's admonitions for candidates to tackle even high-level corruption were often watered down for political reasons in the annual regular reports.[2]

By 2006, things had changed dramatically as EU governments recognized the extent of the corruption problem in Bulgaria and Romania. The Commission reported that only feeble attempts had been made by either government to fight corruption, crack down on organized crime, and strengthen the judiciary. It asked for immediate action, especially on institutional reform. Bulgaria and Romania were held back from concluding negotiations in 2002 and joining the EU in 2004 with eight other post-communist states, due to concerns that their institutions and economies were unprepared to implement the EU's *acquis*. A key component of this concern was widespread corruption, and the lack of transparency and professionalism of state institutions, especially the judiciary. When Bulgaria and Romania did become full members of the EU in 2007, their membership came with an unprecedented condition: an ongoing Cooperation and Verification Mechanism (CVM) that the Commission would use to monitor whether they lived up to their outstanding commitments in satisfying the requirements of EU membership.

The CMV is a tool to maintain the reform momentum in the two countries and prevent reversal of the rule of law reforms enacted during the EU accession negotiations. Every six months, the Council issues a CVM report for Bulgaria and Romania, evaluating progress on the established benchmarks and flagging the most pressing issues that should be addressed before the next report. These monitoring reports have been widely praised for being very detailed and for following the evolution of specific administrative reforms, judicial cases, and political developments. As such, they have played an important role in gathering and disseminating information about the state of reform in both countries (see European Commission 2007–11). The main reports have been published in July, and the so-called interim "technical" reports or updates have come in February.

Are Bulgaria and Romania catching up with the EU CEE eight former communist countries or are they sliding back? Scholars observe relatively little backsliding since accession (as do Levitz and Pop-Eleches 2010; but for a more

---

[2] Personal interviews, officials of the European Commission, 1998 and 2000.

pessimistic view see Andreev 2009; Ganev 2013). However, the mere absence of backsliding is not the desired outcome—from the point of view of democratic consolidation or indeed of the EU—given the sad state of the judiciary and the presence of very extensive, high-level corruption at the moment of accession. So are they catching up? The record here is mixed. Political leaders and parties will only continue and deepen reforms in response to the twin forces of domestic and EU influence (see, among many, Ristei 2010). The domestic incentives for political leaders are primarily electoral ones, and chiefly relate to: the salience of judicial and corruption-related reforms to the voters; the positions of other parties, especially potential coalition partners; and the role of civic groups in publicizing government performance and galvanizing public pressure. The EU incentives stem primarily from the evaluations of government performance made public by the Commission in the twice-yearly CVM reports, and the possibility of punitive actions by the EU, chiefly related to EU funding and Schengen entry. Although it is no silver bullet, the CVM has been useful in pressuring the Bulgarian and Romanian governments to adopt and implement specific institutional reforms.

Domestic incentives to fight corruption are generally tied to getting elected or re-elected. Political parties may choose to build their electoral platforms on improving the rule of law. Once these commitments have been made, the credibility of the political party may hinge upon its capacity to deliver. The chance of re-election may plummet if voters no longer trust that the party will enact and implement domestic institutional reforms to fight corruption and organized crime. Here, the resources of society to hold political leaders to account for the reforms they have (or have not) promised to deliver are critical (see also Noutcheva and Düzgit 2011). A free media and an active civil society are essential for analysing the performance of the governing political parties and highlighting important shortcomings (Primatarova 2010). Ultimately, the CVM can only work in conjunction with strong domestic demand—a point underscored in the Commission's February 2012 interim CVM reports that call for a greater role for civil society in judicial and other reforms (European Commission 2012).

7.2.1 *Bulgaria*

GERB's entry on to Bulgaria's political scene highlights the importance of domestic electoral incentives as a mechanism for translating EU leverage into domestic change. Political developments in Bulgaria since 1989 suggest that clientelism and corruption undermine economic stability and lead to electoral failure. An earlier BSP government that had also vigorously pursued rent-seeking ultimately faced an escalating economic crisis, country-wide protests, and was ousted in early elections (Ganev 2007; Spendzharova 2008;

Vachudova 2009). In 2009, the widespread mismanagement and freezing of EU funds contributed to the electoral failure of the BSP-led coalition government. Under this government, as we show in Figure 7.1 in the next section, the indicators for the quality of governance plummeted. This also made the anti-corruption agenda of the opposition all the more popular and, from the point of view of the citizen and some domestic groups, urgent. A new center-right political party, GERB, seized the opportunity and won the parliamentary elections in 2010 with strong anti-corruption and pro-EU positions. Its leader, Boyko Borissov, became prime minister. Both the European Commission in its July 2010 CVM report and Bulgarian think tanks pointed out a clear shift in the political will of the Bulgarian government to tackle corruption when the GERB cabinet took office (Centre for the Study of Democracy 2010; European Commission 2010).

For the GERB government, the domestic incentives for reform were stronger: it ran an election campaign focused on curbing corruption and limiting the influence of organized crime. Borissov emphatically pledged that prosecuting corruption and abuse of EU funds would be a core priority of his government.[3] To comply with CVM recommendations after 2008, the Bulgarian government increased the transparency of court rulings and access to court decisions. This, in turn, has allowed the Bulgarian media to investigate and publicize striking discrepancies in court rulings on similar cases, in some instances due to corruption (Alegre et al. 2009: 32). In addition to domestic institutional changes, the Borissov government showed more consistent behavioral compliance with EU pressure for high-level prosecutions. As a result, the first CVM report assessing the GERB government recognized that corruption and organized crime was addressed for the first time since the inception of the CVM (European Commission 2010: 3). This is reflected especially in Figure 7.4: Bulgaria's long deterioration as measured by the control of corruption indicator is reversed. The Commission's decision to unfreeze blocked EU funds after a positive CVM report in July 2010 was a big success for the GERB government.[4]

Domestic demand for reducing corruption has grown since Bulgaria's accession to the EU. NGOs such as the Center for the Study of Democracy and Centre for Liberal Strategies have published periodically reports on the state of anti-corruption policy, and together with the media, have highlighted important cases stalled in the judicial system (Alegre et al. 2009; Primatarova 2010). This, in turn, has enabled the EU to put additional pressure on the government to fully comply with its commitments under the CVM. While the Commission commended the GERB government on its

[3] *Sofia Echo*, 6 July 2010.   [4] *Sofia Echo*, 6 July 2010.

pursuit of institutional reform, it pointed out that "the leadership of the judiciary has yet to show a real commitment to thorough judicial reform" (European Commission 2011a: 6). The recruitment process in the judiciary still lacks a convincing assessment of the professional qualifications, managerial skills, and personal integrity of candidates (European Commission 2011a: 4). Furthermore, analyses by the Commission and independent experts have demonstrated serious weaknesses in judicial and investigative practice (European Commission 2012: 4). In the fight against corruption, it concludes that "The track record of decisions and penalties in cases related to high-level corruption, fraud and organized crime under investigation and in court does not yet provide the convincing results needed to provide effective dissuasion" (European Commission 2012: 2). The Commission underscored its concerns about judicial quality in Bulgaria in an "oral update" in February 2013 with the next full CVM report expected in January 2014. The political crisis during the winter of 2012–13, including widespread protests and the fall of the government, are partly a consequence of public anger about the scale and impunity of corruption and state capture in Bulgaria. The peaceful daily protests in the summer and fall of 2013, driven by dissatisfaction with the newly formed coalition government led by the Bulgarian Socialist Party (BSP), are further evidence of the growing civic activism in Bulgaria and domestic demand for a corruption-free political system.[5] From the point of view of the EU, however, Bulgaria performed better in 2012 and 2013 than neighboring Romania.

7.2.2 Romania

In Romania, the political will to tackle domestic institutional reform has been uneven since 2007. There was a surge in activity in the run-up to accession, but much of the political elite responded by closing ranks and working to dilute or remove the curbs on corruption that were implemented at that time. Unlike in Bulgaria, where a new party exploited the failure of the government to fight corruption, in Romania some of the old parties worked to push the issue under the rug. Nevertheless, when the EU has put strong pressure on Romania, the government has responded, mainly by passing legislation in the parliament. President Traian Basescu, in office since 2004, built his reputation on the fight against corruption. His position in Romanian politics, however, has been weaker than that of the GERB as he has battled an uncooperative legislature. Pressured by criticism from the Commission, Basescu's party, the Democratic Liberal Party (PDL) again pushed through

---

[5] *Sofia Echo*, 12 July 2013.

some reforms in 2010; most important was the resuscitation of Romania's anti-corruption agency. As Mihaiela Ristei argues, even in Romania there has been progress in the fight against corruption when EU leverage and electoral pressure have created political incentives for some domestic elites to adopt pro-EU party positions and spearhead reforms (Ristei 2010).

On the eve of Romania's accession in 2007 the EU hailed the creation of the National Integrity Agency (ANI) that had substantial powers to force public servants to disclose their assets, to investigate individuals who could not adequately explain where their assets came from, and to seize unexplained assets. In April 2010, many of the ANI's activities were declared unconstitutional by the Constitutional Court after having also been attacked in parliament. Press reports revealed that seven of the nine judges of the Court were themselves being investigated by the ANI. President Basescu promised in Brussels that Romania would reach its objective of "controlling the income of those in power and investigating the origin of their wealth," even though the ANI had been in practice "annihilated" by the Constitutional Court.[6] The July 2010 CVM report of the European Commission was highly critical, especially of the destruction of the ANI, and declared that Romania was in breach of its accession commitments. The Commission called on Bucharest to "re-establish the ANI's powers to propose the effective forfeiture of unjustified wealth" (European Commission 2010: 7). The Commission also observed that Romania lacks "broad-based political support in favor of transparency and the effective protection against corruption and conflict of interest" (European Commission 2010: 7).

Soon afterwards, in August 2010, both houses of the Romanian parliament voted to resurrect a weaker ANI; this was widely understood to be the direct result of EU pressure.[7] The July 2011 CVM report welcomed the fact that Romania had 'responded swiftly to the Commission's recommendation by adopting a new legal framework for the National Integrity Agency (ANI). It also welcomed an increase in final court decisions in cases launched by Romania's Anti-Corruption Directorate (DNA) from 85 in 2010 to 158 in 2011, including some senior politicians and officials (European Commission 2012b: 3). Throughout the CVM process, the Commission monitored the progress of important cases and helped build pressure on the judiciary and the parliament to act appropriately. Unlike in Bulgaria, parliament was clearly identified as a roadblock to progress, and the Commission called on it to approve the draft anti-corruption strategy and a draft law increasing the penalties for corruption, and to throw out parliamentarians with convictions for corruption (European Commission 2012b). Like in Bulgaria, however, a

---

[6] *EurActiv*, 23 Apr. 2010.   [7] *EurActiv*, 17 Aug. 2010.

rather large "conservative" faction within the judiciary appeared committed to fighting both transparency and accountability as it continued to protect the beneficiaries of widespread corruption in Romania. The performance of government officials in many areas has remained poor since accountability is largely absent and political allegiance is the main determinant of success (SAR 2011).

The parliamentary elections of December 2012 gave a two-thirds parliamentary majority to the center-left Social-Liberal Union (USL) coalition led by Social Democratic Party (PSD) member Prime Minister Viktor Ponta. The USL had already governed as an interim government from May 2012. In a bid to concentrate power in its own hands, it attacked many key democratic institutions not controlled by the parliamentary majority including the presidency, the judicial system, and the ombudsman. It organized a referendum to impeach Basescu, and unsuccessfully used intimidation and fraud in an attempt to make the referendum results valid despite low turnout. As *The Economist* reported, Mr Basescu "repeatedly said that Mr. Ponta's efforts to take him down are linked to the government's attempts to take control of the judiciary and other public institutions. Members of the old political guard are worried about the increasing independence of the general prosecutor and the anti-corruption officer who might go after them. Their wake-up call was the conviction on corruption charges of Adrian Nastase, a former prime minister, who is now in jail."[8] The impression that democracy was under an attack in Romania in 2012 earned the Pontu government a strong round of reprimands from EU leaders abroad, but relatively little protest at home. The recent success of Viktor Orbán and his FIDESZ party government in severely damaging liberal democracy in Hungary had put the EU on its guard. Consequently, the EU acted quickly to check the authoritarian tampering of the Ponta government, insisting on a return to the respect for constitutional norms (Pop-Eleches 2013; Sedelmeier 2014).

Attacks on the independence of the judiciary, however, have continued, prompting the EU to publish a formal CVM report on Romania only in January, turning a page on the worst injuries to the constitutional order but highlighting the continued collusion by many Romanian elites in blocking the prosecution of corrupt politicians (Commission 2013a). The Commission expressed strong concerns again about political tampering with Romania's Anti-Corruption Directorate (DNA) after the politically motivated dismissal of a prosecutor in the run-up to the next CVM report due in January 2014.[9] The attack on democratic institutions in Romania and the struggles with

---

[8] *The Economist*, 25 Aug. 2012.
[9] <http://www.balkaneu.com/european-commission-puts-justice-report-controversial-decisions-romanian-judiciary>.

judicial independence and the fight against corruption have only reinforced the EU's commitment to keeping CVM monitoring in place for Romania—and most probably for Bulgaria, too. Schengen membership remains out of reach as key member states insist on a CVM report that details substantial progress on the rule of law and the fight against corruption before either country can join. In the broadest terms, it is clear that the domestic demand for corruption control is different in the two states: Romanian citizens took to the streets in 2012 and 2013 mainly to oppose economic austerity, while Bulgarian citizens protested against corruption and elite collusion in a sustained manner in 2013.

7.3 Government Effectiveness, Regulatory Quality, Rule of Law, and Corruption in the EU's Accession Queue

Economic integration is an important dimension of the EU integration process. The Union has sought to reduce corruption partly because it is seen as an impediment to a level economic playing field (see European Commission 2003b: 15–19). To assess broader economic governance patterns in East Central Europe, we need to consider how corruption control has evolved in comparison to the related fields of regulatory quality and the rule of law. In this section we compare the performance of EU members Bulgaria and Romania and of EU candidates in the Western Balkans against the performance of the eight East Central European states that joined the EU in 2004 (EU ECE 8 for short). As illustrated in Figures 7.1 and 7.2, Bulgaria and Romania are clearly laggards in government effectiveness and regulatory quality, although they have improved substantially over time. It is important to note this overall positive trend because it can be easily obscured by the often unseemly cut and thrust of domestic politics in both countries. In judicial reform and the fight against corruption depicted in Figures 7.3 and 7.4 they have, on average, performed worse than the EU ECE 8. However, they have performed significantly better than the Western Balkan states that are still in the membership queue, with the exception of Croatia. The data here and in other studies are consistent with the argument that the process of joining the EU did help move Bulgaria and Romania away from the administrative and economic backwardness characteristic of the Balkan region. There is also some evidence that they have improved in certain areas since accession. However, Bulgaria and Romania still have a very long way to go before closing the gap between them and the other post-communist members on the rule of law and other indicators.

The composite measure of government effectiveness from the World Bank in Figure 7.1 shows the gap between the eight post-communist countries that would join the EU in 2004 (the EU ECE 8) and Romania and Bulgaria in 1996 when the dataset was started. Figure 7.2 shows that all post-communist EU candidates have made quite consistent progress in market liberalization over the past 15 years. The lion's share of the EU *acquis* still relates to the functioning of the internal market; removing the state from the economy through deregulation, privatization, and lowering state subsidies has gone hand in hand with improving the way state institutions oversee and regulate economic activity. Thus the steady progress exhibited by Romania, Bulgaria, and also Croatia in Figure 7.2 suggests that the EU has had the most influence in this area, narrowing progressively the gap with the EU ECE 8. Overall, this dovetails with other studies that have shown that post-communist states, as a group, have not reversed course after accession, and are quite good at implementing the *acquis* (Sedelmeier 2008, 2011; Levitz and Pop-Eleches 2009).

Figures 7.3 and 7.4 present the regional trends in domestic institutional change aimed at reforming the judiciary and controlling corruption. This

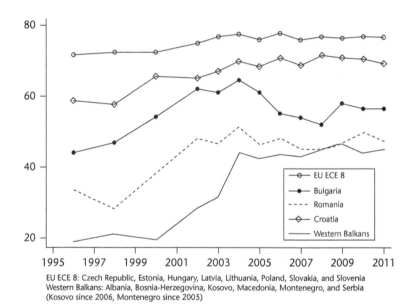

EU ECE 8: Czech Republic, Estonia, Hungary, Latvia, Lithuania, Poland, Slovakia, and Slovenia
Western Balkans: Albania, Bosnia-Herzegovina, Kosovo, Macedonia, Montenegro, and Serbia
(Kosovo since 2006, Montenegro since 2005)

Figure 7.1 Government effectiveness (percentile ranks): higher numbers indicate better performance (Kaufmann et al. 2010). This index combines responses on the quality of public service provision, the quality of the bureaucracy, the competence of civil servants, the independence of the civil service, and the credibility of the government's commitment to policies. The main focus of this index is on "inputs" required for the government to be able to produce and implement good policies and deliver public goods.

Note: World Government Indicators (WGI) 1996–2009, World Bank <http://info.worldbank.org/governance/wgi/index.asp>.

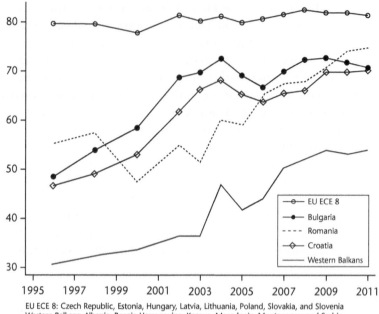

EU ECE 8: Czech Republic, Estonia, Hungary, Latvia, Lithuania, Poland, Slovakia, and Slovenia
Western Balkans: Albania, Bosnia-Herzegovina, Kosovo, Macedonia, Montenegro, and Serbia
(Kosovo since 2007, Montenegro since 2005)

Figure 7.2 Regulatory Quality (percentile ranks): higher numbers indicate better performance (Kaufmann et al. 2010). This index includes measures of the incidence of market-unfriendly policies such as price controls or inadequate bank supervision, as well as perceptions of the burdens imposed by excessive regulation in areas such as foreign trade and business development.

Note: World Government Indicators (WGI) 1996-2009, World Bank <http://info.worldbank.org/governance/wgi/index.asp>.

composite measure of the rule of law paints a much less positive picture of the ability of EU leverage to transform domestic institutions—both before accession and after it. The gap between Romania and Bulgaria, on the one hand, and the EU ECE 8, on the other, is large and has decreased only a little in 12 years. On this measure Croatia is also lagging well behind the EU ECE 8. This is not surprising since the indicators that make up this composite measure include the effectiveness of the judiciary—an institution that was only subject to EU leverage indirectly and which has been notoriously difficult to reform. This composite measure also reflects perceptions about criminality within economic and political activity, which we would expect to be much greater in a country that has high levels of perceived corruption and years of partial economic reform. The figure is consistent with the argument that substantial improvements in the rule of law require a sustained domestic commitment to institutional change (Spendzharova 2008). Helping to create

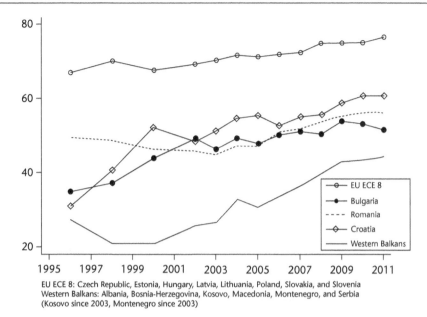

EU ECE 8: Czech Republic, Estonia, Hungary, Latvia, Lithuania, Poland, Slovakia, and Slovenia
Western Balkans: Albania, Bosnia-Herzegovina, Kosovo, Macedonia, Montenegro, and Serbia
(Kosovo since 2003, Montenegro since 2003)

Figure 7.3 Rule of law (percentile ranks): higher numbers indicating better performance (Kaufmann, Kraay, and Mastruzzi 2010). This index measures whether agents have confidence in and abide by the rules of society. It includes perceptions of the incidence of crime, the effectiveness and predictability of the judiciary, and the enforceability of contracts.

Note: World Government Indicators (WGI) 1996-2009, World Bank <http://info.worldbank.org/governance/wgi/index.asp>.

this kind of commitment is one of the purposes of the EU's CVM, as already discussed.

The corruption measure is similar to the rule of law measure, although it shows greater improvement over the last 15 years from a lower starting point, especially in Bulgaria and Croatia. While, in absolute terms, more progress appears to have been made in the area of corruption, the gap between Bulgaria, Romania, and the EU ECE 8 is still considerable (for additional data that show similar results, see Vachudova 2009).

7.4 Western Balkans: Party Positions and Institutional Reform, Eventually?

The commitment to revitalize and integrate the Western Balkan states by offering them a membership perspective has been reaffirmed many times since it was first made by EU leaders in Sarajevo as part of the Stability Pact for South Eastern Europe in 1999. This was seen as a watershed moment for

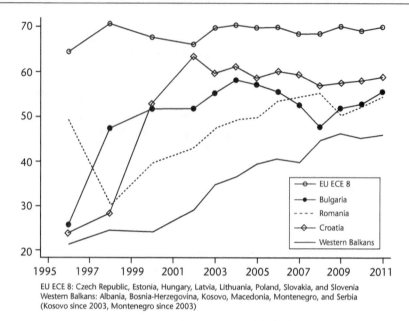

EU ECE 8: Czech Republic, Estonia, Hungary, Latvia, Lithuania, Poland, Slovakia, and Slovenia
Western Balkans: Albania, Bosnia-Herzegovina, Kosovo, Macedonia, Montenegro, and Serbia
(Kosovo since 2003, Montenegro since 2003)

Figure 7.4 Control of corruption (percentile ranks): higher numbers indicating better performance (Kaufmann et al. 2010). This index measures perceptions of corruption, conventionally defined as the exercise of public power for private gain. The survey includes the frequency of additional payments to get things done, the effects of corruption on the business environment, grand corruption in the political arena, and state capture by groups of elites. Note: World Government Indicators (WGI) 1996–2009, World Bank <http://info.worldbank.org/governance/wgi/index.asp>.

EU foreign policy. The EU would use the power of its enlargement process to transform the Western Balkans, opening a new chapter after a shameful decade of failure in the region. EU members have had a strong interest in seeing the EU's "best available tools" work as promised in Western Balkan states: bringing to power moderate, EU-compatible political parties that implement fundamental institutional reforms in order to qualify for membership. Yet with this group of states these reforms have been difficult to come by. There were and there remain high expectations for how this process can spur institutional reform in a candidate country. These expectations, to be sure, have been too high in some areas, such as reform of the judiciary and the public administration. However, the EU's pre-accession process remains by far the most complex and domestically invasive process states have ever gone through to join an international institution. And as the EU integrates further and learns from past enlargements, this process has become somewhat more rigorous.

The Western Balkans pose a greater challenge than Bulgaria and Romania because war, sanctions, and isolation have warped more profoundly the rebuilding of the state after communism (Žilović 2011; see also Dolenec 2013; Šelo Šabić 2003). State capture has been the greatest in post-communist states where a narrow group of elites initially governed with little political competition from other political forces, and with little effective scrutiny from the media and civic groups. All of the Western Balkan states fit the bill. Authoritarian rule gave ruling elites absolute power in Croatia, Serbia, and Montenegro from 1990 to 2000; war and sanctions intensified the grip of organized crime on the economy (Gould 2004). In the three constituent nations of Bosnia the same nationalist parties have controlled the different parts of the state since 1990, and continue to control much of the country's economic activity for the benefit of the few at the expense of the many. There has been greater political competition in Macedonia and Albania, but in conditions of extremely weak administrative capacity and little or no willingness to combat corruption. Throughout the region, elites protect old clientalistic networks and the rewards of a partially reformed economy; they are benefiting from relationships with organized crime, but are also intimidated and pressured into protecting them from prosecution.

The basic equation underpinning the enlargement decision for eligible neighboring states has not changed: The benefits of joining the EU (and the costs of being excluded from it) create incentives for political elites to adopt an EU-compatible agenda and to implement reforms necessary to satisfy the EU's extensive entry requirements. The object of the EU's pre-accession process is to create incentives for governing elites to enact EU-prescribed domestic reforms—and to provide guidance on how to design and implement high-quality versions of these reforms. What, then, have EU member states and institutions learned from the 2004/2007 enlargement that they have applied to the pre-accession process with the Western Balkan states to make this outcome more likely? Have these innovations helped address problems with expertise, legitimacy, and consistency in the process? Taking a broad view, EU actors have learned three things: that leverage works well only *before* accession, that a longer period for exercising conditionality is needed, and that fostering the rule of law and independent state institutions takes finer grained requirements that are also better enforced. While useful, the CVM has not had enough traction to compel comprehensive reform in either country—and everyone agrees that pre-accession leverage is far more powerful (see also Ganev 2013).

To meet these greater challenges and also higher expectations in areas related to the rule of law, judicial reform, and the fight against corruption, EU leverage became more detailed and was delivered earlier in the process for Croatia. The main innovation has been "benchmarking." Once screening takes place to ascertain what needs to be done related to each chapter, the Commission can now choose either to open negotiations right away, or require that certain conditions that are called "opening benchmarks" are met first. For Montenegro the EU has also chosen to start the negotiations with the most vexing chapters—chapters 23 (Judiciary and fundamental rights) and 24 (Justice, freedom, and security)—so that they get the most possible scrutiny. In the future, the Commission is proposing that "these chapters would be opened on the basis of action plans, with interim benchmarks to be met based on their implementation before closing benchmarks are set" (European Commission 2013b). What is perhaps worrying is that the EU rejected a CVM for Croatia as this would signal the failure to reform *before* accession—and yet the Commission's March 2013 report, the last before Croatia joined the EU, pointed to abiding problems related to the rule of law (European Commission, 2013a).

The EU has also created more moments where it can apply leverage well *before* accession. Milestones include: negotiating the Stabilization and Association Agreement (SAA) agreement; having the SAA agreement come into force; negotiating a visa liberalization agreement; being recognized as a candidate country; being given an official date for the start of accession negotiations; and then moving forward through the negotiations with the opening and closing of individual chapters (that now also contain opening and closing benchmarks).[10] The East Central European candidates had to go through some, but not all, of these "conditionality checkpoints."

A problem that the EU has encountered in its efforts to shepherd the Western Balkan states through the pre-accession process is that conditionality is more contested on issues related to national sovereignty and identity (Noutcheva 2012; Bieber 2011). In each case, slow progress can reflect in different parts the strategies of power-seeking elites as well as public and elite conceptions of the national interest. While several East Central European candidates had to comply on issues related to borders, citizenship, and minority rights, some of the issues in the Western Balkans have been more intractable. For example, the EU made full cooperation with the ICTY a precondition for moving forward, usefully lending out its leverage but also stalling the accession process with Croatia and Serbia for several years until ruling elites complied. Serbia's progress has also been stalled by the imperative of regulating relations with Kosovo. EU leaders have learned from admitting a divided Cypress in 2004 that, a decade later, continues to bedevil regional cooperation and economic development. In response, the EU, led by Germany, has prioritized the resolution of issues bearing on national sovereignty, territory, and identity, especially in recent years the Kosovo issue (*Balkan Insight* 2013). It took many years and several governments before the current Serbian government chose

---

[10] For a timeline of these milestones for Serbia e.g. see: <http://ec.europa.eu/enlargement/countries/detailed-country-information/serbia/index_en.htm>.

to move forward decisively—and here the EU's foreign policy team enjoyed a much needed triumph in 2013 by brokering a deal between Belgrade and Pristina that, if it works, will also boost perceptions that the EU acts competently in trying to solve outstanding issues related to sovereignty and territory in the region.

In its relationship with some Western Balkan states the EU has also sometimes been inconsistent in specifying and enforcing the requirements for moving forward in the pre-accession process—and this lack of consistency and also clarity has undermined incentives for elites to pursue reform (Anastasakis 2008). In the most difficult cases, Bosnia and especially Macedonia, the EU—or certain EU member states—have compounded problems of legitimacy with inconsistent conditionality that can reasonably be blamed for sidetracking reform. The most shocking has been the Greek veto of Macedonia's progress due to the tragicomic name dispute that has empowered and unmoored Macedonia's nationalist parties and given them more scope to reverse political reforms. Another example was when the EU cast a unitary police force as a part of the *acquis* instead of accurately as a special requirement for Bosnia, and then walked away once it ran aground. More recently in Bosnia the EU has walked back from some of its requirements for the entry into force of the SAA—not because it is trying to relegate Bosnia to second tier membership, but because it is desperate to see Bosnia move forward in the process since an SAA would give the EU more tools to influence Bosnian politics. The problem, however, is that Bosnian elites believe they have learned to manipulate the EU to get around its requirements, and some argue that EU interference may have retarded the growth of the Bosnian state (Bassuener and Weber 2013; see also Štiks 2013).

Despite the many challenges, EU leverage appears to have worked well in some candidate states. Croatia succeeded in joining the EU in 2013 after shifts in party positions, an overhaul of state institutions, and strengthening of the rule of law. Croatia's political party system experienced a dramatic change after 2000, not just with the ousting of the vicious authoritarian regime of Franjo Tudjman but also, crucially, with the transformation of the agenda (if not the membership) of his extreme right-wing Croatian Democratic Union (HDZ) party. As my model of party behavior in the EU accession queue would predict, the HDZ embraced democratic reforms and preparations for EU membership (Vachudova 2008). This was perhaps easier than in neighboring Serbia because Croatia's belonging to Western Europe had never been questioned by the HDZ (Subotic 2010) and because the destructive grip of authoritarian forces was somewhat weaker (Dolenec 2013). After the HDZ recaptured power at the end of 2003, Prime Minister Ivo Sanader led a government that put preparations for EU membership at the heart of its governing program—and that included reforming the judiciary and bolstering institutions to fight corruption (Konitzer 2011). What Sanader did not apparently consider, however, was that these stronger and more independent institutions might go after him. He was indicted on a colorful array of corruption charges and, in November 2012, he was sentenced to 10 years in prison by a Croatian court.

What the EU would like to see, therefore, is the "Sanaderization" of the other Balkan states (Greece, too). From his jail cell, Sanader symbolizes the possibility that leaders of authoritarian parties will respond to EU incentives and domestic pressures, moderating party agendas in order to stay in the political game (Vachudova 2005). He also symbolizes the hope that these leaders will profoundly reform state institutions and then, if warranted, these institutions will send them straight to jail for their past and current crimes. But this sequence of events is now less likely as entrenched and immensely corrupt political leaders in the region, not wishing to join Sanader behind bars, come to see EU-led institutional reform with much greater caution.

Following in the footsteps of Croatia, the axis of competition in Serbia has shifted quite dramatically over the last decade (Dolenec 2013). The powerful extreme right-wing Radical Party split in 2008, with Tomislav Nikolić bringing many party members into his new Progressive Party. Nikolić proclaimed that it was his support for Serbia's integration into the EU that forced a split from the Radical Party loyal to war criminal Vojislav Šešelj. Meanwhile, the Socialist Party of Serbia, the party of Slobodan Milošević, has also moved toward reform and adopted an agenda supporting Serbia's membership in the EU under its new leader, Ivica Dačić. After the May 2012 parliamentary elections, the Progressive Party and the Socialist Party formed a coalition and Dačić became prime minister, marking a return to power of Milošević's former allies.

Even though Europe's economic crisis had hit Serbia especially hard and the Democratic Party (DS) government in power since 2008 had little to show for its tenure in power, its leader Boris Tadić was widely expected to win the May 2012 presidential elections. Tadić and the DS had long presented themselves at home and abroad as the only hope for a reasonable, pro-Western, pro-EU government for Serbia. With extremists opposing them at every turn, they counseled the EU and the US to expect only modest gains—and then, bit by bit, delivered these gains in highly significant foreign policy areas such as cooperation with the ICTY, remembrance in Srebrenica, and the regulation of relations with neighboring Kosovo. What they did not deliver, however, was domestic reform. Instead, changes to the judiciary filled it with DS acolytes; party control and the sale of jobs in the public sector only increased; the media became less independent; the oligarchs still acted with impunity; and there was little progress in improving Serbia's business environment for small and medium enterprises. Nikolić defeated Tadić in the second round of the presidential elections not because more Serbs embraced the nationalist rhetoric of

Nikolić, but because many supporters of Tadić and the DS were so disappointed that they could not bring themselves to vote at all. Some former DS supporters even voted for Nikolic on the logic that the tempering effect of government could be beneficial for the Progessives, Serbia's largest political party, and that alternating out of power could be beneficial for the DS. After six months, there is some evidence that this could be true: The new leader of the Progressive Party, Alexander Vucić, has had the most powerful tycoon in Serbia arrested on corruption charges, and negotiations on Kosovo continue apace. All together, political developments in Serbia in 2012 and 2013 have been nothing short of dramatic—but the transfer of power has been orderly and peaceful.

The missing piece in Serbia, however, is concerted pressure for reform on the part of voters, civil society, and interest groups (on variation in post-communist Europe, see Pop-Eleches and Tucker 2011; Ceka 2013). Without this kind of systematic pressure, the Vučić/Dačić government may prosecute tycoons and make slow progress on Kosovo even as they build up their own corruption rackets. The EU does have substantial leverage over Serbia—and it is this leverage that explains Serbia's cooperation on the Kosovo issue. But as the EU and especially German leaders continuously prioritize the resolution of the Kosovo issue, they need to also apply sufficient pressure on the Serbian government to pursue high-quality domestic reforms.

As hard as it is to imagine Serbia's current government of Progressives and Socialists bringing positive change, looking back at 20 years of post-communist transition we see that sometimes the formerly authoritarian parties do enact the most difficult and sweeping reforms. We can cling to no such glimmer of hope when it comes to Bosnia. The engagement of citizens and interest groups in politics, so important in helping to improve performance and accountability, is even weaker than in Serbia. Consequently, the costs for politicians of not complying with EU requirements are even lower (Džihić and Wieser 2011). Bosnia's unwieldy, even grotesque institutions create such terrible incentives for politicians at myriad levels of government that it is hard to see how citizens or civil society groups can ever break through. Politics in Bosnia has been reduced to backroom deals between the leaders of the six main political parties—and these parties have been transformed into rigid, authoritarian structures that doggedly pursue personal and party agendas at great cost to the citizens. Sadly, whenever the EU and the US have placed their hopes in a new, less nationalist political leader in Bosnia, be it the Bosnian Serb leader of the Party of Independent Social Democrats (SNSD) Milorad Dodik or the Bosniak leader of the Social Democratic Party (SDP) Zlatko Lagumdžija, they have subsequently become more nationalist, less moderate, and more anti-democratic.

Another barometer for the effectiveness of EU leverage and the EU's commitment to ongoing enlargement is Montenegro. Very small and quite rich, Montenegro was given the green light by EU leaders to start negotiations in 2012. But for these negotiations to conclude successfully, Montenegro's state institutions, especially the judiciary, will need a thorough overhaul that includes dramatic improvements in the fight against corruption and organized crime. The EU is prioritizing rule of law, judicial reform, and the fight against corruption with Montenegro, placing these complex and difficult issues at the start of the negotiations. Montenegro is the first candidate country to which this approach has been applied.

7.5 Conclusion

In this chapter we have explored how the EU has adapted its pre-accession process to tackle the more challenging domestic conditions of later candidates and new members—and how this has played out in terms of party positions and institutional reforms. The CVM is a controversial but successful instance of innovation by the EU as it has extended the EU's active leverage into the post-accession period. The Romanian and Bulgarian governments have both responded to specific demands in the CVM reports, suggesting strongly that in the absence of the CVM there would be less reform. The detailed monitoring and assessment in the CVM reports, coupled with political pressure and concrete sanctions, can deliver substantial results. Given the huge problems besetting the rule of law, judicial quality, and the fight against corruption in the Western Balkans states, the EU would do well to set up a CVM structure for each acceding state. This could always be dismantled rapidly where it was not needed. Some have observed a significant deterioration in the comportment of public officials in the areas of accountability, transparency, and the fight against corruption once their country has joined the EU. A CVM structure would help deter backsliding.

EU pressure can be powerful when it is twinned with domestic incentives related to winning elections and holding power. Civil society groups play an essential role in highlighting corruption and the need for judicial reform. The EU needs to rethink civil society funding that is funneled through government institutions, since this undermines the readiness of civil society groups to highlight corruption. Also, EU leverage tied to the CVM process is more effective in motivating governments if the EU is threatening to withhold something that voters really want. The decision by (some) EU members beginning in 2010 to block Schengen entry, as a sanction for not meeting CVM benchmarks, has helped trigger reform in Romania as in Bulgaria, since Schengen membership is valued by citizens. Linking Schengen entry to satisfying CVM benchmarks has helped trigger reform.

In the Western Balkans the EU has had a strong geopolitical incentive to see its "best available" enlargement tools work to help build stable, democratic, and economically successful states. The EU has responded to more difficult initial conditions in these candidates and as well as the widely acknowledged mistakes in the pre-accession reforms in Bulgaria and Romania. EU actors have learned that leverage works well only *before* accession; that a longer period for exercising conditionality is needed; and that fostering the rule of law and independent state institutions takes finer grained requirements that are also better enforced. The EU has also worked to address problems with legitimacy and consistency in the pre-accession process, although the fiasco of the Greek veto of Macedonia's progress continues to undermine its credibility. All in all, however, the EU can point to important successes at least in Croatia and Serbia where profound changes in the positions of the major parties in support of joining the EU have been followed by important reforms. Whether these changes are locked in in Serbia will tell us a great deal about the durability of the EU's leverage on political party agendas and how they translate into policy for governing parties.

Returning to the four outcomes discussed in the introductory chapter, we have shown that, in compelling institutional reform and combating corruption, the relationship between the EU and the new member states is moving closer to the first ideal-typical outcome, where the transnational rules are adopted and implemented in a way that provides benefits to a broad domestic constituency (see Bruszt and McDermott in this volume). The use of CVM in Romania and Bulgaria has helped put the fight against corruption squarely on the EU. In June 2011, the European Commission launched a new initiative, the EU Anti-Corruption Report, which will be published by the Commission every two years, starting in 2013. The report will be accompanied by country analyses of each EU member state and will contain country-specific recommendations. The thrust of this initiative consists of soft law (i.e. non-binding) measures such as identifying trends and best practice in the fight against corruption, and improving information exchange among the member states (European Commission 2011a). Yet countries will also face scrutiny in the individual reports and will be obliged to take action in response to the Commission's recommendations, which highlights the "common interest regulation" aspect of the CVM.

Part II

Emerging TIRs in the Global South: Blockage and Coordination in the MERCOSUR

8

Informal Drivers of Regional Regulatory Integration

The Auto Sector in Central Europe and Latin America

Moises Costa and Wade Jacoby

8.1 Introduction

The public transnational integration regimes (TIRs) described in this volume are, by definition, formal. Such TIRs vary widely in their capacities, from powerful regimes with their own organizational infrastructure (such as the EU) to the more institutionally sparse (such as NAFTA) to even weakly constituted regimes (like MERCOSUR). Scholars' judgments about regime capacity are typically made by observing regime effects on those territorial or sectoral entities that are party to them. This makes good sense: how better to judge the EU than to look at outcomes under its formal regulatory umbrella? But what if TIRs matter *beyond* their formal domain? What if formal regimes have informal effects? These are the questions taken up by this chapter, the only one in the volume to look in detail at TIRs in two different global regions (Europe and Latin America), leading to the conclusion that regional integration regimes can, under certain conditions, have effects even outside their formal territorial and sectoral scope.

Our principal justification for looking for regime effects *outside* actual regimes is that we want to further develop the Introduction's picture of an interaction between multilateral public regimes (codified as TIRs) and private actors (often embedded in transnational regulatory regimes or TRRs). One persistent worry in the massive literature on regulatory regimes is that such regimes may *codify* existing practices more than they *change* such practices (e.g. Maggetti and Gilardi 2011). Thus, we look for regime effects in areas not formally covered by the regime on the grounds that these are far less likely to simply codify what already exists. Our claim is that some regimes may indeed have spillover effects to neighboring countries and sectors. In some cases, this spillover is a function of anticipated formal enlargement of powerful regimes (e.g. the EU). In others, however, spillover can proceed by the private colonization of weaker regimes (e.g. MERCOSUR). We develop this idea through a case study of the regulation of the auto sector in Europe and Latin America. In one case—Central Europe—the strong formal regime has informal *extra-territorial effects*. In the other case—Latin America—the weak formal regime has informal *extra-sectoral effects*.

In making this case, we strengthen two points central to the overall message of the volume. First, TIRs do vary considerably in their effects even when using the same sector and same firms. Second, the European TIR is indeed far more effective at promoting not merely regulatory convergence but also industrial upgrading. That is, auto assemblers and parts suppliers appear more able to leverage the European TIR into enhanced productive capacities in those areas influenced by the regime but not (yet) part of it.

More surprising are two points not directly anticipated in the broader sweep of the volume. First, notwithstanding massive differences in the regimes in Europe and Latin America, a clear movement toward regulatory integration nevertheless does exist in the automotive sector related to both the EU and MERCOSUR. In each case, private actors can converge on a set of rules, though these rules do differ across regions. This surprise is primarily due to the impressive amount of regulatory change that has occurred in Latin America since the launch of MERCOSUR, shrinking the level of regulatory nationalism that has traditionally governed the auto sector. And second, the bigger surprise is that this change occurs through an informal process by firms and their associations that are not formally part of MERCOSUR, though they clearly use MERCOSUR for mutual approximation of their regulatory regimes.

To develop these claims, we look at two regional organizations with important (if highly unequal) aspirations, namely MERCOSUR and the EU. We use the automotive industry as a case study in both regions due to the sector's significant role in their respective economies and the obvious interest of government in having a hand in the development of the sector. In the EU case, we stress the pre-enlargement process that involved the CEE countries.[1] This period runs from the early post-communist period—when automotive companies first moved east in search of trade and investment opportunities—until enlargement in 2004 when the countries became full EU members. As

---

[1] As the vast majority of auto sector activity takes place in four CEE countries—Poland, Slovakia, the Czech Republic, and Hungary—the current chapter restricts its view to these states. Among the other six post-communist members, only Romania has a substantial automotive industry.

for MERCOSUR, we emphasize its beginnings in the early 1990s, when the automotive sector also tried to expand its markets regionally, but because the sector remains outside MERCOSUR, we also take the story up to the current period.

Empirically, we emphasize two kinds of outcomes, both consistent with the central preoccupations of this volume. The first is regulatory convergence— i.e. do regulatory rules inside these two regions become more similar over time? In Latin America, we show how the interplay between the TIR and the TRR performs a central role in intra-regional regulatory convergence right up to the current time, when the automotive sector is still not a full participant in the formal regional market for reasons we will discuss at length. In the European case, we document largely preemptive behavior by private actors (car producers and suppliers and their associations) who anticipate and, in this case, actually prefer to use regional rules before they are compelled to do so. In South America, private actors are much less ready to preemptively comply with broader regulatory rules than are their European counterparts. Some do, however, instrumentalize MERCOSUR for regulatory advantage.

Beyond the extent of regulatory convergence inside a given region, the second outcome we explain is the effect of these regional movements on industrial upgrading. CEE is the site of substantial industrial upgrading in autos, as both the absolute and relative size of high value-added production has grown markedly. This dynamic holds far less for auto parts, especially indigenous part suppliers. We also report important regulatory convergence in Latin America and, once again, find that the industrial upgrading results for the suppliers are substantially less impressive than for the assemblers.

8.2 Case Selection

To study the informal effects of regimes, we chose two TIRs that differ substantially in their formal powers and institutional architecture. Despite these considerable institutional differences, however, both former EU "candidate states" and current MERCOSUR member states showed a clear movement toward regulatory integration directly related to the presence of their respective TIRs. The differences between the two regional organizations do, of course, impact the scope of such a movement. Regional standardization in MERCOSUR is indeed more limited than in Europe, but it still happens in a significant manner. This runs counter to numerous discussions of MERCOSUR's essential irrelevance (e.g. Bouzas 2001; Malamud 2005), thus making this case an important example of the impact of regionalism outside the EU. Also by varying the type of TIR while focusing on the same commercial actors—the key car firms in Europe and Latin America are almost all the same ones—we can gain some analytical leverage on how the regime peculiarities affect sectoral regulatory and upgrading trends.

There is a large literature on the EU's effects on non-members and prospective members.[2] In that light, the section that deals with the EU and CEE is fairly conventional. We focus on the interplay between the TIR and the TRR in the 14 years between communism's collapse and the beginning of EU membership in 2004. For several years after 1990, EU enlargement was not a foregone conclusion, and private actors from the auto sector—including EU 15-based original equipment manufacturers (OEMs) and parts suppliers, as well as CEE political officials, entrepreneurs, and interest groups—dealt with the influence of EU Single Market rules in the absence of an operative Single Market in the CEE countries. With time, EU enlargement entered a much more formal phase, and actual enlargement then brought the EU rules formally to the region.

Precisely because the story of EU and CEE is so well known, however, scholars often express skepticism that other regional organizations have anything like the requisite prestige and institutional resources to spread their regulatory norms among non-members.[3] And here is where novelty arises. Using the CEE-EU experience as a baseline, one might predict very different regulatory outcomes for the Latin American automotive sector due, in particular, to MERCOSUR's weaker institutional set-up. MERCOSUR is not a regional organization with a supranational dimension analogous to the European Community/Single Market. Instead, it works almost exclusively through intergovernmental mechanisms. Moreover, whatever institutional foundation MERCOSUR does provide for regional market regulation, the auto sector is, for reasons that will be detailed, not formally a part of MERCOSUR.

Nevertheless, despite structural differences, the two regional arrangements have produced parallel trends regarding regulatory integration—a largely comprehensive regional regulatory structure that includes many of the same elements.[4] Important and obvious differences in TIRs aside, these parallels justify comparative interest. Both Central Europe and Latin America saw auto sector regionalism commence cautiously in the 1980s, with profound limits set by authoritarian governments with very different developmental models. In both emerging markets, important technical groups took on the task of harmonizing a host of detailed and specific technical regulations, resulting in a substantially integrated regulatory framework. Finally, in both cases, industrial upgrading has been obvious and sustained.

---

[2] A comprehensive review of this vast literature is Bruszt and McDermott (2012).

[3] For more on this and other issues in the field of "comparative regionalism," see Börzel (2011).

[4] This chapter uses "integration" and "harmonization" interchangeably, except when context makes clear that integration resulted from a *new* regulatory framework that was not the spread of one state's rules to another state ("harmonization").

When comparing the two cases presented here, we recognize and stress the profound institutional differences between the two TIRs. Unlike the EU, MERCOSUR does not have a set of permanent structures that can actually harmonize rules and policies for the region, and its regional effects do seem weaker. However, under MERCOSUR's version of intergovernmentalism, member states still did internalize regional rules. Here, informal practices matter a great deal. In South America, the private sector—mainly through its trade associations—negotiated policies and rules among themselves and with governments, both domestically and regionally, in order to produce (or at least pursue) outcomes they desired. In so doing, they circumvented apparent structural/organizational deficits through a series of de facto ways of doing regulatory business.

A central claim of this chapter is that when we study MERCOSUR, we must take this informal structure into consideration. When we do so, we find that it is exactly because of this institutional difference that the South American arrangement is also able to continue the process of regulatory integration and industrial upgrading despite much weaker formal integration. In this volume's analytical frame, the South American auto sector uses regionalism to move from "stasis" to "private coordination" (see Figure 1.1). But this informal coordination led by the OEMs and their associations is one that later results in national codification and in significant regulatory convergence and upgrading. This is consistent with Bruszt and McDermott's argument that actors from both the TIR and the TRR, acting upon the incentives for regional integration, can produce substantial positive changes to their outcome possibilities. This also gives some leverage to the TIR, improving MERCOSUR's capacity to produce visible results.

Of course, this formal side is much more visible in CEE—no surprise when one considers the powerful formal regulatory structures. We emphasize, however, that CEE—despite strong initial trends to the contrary—did not get stuck with the low value-added production that would have been consistent with "regulatory capture with externally imposed rules" (Bruszt and McDermott in this volume). It too "moved"; in this case, the movement built on informal but well-established preferences of the West European OEMs and their suppliers to eventually consolidate CEE as a regulatory clone of Western Europe. This move both enabled and secured industrial upgrading and moved the case much closer to "common interest regulation" in which employment, education, and growth benefits accruing from the auto sector are more widely spread.

We develop these claims in the next two sections. We first show how the industrial upgrading in CEE provided relatively easy resolution to initial intra-sector and intra-CEE rivalries over which firms would invest where and with what levels of tariff protection. The major firms came, relatively soon after the collapse of communism, to draw the regulatory push of the EU further east and regularize this competition for local markets and, much more important, to secure new low-cost production locations that played by the same rules as those in the OEMs' home markets. We then turn to South America, where the much weaker regional organization played a more informal but, we think, still decisive role in both regulatory integration and industrial upgrading. The final section concludes with implications for the comparative study of transnational integration regimes.

8.3 Transnational Regulatory Integration in the CEE Auto Sector: How Upgrading Dampens Conflicts

This section establishes two points consistent with prior research but also constitutive of a substantial puzzle when combined with the Latin American research to follow. The first point is that the EU TIR could motivate partial regulatory convergence even before such convergence was formally obliged. The formal regime had informal effects. The second point is that this regulatory convergence went hand in hand with industrial upgrading. Competition drove OEMs to establish modest production footholds in CEE, but the OEMs' subsequent realization of substantial opportunities for business reorganization led them to seek the shelter of the familiar regulatory environment as a secure legal basis from which to exploit these opportunities. Regulatory convergence to advance global goals quickly became more attractive for OEMs than regulatory arbitrage for local advantage.

Car production has been one of the great post-communist success stories. Auto production accounts for about 10 percent of the region's GDP, and a substantial amount of this is high value-added manufacturing (Scepanovic 2011: 9). This transformation was unexpected by most observers and indeed was not part of the initial OEM strategy in the region. After 1990, Western OEMs initially merely sought new sales markets in the CEE states, which, in turn, protected their own auto producers. CEE tariffs on new and used cars motivated Western OEMs to undertake FDI to meet new local content laws, and, in turn, these OEMs often benefited from protective regulations once inside the CEE national markets. But a combination of broader moves towards free trade (the 1991–2 Europe Agreements) plus a sharp recession in 1992–3 induced OEMs to seek much more substantial reorganization of production on a pan-European (and even global) level (Schamp 2005; Bluhm 2007). The modest benefits of existing tariff schemes were far less interesting to individual producers than a predictable and familiar regulatory environment for long-term production.[5] OEMs thus increased their support for bringing the single market rules to CEE, much of which was accomplished well in advance of the 2004 enlargement. Despite important adjustments before and since the 2008 onset of the financial crisis, the regulatory state of affairs has not fundamentally changed.[6]

Economies of scale are critical in auto production, and this gives an important regional impulse to firms for investment that allows entry to new markets and new production sites, including sites that lay beyond the established regulatory regime (Rhys 2004; Schamp 2005). For example, while Fiat started in Poland—where it had a production history stretching back into the communist period—with a regional CEE-focused production and sales strategy, by the mid-1990s it moved to a much more integrated regime in which linkages between Western Europe and CEE production boosted the productivity of its European production more generally (Balcet and Enrietti 1998).

The initial post-1990 OEM moves into selected CEE markets were primarily efforts to explore territorially contiguous and newly available sales locations. This generated relatively little concern about the regulatory environment since immediate production in CEE was not a high priority. Instead, trade rules were the focus. The EU signed the so-called Europe Agreements (EAs) with Hungary, Poland, and Czechoslovakia on 16 December 1991. The EAs called for a phased-in liberalization of trade between the EU and the CEE signatories. Yet this certainly did not mean the end of non-tariff barriers (NTBs). For example, Kaminski calculates that as late as 1995, 99 percent of Poland's auto sector was still covered by NTBs, and auto sector NTBs accounted for over half of all NTBs in Poland (2001: 15). These auto sector NTBs covered nearly half a billion dollars in goods, 90 percent of which came from the EU. Hungary used a global quota for both new and used cars, and a 1995 law prohibited the import of used cars more than four years old on safety and environmental grounds (Kaminski 2001: 16). There was little incentive for OEMs focused on sales alone to informally push for the EU-15's regulatory framework and, with post-communist reform in its early stages, virtually no reason for CEE states to seek to expose themselves to it.

But important changes were already afoot. The gradual liberalization of trade—and the pressure of steep recession in the early 1990s—motivated OEMs to begin locating CEE production sites not merely on the pull of regional consumer preferences and the push of trade restrictions, but now on the basis of a more Europe-wide production strategy. This profoundly

---

[5] To be sure, this trade off is not absolute. Since both the EU and WTO prefer tariff barriers over non-tariff barriers, regulatory harmonization could, in principle, go hand in hand with higher tariffs to compensate for regulatory integration. We thank Vera Scepanovic for this qualification.

[6] The EU's primary regulatory instrument is an omnibus directive known as 2007/46/EC. During the period investigated here, that instrument was known as 70/156/EEC.

changed the game in CEE. For now, OEMs could integrate CEE production sites into a matrix of facilities that ran from Iberia to Ukraine. This unleashed a new wave of FDI for new (usually greenfield) sites, and a race among some CEE countries to attract as much of this FDI as possible (Drahokoupil 2008; Scepanovic 2011; Pavlinek 2008). It also led OEMs to lend their support to the growing momentum for what was euphemistically called an "enlargement perspective" for the states of the region.

This trend, in turn, put a major bureaucratic undertaking on the agenda. For while the EAs regulated trade between the EU and its bilateral partners in CEE, the "pre-accession process for candidate states" sought to regulate all manner of politically sensitive issues *inside* the prospective member states. As the auto sector has long been an important part of the European Single Market, it has accumulated a large number of such rules. Between 1970 and early 2012 the EU has issued 211 directives and 28 further regulations governing a wide range of sectoral activities.[7] This complex of regulation contributes to the EU's *acquis communautaire*, or body of law. Beginning already in the mid-1990s, the candidate states in CEE began work to identify and transpose the regulatory framework of the EU, including the accumulated regulatory framework of the auto sector.[8]

The best evidence of this claim is the legislative history of the "transposition"—the EU's term for the process of turning a directive into a specific national law or laws—of individual directives. For example, the core EU directive on automobiles (70/156/EEC) was already substantially in place in Hungary by May 2000 and in Poland by December 2002. Slovakia's major transposition did take place around the time of enlargement, but it had engaged in two prior regulatory changes in December 1996 and April 1997 that brought Slovak regulations closer to those in the EU.[9]

The presence of West European OEMs meant that sectoral familiarity with these rules was already quite high, and the OEMs became important advocates for the extension of their familiar regulatory framework. EU Commission officials met regularly with responsible officials from the candidate states to discuss the regulatory framework of about 30 policy sectors and institutional domains. The auto sector *acquis* was the subject of discussions in a number of such areas, including competition policy, state aids to industry, skills formation, and labor markets. These discussions primarily served to inform candidate states about the *acquis* and to identify apparent legislative

---

[7] <http://ec.europa.eu/enterprise/sectors/automotive/documents/directives/motor-vehicles/index_en.htm>. Around 2007, the EU began using far more regulations, so the composition of these two tools has changed substantially over time. Directives gave states too much scope for protectionist regulations.

[8] Many of the directives and regulations superseded earlier ones.

[9] <http://eur-lex.europa.eu/LexUriServ/LexUriServ.do?uri=CELEX:71970L0156:EN:NOT>.

and regulatory gaps that required a specific policy response from the CEE state in question (Jacoby 2004).

To gauge the candidate states' progress, the Commission released an initial "opinion" in 1997 and then annual reports between 1998 and 2003 (just before the May 2004 enlargement). These documents often contained very blunt EU criticisms of the legal and regulatory environment of many policy sectors in the candidate states. It is, therefore, notable that the opinions on the main auto producing states expressed no real alarm even in 1997, suggesting further indirect evidence that already by then the formal TIR had been informally influential in the candidate states before the onset of the formal enlargement process. For example, the Opinion on the Czech Republic noted, with reference to the 1958 UN Economic Commission for Europe (UN-ECE) agreement that is the baseline for upwards of 120 common auto sector regulations, "the Czech Republic is a signatory of the UN-ECE 1958 Agreement and applies more than two thirds of UN-ECE regulations" (European Commission 1997: 35). On the Hungarian auto sector, the Commission noted, "Hungary has announced plans to transpose the framework directive [70/156/EEC] as well as the separate technical directives for the European type approval system into national law by the end of 1997" (1997). The Opinion on Poland was the most blunt, arguing more work was needed on transposition of auto sector directives and also explicitly mentioning exiting "trade obstacles" in connection with the auto sector (1997: 9, 43, 97). Only in the case of Poland can we find evidence that formal enlargement played a key role in sparking substantial additional regulatory convergence in the auto sector.

In part because OEMs that invested most in CEE had long functioned inside this regulatory environment in their home markets in Germany, France, and Italy, they supported the CEE states' efforts to converge on the EU-15 regulatory corpus. Thus, the negotiations over autos were not terribly controversial. To be sure, the Commission's 2002 report signaled that Hungary would need to generate more "transparency" and phase out "implicit support through tax breaks in favour of explicit budgetary support" in the auto sector (2002a: 46). This was a thorny issue. CEE states had often promised Western OEMs large and long "tax holidays" as a condition of their investments. Many of these commitments made in the early or mid-1990s were still in force as enlargement approached and would have violated the restrictions on state aids to industry. For example, for its $840 million investment in the Czech Republic, PSA (Peugeot-Citroën) received a 10-year tax holiday, €16 million in cash for factory construction, €28 million for infrastructure, €13 million for land acquisition for suppliers, and €2,500 for each job created and training costs (Rhys 2004: 888). The broader point is that the regulatory environment from the EU-15 was not flexible, and CEE states in violation of any parts of it needed to find a solution that was *acquis* compliant (Medve-Balint 2014). As we will develop, this marks a major difference between the EU and MERCOSUR. The latter continues to function as an intergovernmental body whose norms are incorporated by each member state in its own way, and this flexibility goes well beyond what an EU member state might enjoy in transposing an EU directive into national law.

Aside from a few difficulties with Poland, there were no major concerns flagged in the annual reports. In 1998, the Commission worried about the Polish licensing system for the import of duty-free parts and about tariff levels (29). The 1999 report on Poland noted, "Closer scrutiny is required for the application of Community rules on public aid in sensitive sectors such as the steel and automotive sectors" (33), a warning repeated in 2000 and again in 2001, although the report went on to note that the 1998 problem on licensing had been resolved by moving to a tariff system (where EC imports were exposed to zero tariff) (2000: 61). In sum, the Commission reports confirm there were relatively few outstanding regulatory problems in this sector. The auto sector is barely mentioned in the 1998–2003 Czech annual reports, and meanwhile, there are long discussions of seemingly intractable problems in other sectors, such as textiles, banking, or steel. By the eve of enlargement in 2004, the process of regulatory integration in the auto sector was complete.

Given the clear initial evidence of intra-sectoral rivalries among OEMs and a ferocious competition among CEE states to attract FDI, how do we account for this remarkable easy road to regulatory integration? After all, many other sectors traveled a far more contentious path under the very same TIR. We would point primarily to the strong and largely unexpected growth in industrial sophistication as a key lubricant for this otherwise potentially contentious process. While other struggling sectors filled the annual reports with sustained brawls over subsidies and market share, the sections on the auto sector betray almost no such anxiety. Interviews with sectoral officials confirm the picture of largely "unproblematic" regulatory adaptation while adding evidence that CEE states were far less disposed than EU-15 states to embellish the common regulatory framework with national idiosyncrasies (Ketzer 2013).

The evidence is strong that this smooth regulatory convergence is primarily because the OEMs were doing very well by their steps to integrate new CEE locations into their broader production empires (Schamp 2005; Rhys 2004; Scepanovic 2011). Indeed, as regulatory problems receded, the evidence of upgrading grew very substantial. Bernaciak and Scepanovic (2010) show that already by 2006 the percentage of high value-added exports from the region was approaching the levels in Germany. Thus, in 2006 nearly 40 percent of CEE component exports were high value-added, a figure actually slightly higher than that in Germany, albeit based on total component exports of €30 billion compared to €42 billion in Germany. Medium and low value-added figures were also very close to German figures. In some cases, the upgrading of products was very stark. Poland's high value-added share was 4 percent in 1996 and rose to 33 percent by 2006 (Pavlinek et al. 2009: 49). To be sure, this trend was far more pronounced among foreign assemblers than among indigenous suppliers. For example, Pavlinek (2008) shows that upgrading happened in the production profile of both OEMs and suppliers in the Czech case, but there was little spillover to indigenous suppliers, who continued to produce mostly at the lower value-added end of the spectrum. The region has at least 26 R&D centers for the auto sector, more than half established since EU membership in 2004 (Pavlinek et al. 2009).[10]

Another measure of upgrading lies in the situation of workers. OECD data on total labor compensation per employee measures wages, bonuses, and social contributions. In a period of upgrading, we would expect some growth in this measure, even when taking into account the weakness of unions in CEE (Jürgens and Krzywdzinski 2009). While German data for all manufacturing—separate data for the auto sector are not available—show an annual rise of 3.3 percent between 1995 and 2010, these figures are higher in the major CEE auto-producing states. In Hungary, total compensation rose 3.9 percent annually, while Poland (5.0 percent), Czech Republic (7.2 percent), and Slovakia (10.2 percent) posted even stronger annual gains.[11]

While upgrading is an uneven story that benefited OEMs more than suppliers and foreign firms more than indigenous ones (Fortwengel 2011), the growing sectoral pie helped lubricate the initial rivalries and helped make regulatory integration relatively uncontroversial. Stepping back, when considering the experience of CEE countries during and after the EU enlargement process, there were key turning points when the *informal* effects of the TIR gradually gave way to increasingly *formal* regional structures that then became the effective regulators for the private sector. As described, these critical turning points were, first, the European Agreements of the early 1990s and, second, the harmonization of CEE states' regulatory frameworks with Single Market rules between 1997 and 2004. When private companies in the automotive sector saw initial market opportunities in CEE, they moved east, bringing new regulatory standards and the hopes of further integration between the markets.

Prior to enlargement, private firms already invested in CEE countries, and incorporated regional regulations as an attempt to preempt future formal regulations in CEE states that might require the OEMs to deal with a new set

---

[10] Still, Bernaciak and Scepanovic note that R&D spending is still below 1 percent of GDP in the CEE states (2010: 17; see also Winter 2010).

[11] <http://stats.oecd.org/Index.aspx?queryname=430&querytype=view>. Author calculations (PPP). See also Fortwengel 2011: 17.

of standards. When enlargement actually happened, EU regional authorities then acquired direct regulatory authority, which drove regulatory integration from that point onwards, making it a much more institutionalized and formal procedure. This regulatory integration was driven in important ways by the experience of European OEMs with longstanding European car regulations. They were used to them and, far from fighting them, generally welcomed their extension to CEE.

8.4 Integration through the Backdoor: Transnational Regulatory Integration in the MERCOSUR Auto Sector

The MERCOSUR case is, of course, quite different, but although the story varies markedly from its European counterpart, regulatory integration is still a surprising reality. To be sure, this outcome is undoubtedly at least partly a result of similar actors—the leading car companies in South America are not all that different from the leading firms in Central and Eastern Europe, and they want many (though not all) of the same things. But this section pushes the argument beyond an institutionalism that is merely the vector sum of the preferences of the leading car companies. South American regionalism is more than that. We also stress the preemptive mechanism far less and a series of unintended consequences and institutional feedback loops far more.

The 1991 Treaty of Asunción, signed by Brazil, Argentina, Paraguay, and Uruguay, established MERCOSUR.[12] With the signing of the Protocol of Ouro Preto in 1994, the institution gained a more developed structure, giving MERCOSUR much of its current institutions and formal powers. The resulting structure includes the exclusively intergovernmental nature of all of its deliberative and representative institutions, which only meet a few times a year (Moschen 2006). In that regard, the South American project's composition differs in very basic ways from that of the EU, especially in that it lacks a supranational structure (Malamud 2005). Although a few subsequent protocols have since refined its structure in an attempt to help the region move beyond a free trade area, the intergovernmental configuration of MERCOSUR, coupled with the disproportional sizes of the economies of the member states and the requirement of unanimity in all decisions taken in regional matters, creates constant gridlocks and politicizes almost every issue

---

[12] Venezuela joined MERCOSUR in 2012 after bypassing a long-standing Paraguayan block to its entry. Paraguay's voting rights in MERCOSUR were suspended after anti-democratic allegations around a messy presidential impeachment process. MERCOSUR's three remaining members took advantage of Paraguay's inability to sustain its blocking against Hugo Chávez's government. Because the impact of Venezuela's entry is unclear, it will not be considered in this chapter.

dealt with by the organization (Veiga 2004; Barbosa 2009; Doctor 2012). In practice, MERCOSUR still has an imperfect customs union and a less than ideal free trade area, with no indication of moving toward a common market, which is what the original treaties foresaw (Barbosa 2009; Vaz 2003; Gardini 2011).

The private sector began to show interest in a more integrated region as an opportunity to advance its businesses long before any formal regional project was introduced (Casella 2007; Vaz 2003; Veiga 2004). As in the CEE case already discussed, we see the potentially powerful impulses towards integration driven by "domestic" firms and their associations. Immediately before the formative years of MERCOSUR, its future member states had begun to open their economies after a long period of protectionist policies and import substitution programs, especially after the fall of dictatorial political regimes in the early and mid-1980s (Barbosa 2009; Gardini 2011; Shapiro 1994).

In the mid-1980s, Argentina and Brazil took advantage of the new economic and political mood in the region and began a bilateral process of integration that was gradual, sectoral, and flexible (Gardini 2011). The process happened much like the future development of MERCOSUR, with numerous protocols gradually promoting integration, directed only at specific important economic sectors and replete with flexible exceptions. This process bore early fruit in a key economic sector with the 1987 creation of AUTOLATINA, a joint venture between Volkswagen do Brasil, Ford do Brasil, Volkswagen Argentina, and Ford Argentina. AUTOLATINA came, in part, as a strategic answer to the financial problems faced by both Ford and Volkswagen at a time of high inflation and foreign debt as well as meager growth in Argentina and Brazil (ADEFA 2010; Fenianos 2009). This experiment showed the automotive industry that integration could bring strategic market benefits, leading the sector to participate more fully in discussions with government about the MERCOSUR project, which began at this time. Other sectors such as sugar, textile, chemicals, etc., soon joined in the conversations, creating weight in support of regional integration. However, not to be mistaken, the initial pressures for a formal process of integration came from government officials, which had been the standard order of business in the region for decades (Niel 2012).

Once MERCOSUR became a reality, the sector's tariff lines remained outside the original treaties and still have not been fully integrated into the regional accords to this day. To understand why, one must remember that during the formative years of MERCOSUR, Brazil had a much stronger automotive industry than Argentina. Moreover, because the sector enjoyed independent domestic supply and production networks in both countries, the two national sectors did not need each other to survive (Triches 2003). Although the OEMs generally favored deeper sectoral integration, the Argentine government opposed immediate liberalization because of the potential huge trade imbalance in a strategic sector. Instead, a 1990 bilateral economic complementation treaty (ACE 14) regulated trade exclusively for the auto sector, providing virtually a zero-tariff environment. That treaty still remains the basis for automotive trade between Brazil and Argentina, given their subsequent inability to resolve their historic disputes. Similar bilateral treaties were signed between all four original members of MERCOSUR, all originally to expire in 1994, when the Asunción Treaty predicted free trade would be generalized for all tariff lines in all member states and when all fears of possible trade imbalances had to be resolved. As noted, this assumption proved far too optimistic, but the goal of bringing the auto sector under the MERCOSUR agreements was never tossed out officially.

Even with the automotive industry initially—and surprisingly, given its pioneering efforts at regional integration—outside MERCOSUR, the sector still believed it would reap the benefits of regional integration once 1994 arrived. With that objective in mind, the discussions between private and public sectors intensified, especially in the involvement within important working groups within the Common Market Group structure (MERCOSUR's executive body, also known as the GMC) that would help pave the way for a smoother eventual entrance of the sector into the regional agreement. SGT-3 (Technical Norms) is especially relevant because it dictated the formalization of MERCOSUR technical norms for all other original working groups, which ranged from health and communications to agriculture and industry. This is the case because all technical norms had to go through SGT-3 before the GMC could propose a normative resolution to later be adopted by member states. Critically, although the automotive sector stayed outside the treaty, technical norms regarding its products were still discussed in SGT-3 meetings, and dozens of regulative norms were enacted by the GMC during its early years.

The logic behind the creation of SGT-3 is that, once all MERCOSUR member states adopted and followed harmonized norms and regulations, commercial discussions would become simpler and trade obstacles would diminish, paving the way for freer trade for all sectors (Ferman 2006). Since MERCOSUR operated intergovernmentally, technical and regulatory bodies from each member state represented their country whenever the group met. This structure allowed for an informal network where the private sector regularly brought issues to their respective governments, along with arguments to support their views on questions discussed by the technical bodies forming the SGT-3.

While this never approached the regulatory density of the EU auto *acquis*, the Automotive Industry Commission, within the SGT-3 structure, developed rules on dozens of issues. Such norms, however, were only binding after being voluntarily approved and transcribed into law by the responsible domestic institutions of each member state. Since domestic institutional capacities varied a great deal among member states, this process had the potential to produce widely different regulatory outcomes in the region *even when states sought to harmonize.* Moreover, unlike an EU directive—which also requires the national "transposition" of more general language into specific national laws—there was absolutely no obligation of MERCOSUR states to engage in this process.

As noted, private sector interest in regionalism was substantial, especially after government officials pushed openly for greater industrial integration and complementarity in the region (Santana 2012). The automotive sector, eager to be included in the proposed regional treaty, began as early as in 1991 to bring issues to be discussed by the SGT-3, giving room for the main trade associations of the member states to discuss which norms should be emphasized for regional harmonization. This process became the *modus operandi* of SGT-3 discussions throughout the 1990s and into the early 2000s. It mended some of the institutional gaps of MERCOSUR due to a lack of supranational bureaucrats who would give focus to the discussions envisioned by SGT-3. It also unintentionally allowed the new and very partial regional agreement to affect sectors in the signatory countries that were not yet party to the agreements. Although the formal representatives from each country at SGT-3 discussions were from public entities, private sector representatives, especially when acting in the name of domestic trade associations, provided ammunition for formal discussions in the group. This public/private interaction helped SGT-3 discuss timely issues based on real domestic needs from each member state (Bezerra and São Thiago 1993). Considering the institutional weaknesses of MERCOSUR, the TRR was surprisingly willing and able to strengthen the formal capacity of the TIR in order to play a larger role in regional regulatory change. Though modest when compared to the European experience, this mechanism is fundamental to regulatory integration in South America.

GMC norms that originated from SGT-3 decisions were much more likely to receive serious subsequent attention at the domestic level simply because the key public and private stakeholders had already engaged the matter at the SGT-3 level and had created mutual expectations regarding the subsequent adoption of such regulations. Legal adoption did vary by country, however. Brazil had a well-developed regulatory structure and already followed international standards on a number of issues, while the other member states had extremely limited rules in most areas discussed by SGT-3 (or any other working group, for that matter).[13] In Paraguay, for example,

---

[13] As further auto sector integration stalled, the SGT-3 gradually grew dormant by the mid-2000s.

technical norms regarding vehicle quality and safety were only introduced in the early twenty-first century and then only because of MERCOSUR decisions. The best evidence for this is that GMC norms were all transcribed word for word, despite the fact that they were *not* mandatory. Paraguay does not have a relevant domestic automotive industry, yet it still ended up adopting *all* MERCOSUR norms affecting the sector. We credit this resulting regional integration to the fact that the TIR used the capacity offered by the TRR and pushed for the adoption of such norms according to the expectations set during the SGT-3 meetings. With the intergovernmental setting, the TIR officials that received support from the TRR are, in effect, domestic public servants, thus more likely to have leverage in the domestic transposition of MERCOSUR norms.

Along with steady integration came a clear, if partial, convergence of regulatory standards. Indeed, the premise of all discussions about industry norms was the strictest standard among the participating parties (Saltini 2012). This strategy was, in fact, controversial. The main source of tension was that, in nearly every automotive standard discussed by the group, the strictest version came from the Brazilian side. To some extent, this occurred because the three other member states either did not have a specific national norm in the areas discussed—such as in the Paraguayan case just noted—or had very general and relaxed ones. For the private sector, this unruly environment was seen as a potential threat since newcomers could enter those markets without having to incur the costs of compliance to the technical norms present in markets like Brazil, a natural exporter to its neighbors. This fear became very real when Chinese auto makers began producing in the region later on.

Not all such disputes could be resolved, however. Take, for example, emission standards for petrol engines, which was one of the earliest topics of discussion by SGT-3 already in 1991. In this area, Brazil had long exclusively adopted American emission standards, while Argentina only developed pertinent legislation in 1994 and accepted either European or American standards after the initial discussions resulted from the integration process. Throughout negotiations during the SGT-3 discussions, Brazil was reluctant to accept any European norms, which angered the Argentines. In 1995 Argentina changed its legislation to accept *only* European standards, thus moving further away from agreement as a clear provocation to the Brazilian reluctance to compromise (Saltini 2012). When the issue was negotiated, the Brazilian government argued for the American standard on the grounds that it was the strictest one. The Argentine government said it would only accept that standard if Brazil also recognized the European norms as well as the American ones. It was even suggested that both sides adopt a neutral standard championed by the UN, but no agreement was reached. The topic has been discussed numerous times since, but the dispute still exists even though the resulting emission levels from both standards are virtually the same. The differences lie in the technical tests performed to reach the standards, which measure different aspects of emissions and, therefore, are not technically compatible despite their clear functional similarity (Saltini 2012).

Despite such occasional deadlocks, SGT-3 was able to produce a number of decisions that were later translated into GMC resolutions. On the one side, there were the public officials interested in the political and distributive implications of each regulatory decision. On the other side, there were the private sector representatives wanting to use regulatory harmonization to facilitate production integration and complementarity in the region (Melo and Goulart 2003). The steady development of SGT-3 helped in that process, but that body still had limited power due to its lack of formal capability to produce legal norms at the domestic level based on its decisions at the inter-governmental level.

And what about industrial upgrading? Here again, the story is surprisingly positive, though admittedly harder to link to the regional TIR than was true in the European case. This is especially true since there is no explicit regional policy aimed at upgrading, but we can see how deeper integration has brought positive spillover effects that have contributed to industrial sophistication as explained below. Before MERCOSUR, only Brazil and Argentina even had an auto industry in the region. But the dominant OEMs in one national market were not necessarily the same as in the other, or at least not with the same strength. With the closer relations after the MERCOSUR talks were launched, OEMs started expanding across the border. Once established there, they began revisiting their production strategies to take advantage of the regional market. Today, companies present in one country have a secure presence in all MERCOSUR neighbors. All post-MERCOSUR new entrants have adopted that strategy, making the region a much more homogeneous and competitive environment, much like in Europe.

In Uruguay, for example, by the time newcomers like Chinese auto makers Lifan and Effa and South Korean Kia saw the potential of using Uruguay as a new production base for the region, both regulatory integration and industrial upgrading were long underway. This environment more or less obliged the new entrants to raise their industrial standards in order to both produce and sell in the region. Without MERCOSUR it is doubtful that Uruguay would have adopted such a high number of regulatory standards as it did in such a short period of time. It is also not clear firms investing there would have chosen such high production standards, which go beyond what they use in their home markets.

Today, regional stakeholders regard the automotive market as a regional business. OEMs see MERCOSUR as an integrated production platform for regional consumption as well as an export base. That is anecdotally evident from the fact that one of the major automotive magazines in the region, *Quatro Rodas*, as well as most other specialized publications, publishes a periodic price list which is divided into two: one is "imported vehicles" and the other is "domestic, MERCOSUR, and Mexican vehicles" (Mexico enjoys free trade agreements with MERCOSUR). This illustrates how the complementarity strategy has been adopted in the region. What this means for industrial upgrading is that, with the possibility of larger production volumes for vehicles that could not otherwise be produced in any individual MERCOSUR country, OEMs are willing to invest in more advanced production platforms in order to take advantage of the new enlarged regional market. The story, however, is different for auto part suppliers, where—as in CEE—much less industrial upgrading occurred. As the more technologically advanced vehicles are produced in more modest numbers, OEMs concentrate their parts purchases either from their headquarters or China, rather than investing in expensive plants in South America. In general, only large tier-1 suppliers have made major investments.

Also as in CEE, OEMs used cross-investment to put their regional production on far more efficient footings. Put simply, Brazilian subsidiaries were increasingly favored for higher volume production of smaller cars due to its larger production capacity, while the Argentine side started to produce more complex vehicles with lower volumes (Triches 2003). This strategy was adopted by most companies, leading them to either open new plants in the neighboring country or to expand their already extant business on the other side of the border. One important difference between the European and the South American stories, however, is that, in the former, Western Europe was the target market, thus the initial reason and standard pushing for upgrading. In the latter, Brazil was the benchmark. That means that the ceiling was much higher for CEE countries, which partially explains the extent of upgrading that happened there.

The SGT-3 decisions that later became GMC resolutions formed a new regional basis for the industry, but the process of internalization of its norms was contentious, sensitive, and ultimately incomplete. For example, the Argentine government was quite reluctant to adopt Brazilian norms when updating their national road and vehicle safety regulations. Instead, Argentina enacted Law 779 in 1995 and incorporated all GMC resolutions worked by SGT-3 up to that point. It turned out these, too, were mostly based on Brazilian standards. However, the Argentine government and industry insist that, rather than having adopted Brazilian-inspired norms, they had drafted a new set of indigenous rules responsive to their particular needs. Whatever the rhetorical stance, the GMC resolutions are transcribed nearly word by word into Argentina's legislative framework, retaining even the recognized technical problems and wording of the Brazilian inspired norms so criticized by them during SGT-3 discussions.

Absent well-developed auto sectors, regulatory harmonization was less contentious for Paraguay and Uruguay, but they were still reluctant to follow the path of upgrading based on regional rules. Paraguay did so in 2006, when it enacted a law (Resolución 8064/06) that adopted the recommended MERCOSUR technical norms for all sectors word for word, which included all points related to the automotive sector already incorporated by Argentina. Uruguay's strategy was to first create the necessary domestic institutions, including thematic working groups and technical commissions to update the already existing legislation in order to address issues raised by MERCOSUR discussions, which happened in 1994 through Law 16.585. These newly created structures allowed for a patchwork on a number of laws and articles within those laws, adapting their norms to the newly created MERCOSUR demands. This process culminated in the formulation of a new road and vehicle safety code in 2007 (Laws 18.113 and 18.191) in which they incorporated most of the norms internalized by Argentina and Paraguay.

One might argue that regulatory integration was a natural process due to the growing internationalization of markets of the 1980s or that, since the private sector was represented largely by the same actors throughout the region, it was in their interest to develop common standards. To an extent, this is true, as we have already noted in several places. Firm strategies play a very important role, and this point is consistent with the introduction's focus on the need for certain parallel tendencies at domestic and international levels for regulatory integration to occur. However, we have also tried to show that, despite MERCOSUR's very loose institutional structure, it helped produce substantial regulatory integration in this sector after open discussions brought together relevant stakeholders from all member states. No MERCOSUR nation was obliged to incorporate GMC resolutions, but they generally did so anyway. More importantly, this happened in a sector not yet completely integrated into MERCOSUR and whose tariff lines still lie outside the regional project. If the private sector had moved alone toward closer harmonization of standards, governments would not have enacted legislation so uniformly across the region.

That said, and very unlike the CEE case, regulatory integration did not happen all at the same time and through the same processes, showing that MERCOSUR's loose intergovernmental processes are a far distance from the EU. In South America, the key policy-makers are often not regional authorities representing member states and far less supranational officials representing the regional organization. Rather, they are more frequently private sector actors working in close concert with their own national officials and with counterparts in other MERCOSUR countries. Far from an ad hoc process, however, this repetitive and regularized set of practices involves informal relationships and actions that can lead, and has already led, to substantive formal outcomes, where the interaction between the relevant regional TRR with the TIR is able to bridge institutional gaps and create enough clout for the TIR to push its agenda forward.

Once the automotive sector realistically understood it still had a long way to go before its tariff lines were incorporated into the MERCOSUR agreements due to the ever-present political and economic volatility in the region, it did become less enthusiastic about harmonizing regulations. This situation was aggravated by the fact that no regional body could guide the process in the name of MERCOSUR. In subsequent years, SGT-3 slowed its pace, and only a few resolutions were produced after the initial batch that dictated most of the domestic legal changes just discussed. In total, SGT-3 produced 44 MERCOSUR Technical Regulations affecting the auto sector, of which 26 came in the early years between 1991 and 1994, showing the initial enthusiasm toward integration.[14] Its role also diminished due to a feeling that most major issues had already been addressed by the existing regulations and that newer ones would be too specific and irrelevant unless greater integration happened first.

Currently, old disputes between Argentina and Brazil, as well as simpler ones involving Uruguay and Paraguay, have brought tensions to the parallel agreements designed to dictate the rules for the automotive sector between all four members of MERCOSUR. Without a larger treaty that includes dispute settlement systems and a formal bureaucracy that can lead discussions important to the region, the weaker bilateral agreements suffer the economic and political pressures of critical times (Barbosa 2009). In January of 2011, for example, the Argentine and Brazilian presidents released a joint statement in Buenos Aires that stated their formal commitment to support further integration between the two countries and the region, as well as a determination to eliminate trade barriers between the two countries. A few months later, the Argentine government enacted a series of protectionist regulations making bilateral trade ever more difficult, followed by Brazilian retaliation in the form of increased import taxes, especially geared toward the auto sector (AutoData 2012a; Fiesp 2012). Once the quarrels between Brazil and Argentina seemed to soften, Uruguay announced its intention to break the agreement that dictates rules for trade in the automotive sector, due to allegations of unbalanced bilateral trade (AutoData 2012b).[15]

During the early years of MERCOSUR, when the 1994 goal of full incorporation of the auto sector was still alive, government officials had a much easier time persuading the private sector to follow their plans. Once it became

---

[14] The last SGT-3 regulation came about in 2002. Since 2003, SGT-3 stopped meeting, mainly due to the uncertainty regarding the standing of the automotive sector within MERCOSUR.
[15] This agreement is known as ACE 57.

clear the auto sector would stay out of the regional accords for some time, one might predict a total halt to integration. That was not the case, however. While the pace did diminish, almost half the technical norms produced by SGT-3 that were later adopted by member states came after 1994. The private sector also continued to regard MERCOSUR as important. The trade associations of the OEMs continue to meet to discuss MERCOSUR, including the formulation of a unified automotive policy to be handed to each national government to guide future discussions. Working groups across the different trade associations continued to work under active deadlines in 2013. In short, MERCOSUR remains a relevant agenda for the private sector and very much a reality for government actions in the region and abroad. Indeed, whenever a topic is to be discussed with national government related to foreign trade and autos, the private sector nearly always seeks out the government official holding the title for the MERCOSUR automotive commission.

Once the TRR strengthened the capacity of the TIR, it built a link that would only be extinguished with the formal dissolution of MERCOSUR. Considering how volatile the governments in the region are, the auto sector believes it can never be too prepared, and that is why it is working on a MERCOSUR automotive policy during a time even when most observers claim that the organization is nearly dead.

For the auto parts industry, we have to consider the creation of Mercopartes in October 2004. This is a council composed of the trade associations representing auto parts producers from all MERCOSUR members. It meets quarterly to coordinate policy positions. Although Mercopartes has the potential to strengthen the regional TRR and provide leverage against the auto producers, the results to date have been modest. Partly, this is because of the lack of a supranational authority to whom they could address joint appeals. Thus, each trade association in Mercopartes invariably goes to their domestic governments at the end of the coordination process. During Mercopartes's latest 2013 seminar, government officials that compose MERCOSUR's SGT-7 (working group representing industry) noted the significance of Mercopartes and urged the auto producers' trade associations to build a similar grouping. The very existence of such a grouping and the desire by public officials to expand such an initiative are indications of the deeper roots that regional integration has taken in South America.

8.5 Conclusion

This chapter has developed one central claim, which is that regional integration regimes can, under certain conditions, have effects even outside their formal territorial and sectoral scope. We show this through case studies of the auto sector in Latin America and Europe, demonstrating that regulatory integration happens differently in MERCOSUR than it does in the EU, but it still happens. In making this case, the chapter also has made four subsidiary points. First, these two TIRs vary considerably in their effects even when using the same sector and same firms. Second, the European TIR is more effective at promoting not merely regulatory integration but also industrial upgrading as well. Third, notwithstanding the massive differences in the regimes in Europe and Latin America, a surprising parallel movement toward regulatory integration nevertheless does exist in the auto sector. This surprise is primarily due to the impressive amount of regulatory change that has occurred in Latin America since the launch of MERCOSUR. Finally, and more surprising still, this change occurs through an informal process by firms and their associations that are not actually part of MERCOSUR, though they clearly use MERCOSUR for mutual approximation of their regulatory regimes.

Indeed, there are a number of parallels across the two cases. Both saw auto sector regionalism commence cautiously in the 1980s, limited by authoritarian governments with very different developmental models. Both saw informal use of formal TIRs to leverage a process of regulatory convergence on a regional level. Technical groups such as SGT-3 have their European counterpart in the extensive Commission-run process that harmonized dozens of detailed and specific regulations. To be sure, the extent of this common regulation is greater in Europe than in Latin America; still, in both sectors, regulatory convergence was obvious and sustained. Sectoral standards were diffused not only to the key producing states but also to newcomer states like Uruguay, Paraguay, Romania, Estonia, and Lithuania. These states, in turn, often initially specialized in parts production, but have moved towards final assembly in some cases, fueled mostly by Asian investment.

The big differences, however, stand out just as much. The most important difference we found lay in the potential of the two TIRs to stimulate industrial upgrading from low value-added to high value-added manufacturing. It is clear that determined private actors—especially if they are powerful OEMs—can encourage a process of regulatory integration in which rules for safety, consumer protection, and a wide range of other issues are harmonized across a region. At the same time, absent a more robust regional architecture capable of designing pertinent policies, it seems industrial upgrading will be more limited. Certainly, that was the pattern from CEE, where substantial investment in the sector generally occurred only once the promise of EU membership was extended to the states of the region.

From the beginning, South American regional coordination was hard to achieve due to the absence of supranationality. Having to deal with this complex environment, the private sector, which was enthusiastic about the early years of economic growth attributed to regional integration, had to find a new way of making the regional decision-makers hear their demands in order to achieve higher profit and market gains (Cason 2011; Shapiro 1994). This particular interest on the part of the private sector forced a higher degree of auto sector involvement in the decision-making processes of MERCOSUR.

Without supranationalism, the sector found "workarounds" for some areas. For instance, since there was no supranational bureaucracy to coordinate regulatory matters, domestic governments consulted their private sectors through the respective trade associations. But since the private companies had cross-border representation and multi-faceted connections in the region, they were able, after initial consultations, to present harmonized positions to all domestic governments simultaneously. To compound the irony, these initial consultations usually happened in all member states during and right after MERCOSUR meetings. This system effectively substituted the role of a supranational authority, producing a de facto regional structure where figures from the private sector played critical roles in shaping power at the regional level. The peculiar interaction between the public and private sectors in the region has provided institutional bridges for deep intergovernmental divides specific to the formal structure of MERCOSUR.

In short, while the informal territorial effects of the powerful EU are consistent with much received wisdom about regionalism, the unusual story of informal sectoral regionalism in Latin America breaks new ground. And in both cases, informal regulatory integration tended to broaden rather than narrow the benefits of regionalism.

9

Multiple Paths toward Regime Building? SPS Regulation in the MERCOSUR

Miguel F. Lengyel and Valentina Delich

9.1 Introduction

International competitiveness in agri-business today is strongly determined by the capacity of building competitive advantages based on food quality and safety as well as the certification and management of quality standards (Jatib 2003). In the food chain, while the development of safety standards is mandatory, quality standards are voluntary. Implementing food safety systems, such as Good Manufacturing Practices (GMP), Sanitation Standard Operating Procedures (SSOP), and Hazard Analysis and Critical Control Points (HACCP), is not the same as implementing quality systems, such as ISO 9000 and total quality and continuous improvements, which together seek to satisfy consumer preferences. Within the food industry, food safety and quality management are closely intertwined, and both fields build upon and nurture technological innovations for competitiveness (Jatib 2003; Baldwin 2012; Sterian 2013).

Against this backdrop, the role of sanitary and phytosanitary (SPS) standards in agri-business has qualitatively changed over the past decade from a technical means to reduce market transaction costs of homogeneous commodities to a strategic tool to compete by increasingly differentiating products or developing new ones (Reardon et al. 2001). Simply put, the traditional goal of SPS standards of homogenizing/standardizing commodities in order to generate scale economies was challenged in two ways: on the demand side, by the shift from mass to niche markets comprising consumers with higher purchasing power and/or changing and more demanding tastes; on the supply side, by product, process, and distribution technologies that enhance firm capacities for product differentiation and customization to attend to increasingly segmented markets (Reardon et al. 2001).

How have governments in emerging economies responded? The general answer has been to make mandatory standards such as HACCP or ISO 9000 for exports to some destinations while keeping lower standards for domestic production and consumption. By doing so, governments have faced a dilemma. On the one hand, setting "inclusive" standards for local firms would not sufficiently motivate public and private actors to adjust the SPS standards to the more dynamic source of demand (the global market). On the other hand, using higher, more "exclusive" standards would pose the risk of allowing only a few firms to access external markets. An additional challenge is the continued growth of private standards, which give competitive advantages in increasingly contested markets (Reardon et al. 2001).

How has MERCOSUR managed these challenges? Has it been a working platform for helping member countries to strengthen their standard-setting and enforcement capacity? And which factors are driving these issues? The answer to such questions is neither straightforward nor conclusive, especially if addressed through the lenses of the analytical framework suggested by Bruszt and McDermott in the Introduction of this book.

As this chapter attempts to show, the MERCOSUR is a transnational integration regime (TIR) with no clear hegemon for the time being. There are considerable veto powers for rule-making coming from the private sector and government bureaucracies. There are weak incentives and moderate government capacities to craft new or harmonize existing rules. And there is an overcrowding of regulations with scarce monitoring capacities. As a TIR, the MERCOSUR could therefore easily be placed in the lower middle-right of Figure 1.1. At the same time, the situation of blockage does not mean, however, total paralysis. On the contrary, avenues for coordination of SPS setting are taking place, some with concrete results, at the regional, national, and subnational levels through different mechanisms and with different rationales. In other words, although the larger picture appears as one of stagnation, it is punctuated by different episodes of rule creation, redefinition, and even implementation. SPS standards in the MERCOSUR could thus be better conceived as following a multiple, patchwork pattern of rule adaptation and creation coming from different sources.

This chapter addresses these questions by exploring two main issues: (1) the MERCOSUR's key regulative integration strategies in the SPS area, and (2) the different top-down and bottom-up rule-making mechanisms. We address the first question by focusing on regional (public) action and thus mostly on public SPS rules and standards. We address the second by analyzing the "SPS dynamics" mainly driven by market considerations and, in selected products, especially in terms of the development and impact of private SPS standards and of their interaction with public standards and policies.

The first section presents a brief description of MERCOSUR objectives, achievements, and weaknesses concerning cross-border rule-making and SPS standard setting at the regional level. The second section examines various venues of cross-border standard setting—some "top-down" and others "bottom-up"—coming from quite different sources and driven by different forces and actors: the "brazilianization" of national standards within MERCOSUR; the "alignment" of regional-level standards to those set in international agencies; and some "product-based" experiences of standard setting—the case of quality standards and export performance in key fresh fruit and rice products. The latter reveals pioneering steps toward public-private collaboration and innovation. Along the way, we consider the public policy responses to these diverse processes of standards setting. In the concluding section, the chapter discusses the interaction between regional (MERCOSUR) and domestic regulatory dynamics on SPS and its implications for building a transnational regulatory regime in this policy field.

9.2 MERCOSUR in Brief: The Regional SPS Institutional Setting and its Implications

Since the creation of the MERCOSUR in 1991, South America has drastically changed its economic, political, and social profile and policies: from indebtedness to lenders in countries, from negative to positive rates of growth, from the Washington consensus model to more locally coined (still quite experimental) models of development. The MERCOSUR has been part of these changes, although it still remains—at least in the political discourse and social imaginary—as a strategic regional project for a common market fostering long-term growth. In other words, it is still seen as an institutional device for articulating integration in international markets with development at home.

The MERCOSUR's institutional design was understood from its creation in 1991 as a case of "open regionalism," i.e. an integration endeavor not intended to build up a trade fortress or to be a device for ambitious import substitution policies. Accordingly, MERCOSUR trade liberalization among its members (Argentina, Brazil, Uruguay, and Paraguay) was the agreement's linchpin in the Washington consensus mood of the 1990s and proceeded very fast and with few exceptions over its first years of life. Yet, it soon became difficult to deepen the Southern Cone economic integration process: the lack of a clear leadership (or hegemon in Bruszt/McDermott's framework) and strategy, divergent economic policies between the main partners, Brazil and Argentina, and the Argentine crash of 2001–2. On top of that, MERCOSUR members were unable after 1995 to implement the customs union. Intra-regional trade declined, and an uncoordinated, centrifugal dynamic of rule-making took over as members began to create norms at the MERCOSUR level that were never internalized into the domestic legal systems, and thus never became operational. The MERCOSUR then became more of a discourse than an operative transnational legal system based on a functional distribution of power, shared strategic policy concerns, and incentives for actors to establish common regulations.

This situation did not drastically improve when regional economic growth restarted in 2003 under renewed political leaderships (from left-wing parties) in the member countries and the integration initiative was relaunched with the participation of Venezuela and Bolivia as guest nations. The emphasis was then placed on the need to deepen the "political MERCOSUR." Consequently, its new agenda was built upon issues such as democratic compromise, protection of human rights, and the like (Fundación Exportar 2009).[1]

Finally, the MERCOSUR's institutional architecture is usually described as "soft" or "flexible" in that its organs are formed by governmental delegates, instead of permanent MERCOSUR officials,[2] and decisions are made by unanimous consensus. In effect, the MERCOSUR has three main decision-making instances and in all of them consensus is necessary to make binding decisions, i.e. to create a norm. At the same time, all members must "internalize or incorporate" the MERCOSUR norms at the domestic level in order for them to become operative.[3]

9.2.1 MERCOSUR Institutional Architecture and Dynamics of Norm Creation: The Unfulfilled Expectations of SPS Policy

The MERCOSUR has a multi-layered institutional architecture, which is bureaucratically complex but whose decision-making dynamism and leverage do not fully follow suit. The Common Market Council (CMC) is the highest political organ, in charge of giving political direction to the integration project; the Common Market Group (CMG) is the executive organ, supported by two technical instances, the sub-working groups (SGT) and technical committees (CT). In addition, the MERCOSUR Trade Commission (MTC) was created in 1994—when the custom union was achieved—to deal with issues

---

[1] Details available at <http://www.exportar.org.ar/informes_estadisticos.html>.

[2] Except for a minimal staff at the MERCOSUR Secretariat in Montevideo.

[3] In terms of dispute settlement, the original system was GATT-like (instead of being inspired in the European Union or the Andean Pact, i.e including permanent tribunals). The MERCOSUR treaty on dispute settlement foresees consultations and claims before the Common Market Council (CMC) and Common Market Group (CMG) and, if no solution is found, the case can be submitted to an ad hoc arbitral tribunal. In 2002, some changes were made to the dispute settlement system, by which a permanent tribunal was set up as a second instance that also can, under request, give non-binding opinions.

concerning the custom union's implementation. Notably, all these organs have the power to take binding decisions, i.e. to create norms.[4]

The legislative process in the MERCOSUR is also complex, involving three stages: the elaboration/negotiation of the norm within the technical groups, its approval as a regional norm at the CMG or CMC (depending on norm's content), and the incorporation of the norm into the domestic legal system by an administrative or legislative act (depending on the national juridical system's requirement). Yet, at the same time, the system is quite ineffective: while it has regulated in a detailed way the norm-building and approval processes at the regional level and has mandated regional norm internalization by all domestic legal systems to make the rule operative as well, it has not created specific mechanisms or instances to jointly monitor how members implement regional norms at the domestic level.

In the SPS field, the structure and process of norm building are not an exception to the general pattern, involving various technical groups: the Sub Working Group No. 8 (SGT8 Agriculture), the Sub Working Group No. 3 (SGT3 Food), the Plant Protection Committee, and the Animal Health Committee. Each group comprises delegates from each member country (named "national coordinators" or just "coordinators") and is in charge of harmonizing differing national norms in its specific domain or suggesting requirements within MERCOSUR or for imports from non-MERCOSUR countries (e.g. on plant or animal health). Once the regional norm is drafted at a CT, the SGT8 "elevates" the norm to the CMG for treatment and approval.

As on some other MERCOSUR fronts, however, a gap between rule and practice usually prevails. Indeed, notwithstanding that CMC Decision 20/02 establishes the general negotiation and approval regime of MERCOSUR norms, some stages are not complied with in practice (at least in SGT8 practice) in order to speed up the decision-making process.[5] In turn, mandatory domestic consultations take place in practice only for few days.

All this could give the impression that the MERCOSUR norm creation process is detached from national institutional influence, but actually the opposite turns out to be the case. Specific national consultations are not crucial because MERCOSUR delegates are national officers whose main work is at the

---

[4] A norm organ origin is denoted by their technical name. Formally, CMC binding decisions are "Decisions," CMG binding decisions are "Resolutions," and MTC binding decisions are "Directives." Most SPS norms are Resolutions.

[5] In effect, once the SGT8's Technical Committees (Animal or Plant) agrees on a norm project and passes it to the SGT8, SGT8 (1) verifies the translation of the norm (Spanish and Portuguese), (2) checks for possible legal or trade issues that may justify a norm revision before sending it for approval, and (3) establish a deadline as well as the kind of act required to internalize it in each country. It is noteworthy that the SGT8 does not "decide" the kind of act (administrative or legislative) needed in each country to internalize the regional norm. The SGT8 takes note of what each country member delegate says is needed to internalize the norm in his or her respective country.

national level within national structures. Each officer is, basically, a national officer who participates at the regional level with soft decision power. There is direct participation of national officers in the creation of regional norms, as they are members of the agencies that enact SPS national policies with an ensuing de facto veto power on decisions at the regional level. This somehow ironically suggests that there is no such a thing as a MERCOSUR SPS policy, except for the mandate not to obstruct trade unjustifiably and eventually to harmonize norms if required.[6]

This breach in the regional process of norm creation/harmonization is aggravated by the lack of enforcement capacities. That is, there is a gap between the created and internalized norms, or, to put it slightly differently, between created and implemented commitments (Bouzas and Fanelli 2001; Peña and Rozemberg 2005). Finally, to aggravate the "incorporation issue" even further, Brazil interprets that norms are valid in its territory once incorporated in its domestic legal order, while Argentina interprets that the norm is not valid even if passed at the domestic level until the other three countries have passed the norm at their domestic level and communicated it to the MERCOSUR Secretariat. So, Brazil basically applies MERCOSUR norms after internalizing them in its legal order even if other members have not yet put them in place.

In light of these trends and factors, it is not surprising that, in the SPS field, the MERCOSUR went from a full to a narrow harmonization process, downgrading initial expectations and aims.[7] In effect, in the early MERCOSUR, the harmonization strategy included the elaboration of a "MERCOSUR Code" grounded on the idea of harmonizing all of the operative sanitary and phytosanitary norms in each and every MERCOSUR member country. This is why some authors have interpreted MERCOSUR SPS policy as "European type" (Berlinksi 2003), while others have seen the roots of such "interventionism" in MERCOSUR's legal tradition, namely, Continental law, and have exemplified this deep and detailed regulation policy preference with the case of dairy (Duina 2006).

Even at the beginning, total liberalization of agricultural trade elicited much tension. There were many formal consultations among members and it is not surprising at all that most of them were in the agri-food sector (39 percent). As trade among members declined in the following years, the strategy of total harmonization was under pressure to be sharply changed.

---

[6] Before getting into the nitty-gritty of MERCOSUR SPS dynamics, it must be noted that at least three of its members, Argentina, Brazil, and Uruguay, have pretty good sanitary services, as they are very efficient global agri-food exporters. Thus, these countries are usually reluctant to set apart their national practices and standards.

[7] This is part of a general trend in MERCOSUR. Indeed, The TIR foresees the creation of a common market, establishing to that end that members should achieve free circulation of goods, services, and productive factors. Free circulation of goods, a central pillar of the economic integration process, would be achieved by the elimination both of tariff and non-tariff barriers or equivalent restrictions.

In addition to market dynamics, the MERCOSUR SPS policy of full har-monization was revised because of the technical complexity of carrying it forward. A kind of "by default" strategy replaced the ambitious aspiration of total harmonization: countries would only harmonize those regulations strictly necessary to facilitate intra-bloc trade. The harmonization need may arise from the volume of trade at stake or due to particular difficulties and, therefore, there is no more ex-ante harmonization but ex-post, ad-hoc har-monization linked to export prospects or concrete operations. This move is of course functional to the reluctant position of MERCOSUR member coun-tries on harmonizing norms, as they consider current practices and stand-ards to be sufficient and successful.

The upshot of the dynamics and forces at work in the public policy domain is a very narrow SPS harmonization process at the regional level: just what is needed to keep intra MERCOSUR trade flowing. In this light, it could be fair to say that MERCOSUR SPS policy is still essentially defined at the national level, as domestic standards and practices are brought and power-fully defended by national officers in MERCOSUR meetings. With respect to Bruszt-McDermott's analytical framework, it thus seems that the MERCOSUR story of standard harmonization in the SPS field is one of severe restrictions, if not outright blockage, as it has more to do with national influence and con-trol over the trade integration agreement. The MERCOSUR was less and less a distinct institutional entity, acting as a supranational platform helping or inducing to craft shared national standards and practices or even providing a space for mutual policy learning in and across member countries.

At the same time that substantive harmonization is minor, there is no com-mon or unified control or information system with respect to SPS measures. The MERCOSUR has not developed any kind of regional animal and plant health surveillance system or a harmonized or equivalent food control system among their members (a kind of a regional unit of risk analysis). In addition, the MERCOSUR does not have specific norms for the HACCP system and, fur-thermore, MERCOSUR countries differ in their implementation of the HACCP (Codex Alimentarius 1985). Finally, the same can be said for sanitary services auditing proceedings at MERCOSUR level. Although there is a proposal for a Guide of Auditing Proceedings to be used as a model by animal and plant health and food safety services, it has not been adopted by MERCOSUR members.[8] This

---

[8] Proyecto UE-MERCOSUR de cooperación para la armonización de normas y procedimientos veterinarios y fitosanitarios, inocuidad de alimentos y producción agropecuario diferenciada. This is an extensive two-year project that has worked on MERCOSUR SPS issues. In this para-graph in particular, we benefited from three Project reports: one on HACCP, another on com-mon auditing procedures mechanisms, and the other on common surveillance systems. In turn, this chapter'sr authors have worked on four reports: Monitoring, Transparency, Institutional Dynamics Practical Guide, Negotiation and Coordination of National Positions.

lack of monitoring capacities impairs gathering information on the impact of the TIR on their members, while weak transparency and information availability constrain informed decisions. Thus, although there are three organs entitled to create norms through binding decisions (CMC, GMC, and MTC), most norms come from the work in the technical bodies.

Do the severe limitations of MERCOSUR as the sphere for coordinating SPS regulations mean that no other sources push for the generation of cross-border rules and standards? The answer is no, in that various venues of regional standard-making exist in the SPS field, even at an incipient or experimental stage. Exploration of these venues allows one to consider how they may contribute to the process of building a regional standards regime in that policy domain.

9.3 The Multiple Paths to SPS Regulation in MERCOSUR: Public Policies and Private Standards at Work in a Multi-Level Game of Rule Setting

9.3.1 *Top-Down Incentives and Pressures*

SPS regional (public) standards have many sources. Since this chapter looks through a regional lens, some regional norms appear similar, even identical to national standards, others incorporate internationally adopted standards, and still others reflect harmonization performed to fix intra-bloc trade problems.

As discussed in the previous section, the MERCOSUR in its actual institutional shape is not the locus of SPS norm creation or deep revamping. At best, it has moved away from processes of harmonization and toward adjudicating SPS controls and facilitating trade. For instance, in the cases of apples and pears, to be further examined shortly, early in MERCOSUR there were negotiated quality norms for apples (GMC Resolution 117/96) and pears (GMC Resolution 118/96) for intra MERCOSUR trade. This reflects the first MERCOSUR policy towards its institutional role and standing on SPS matters: harmonization of both safety and quality standards. Then, when MERCOSUR had already shifted to the problem-solving policy, the issue of Carbocapsa (a plague affecting both apples and pears) took shape, and there was a negotiation in the MERCOSUR sphere, since Brazil is one of Argentina's main destination markets. According to an agreement between Brazil and Argentina, Brazil has sent inspectors to the production site (origin) instead of controlling at the frontier. This agreement worked until the end of 2010, when it had to be renegotiated since Brazil refused to send inspectors due to the costs. Finally, and more recently, there was the issue of apples and pears (among others) being hostages of bilateral trade problems between Argentina and Brazil. As a response to license requirements Argentina imposed on several Brazilian products, Brazil issued "Instrucción Normativa 12" in June 2012, according to which, due to phytosanitary concerns, apples and pears (among other items) would need previous authorization to enter Brazil. The blockage of apples was really damaging to Argentina since Brazil accounts for almost 25 percent of Argentine production, representing around $63 million. After further negotiations, the Brazilian market was reopened in July 2012.

This example points to a first, regional-level, market-driven stimulus for some sort of coordination of standard-setting, namely, the "mercosurization" of Brazil's norms or, even better, the "Brazilianization" of MERCOSUR SPS regulations. Indeed, as the SPS harmonization process is limited, amounting to just what is needed to keep intra MERCOSUR trade flowing, and as Brazil exerts increasing market power in intra-bloc trade, this country acts as a dominant importer and attempts to use its local legislation as regional legislation. In turn, the situation in MERCOSUR is basically one in which the most dynamic source of standards creation is not harmonization policy or sanitary crisis, but market circumstances: public and private requirements at export destinations. Under such conditions, as intra-bloc trade is directed mainly to Brazil, the MERCOSUR's main activity is largely devoted to making national legislation compatible with Brazil's.

A second source of "top-down" regulatory coordination emerges from the issue of "rules, principles or SPS disciplines." There is increasing influence at the national level of international standard bodies such as the OIE and the Codex Alimentarius as well as of private standards. In the case of SPS disciplines, the WTO stands out as a decisive, almost unique actor. A few years after the creation of the MERCOSUR, in 1995, the WTO (and the SPS agreement) took stage. The MERCOSUR was registered at the WTO as a regional agreement under Article XXIV of the GATT (custom union) and thus it is not a WTO member. All MERCOSUR members are individually WTO members, and so they have also signed individually the SPS agreement. However, MERCOSUR has made the SPS agreement a MERCOSUR norm (i.e. Decision CMC 6/96).

Adopting the WTO SPS agreement effectively challenged the regional project in so far as it provided a set of more articulated and deeper rules than those available at the regional level, as well as a forum to debate, negotiate, and eventually solve conflicts on SPS matters. In effect, when the SPS agreement came into force (1995), MERCOSUR did not have a SPS norm covering principles that the SPS agreement does. It is true that it had Decision 6/93, but this just replicated the SPS draft agreement (as it was in 1993!). Later on, in 1996, MERCOSUR adopted (through CMC Decision 6/96 that replaced

Decision 6/93) the WTO SPS agreement as a MERCOSUR norm. Since the SPS agreement is in force, dialogue over a lot of SPS issues has moved to the multilateral forum, and many conflicts have been brought to the WTO dispute settlement system. Moreover, the SPS agreement works as the "floor"—the minimum regulatory matrix every WTO member must have and respect. In turn, current SPS negotiations at bilateral or regional levels are viewed as WTO plus or WTO compatible or WTO standards, etc. Thus, the SPS agreement has given MERCOSUR a common and shared legal framework, has opened a new instance for debating and negotiating SPS issues, and has offered a dispute settlement forum.

The WTO SPS agreement also could induce the MERCOSUR to coordinate more its policies and procedures. Beyond the obvious case of negotiations (MERCOSUR coordinates its negotiating position at the WTO in almost all areas), a good example comes from an SPS agreement pillar—the transparency principle. According to the transparency principle, WTO members must notify, as early as possible, SPS draft measures if they differ from international standards and affect a considerable portion of trade.[9] The idea is that early notification would allow other members to comment on it and eventually call for modifications if the norm unjustifiably obstructs trade. This obligation does not distinguish norm's origins: it makes no difference if the norm has been created at the regional or domestic level (i.e. if Argentina applies a norm, Argentina has the obligation to notify it whether it is a MERCOSUR norm that has been internalized or whether it is a local norm that never went through the MERCOSUR legislative process).

However, the MERCOSUR does not have a particular system or process to jointly or in a coordinated way notify regional (SPS) norms. Thus, each member notifies MERCOSUR SPS norms. The upshot is that each country has notified different norms at different stages, according to their own interpretation of norms and procedures. In effect, some countries have notified norms once they are created at the regional level by the CMG while others have notified them once they are internalized. In addition, members have not notified the same norms. There is not one norm out of all notified norms by MERCOSUR members to the WTO notified by all four members. According to notifications to the WTO in the period 1995–2009, Argentina has notified 126 measures, Brazil 538, Paraguay 22, and Uruguay 13 (Lengyel et al. 2010).

Incredibly enough, although the SPS agreement is the axis of MERCOSUR SPS legislation (in terms of principles), WTO issues are not widely managed by SPS national officers (with the exception of international units within

---

[9] International standards are those made by the World Organization of Animal Health (OIE), Codex Alimentarious, and the Secretariat of the International Plant Protection Convention (IPPC).

ministries). This is so because the WTO does not impose standards as the Codex, the OIE, and the IPCC do and so veterinarians, for instance, rarely know or read the SPS agreement before or during regulation drafting. But they know very well the MERCOSUR as well as these so-called "three sisters."

The "three sisters" are quite a powerful additional source of MERCOSUR shared standards as well as for MERCOSUR members' standards, as cogently pointed out by some authors (Leavy and Saenz 2010). For instance, the Animal Health Technical Committee works in permanent contact with the World Organization of Animal Health (OIE), as the Committee limits itself to establish OIE standards. In effect, norm production at the Animal Health Committee has developed towards unifying standards for intra-bloc trade and imports from third parties using OIE standards. However, as not all countries have the same sanitary status, it is not always possible to refer to the OIE standards. In this sense, when the OIE standard would impede intra MERCOSUR trade, MERCOSUR members at the MERCOSUR level create the same norm but with an "escape clause" by which countries may allow imports to proceed even if they do not meet OIE standards.

But the public sector is not the only one pressed to adopt the standards of international organizations. The private sector in developing countries is heavily influenced, if not determined, by IO standards if it wants to get into export markets. Actually, there is at present such a web of standards that countries and firms usually have more than one strategy to deal with them (other than just complying with them). For example, in the case of olive oil, the parameters for a product to be considered as olive oil are set up at the COI, the International Olive Oil Council, mostly reflecting Spanish and Italian production parameters. While Argentina, working closely with the private sector, decided to try to modify those standards from inside by becoming a member of the COI in 2009, Australia decided to try to modify them at the Codex.[10]

Against this backdrop of few and broad shared norms combined with a reactive policy, private standards did develop in the MERCOSUR geographical ambit, of course, not as result of a regional policy but because of the lack thereof. Even if private standards extended throughout the MERCOSUR, they did not receive a regional coordinated common policy response. There is no record of formally discussing private standards in MERCOSUR organs as a specific MERCOSUR policy. However, MERCOSUR negotiators hotly debated the issue of private standards when they faced Europeans in the EU–MERCOSUR negotiations. Also, MERCOSUR delegates to the SPS Committee

---

[10] COI is an intergovernmental organization bringing together olive oil producers. For more on the olive oil Argentine strategy, see Delich 2012.

at the WTO coordinated their views around private standards to discuss the issue at Geneva.

The first wave of private standards in the agri-food chain in MERCOSUR occurred during the 1990s as trade liberalization and deregulation policies consolidated in the region, MNCs brought their own standards into the region, and supermarkets elevated their criteria. Some authors have suggested that it was the lack of regional policy (or "disharmony") in this domain that may have spurred private standards (Farina and Reardon 2000). In a context of liberalization of markets and increasing competition "firms and associations had strong incentives to create and enforce standards and communicate them to consumers via labels and certification in order to capture rents from quality and safety and product differentiation" (Farina and Reardon 2000: 7). In other cases, Farina assesses the existence of regional standards which were too low to allow product differentiation: she identified nine Brazilian agribusiness systems, including seven commodity systems, such as corn and soybeans, where this situation occurred, even after a decade of deregulation (Farina et al. 1999, cited in Farina and Reardon 2000).

9.3.2 *How do Private Standards Interact with Public Standards and Policies in the MERCOSUR Today?*

Over the past 15 years, there has been a strong growth in the power and number of private voluntary standards (PVS) affecting agri-food trade, particularly from developed country markets. Examples of company PVSs are Tesco Nature's Choice and Carrefour Filiere Qualité; those from national collective systems are the British Retail Consortium Global Standard, the Label Rouge, and the Food and Drink Federation, and those from international collective systems are the EuropGAP, ISO 22000, and ISO 22005 (WTO 2007). Harmonization within a sector (along the production chain) and merging between voluntary private and public norms tends to occur whenever the former becomes widely accepted and required for market access (WTO 2007). According to a WTO Survey, governments have two concerns associated with private norms: its content in terms of (lack of) scientific justification and the (in)capacity of developing countries to comply with them (WTO 2007). In Argentina, while some producers and firms point to the benefits of private standards in terms of market access, improved production or firm management, new and more awareness on the environment, product differentiation, and better prices and traceability, others emphasize their increasing costs and requirements, lack of harmonization of different standards, lack of resources to carry standards forward, and sometimes no differentiation of the product (Alonso and Idigoras 2011). The most affected products worldwide are fresh fruits, vegetables, and meat, while the most influential markets are those of Australia, Canada, the European Union, United States, and Japan (WTO, G/SPS/GEN/932). As seen from the standpoint of Argentina's export basket, development of the EU's private standards affects products such as fruits, soy, oils, and meat, while the United States has impact on products like pears, concentrated apple juice, and lemons.

Policy responses in Argentina to the growth and consolidation of private standards have not been homogeneous: while the government has not implemented so far an across-the-board policy related to private standards at the domestic level, it sometimes has accompanied the development of private standards by incorporating them in some circumstances or products (e.g. HACCP is still voluntary within the domestic market but is mandatory for meat exporters). In other cases, it has created specific programs to work with the private sector in the development of new varieties to gain quality and institutional "networking" to improve access to knowledge resources for key stakeholders (for instance, the Fundación Pro Arroz program). The private sector's response to the increasing number and importance of private standards and certification is heterogeneous as well, depending on the structure of the sector and the size, innovation culture, or capacity of the firms.

The next subsection will explore selected products in more detail to shed light on the relationship between private and public standards and the public action. It will do so by considering two cases, namely, fresh fruit and rice, which provide insights on different export performances with differing institutional and policy dynamics underlying them. How did Argentina lose its competitive position in the world market for fresh apples? Why have pears, which are produced in the same region as apples and sometimes by the same producers, improved their value in international markets? How has rice production in the province of Entre Rios moved in 10 years from a low-quality, commodity-oriented, inward-looking pattern into a high-quality, increasingly sophisticated market-niche, export-oriented strategy?

9.3.3 Bottom-up Experiences: Fresh Fruits and Rice Production

State intervention is usually high in the fresh fruit sector: sanitary certifications, quality standards, pest control, import restrictions, international negotiations for market access, and development of a country trademark, among others. In addition, research on innovation and new varieties as well as productive technology is usually led by public sector institutions (de Tappatá 2003).

Argentina's state actions cover all these areas. However, its actions to deal with quality standards across fresh fruit products are limited, mostly devoted to combating pests, and poorly articulated with other state interventions as well as with private sector initiatives. In addition, policy-making is at best ambiguous in respect to private standards since there are arguments against intervention on grounds that state promotion or adoption of current PVS would validate them without scientific justification, just for the sake of attaining richer consumption niches. At the same time, there are some private coordinated (re)actions—as shown by producers participating in the Southern Hemisphere Association of Fresh Fruit Exporters—that have reacted to the overproduction of standards by the EU.

To make things more complex, as the number of private standards increase, there is no clear hierarchy between them and the public ones. Also, firm choices vary across the broad gamut of available options of private standards. For instance, one of the most used standards is Global Gap (which emerged from EUREPGAP). However, some firms use Tesco´s Nature's Choice (for primary production), British Retail Consortium (BRC) and HACCP for the fruit packing process, and ISO 22.000 and 14.000 (Management Systems of Food Security and Environment). When it comes to Corporate Social Responsibility (CSR) firms use Fair Trade and SEDEX (in the latter the auditor does not certify but his report goes to the SEDEX in England to be consulted by SEDEX clients).

In this complex and dynamic setting of private standards, Argentine producers agree that there is a lack of harmonization and that initiatives to address it, such as agricultural good practices handbooks, usually provide minimum standards that are not enough to export. In addition, there are private standards that the state often has to promote, such as with the management of pesticides. Finally, producers and firms are concerned about the increasing demands of private standards that include as well issues of environmental hazards and corporate social responsibility. These are perceived as entry barriers, stronger than any safety protocol (Alonso and Idigoras 2011).

Apples and pears are, together with lemons, products with the greatest economic relevance within the fresh fruit sector in Argentina. While apples and pears are produced in the south of Argentina (through 3,000 producers, 300 packaging companies, 250 cold storage firms), lemons are produced mostly in a tiny province, Tucuman, in the northwest part of Argentina, through a highly integrated and concentrated type of production. Argentina is by now the second pear exporter; it is also rapidly gaining positions in lemons; while in apples it has fallen from the second to the ninth world position over the last two decades.

Their differing production and trade performances can be attributed to their different value chain configurations, as well as to Argentina's macroeconomic conditions. However, it could also be explored from the standpoint of what makes those products competitive: since Argentina is a price taker in all the three products—apples, pears, and lemons—their quality makes them attractive/decisive for importers. In turn, quality is increasingly related to a fruit's variety, which brings to the surface the issue of variety innovation and of novel legal and business models of marketing.

In terms of SPS standards, safety ones (for human, plant, or animal health) refer to diseases/pests affecting the fruit and the minimum level of pesticide residues permitted, while quality standards relate to the appearance, firmness, color, size, and taste. Some of the quality standards within the control of the producer, and many of them are attached to the kind of variety produced. In order to distinguish, create, produce, and sell a new variety successfully today, firms must spend significant time and resources in research and innovation. They also need a competent public institutional setting to intervene in the international rule/regulatory making game and to network domestically with the private sector, both to set up safety and quality improvement programs and to push forward marketing strategies.

The "variety strategy" to penetrate markets was started some 15 years ago by fresh fruit exporters with higher labor costs. It was a way to improve their competitiveness and value-added through a varietal differentiation. Differentiating varieties requires time, labor, and knowledge, if done "naturally or in the traditional way," and it also demands research infrastructure and investment if done through genetic modification. This kind of strategy would require some kind of appropriation of the innovation to recover investments made and measures to administer supply and introduce and place firmly the new variety in the market.

In the case of apples, a highly successful export 10 years ago, the policy of SENASA, the Argentine food safety regulatory agency, focused only on safety aspects (basically to fight *carpocapsa* because it impeded trade with Brazil), but there were no public or public-private initiatives to deal with quality issues or variety renewal (using financial mechanisms). So SENASA fought to ensure apple and pear safety regarding *carpocapsa,* but no state agency helped to finance or promote strategies to deal with the quality of apples or pears. Because pear plantations are younger (less than 20 years old) and the "variety strategy" attempted by some countries has not been successful in the global market, the old classic varieties of pears continue to be successful. We now examine in greater detail the ongoing complex dynamics between production patterns and regulation/standard setting.

There are six important apple producers in the world: Chile, Brazil, Argentina, Australia, South Africa, and New Zealand. These harvest 4.8 million tons per year. Argentina shares today 20 percent of the total production but it used to be 37 percent two decades ago.[11] Furthermore, 50 percent of apples go to the concentrated juice industry, 21 percent to export, and

---

[11] <http://www1.rionegro.com.ar/diario/rural/2010/01/30/22322.php>.

29 percent to the domestic market. Apples sold to the juice industry do not meet quality standards to be sold fresh, and thus have low value. The main export destinations of Argentina's apples are Brazil, Russia, the EU, and the US. But the EU absorbs 46 percent of fresh apples, while 95 percent of concentrated juice goes to the United States. Argentina is right now redirecting exports of fresh fruit to Brazil and Russia and leaving the EU, where the quality required is higher. According to the 2008/2009 harvest, Chile is the first producer in South America with 1.3 million tons a year, followed by Brazil with 1.1 million and Argentina with 940,000 tons. In terms of the amount of discarded production, Argentina leads by far, with 50 percent going to the concentrated juice industry.

As mentioned, there are two problems with apples and pears—*carpocapsa* and variety renewal. Regarding the former, in the Patagonia region, annual losses caused by that pest for pears and apples had been estimated in $19 million in 2004. According to a report, the adoption of pest control practices more friendly to health and the environment by producers in Argentina was very low. Out of six good practices assessed at the National Agriculture Census in 2002, only one had a high frequency (pest monitoring, 40 percent of registered farms) and the key factor explaining the adoption or not of pest control techniques was the producer's socio-economic level. As an example, the same report cites the case of fresh fruits in Alto Valle, Rio Negro, particularly in apples and pears, where they found a clear division between producers who had adopted proper practices and small- and medium-sized producers who had not invested in new technology (in part because they are "just survivors" of the Argentine crisis of 2001/2 (Huerga and San Juan 2004).

In this context, SENASA started the National Program on Vegetal Health (Programa Nacional de Sanidad Vegetal, PROSAVE) in 2004 to deal with fruit sanitary aspects. Three priority issues were defined: fruit flies, *carpocapsa*, and citrus cankres. The general objective of the *carpocapsa* program was to eliminate the plague, achieving a less than 0.1 percent incidence, and to change the way of fighting it: from chemical control to the pheromone confusion technique (PCT), combined with chemical, cultural, and legal control.

At the national level, SENASA was the program's executing agency. FunBaPa[12] was in charge of implementing the program at a local level (and is in charge of control and assistance post-program actions). Financing came from the IDB and from public national and provincial sources as well as from fees charged to producers. The program's actions started in 2006. Producers interested in participating had to coordinate and cooperate with each other

[12] FUNBAPA is the acronym for Fundación Barrera Zoofitosanitaria Patagónica (Patagonic Zoo-sanitary Barrier Foundation). FUNBAPA is an NGO created in 1992 that works with the public and private sector (formed by SENASA, producers' associations, and provincial authorities).

in order to achieve a territory large enough to work over (named "blocks") and had to present detailed information on the sanitary characteristics of their orchard as well as the following three-year actions. Priority was given to those producers that had already adopted PCT and to zones considered "red". From 2006 to 2008–9, the cost involved amounted to 58.3 million ARS, of which, without considering producers' fees, 58 percent was funded by the IDB, 30 percent by provincial funds, and 12 percent by federal funds. In terms of the program's results, the average damage level in 2008–9 was 0.5 percent, much lower than 2000 when it was evaluated at 6.1 percent (Villarreal 2009, cited in FunBaPa 2010). Moreover, in the 2009 season there were included around 12,000 ha in the PCT, seeking to include almost 100 percent of the productive territory in the program. Monitoring reports of "blocks" with a three-year application of the program have reported damage in values around 0.2 percent. One way of measuring the benefits is considering that, without implementing the program, the sector would have lost 49.5 million ARS every season as a result of the price difference between the juice industry and the cost incurred in the production, packaging, and conservation of pears and apples with *carpocapsa*. In addition, one of the findings for the three-year report by FunBaPa is that the implementation of the program meant an increase of income as a consequence of redirection of fresh fruit from industry to the fresh market in around 109 million ARS (U$S 33.680.613) (FunBaPa 2010).

However, apples had at least two problems in keeping up in the global market: safety issues (*carpocapsa*) and quality issues (varieties). With respect to varieties, Argentina was slow to react, as competing markets like South Africa and New Zealand started programs of genetic improvement while restricting the use of some varieties in order to stimulate diversification. Several countries imitated New Zealand's experience of differentiating instead of homogenizing varieties, adding to this strategy the formation of exclusive alliances with distributors. In this way, they coordinate and limit the supply of some varieties (such as Pink Lady or Cameo). The key factor allowing this strategic move has been the development and institutionalization of collaboration along the production chain, allowing –(as in New Zealand) all main aspects concerning production, harvesting, and marketing to be coordinated through Government Regulatory Committees (Preiss and Diaz 2003).

Argentine apples also face challenges related to new levels of exigencies in terms of residue levels and quality from the European Union and the United States; a high percentage of areas with old plants; apple varieties less demanded; a low degree of cooperation and vertical integration. Even if reduced to very niche markets, varieties protected by different forms of intellectual property (patents and trademarks) and administered (in certification and trading terms) by clubs are gaining in importance. The case of Pink Lady in apples is one of those cases. According to the Pink Lady Alliance web page,

> The Pink Lady trademark is one of the great success stories of the fruit industry—now used under license across four continents on a range of food products. The Pink Lady® trademark was originally established for use on apples of the Cripps Pink variety that met specified quality standards. This created a mechanism for growers worldwide to sell premium quality apples from the variety Cripps Pink at a premium price. The Cripps Pink apple variety was developed by plant breeder John Cripps at Manjimup in Western Australia as part of a breeding program administered by the Department of Agriculture Western Australia. In countries where the trademark is registered, apples sold under the Pink Lady brand must meet rigorous and specific standards. The Pink Lady trademark can only be used under license whose holders pay royalties which cover management of the trademark—including auditing of fruit quality, branding, brand promotion and protecting the trade mark against illegal use.[13]

Thus, Argentina led apple production and exports in the 1980s in South America, then consistently lost market share due to increasing costs, lack of state coordinated actions to promote exports, quality decline, and exchange rate overvaluation during the 1990s. By the beginning of the 2000s, new varieties and business models took off at the global level, but Argentina's most articulated policy focused only on apple safety conditions, while the MERCOSUR institutions were only used to guarantee Brazilian imports. As some authors have rightly pointed out, "Countries that have generated competitive capacities in apples, and specially New Zealand, show that those firms, sector, regions or nations that can learn faster and better become competitive because their knowledge is scarce and cannot be easily replicated or transferred through formal channels to other firms, regions or competitors. Thus, actually, the more general and deep way to assess the logic of the most advanced forms of economic competition is learning" (Preiss and Diaz 2003).

The situations of apples and pears differ, although they share the same productive territory, the same diseases/pests, and the same export destinations. However, on the one side pears producers do have younger plantations (less than 20 years) and on the other side new varieties developed abroad have not rooted in the global market. In turn, Argentine producers do produce Williams, still highly required, and of an excellent quality. Thus, pear production and exports instead of declining have been increasing.

Pear production has been increasing since 2000 mostly due to new plantations and technological innovations. Right now, Argentina is the fifth pear producer and first pear exporter in the world, basically Williams

---

[13] <http://www.pinkladyapples.com/about/about.html>.

and Packham Triumph varieties that enter the European Union. In South America, Argentina is the first producer and exporter, with the main export markets of Brazil, the European Union, and Russia.

As in the case of apples, some world pear producers have higher labor costs when compared to Argentina or Chile (such as the United States and the European Union). Their strategy has been to reinforce the mechanical dimension of the production process to lower costs. And even though there are many programs developing pear varieties, and some new varieties have been tested in the market, they have not been accepted by consumers. In addition, some countries, particularly in Europe, are using differentiation strategies via geographical indications, such as "Rincon de Soto" in Spain. But the bulk of the pear trade is still in traditional varieties.

In contrast to apple and pear production, lemon production in Argentina involves a set of highly concentrated and integrated large firms that produce, pack, industrialize, and export from the province Tucuman. Lemons are basically a product for export, both in fresh and processed forms (concentrated juice, essential oils), since local demand is not significant. In the beginning of the 1970s there were around 6,800 ha sowed that included around 1,000 producing units. By the beginning of the 1990s, there were 16,000 ha sowed involving 593 productive units. In 1995 there were around 23,300 ha sowed with 515 productive units and in 2002 there were only 362 productive units. Increased ha sowed came with increased productivity due to the new technological packages: while at the beginning of the 1990s each sowed ha produced 24 tons, by 1999 it produced 50 tons. But technology is very expensive and so only affordable by large producers and firms (Rivas and Zamora 2010).

The process of land concentration and the disappearance of small producers in Tucuman is notorious today. The increase of the efficient production unit to at least 50 ha has eliminated small producers (less than 10 ha size), while medium (50 to 300 ha) and large producers (more than 300 ha) concentrate more than 90 percent of the production. In terms of firms, the degree of concentration is very high: only four producing firms account for 50 percent of the sowed area (MECON 2010). Some consider the case of Tucuman as one of non-traditional production, with expulsion of small farmers caused by higher production costs and differential access to technology (Rivas and Zamora 2010).

Today, Argentina produces around one million tons a year, mainly of the Genova and Eureka varieties. Taking the world production (around 6 million tons), Argentina's share is 20 percent and ranks sixth after large producers such as China, Brazil, US, Mexico, Spain, and Italy. In terms of exports, Argentina's share of world markets is 17.62 percent (FEDERCITRUS 2011). In the past couple of years, a relatively high proportion of lemons were directed to the industry by an industry decision to export only fresh lemons meeting the highest quality standards, thus restricting the export supply and preventing a steep decrease in international prices (USDA 2011). So, the lemon industry's path of expansion has had various steps and periods that basically involved, first, a deep process of vertical integration, then a process of capital concentration in primary production, and finally an association between importers and wide-scale distributors of fresh fruits in destination markets.

This organization of production only partially accounts for the successful "lemon case." Key factors also are that Tucuman is free of citrus cankres, it has been able to implement a trusted Certificate of Origin, and the private sector has successfully coordinated to create its own quality seal. In public policy language, we could call this public action: the National Program for the Citrus Health promoted by SENASA; the Program of National Certification of Citrus from INASE, the Program of Provincial Agricultural Services, the Program of Fresh Fruit Certification for Export to the EU (citrus cankres and black spot), and the Export Program to Russia to address new exigencies regarding Maximum Limits of Residues.

Second, there is also public-private coordination, such as in the case of the citrus cankres. AFINOA (a Northwest Phytosanitary Association) is the agency in charge of controlling the sanitary barrier. And even if private firms do R&D, they receive important support from EEAOC (Estación Agroambiental Obispo Colombres) and INTA Faimalla (both public entities) and from FEDECITRUS (private sector association) at the national level.

Finally, there is also private cooperation as shown by the work of the Tucumán Association of Citrus (Asociación Tucumana de Citricos, ATC) which links citrus producers and industries in order to gain international markets. The quality seal AllLemons was created three years ago by the largest 11 lemon-exporting firms (accounting for 80 percent of the Argentinean sales abroad). AllLemons was created to promote compliance with international standards and has a quality protocol specially designed by public and private experts. The main lemon qualities certified are: high content of juice, firmness, freshness, traceability, balanced color, skin's optimal conditions, and uniform format.

To be sure, there is a myriad of SPS public policies, in a wide sense, involving critical dimensions of lemon production and export. But above all, there is a great degree of cooperation, learning, and coordination among actors, for sure eased by the fact of being a highly integrated and concentrated value chain. But the point is that SPS issues are understood in a broad sense, including safety, quality, legal, and even marketing dimensions. Some SPS policies are purely implemented by the state while others require cooperation and coordination with the private sector (like maintaining the status of free of citrus cankres). There are coordinated private and public-private actions dealing with export markets requirements in terms of quality, product origin, and sanitary conditions.

Our working hypothesis is that, even if the level of concentration between lemons and apples differs and could be used to explain differing production and trade performances, it is their differing public private institutional setting and dynamics which is key to identify export failures and successes. These differences become essential when comparing the fresh fruits to the case of rice.

During the 1990s, Argentine rice production went from hope to despair in a few years. It temporarily boomed in the first half of the decade, largely driven by exports to Brazil within the total agricultural liberalization framework of the newly born MERCOSUR. This phase of fast growth vanished, however, in the second part of the decade: within the context of a fixed exchange rate regime with a grossly overvalued local currency, small producers found it more and more difficult to maintain external markets (and there was a low level of rice consumption in the country), while larger national and foreign producers chose a specialization strategy combining export of paddy rice with the import of parbolized rice. The situation became even stiffer by the end of the decade as a result first of the 1997 Asian crisis and then of Brazil's devaluation of its currency in 1999. In this context, the situation became much tougher for small producers in the domestic market as well, as they had to face greater competition from the bigger players. These market movements were particularly distressing for small and medium producers since the prevailing local production pattern was based on low-quality, low-resistance commodity rice and thus heavily dependent on price competition.

In the particular case of the Entre Rios province, one of the largest rice producers in the country, production, land sowed, and employment had sharply fallen by the year 2000 compared to the levels of the mid-1990s, and operations were plagued by high levels of idle capacity. Profits, of course, sank dramatically. However, 10 years later, the situation turned around, as shown by some figures and developments. At the macro level, in the 1989/90 and 1990/1 campaigns 16 varieties of low-quality rice were sowed in Entre Rios for a total output of 350,000 tons per paddy, with average yields of 4,500 kg/ha, which made it impossible for the local industrial sector to provide good quality products both for the domestic and external markets. In 2011, however, the province had become the first high-quality rice producer in Argentina, with a volume of 712,000 tons (41 percent of total national production, followed by the provinces of Corrientes, Santa Fé, Formosa, and Chaco), although it is the second after the province of Corrientes in sowed area. This means that it is also the most productive province with about 7.15 tons/ha vis-à-vis the 6.67 tons/ha of Corrientes. In addition, Entre Rios accounts for about 70 percent of the capacity for rice industrialization all over the country.

Between 2004 and 2011 three new varieties of rice seed were developed with stunning market success, using both traditional improvement methods as well as the latest technologies based on molecular biology (INTA 2011). In addition, improvements in the management of rice farming by a large number of producers through the diffusion of the latest methods and procedures—applied for instance, to fertilization and sowing—also contributed to the successful shifting gears and upgrading of Entre Rios's rice production model. This allowed local rice producers to almost double exports in the last five-year period and diversify target markets (Chile, Iraq, Senegal, Puerto Rico, Spain, and lately the Netherlands and China), reducing their "Brazil dependency." It also allowed a great expansion in the share of the new varieties (Camba INTA-Pro Arroz, Puita INTA CL, and lately Guri INTA CL) among the seed varieties being sown in Entre Rios (60 percent) and in Argentina's other rice-growing provinces, and to capture with one of them (Puita INTA CL) a big share of the sown field in Brazil in just a few years (from 0 percent in the 2007–8 campaign to 50 percent in the 2009–10 campaign).

The key factor explaining this impressive performance improvement was a shift of the Entre Rios production model (mostly small- and medium-sized firms) implemented from the late 1990s onwards. This involved moving away from the prevailing but declining commodity production model, heavily dependent on the Brazilian market, to a strategy based on high-quality, high-performance seed varieties to reach increasingly diversified market niches. Underpinning this shift was, in turn, continuous technological upgrading and innovation both in seed production and in farming management.

These developments in Entre Rios's rice production could not be understood, however, without the simultaneous development of an institutional exoskeleton in the province, Fundación Pro-Arroz (FPA), geared to promote rice, coordinate the rice production chain, and improve the value-added, quality, and efficiency of the local rice production. Created in 1994, FPA is a public-private organization whose institutional configuration has some traits worth noting: a highly inclusive, representative, and participatory decision-making system, that includes all components of production and ensures that all relevant stakeholders have a voice in the strategic decisions; consensus rule for decision-making; a network (led by INTA) of different but complementary capabilities to search for, develop, and diffuse new technological options and innovations; and—as a result of all the former—a two-tier, macro and micro systems of governance that nurture each other, generating a virtuous circle of institutional development concerning not only the organization's technical capacities but also its capacity to align the interests of all actors of the rice production chain, streamline incentives to mobilize those actors behind new productive options, and coordinate their contributions and actions to put them into practice.

227

The crucial contribution of FPA has been to help Entre Rios's small- and medium-sized rice producers[14] to effectively serve increasingly segmented, differentiated, and "democratized"—i.e. open to direct trade between small/medium-sized producers and end consumers—international markets. The crux of its work to that end consists in the very effective provision of public goods for inducing and enabling producers to continuously adopt improved seed varieties and upgrade farming management practices instead of traditional protection or market intervention measures. These public goods are tailored to address knowledge, resource, regulatory, or infrastructure bottlenecks or constraints that producers would find extremely difficult, if not impossible, to overcome by themselves, especially if working alone. The most relevant of these public goods are, on one hand, the technical expertise and systematic R&D efforts to "design" new rice seed varieties as production conditions (agronomic, technical) or market requirements (tastes, quality, health, ecological) shift; on the other, the search for new market opportunities and the generation of the required conditions to meet them (quality and phytosanitary standards, product specifications, and the like).[15]

More specifically with regards to SPS regulations, FPA's work concerns three fronts. At the level of rice production, FPA is concluding at present the elaboration of a good practice guide including criteria and guidelines (like MERCOSUR's "horizontal norms") mainly for the management of herbicides, the use of fertilizers, and soil analysis and treatment. These guidelines set standards well above those established in MERCOSUR GMC Resolutions concerning rice directly or indirectly. It is voluntary but it is intended to be a central component of a certification system in the near future. At the level of rice mills, FPA is accompanying with technical assistance the efforts firms are making to improve their production processes in order to certify quality through ISO norms. Finally, with regards to exports, FPA is supporting firms to increasingly differentiate their products on phytosanitary grounds, stressing in particular the low use of herbicides as a central distinguishing trait (from Brazilian production in particular); the promotion of production of organic rice varieties is also part of this differentiation strategy. An additional FPA contribution, on a destination market basis, is to support the

[14] According to the last census (2010) of rice producers in Entre Rios, 39 percent of them work on sew slots under 100 ha, 86 percent on slots of under 500 ha and only 11 percent on slots over 500 ha, revealing a stratification clearly skewed towards a small-, medium-size production unit structure. Almost the opposite is the case in the second largest rice province, Corrientes.

[15] Other important cases include the satellite geo-referencing of water wells to build the matrix for the electrification of rice irrigation in the whole province—a critical input to drastically reduce production costs; stockpile infrastructure as the growing number of rice varieties and types demands increasing capacity of seed selection and classification; and new human resource skills on rice sowing in order to meet the increasingly specialized knowledge this activity is demanding.

practice of some exporting firms of working together with potential or actual clients in the implementation of traceability schemes along the whole production chain.

Thus, it could be said that the MERCOSUR, in a way, is central to the rice story. It was the MERCOSUR agricultural liberalization (zero tariffs) that opened the Brazilian market to Argentina. And Argentina is still Brazil-dependent. As in the case of fresh fruits, the MERCOSUR brought about—in its beginnings—a technical norm on the identity and quality of rice.[16] However, by the end of the 1990s, MERCOSUR became the means to solve recurring trade tensions deriving from increasing Argentinean rice exports to Brazil (consultations at the Trade Commission and negotiations) instead of becoming a space or platform to discuss and plan medium-term safety/quality policies. The Argentine crisis of 2001–2 sank Argentina's production and trade across the board. For the last 10 years though, Argentina has not only reassumed rice production, but in the case of Entre Rios it has changed its production model. Brazil was Argentina's main destination market over that time and there weren't important market access or safety/quality issues, except price determinants.[17] But MERCOSUR, with its institutional proceedings, organs, or technical bodies, has not been the locus for such revamping. Interestingly enough, this public (led)-private quality upgrading strategy could be the way to successfully deal with the "Brazilian dependency," making possible the opening of other markets by offering more quality.

Therefore, this chapter does not claim that other important dimensions of the rice production, industrialization, and marketing are not determinants in successful economic performance (tax policy, energy costs/issues, more cooperation along the value chain, or infrastructure needs). What we suggest is that in the (successful) Entre Rios rice story competitive advantages were built upon knowledge, coordination, and cooperation among public-private actors and institutionalization of incentives (including a local tax for R&D on rice varieties). Cooperation in the setting of some key standards is also part of this story.

9.4 Final Reflections: Regional Regime Building and the Complex Web and Dynamics of SPS Standards

The MERCOSUR as an integration project is more than a free trade agreement or a customs union. It is a wider political project that is solidly rooted in the

---

[16] Res. 5/97, Reglamento tecnico MERCOSUR de identidad y de calidad del arroz beneficiado.

[17] Brazil, in turn, has also increased its production during recent years and is close to fulfiling the demands of its domestic market; in turn, it has launched some controversial measures, such as detailed border inspections of residue levels of imported products.

political discourse and our societies' visions. However, the regional setting is not the source of common and consistent regulatory regimes in key policy areas. The field of SPS policy is, as shown in this chapter, one such case: while MERCOSUR rules and principles have been defined at the WTO, standards are defined at the national level, largely driven by export market requirements, both public and private. In turn, the standards of international organizations (CODEX, OIE, and IPPC) are also becoming part of the regional *acquis* mostly through a top-down course of action (when for instance SENASA dictates a norm where the CODEX standard is applicable by default) or following a top-down channel through the WTO (the SPS committee) to MERCOSUR (as the SPS agreement). However, the MERCOSUR does provide an institutional platform for harmonization in cases of intra-bloc trade conflicts.

When compared with other TIRs, such as the European Union, the MERCOSUR is still in a nascent stage in terms of common constructions: it does not have institutional proceedings that are properly "mercosureñas," since all its more important and decisive organs are formed by governmental officers who take binding decisions by unanimous consensus (just to name one difference). What is most relevant to the discussion in this volume is that it also lacks the EU institutional architecture geared to get acquiescence from member countries (old and new) with common rules, as well as to help them to build the institutions and capacities to deal with the supranational regulatory wagon. In this sense, MERCOSUR has not built up regional instances to share information or coordinate activities such as surveillance, monitoring, auditing, or control of pests, diseases, food safety, etc.

When compared to NAFTA, the MERCOSUR distinguishes itself first and foremost by its membership: all MERCOSUR countries are developing countries. Given its size and trade relevance, does Brazil play in the MERCOSUR the role the United States does in NAFTA? No, it does not and it is dubious whether it will seek to play the role of a hegemon anytime soon. It is neither an international rule-maker nor an actor with strong sanctioning powers. Being an emerging power or a global player is not the same as being the hegemon.

However, Brazil is the main market within the MERCOSUR and, as an importing country, it pressures other members to use its SPS standards at the regional level. Since norms within the MERCOSUR institutional setting are adopted by unanimous consensus, there is a certain degree of negotiation (and concession) among members, including Brazil. In other words, within the market rationale that drives the MERCOSUR dynamics of SPS regional standard setting, there is no public stakeholder with the leverage of a hegemon. In addition to these traits, SPS in the MERCOSUR is a field in which public actors, and some private actors as well, have strong capacities. The existence of "common interest regulation" or "transnational regulatory capture"—two of the possible outcomes of regulative integration Bruszt and McDermott suggest—are situations in which the case of MERCOSUR does not comfortably fit.

From a more dynamic point of view, as the introduction of this volume suggests, consideration of recent experiences with private standards in Argentina brings about a more nuanced picture that places the MERCOSUR case of SPS closer to what has been labeled a "regime complexity space," with different lines of influence for standard setting coexisting most of the time uneasily; as a result, the MERCOSUR situation casts serious doubts on the feasibility/ convenience of building a unified regulatory apparatus at the regional level.

As shown in this chapter by the fresh fruit and rice cases, the private standard dynamic is characterized by a strong heterogeneity in terms of the initiatives, leading actors, and institutional arrangements involved. To be sure, the emergence, expansion, and strengthening of private SPS standards present public policy with the need to address them in order to avoid the marginalization of products from profitable markets. At the same time, the public response is neither obvious nor easy, especially if the goal is to meet the double benchmark of integration and development.

Traditional forms of SPS policy intervention, such as specific timely programs to fight disease/pests (e.g. the *carpocapsa* program in the apple sector) does not tackle the problem of developing new varieties, increasingly praised and valued in international markets. It thus fell short of bringing positive competitive and development pay-offs. On the other hand, more sophisticated and innovative policy initiatives, geared both to deal effectively with phytosanitary problems but also to initiate product upgrading and differentiation (such as the ones the public sector implemented in the lemon industry in collaboration with producer associations), cannot also avoid suboptimal development results if not framed within an "inclusive" (or "multiplex" in Bruszt and McDermott's formulation) approach. Finally, successful policy interventions deeply anchored in public-private cooperation, such as the rice case, seem to call for complex regulatory mechanisms and institutional coordination arrangements that buttress continuous improvement, whose construction cannot be taken for granted.

Our underlying assumption throughout the chapter has been that, even if the success/failure of some products performances could be explained by factors such as the level of coordination/concentration of the product chain, macroeconomic conditions, and so forth, differing production and trade performances could be appraised through their differing public-private institutional settings and dynamics. These differences become important when comparing some fresh fruit cases with the experience of rice, since in the latter it is noteworthy how public goods are tailored to address knowledge, resource, regulatory, or infrastructure bottlenecks or constraints that producers would find extremely difficult, if not impossible, to overcome by themselves.

It is reasonable to ask whether it would be the soundest strategy to give MERCOSUR (or any other integration agreement) the task of catching up with taken-as-given private developments and canvass them through harmonization. Rather, it could well be more productive to conceive the MERCOSUR as providing an experimental space to learn how to manage, and to somehow reduce, the diversity and duplicity of SPS standards (the Chile Gap initiative may provide clues to this end) as well as to strengthen capacities for product innovation where competitive advantages increasingly rest.

Part III
Fragmentation and Regime Complexity in TRRs

10

Assembling an Experimentalist Regime

Transnational Governance Interactions in the
Forest Sector Revisited

Christine Overdevest and Jonathan Zeitlin

10.1 Introduction

It is a commonplace of international relations theory that effective, integrated regulatory regimes cannot easily be constructed in issue areas characterized by divergent interests and beliefs among key actors, where there
is no hegemon with the power to impose a single set of rules (Keohane and
Victor 2011; Hasenclever et al. 2000).[1] The result in such conditions is typically regime complexity: a proliferation of regulatory schemes operating in
the same policy domain, supported by varying combinations of public and
private actors, including states, international organizations, businesses, and
NGOs. Where these parallel, overlapping, or competing initiatives are not
joined up into a coherent hierarchical system, the ensuing fragmentation
has often been held to undermine the effectiveness of transnational regulation (Raustiala and Victor 2004; Alter and Meunier 2009). Recently, however,
some scholars working in this area have identified the possibility of productive interactions emerging or being deliberately orchestrated among the
components of such transnational regime complexes (Keohane and Victor
2011; Abbott and Snidal 2009b, 2010; Alter and Meunier 2009). A special

[1] An earlier version of this chapter appeared as "Assembling an Experimentalist
Regime: Transnational Governance Interactions in the Forest Sector," *Regulation and Governance*,
8(1) (Mar. 2014): 22–48, first published online 29 Mar. 2012. We also draw on material from
Overdevest and Zeitlin (2013). Jonathan Zeitlin gratefully acknowledges the support of the EU
FP7 large-scale integrated research project GR:EEN—Global Re-ordering: Evolution through
European Networks, European Commission Project Number: 266809.

issue of *Regulation and Governance* on "Transnational Business Governance Interactions" takes such rethinking a step further by proposing a new conceptual framework for analyzing both positive and negative interactions between transnational business governance initiatives operating in the same economic sector or policy domain as the product of "a dynamic co-regulatory process involving actors with different stakes and competencies. . . who perform different regulatory functions" (Eberlein et al. 2014).

In this chapter, we build on such rethinking to outline a theoretically informed route to the stepwise construction of a joined-up transnational governance regime in hotly contested policy fields where no single actor can enforce a unilateral solution. We use the case of the European Union's Forest Law Enforcement Governance and Trade (FLEGT) initiative, interacting with private certification schemes and public legal timber regulations, including those of third countries such as the US and China, to illustrate how an increasingly comprehensive transnational regime can be assembled de facto if not de jure by linking together distinct components of a regime complex. We highlight the experimentalist features of the FLEGT initiative and its regulatory interactions, arguing that it is precisely these features, which accommodate local diversity and promote recursive learning from decentralized implementation experience, that make it possible to build up a flexible and adaptive transnational governance regime from an assemblage of interconnected pieces.

10.2 Complexity and Experimentalism in Transnational Regime Formation

10.2.1 *Regime Complexity*

Regime complexity may be defined as a situation in which there is no single, unified body of hierarchically imposed rules governing a transnational issue area or policy domain, but instead a set of parallel or overlapping regulatory institutions. In a recent survey, Alter and Meunier (2009) sketch out the possible consequences of such plural institutional arrangements for transnational governance. Like most previous commentators, they argue that regime complexity increases the likelihood of "cross-institutional political strategies," such as forum shopping, regime shifting, and strategic inconsistency. Faced with competing institutions and rules, actors will exploit regulatory diversity to pursue self-interested goals and particularistic advantages. In forum shopping, actors strategically select from among a set of institutional venues in hopes of obtaining a decision that will advance their own specific interests. In regime shifting, they try to move the regulatory agenda for a particular issue from one institution to another in order to reshape the global set of rules. In strategic inconsistency, actors intentionally create a contradictory rule or exploit contradictions between overlapping institutions in order to weaken the effect of existing disadvantageous rules. Alter and Meunier argue that regime complexity creates greater structural opportunities for these cross-institutional strategies and suggest further research to evaluate their frequency and impact.

Although Alter and Meunier (2009) focus primarily on the negative consequences of regime complexity, they also suggest that it may generate more positive interactions between parallel or overlapping institutions. Thus competition between regimes can promote productive experimentation by actors pursuing different approaches, reduce the risk of failure of any single institution, stimulate cross-fertilization and horizontal learning, and enhance accountability by creating new opportunities for dissatisfied parties to challenge existing rules. But Alter and Meunier do not specify under what conditions such competition can produce these positive effects, nor do they identify institutional strategies for promoting them.

Keohane and Victor (2011) elaborate further on the potential for regime complexity to generate positive interactions in transnational governance. In their view, "loosely coupled" regime complexes, or sets of interlinked institutions without an overall architecture, often emerge as a creative response to the failure of attempts to create a more comprehensive and integrated international regime. Where the interests and beliefs of key actors persistently diverge and there is no hegemonic power, a weak or non-existent international regime is the most likely result. Under these conditions, groups of actors may create narrower institutions in order to move parts of the regulatory field forward. These uncoordinated moves may actually produce a stronger de facto regulatory regime. For instance, regime fragmentation increases the probability that individual components of complex problems such as climate change can be tackled separately and solutions adapted to local or regional conditions and concerns. In this way, if the first-best world of a coherent, broadly agreed global regulatory regime proves politically unfeasible, there may be a second-best world in which a loosely coupled regime complex improves regulatory outcomes in comparison with the real alternative of a weak or non-existent overarching regime.

In a more radical departure from standard regime theory, Keohane and Victor go on to argue that such loosely coupled regime complexes may also be more flexible across issues and adaptable over time than a hierarchical system of rules imposed by a monopolistic international institution. Rather than representing a second-best alternative to a broadly agreed global regulatory regime, regime complexes may thus offer a superior starting point for building a joined-up, sustainable set of transnational governance institutions.

Keohane and Victor set out a number of criteria for evaluating actually existing regime complexes in terms of their coherence, accountability, determinacy, sustainability, epistemic quality, and fairness. But they do not provide a road map for the emergence of regime complexes with these beneficial features, nor do they identify a governance architecture within them for learning from local experimentation.

Recent work on transnational private, public-private, and multi-stakeholder regulation reaches similar conclusions. Thus Abbott and Snidal (2009a, 2009b) observe that the proliferation of Regulatory Standard Setting (RSS) schemes in fields like labor rights, human rights, and the environment can undermine the effectiveness of transnational governance by raising compliance costs for firms, creating opportunities for both firms and states to shop around for the weakest or most favorable standards, and confusing consumers and other public audiences. But they also argue that the multiplicity of competing RSS schemes has a number of salient virtues in comparison to "International Old Governance" (hierarchical regimes led by intergovernmental organizations or IGOs): facilitating adaptation of standards and procedures to local circumstances; promoting regulatory experimentation; and avoiding institutional capture, by obliging RSS schemes to compete with one another for legitimacy and public support (Abbott and Snidal 2009b). To retain the benefits of multiplicity within "Transnational New Governance" while minimizing the disadvantages of complexity, Abbott and Snidal recommend that states and IGOs should "orchestrate" RSSs by establishing substantive and procedural criteria for approved schemes, and publicizing the results to consumers and other audiences; providing material benefits to firms meeting the standards of approved schemes such as relaxed administrative requirements or preferential access to loans, grants, and contracts; and fostering collaboration and comparison among competing schemes to identify, diffuse, and scale up effective practices and approaches (Abbott and Snidal 2009b, 2010). Like Keohane and Victor, however, Abbott and Snidal do not delineate a governance architecture within which local experimentation and dispersed expertise can be systematically combined with coordinated learning and regime coherence.

10.2.2 Experimentalism

Experimentalism, we argue, provides just such a governance architecture. Defined in the most general terms, experimentalist governance is a recursive process of provisional goal-setting and revision based on learning from comparison of alternative approaches to their advancement in different contexts. Experimentalist governance in its most developed form involves a multi-level architecture, whose four elements are linked in an iterative cycle.

First, broad framework goals (such as "sustainable forests" or "legally harvested timber") and metrics for gauging their achievement are provisionally established by some combination of "central" and "local" units, in consultation with relevant stakeholders. Second, local units are given broad discretion to pursue these goals in their own way. These "local" units can be public, private, or hybrid partnerships. In regulatory systems, they will typically be private firms and the territorial authorities or branch organizations to which they immediately respond. But, third, as a condition of this autonomy, these units must report regularly on their performance and participate in a peer review in which their results are compared with those of others employing different means to the same ends. Where they are not making good progress against the agreed indicators, the local units are expected to show that they are taking appropriate corrective measures, informed by the experience of their peers. Fourth and finally, the goals, metrics, and decision-making procedures themselves are periodically revised by a widening circle of actors in response to the problems and possibilities revealed by the review process, and the cycle repeats (Sabel and Zeitlin 2012).

These four key elements should be understood as a set of necessary functions which can be performed through a variety of possible institutional arrangements. There is in such an experimentalist architecture no one-to-one mapping of governance functions to specific institutional mechanisms or policy instruments, and vice versa. A single function, such as monitoring and review of implementation experience, can be performed through a variety of institutional devices, operating singly or in combination. Conversely, a single institutional mechanism, such as a formal peer review, can perform a number of distinct governance functions, such as assessing the comparative effectiveness of different implementation approaches, holding local units accountable for their relative performance, identifying areas where new forms of national or transnational capacity building are required, and contributing to the redefinition of common policy objectives (Sabel and Zeitlin 2008). Experimentalist governance regimes, moreover, are often underpinned by "penalty default" mechanisms that induce reluctant parties to cooperate by threatening to impose sufficiently unattractive alternatives (Sabel and Zeitlin 2012; de Búrca et al. 2013).

Experimentalist governance architectures of this type have become pervasively institutionalized across the European Union and the United States, covering a broad array of policy domains, including risk regulation, public service provision, and protection of fundamental rights (Sabel and Zeitlin 2012). Transnational experimentalist regimes likewise appear to be emerging across a number of major issue areas, such as disability rights, data privacy, food safety, and environmental sustainability (Sabel and Zeitlin 2011; de Búrca et al. 2013).

Experimentalist governance architectures have a number of salient virtues. First, they accommodate diversity in adapting general goals to varied local contexts, rather than imposing uniform, one-size-fits all solutions. Second, they provide a mechanism for coordinated learning from local experimentation through disciplined comparison of different approaches to advancing broad common goals. Third, both the goals themselves and the means for achieving them are explicitly conceived as provisional and subject to revision in the light of experience, so that problems identified in one phase of implementation can be corrected in the next. For each of these reasons, such governance architectures have emerged as a widespread response to turbulent, polyarchic environments, where strategic uncertainty means that effective solutions to problems can only be determined in the course of pursuing them, while a multi-polar distribution of power means that no single actor can impose her own preferred solution without taking into account the views of others.

The scope conditions for experimentalist governance are thus precisely the opposite of those for regime formation in standard international relations theory. For the latter, as we have seen, the formation of a comprehensive international regime depends on a convergence of interests and beliefs among the key actors, or the capacity of a hegemonic power to impose her preferred rules. Experimentalist governance, by contrast, depends on strategic uncertainty, a situation in which actors do not know their precise goals or how best to achieve them ex ante but must discover both in the course of problem-solving, as well as on a polyarchic or multi-polar distribution of power, where no single actor can enforce a unilateral solution. Thus under conditions of polyarchy and disagreement among the parties, where standard international relations theory sees bleak prospects for creating a unified, effective multilateral regime, experimentalism discerns instead the possibility of building a new type of transnational regime with a different governance architecture. Because of their reflexive, self-revising capacity and deliberately corrigible design, such experimentalist governance architectures are also well-adapted to cope with volatile, rapidly changing environments characterized by deep uncertainty, which prominent theorists like Young (2006: ch. 7) and Keohane and Victor (2011) consider the critical contemporary challenge to sustaining effective international regimes.

10.2.3 *Emergent Pathways and Causal Mechanisms*

Experimentalist governance appears particularly well-suited to transnational domains, where there is no overarching sovereign with authority to set common goals, and where the diversity of local conditions and practices makes adoption and enforcement of uniform fixed rules even less feasible than in domestic settings. Yet the very polyarchy and diversity that make experimentalist governance attractive under such conditions can also make it difficult to get a transnational experimentalist regime off the ground. Thus, too many participants with sharply different perspectives may make it hard to reach an initial agreement on common framework goals. Conversely, a single powerful player may be able to veto other proposed solutions even if he cannot impose his own. Hence some kind of penalty default may be required to induce reluctant parties to cooperate in the construction of a transnational experimentalist regime.

In some cases, an experimentalist regime may nonetheless be created through the established multilateral procedures for negotiating international agreements, as a result of reflexive learning by state and non-state actors from the failures of more conventional approaches. The clearest example is the 2008 UN Convention on the Rights of Disabled Persons. Traditional regimes of this kind contain catalogues of specific obligations for states and sporadic international monitoring, understood as an analogue and (ideally) precursor to judicial enforcement. The CRDP, as de Búrca (2010) documents, arose out of a sustained debate among participating governments and NGOs about the deficiencies of such international human rights treaties. It departs from the model of formalist law strictly enforced by a court by incorporating many experimentalist features, including broad, open-ended goals such as "reasonable accommodation" for the disabled; participation of national NGOs and human rights institutions in implementation monitoring; and annual review of its operations on the basis of comparative national data by an inclusive conference of stakeholders.

Conversely, a transnational experimentalist governance architecture may also emerge through "cooperative decentralization" of an established international regime in response to failed attempts at imposing uniform universally applicable standards. Something of this kind may be occurring in the field of financial regulation, where pervasive differences in national and regional circumstances have led in the past to "sham compliance" with tightly harmonized global rules. Thus the new Financial Stability Board, as Helleiner and Pagliari (2011) argue, appears to be moving fitfully towards "the development and promotion of broad principles-based regulatory standards." These would allow for a substantial margin of policy autonomy to accommodate regional and national diversity, supported by "activities such as information-sharing, research collaboration, early warning systems, and capacity building." Compliance with these broad regulatory standards would then be secured through a combination of regular peer reviews, periodic assessments by international financial institutions, and restriction of market access for non-conforming jurisdictions.

Often, however, the familiar coordination and collective action problems discussed earlier will block the initial formation of a comprehensive multilateral experimentalist regime. But that is only the beginning, not the end of the story. Because they are defined in functional rather than structural terms, experimentalist governance architectures can take a variety of institutional forms. They can be built in multiple settings at different territorial scales, which can be nested within one another vertically and joined up horizontally. A number of emergent pathways and causal mechanisms can be identified through which transnational experimentalist regimes may be assembled piece by piece in this way, rather than being constructed as a unified whole through conventional multilateral procedures. These pathways should be understood analytically as stylized, ideal-typical trajectories leading from a characteristic starting point (national or international, public or private) towards the emergence of a transnational experimentalist regime, while the mechanisms should be understood as recurrent causal processes that explain the movement along these trajectories.[2]

There is no reason to believe that these ideal-typical pathways and mechanisms exhaust the full range of possible routes to a transnational experimentalist regime, nor are they mutually exclusive, since they can often be found in combination with one another in specific empirical cases. Whether these pathways originate with public or private actors, or at the national or the international level, they converge on a multi-level, multi-actor governance architecture which in practice should efface the relevance of these distinctions and thus the relevance of particular starting points and development patterns. In this sense, these experimentalist mechanisms can also be understood as devices for overcoming the path dependency and institutional inertia which many standard theorists consider endemic to transnational regimes, both public and private (Keohane and Victor 2011; Büthe and Mattli 2011).

In our analysis of the emergence of a transnational experimentalist regime for sustainable forestry and the control of illegal logging, we will focus on four such ideal-typical pathways. The first involves the creation of private experimentalist regimes (transnational regulatory regimes, or TRRs in the language of this volume) in response to impasses in multilateral negotiations and inaction by public authorities, followed by their diffusion vertically along supply chains and horizontally within industry associations. In forestry, as we will see in the next section, a transnational coalition led by environmental NGOs established a private scheme to develop sustainable management standards and certify their application in response to the governance gap resulting from the failure of earlier intergovernmental efforts to agree to a

---

[2] For a preliminary inventory and analysis of these pathways and mechanisms, see Sabel and Zeitlin (2011). For an overview of the social-science literature on explanation through mechanisms, see Mayntz (2004).

binding global forestry convention. The Forest Stewardship Council (FSC), as we shall also see, has many experimentalist features, including not only its multi-stakeholder governance structure and deliberative decision-making procedures, but also its broad, principles-based standards, adapted to local conditions by national or regional chapters; continuous monitoring, independent verification, and revision of individual forest management plans; and full traceability of certified wood from initial harvest to final point of sale.

One mechanism through which private forest certification has expanded and developed is vertical diffusion along supply chains from downstream customers to upstream producers. Thus retailers, branded manufacturers, and government procurement agencies have responded to NGO campaigns for responsible sourcing by pressing and sometimes assisting their suppliers to upgrade standards and achieve sustainable forestry certification. A second such mechanism is horizontal diffusion within industry associations. In some cases, industry associations have accepted FSC standards and promoted certification among their members. In others, they have established alternative business-dominated schemes with weaker initial standards and verification requirements. Either way, industry associations have proved important institutional devices for recruiting forestry firms into certification schemes, coordinating their responses to changing demands from external actors, and pooling learning from implementation experience.

A second pathway towards a transnational experimentalist regime involves unilateral regulatory initiatives subject to procedural requirements imposed by multilateral institutions like the World Trade Organization (WTO). Thus a large jurisdiction such as the EU or the US may unilaterally seek to extend its internal regulations to transnational supply chains as a condition of market access (thereby extending the geographical scope of its transnational integration regime or TIR, in the language of this volume). WTO rules permit member states to restrict imports in order to protect public health and the environment. But as interpreted by the WTO Appellate Body in its landmark Shrimp-Turtle decisions (1998, 2001), they also require states wishing to restrict imports on these grounds to ensure that their proposed measures are non-discriminatory and proportional to the intended goals, take account of relevant international standards, and consult with their trading partners to minimize the impact on affected third parties (Weinstein and Charnovitz 2001; Scott 2007). These disciplines, when they permit such extensions at all, can thus provide a reflexive mechanism for transforming unilateral regulatory initiatives by developed jurisdictions into a joint governance system with stakeholders from the developing world, capable of providing common interest regulation in the language of this volume, if not a fully multilateral experimentalist regime.

The EU's FLEGT initiative offers a clear illustration of this pathway. As we will see in section 10.4, FLEGT seeks to control exports of illegally logged wood by negotiating Voluntary Partnership Agreements (VPAs) with developing countries to create export licensing systems, based on jointly defined legality standards, regular monitoring and performance review, and third-party verification. Domestic civil society stakeholders participate both in the definition of "legally harvested wood" and in monitoring its certification, each of which are explicitly conceived as revisable in light of the other, while the EU provides development assistance to build up the regulatory capacity of both public and private actors. But the effectiveness of this experimentalist initiative depends on the willingness of individual developing countries to sign such agreements. To reinforce FLEGT's effectiveness and extend its geographical scope, the EU has therefore enacted legislation requiring all businesses placing wood products on the European market from whatever source to demonstrate "due diligence" in ensuring that they had not been illegally harvested. The EU's approach to combating illegal logging appears likely to be accepted as legitimate not only by the WTO but also by developing countries, because it offers them an opportunity to participate in a jointly governed system of legality assurance, while imposing parallel obligations on European timber firms to exercise due diligence in respecting local legal standards.

A third pathway arises where multilateral treaty obligations do not impose procedural constraints on unilateral regulation, but there is transnational pressure for coordination of separate national and/or regional regimes. Under these circumstances, convergence towards an experimentalist regime can emerge via mutual influence, transmitted through thin links such as the operation of multinational corporations within each other's territory, or interchange within transnational advocacy networks. In forestry, as we will see in section 10.5, the US has recently adopted legislation subjecting trade in illegally harvested wood to criminal prosecution, with harsher penalties for violators who fail to exercise "due care" in acquiring such products, and obligations for importers of timber products to declare their species and place of origin. Although the US Lacey Act lacks many of the experimentalist features of FLEGT and the EU Timber Regulation, civil society activists and public officials from both jurisdictions are exploring opportunities for synergy between the two regimes through exchange of information and experiences on the one hand, and joint pressure on their trading partners to adopt similar schemes on the other.

A fourth pathway to the development of transnational experimentalist regimes works through benchmarking and public comparison of competing components of regime complexes. In private forest regulation, as we argue in section 10.3, both the governance arrangements and substantive standards of the FSC and its business-led rivals have converged as a result of what we call "benchmarking for equivalence," conducted by retailers, government procurement agencies, and industry associations in response to pressure from NGOs, which has pushed the industry schemes to raise their standards and the FSC to make certification less costly and more practically feasible, even if they remain some distance apart on key issues. Without such processes of public comparison, which obliged each "private" certification scheme to justify and where necessary revise its standards to meet the assessment of external actors, the competition between them could easily have degenerated into a race to the bottom, rather than upward harmonization through mutually productive interaction. FLEGT VPAs and the EU Timber Regulation extend and formalize this logic of accountability by providing for public recognition of private certification schemes, subject to comparative assessment of their legality standards, monitoring systems, and verification arrangements. A weaker form of such public recognition is also implicit in the US Lacey Act, where participation in a bona fide private certification scheme may serve as mitigating evidence of "due care." Both the EU and the US, finally, are likely to have a similar impact on their major trading partners such as China by pressing them to adopt equivalent legality assurance regimes, whether public or private, as a condition of market access.

Taken together, we conclude, these four pathways and the mechanisms underlying them appear to be leading to the de facto emergence of a joined-up transnational experimentalist regime for sustainable forestry and control of illegal logging, capable of providing common interest regulation in the language of this volumes, which blurs and may ultimately efface standard distinctions between public and private authority, as well as between TIRs and TRRs.

10.3 From Failed Public Governance to Private Experimentalism

Transnational efforts to build a regulatory regime for forestry date back to 1992, when environmental groups and northern countries concerned with high rates of tropical deforestation proposed a binding global convention at the UN Conference on Environment and Development. Developing countries led by Malaysia rejected that proposal, fearing that their capacity to achieve economic development would be constrained by northern demands for conservation, which they also viewed as a disguised form of protectionism (Bernstein and Cashore 2004). The Rio Earth Summit produced only a set of non-binding forest management principles, which enshrined the principle of national sovereignty over forest exploitation. Over the ensuing 30 years, several additional attempts, including the UN Intergovernmental Panel on Forests (IPF) and its successor, the Intergovermental Forum on Forests (IFF), created international dialogues on forest sustainability but, as at Rio, "the IPF delegates failed to agree on major issues" (Rosendal 2001: 450; Humphreys 2006).

Efforts by some northern governments to tackle this issue by imposing unilateral environmental standards or mandatory eco-labeling systems for imported timber were likewise blocked by their incompatibility with the rules of the global trade regime. Thus, for example, the Austrian government was obliged to withdraw a law banning import of unsustainably harvested tropical wood products in the face of complaints by developing countries to the WTO's predecessor, the General Agreement on Tariffs and Trade (GATT). An earlier effort during the late 1980s to develop a system for certifying ecologically acceptable forest products through the International Tropical Timber Trade Organization (ITTO) similarly foundered on opposition from timber-exporting countries and charges of GATT-incompatibility (Bartley 2007).

10.3.1 *Experimenting with Private Certification*

Such failures of multilateral agreements and national public governance, however, can create openings through which non-state actors creatively move parts of a complex issue forward. Forestry provides a clear illustration. Thus in response to the failure of nations to agree on common global rules at the 1992 Rio conference, civil society groups began developing private standards and certification systems. A year after the Rio debacle, environmental NGOs, businesses, foundations, and social organizations launched the Forest Stewardship Council. The FSC has a number of experimentalist features which explicitly address the impasse at Rio by establishing a deliberative, multi-stakeholder process for setting and revising broad, principles-based standards for sustainable forest management, adapting them to local conditions, certifying their voluntary application by firms, independently verifying the results, and requiring corrective action where needed.

In order to overcome the mistrust and resentments that blocked agreement at Rio, the FSC creatively balanced the influence of environmental, business, and social organizations, as well as southern and northern interests, in its central standard-setting and revision body. Standards and procedures are determined through deliberation and supermajority voting by three equal chambers representing environmental, economic, and social interests, with equal weight within them for members from the global north and the global south.

The FSC's principles include respect for labor and indigenous peoples' rights, as well as biodiversity, ecological sustainability, and environmental management requirements. These general principles are elaborated through more specific global standards and criteria, which are in turn adapted to local conditions by national or regional chapters.

Monitoring of compliance with FSC principles and standards is verified by independently accredited third-party auditing organizations. Audit teams review forest management planning documentation, contracts for services (such as chemical applications), and firm financial data, as well as conduct consultations with forest employees and other local stakeholders, such as NGOs, community leaders, resource managers, and neighbors in order to open spaces for local deliberation about the certified forest's management.

FSC audits also enable continuous learning at the forest management unit (FMU) level. Principle 8 states that certified management units must continually assess the condition of the forest, monitoring harvest yields, growth rates, compositional changes in flora and fauna, environmental and social impacts of harvesting, and costs, productivity, and efficiency of forest management. Results of such monitoring must be incorporated into the revision of management plans. In theory, therefore, the FSC establishes a process of continuous learning whereby firms should be able to assess regularly updated information on environmental impacts, growth rates, yields, etc. This also means that auditors have access to information about the relative effectiveness of forest management practices, which they could use to develop performance-based comparisons across certified units. Such comparisons could be used to put additional pressure on laggards and leaders and to inform the regular three-year General Assembly Meeting of the FSC, where the chambers vote on any changes needed in the standards. To date, however, the FSC has inadequately developed its own capacity for experimentalist "learning by monitoring" (Sabel 1994), even if the institutional preconditions for the functioning of such a system are already in place, because it fails to pool, compare, and thereby induce greater reflection on learning.

To promote accountability of both certified forests and monitors, the FSC requires accredited auditors to publish public summaries of the audit reports on their websites. Descriptions of the forest are recorded (location, management objectives, size of holding, types of sites) and documentation of the audit findings are provided, including major and minor non-conformances, summaries of field and office assessments, and stakeholder interviews. These audit summaries have enabled watchdog groups and activists to monitor the functioning of the FSC and thereby contribute to securing the FSC's accountability to the broader forest governance community.

The FSC also certifies supply chains. In order for retail products to carry an FSC label, each step along the supply chain must be certified. Traditionally, chain of custody audits have been built on "paper-based" systems, where checkers evaluate whether companies have systems in place to track FSC certified wood through the supply chain. Recent advances, however, suggest that DNA fingerprinting technologies may soon enable genetically based spot checks to supplement paper and system audits (Auld et al. 2010).

The FSC thus displays several key features of an experimentalist governance architecture. Its global organization establishes broad framework goals for "sustainable forests." The national and regional chapters are given discretion to customize these goals to local conditions. Individual FMUs apply these standards and report regularly on their performance through audits. Theoretically, the FSC can orchestrate a process of information pooling and review in which the results of local experimentation with sustainable forestry are compared with those of others employing different means to the same ends. Auditors do in fact require that local units show that they are taking appropriate corrective measures, although the FSC could do more to require continuous improvement from experience-based learning across as well as within FMUs, by endogenizing lessons learned from implementing the standards in regular revisions at General Assembly meetings.

10.3.2 *Productive Interactions or Regime Fragmentation?*

The emergence of private certification schemes could have led to a highly fragmented regime in which high-standards forest operations joined the FSC for strategic advantage while others looked to weaker schemes to shield themselves from public regulation (Bartley 2007). In fact, as competing industry certification schemes emerged, progressive firms and those under strong state regulatory standards did join the FSC for strategic advantage, while many large forest industry companies and small forest landowners joined weaker competing schemes, creating an apparently fragmented governance space (Cashore et al. 2004).

However, three key mechanisms have combined to encourage more positive interactions between the FSC and its competitors (Overdevest 2004). Rather than fragmentation, competition among private schemes instead resulted in mutual adjustment, learning from experience, and increased accountability of schemes to one another and to external audiences. This accountability, initiated by downstream customers, government procurement offices, and NGOs through "benchmarking for equivalence," enhanced the social nature of their rationality, explaining how a reflexive competition emerged which yielded productive interactions rather than a race to the bottom.

These regime dynamics thus call attention to how issue areas characterized by strategic uncertainty and complex interdependence, in which actors like forest companies cannot achieve narrow self-interested goals because they depend on the approval of others (such as consumers, retailers, regulators), may generate conditions for a more other-regarding rationality to emerge. Rather than shielding participants from public scrutiny, private certification schemes thus subjected them to broader demands for mutual accountability. We argue in subsequent sections that as EU FLEGT and potentially the US Lacey Act start to recognize private forest certification schemes as evidence of legality and subject them to a measure of public oversight, further productive interactions and a more coherent transnational governance regime can be expected to emerge, cutting across conventional distinctions between public and private authority.

One mechanism through which private forest certification has expanded and developed as an alternative to the weak international regime created by states following Rio is vertical diffusion along global supply chains from downstream customers to upstream producers. Retailers, branded manufacturers, and public procurement agencies have responded to NGO campaigns for sustainable sourcing by pressing and sometimes assisting their suppliers to upgrade standards and achieve forestry certification. Initially, such large end-of-chain retailers only adopted FSC-preference policies after being targeted by NGO campaigns. NGOs thus played an important role in pushing economic actors to discover a "self-interest" in adopting higher standards so that they could put an end to the forest campaigns. Over time, however, such standards have become more broadly institutionalized as good business practice.

In addition to these commercial supply chains, government purchasing policies provided a major stimulus for the adoption and diffusion of private forest certification standards. Denmark, Belgium, France, Germany, Netherlands, the UK, Japan, and New Zealand all accept private certification as evidence of legality and/or sustainability in meeting green public procurement standards (Gulbrandsen 2011). In combination, public and private supply chains have thus proved an important conduit for partial and selective transnational forest regulation in the absence of a multilateral regime.

A second mechanism through which private certification has expanded and developed as an alternative to the weak public international forestry regime is horizontal diffusion within industry associations. As of April 2011, for instance, the Program for the Endorsement of Forest Certification Schemes (PEFC), which historically has been much more closely associated with industry associations, had certified 60 percent more hectares than the FSC.[3]

The PEFC's larger share of certified acreage reflects its emergence as the standard of choice among national forest industry associations, sometimes even becoming a requirement for associational membership, as with the

---

[3] <www.fsc.org>, <www.pefc.org>, respectively, accessed May 2011.

US Sustainable Forestry Initiative (SFI). The PEFC, like the FSC, endorses nationally customized certification systems. But it originally appealed to non-industrial landowner associations who found the FSC's model of regular annual audits economically impractical, because many small-scale forest operations do not harvest every year and because they worried that the FSC was dominated by environmental advocacy organizations which knew little about silviculture. Small landowners' associations in countries dominated by fragmented, small-scale ownership, but generally quite strong environmental regulations like Finland, Sweden, and Germany created the PEFC in order to combat pressure to join the FSC. Later however, the PEFC enrolled industrial landowner associations whose members harvest thousands of acres on an annual basis in countries such as the US and Canada, as well as industrial forestry associations in the global south, such as Argentina and Brazil (Cashore et al. 2004).

The high rate of adoption of private standards through associational channels suggests the comparative organizational advantage of horizontal diffusion strategies for private standards, although in forestry this has arguably benefited industry-sponsored certification schemes more than their NGO-sponsored counterparts. A key mechanism engendering more productive interactions in the face of such forum shopping is public comparison and benchmarking for equivalence. In the following discussion, we show how such benchmarking generated positive interactions and upward convergence of standards among private certification schemes. The results presented here suggest that a narrow, asocial strategic rationality leading to races to the bottom is not a necessary outcome of competition within regime complexes.

Impressed by the differences between the FSC and its competitors and concerned that these would not be readily apparent to others in the broader governance field, NGOs, retailers, government procurement agencies, and international organizations like the World Bank began to benchmark the standards of these schemes against one another. NGOs supporting the FSC took the lead in generating comparative studies in which operational details of different emerging schemes were exposed to public debate. In each major location where competitors emerged NGOs produced detailed comparisons, showing how FSC and competitors differed in terms of substantive and procedural standards, emphasizing how the weaker rival schemes lacked the FSC's balanced governance, annual and independent audits, stakeholder consultations, regular revisions, and performance-based principles and assessment criteria.

These reports generated unexpected reactions from weaker industry schemes, which became concerned that such contrasts would delegitimate them with external audiences. But this benchmarking process also generated learning by the FSC about the relative strength of competing systems, such as the PEFC's greater accessibility and affordability for smaller landowners. The NGOs did not intend their reports to guide internal changes in the standards, but hoped instead that external audiences would reject the FSC's competitors. But these comparisons instead ended up producing substantial adjustment on both sides.

The explanation for this unexpected development can be found in the legitimacy dynamics of private governance schemes. Both Cashore et al. (2004) and Black (2008) argue that, because private certification schemes do not enjoy the same taken-for-granted legitimacy of public authorities, they need to gain it from legitimacy-providing communities such as supply chain actors, industry associations, academics, international organizations, etc. Their need to be accepted by such legitimacy communities gives the latter significant power to influence private certification standards in accordance with their own narrow rationality, a point emphasized Black and Cashore et al. But it also creates interdependence and strategic uncertainty among the participants in these relationships.

By strategically targeting public and private supply chains' reliance on "demonstrably questionable" forest management or certification systems, NGOs not only rendered the differences between the FSC and its competitors transparent, but also highlighted to downstream customers their deep dependence on the trustworthiness of upstream suppliers. This exposed the interdependence and uncertainty in the system. End-users' reputations depended on how seriously suppliers took their standards. Rather than reinforcing a narrow self-interested rationality, weaker certification schemes were forced to justify their standards publicly, at the same time as retailers, manufacturers, and government procurement agencies came under pressure to live up to their commitment to high standards. These comparisons therefore had the effect of broadening the rationality of industry certification schemes vis-à-vis retailers and other end-users, as well of the latter vis-à-vis their own standards.

The results of benchmarking for equivalence can be seen in the often dramatic responses by industry schemes. The FSC and its competitors started off far apart in both substantive and procedural standards. Thus the industry-sponsored schemes initially lacked multi-stakeholder governance structures, independent audits, stakeholder consultations, regular revisions, and performance-based principles and assessment criteria (Overdevest 2005, 2010). Table 10.1, adapted from Fernholz et al. (2010), shows that competitors have all moved closer to the FSC on these dimensions.

The FSC also made adjustments during this early competition, moving towards PEFC practice on key issues where its original approach proved to be incongruous with the organizational realities of the forest industry. For instance, the FSC changed its 100 percent label requirements for paper,

Table 10.1 Forest certification program characteristics

Program	Third-party auditors?	Chain-of-custody?	Public reporting?	Stakeholder consultation	Independent governance	On-product label?
American Tree Farm System	Yes	Yes	Yes	Yes	Yes	No
Canadian Standards Association	Yes	Yes	Yes	Yes	Yes	Yes*
Forest Stewardship Council	Yes	Yes	Yes	Yes	Yes	Yes
Program for the Endorsement of Forest Certification	Yes	Yes	Yes	Yes	Yes	Yes
Sustainable Forest Initiative	Yes	Yes	Yes	Yes	Yes	Yes

* CSA has adopted the PEFC on-product label and discontinued use of the original CSA on-product label.

realizing that it could not produce FSC-certified paper unless it certified a critical mass of all the pulp entering a mill (i.e. separation in a pulp mill is not easily achieved; production is not small batch). Instead, they eventually adopted the (previously much criticized by NGOs) PEFC percentage-in/percentage-out system, which allowed the percentage of certified paper coming out of a mill to equal the quantity of certified pulp entering. The FSC likewise adopted PEFC-style audits of small and low-intensity forests, which by definition harvest less frequently and so make regular annual surveillance audits an inappropriately scaled response to the problem (although NGOs originally argued for the PEFC to have high standard annual surveillance audits for all forests). Generally speaking, these adjustments reflect learning by the NGO-led FSC from practical experiences of their large and small industry counterparts.

Other studies of competing forest certification schemes, while acknowledging this trend towards cross-scheme convergence, also emphasize continuing divergences in substantive standards not only between the FSC and its competitors, but also among the national and regional standards of the FSC itself. But these studies tend to assume that more stringent and prescriptive substantive standards, e.g. regarding riparian logging exclusion zones or clear-cutting bans, are inherently superior, without reference to their practical effectiveness in promoting environmental sustainability in specific local contexts, which would be the key evaluation criterion from an experimentalist perspective. Conversely, such studies also tend to consider any adaptation of FSC standards to forest firm concerns as a sign of weakening in conformity to market pressures, irrespective of whether changes, such as reducing the frequency of audits of small landowners or introducing a secondary "percentage-in/percentage-out" label for certified wood, may enhance rather than compromise their fitness for purpose (Cashore et al. 2004; McDermott et al. 2009).

Responses to recent comparisons suggest that these dynamics remain effective in the sense that the gaps between the PEFC and FSC continue to close. Thus a recent World Wildlife Fund (WWF) study concludes that the 2010 revision of the PEFC international standard brings it "much closer" to the International Social and Environmental Accrediting and Labeling (ISEAL) Alliance code of good practice, endorsed by the FSC, which sets minimum criteria for a credible voluntary standard system, including stakeholder consultation, balanced participation, and adaptation to local conditions (Walter 2011).

These comparisons however are largely based on analyses of the paper standards. As such, they lack the capacity to generate disciplined assessments of how well the schemes are working on the ground, which could feed into public accountability, recursive learning, and external pressure for improvement. This is a crucial issue and the next generation of evaluations of competing forest certification schemes—and thus their future interactions—would be better served if they were based on performance rather than paper-based comparisons. Such comparisons are necessary both to keep the FSC and its competitors responsive to their own standards as well to forestall growing gaps between them. Until recently, however, few legitimacy communities from NGOs through industry and governments to academics have focused systematically on evaluating implementation and impact across schemes. Fortunately, there is recent evidence of at least one organization taking on a meta-standard-setting role in pressing for greater use of impact data and performance evaluation along experimentalist lines.

The ISEAL Alliance, the global umbrella association of sustainability standard-setters, is playing a new meta-organizational role. In an apparent effort to close the paper–practice gap and raise the benchmark for competitors, ISEAL is requiring member organizations to undertake impact assessment in order to reliably assess the impact of sustainability standards on the ground. If ISEAL is successful in fostering a robust system of ongoing impact assessment, the member organizations will move (1) one step closer to becoming real experimentalist institutions and in the process (2) enable a new source of comparative pressure on rivals to take their own impacts seriously in order to maintain their public legitimacy. In this way, ISEAL may play an important role in the otherwise anarchic world of competing standards, by serving as a virtual meta-center which does not specify first-order standards but instead sets second-order standards for their assessment.

The new ISEAL Impact Code ("Code of Good Practice for Assessing the Impacts of Social and Environmental Standards Systems") requires standards organizations to evaluate their progress in achieving stated goals. The Code requires organizations to develop Monitoring and Evaluation (M&E) systems in order to ensure that sustainability standards become more results oriented, to publicly demonstrate impacts, and to maintain credibility with donors, companies, civil society producers, and other standards supporters.[4] To achieve these ends, member organizations are required to define monitoring indicators grounded in the outcomes they seek to achieve in both the short and long term, and to track them on an ongoing basis.

So far the FSC has participated in the construction and first revision of the ISEAL Code of Good Practice. It has created draft "Theory of Change" and "Intended Impacts" documents along with a set of indicators to be used to assess the effectiveness of FSC standards. A public consultation on these documents closed on 20 October 2013.[5] If the FSC uses this self-assessment

---

[4] ISEAL Alliance "A Snapshot of the ISEAL Impacts Code," <http://www.isealalliance.org/sites/default/files/ISEAL%20Impact%20Code%20Brochure%20(low%20res).pdf>.

[5] <https://ic.fsc.org/fsc-theory-of-change.657.htm>.

process as an opportunity to render the quality and impacts of its certification scheme more credible and publicly accountable, it will also open up possibilities for new comparisons to put pressure on the PEFC about its own failures to demonstrate the impact and effectiveness of its operations on the ground. As the ISEAL documents rightly point out, a variety of external actors or communities has an interest in performance of these schemes, from states and firms, to NGOs and donors. It is important to the success of such benchmarking exercises that these actors mobilize to consider the quality of competing standards.

Over the past two decades, private forest certification has offered a creative but incomplete response to the failed multilateral forest regime by extending vertically down supply chains and horizontally across industry associations. Over 25 percent of managed forest lands worldwide have been enrolled in one of the competing forest certification schemes. But the global south's share of certified acreage has been far smaller, as most developing country producers could not afford the associated costs, needed external support to adopt high forest sustainability standards, and faced little domestic demand for certified forest products. Whereas over half the forests in the US, Canada, and Europe are now certified by FSC or PEFC, these schemes cover just 2 percent of tropical forest land (UNCECE and FAO 2012: 108). Furthermore, through benchmarking for equivalence the standards of the weaker industry schemes' standards have been raised, although inadequate attention has been paid to comparisons of on-the-ground performance. Yet despite these mechanisms of vertical, horizontal, and competitive diffusion, private experiments with forest certification have not so far produced a coherent, joined-up transnational governance regime.

10.4 FLEGT as an Experimentalist Transnational Regime

By the early 2000s, private certification schemes had thus achieved high rates of coverage among industrial forest companies in developed economies.[6] But

---

[6] Except where otherwise indicated, the analysis in this section is based on the following sources: FLEGT VPAs, <http://ec.europa.eu/environment/forests/flegt.htm>; FLEGT VPA briefing notes, prepared jointly by European Commission delegations and signatory governments, <http://www.euflegt.efi.int/portal/home/vpa_countries>; "Regulation (EU) No. 995/2010 of the European Parliament and of the Council of 20 October 2010 laying down the obligations of operations who place timber and timber products on the market," *Official Journal of the European Union*, L 295/23, 11 Dec. 2010; interviews with officials of the European Commission (DG Environment), FERN, and the European Forest Institute FLEGT Facility, Mar. 2011; FERN *Civil Society Counter-Briefs*, <www.fern.org>; DG DEVCO (2011); Leal Riesco and Ozinga 2010; Beeko and Arts 2010; presentations and discussions at Chatham House Illegal Logging Stakeholders' Forum, London, 10–11 Jan. 2011, <http://www.illegal-logging.info/item_single.php?it_id=206&it=event>, and 4th Potomac Forum on Illegal Logging and Associated Trade, Washington, DC, 4 May 2011, <http://forest-trends.org/event.php?id=547>, respectively.

their take-up by developing countries remained limited, especially in the tropical forests whose deterioration sparked the original campaign for global regulation. In response, NGOs, governments, and international organizations have focused increasingly on combating illegal logging, an endemic problem in many countries, which depresses prices for legally harvested wood and undercuts the adoption of sustainable forestry practices (Humphreys 2006: ch. 7; Cashore et al. 2007; Lawson and MacFaul 2010).

The most ambitious such initiative is the EU's FLEGT Action Plan, adopted in 2003, and buttressed by the enactment of a voluntary import licensing scheme in 2005 and the EU Timber Regulation in 2010. Like private certification itself, FLEGT arose from dissatisfaction with the lack of progress in tackling the problem of forest degradation through multilateral institutions. During the mid-1990s, environmental NGOs had successfully pushed the issue of illegal logging onto the agenda of the UN Intergovernmental Panel (later Forum) on Forests, which called on participating countries to consider national action and promote international cooperation to reduce illegal trade in forest products. The G8 then included illegal logging in its 1998 Action Programme on Forests, and proposed a set of measures to improve domestic forest law enforcement and reduce illegal international trade in forest products, which were echoed in turn by the Johannesburg World Summit on Sustainable Development in 2002. Beginning in 2001, the World Bank sponsored a series of regional dialogues on Forest Law Enforcement and Governance (FLEG), which brought together governments, businesses, and NGOs from timber-producing and consuming countries to discuss domestic and international actions aimed at tackling illegal logging and trade. These initiatives, particularly the FLEG processes in Asia and Africa, produced a growing political and epistemic consensus on the problem of illegal logging and appropriate policies to combat it, including improvements in domestic law enforcement and forest management capacity, involvement of stakeholders and local communities in forest decision-making, monitoring of forest resources, and coordinated efforts to control international trade in illegally harvested timber. They also stimulated bilateral agreements of producing countries with consuming countries, international donors, and NGOs to implement some of the proposed measures. But none of these processes generated binding commitments among the participating countries, nor the creation of systematic mechanisms for monitoring progress towards their agreed aims (European Commission 2003; Humphreys 2006: ch. 7; Cashore and Stone 2014).

Under these circumstances, the EU decided to proceed unilaterally, by linking the improvement of forest law enforcement and governance (FLEG) to regulation of trade (T), but in ways shaped by the need to comply with WTO rules, as well as to obtain the consent of developing countries themselves.

The centerpiece of the FLEGT Action Plan was the negotiation of bilateral Voluntary Partnership Agreements with developing countries to establish licensing systems for the export of legally harvested wood to the European market, where legality includes reference to the social and environmental conditions of production. Because they are voluntary and jointly agreed, such licensing systems were expected to be fully WTO-compatible, unlike the unilateral eco-labeling requirements for imported tropical wood proposed by some northern governments a decade earlier (Brack 2009). But the VPAs were also designed to win the active cooperation of developing country stakeholders by promoting "equitable and just solutions" for all concerned interests, engaging local communities and NGOs in forest sector governance reform, and providing capacity-building support for civil society and the private sector as well as for public fiscal, law enforcement, and forestry authorities. Given the "important but not dominant" place of the EU in the world market for wood products, the FLEGT Action Plan underlined the need for continuing efforts to build an effective multilateral framework for controlling illegal trade in collaboration with other major importers. But "in the absence of multilateral progress," the European Commission would eventually consider further measures, including "legislation to control imports of illegally harvested timber into the EU" (European Commission 2003b).

The first FLEGT VPA was signed with Ghana in September 2008, followed by the Republic of Congo (2009), Cameroon (2010), the Central African Republic (2010), Indonesia (2011), and Liberia (2011). Negotiations are currently underway with the Democratic Republic of Congo, Gabon, Côte d'Ivoire, Guyana, Honduras, Malaysia, Thailand, Laos, and Vietnam.[7] These agreements have taken years to negotiate, not only because of the technical complexity and political sensitivity of the issues concerned, but also because the EU has insisted on an open and deliberative multi-stakeholder process, with full participation of domestic civil society in their design and implementation. To facilitate this process, the EU has provided extensive support to partner country governments, civil society organizations, and indigenous forest communities through capacity-building projects organized by international NGOs and consultancies.

At the heart of each VPA is a national Legality Assurance System (LAS), based on jointly agreed definitions of legally harvested timber; a legality "grid" or "matrix," with indicators and verifiers defined for each obligation; and a comprehensive, integrated system for controlling the flow of logs from the forest to the point of export, ensuring that no illegal wood enters the supply chain. Wood conforming to these standards will receive FLEGT export

[7] A further 11 countries in Latin America, Asia, Oceania, and Africa have also expressed interest in entering into VPA negotiations: see <http://www.euflegt.efi.int/portal/home/vpa_countries>.

licenses, subject to verification of individual shipments, and monitoring of the operation of the LAS as a whole by independent auditors and civil society organizations, as well as by government officials. Each VPA is overseen by a joint committee comprising both EU and partner country representatives, which is responsible for resolving disputes; monitoring and reviewing implementation of the agreement; assessing its broader social, economic, and environmental impacts; and recommending any necessary changes, including further capacity-building measures. The European Commission and EU member states commit to providing financial and organizational support for implementation of the agreement, and to helping partner countries raise additional funding from other international sources as needed.

FLEGT VPAs are designed to incorporate key experimentalist features such as deliberation, revisability, and recursive learning. Thus the legality standards in each agreement are the product of a deliberative, multi-stakeholder review process, requiring reconciliation and consolidation of conflicting regulations from different sources, including international treaty commitments as well as domestic law. They cover not only fiscal, forestry, and environmental regulation, but also labor law, worker health and safety, and the rights of indigenous communities. In many of these areas, the review process revealed significant inconsistencies and gaps in existing regulation, which the signatory governments have committed themselves to rectify through legal and administrative reforms. The legality definitions themselves are explicitly subject to periodic review and revision in light of new developments and experience with their implementation.

Verification and monitoring, similarly, are conceived as mechanisms for learning and continuous improvement of forest management and governance, as well as compliance enforcement. Thus for example, the role of independent monitoring is understood as "not just to find infractions as they occur, but to investigate the root causes of the infraction by analyzing information channeled from various sources in a systematic manner and to document governance problems" (DG DEVCO 2011: 28; Resource Extraction Monitoring 2010). Transparency and public disclosure of information on verification of the LAS are likewise regarded as crucial provisions aimed at enabling civil society networks to participate actively in monitoring its operations at all levels. The joint implementation committees, which operate by consensus but may refer unresolved disputes to arbitration, are constituted as deliberative problem-solving bodies responsible for sustaining the agreement through improvements based on learning by monitoring of its implementation.

Although FLEGT VPAs are becoming increasingly standardized, they differ from one another in several areas, reflecting both specificities of the local setting, and the sequence in which they were negotiated (for a comprehensive review, see FERN 2013). Thus for example the Republic of Congo is creating two separate legality grids, one for forest timber and the other for commercial plantations, while Cameroon, which is a major processor of imported wood, has led the way in developing a sophisticated traceability and chain-of-custody system to prevent illegal timber from neighboring countries entering its supply chain. Although the LAS in each VPA applies to all timber exports, not just those to the EU, countries vary in how they are integrating production for the domestic market into these systems in order to avoid creating a double standard of legality. Institutional arrangements for participation of civil society actors in implementing and monitoring the VPAs likewise vary cross-nationally, becoming progressively more extensive and specific in later agreements. Negotiating FLEGT VPAs has thus been a "learning-by-doing process," with transfer of knowledge and experience not only between countries, but also across regions (e.g. between Cameroon and Vietnam, which is a major processor of imported timber from the Mekong Basin). This adaptive learning and knowledge transfer process has been supported by the development of a rich and variegated expert community of research and policy institutions, consultancies, and NGOs.

FLEGT VPAs were attractive from the start to some developing countries because of their potential to enhance consumer confidence, improve access to European markets, increase tax revenues, and open up new sources of development assistance. But these agreements are also quite challenging, both politically and administratively, in terms of their demands for multi-stakeholder participation and reform of forest-sector governance. The first round of VPA negotiations accordingly proceeded slowly, with some developing country governments remaining initially reluctant to move beyond exploratory talks, particularly as their competitors continued to be able to export timber to the EU with no legality checks.

In response to these concerns, the EU enacted new legislation in 2010 requiring all businesses placing timber products on the European market from whatever source (domestic or foreign) to demonstrate "due diligence" in ensuring that they had not been illegally harvested. Exercising due diligence includes securing key information describing the timber products (including country of harvest, species, details of the supplier, and information on compliance with national legislation), undertaking a risk assessment, and creating and implementing a risk mitigation plan.

There are three possible pathways to demonstrating due diligence laid down by the EUTR. The first is possession of a valid FLEGT VPA license. Second, operators can develop their own due diligence system, with full risk assessment, risk mitigation, and regular evaluation procedures. Third, they can use a turnkey system developed by a third-party "monitoring organization" (MO) recognized by the EC. The MOs' functions are to create, evaluate, and improve systems for information gathering, risk assessment, and risk mitigation; verify their proper use by participating operators; and take corrective action in case of improper use.[8] The EUTR provisions for the recognition of MOs state that these will be subject to scrutiny by both the European Commission and the national "competent authorities" responsible for administering the EUTR in the member states. The MOs will be subject to audit by the Commission at least every two years, and will experience additional scrutiny if the "operational due diligence systems" they provide to operators fail to exclude illegal material.[9] In addition, civil society organizations are expected to play a watchdog role, as the EUTR requires competent authorities to investigate substantiated complaints by third parties.[10] EU member states are responsible for setting and enforcing penalties on companies contravening the regulation, but the Commission will orchestrate a dialogue network among the national competent authorities to ensure that implementation does not vary too widely. The Commission will produce regular progress reports on the operation of these rules based on information provided by the member states, and the regulation itself will be reviewed, and if necessary revised, at the end of five years.

Like FLEGT, the EU Timber Regulation (EUTR) is carefully designed to comply with WTO rules, because it applies the same requirements to domestic operators placing wood products on the European market as to importers. By making FLEGT export licenses a "green lane" into the European market, the EUTR significantly increases the incentive for developing countries to sign VPAs. For processing countries and export businesses, the cost per unit of legality verification and traceability is likely to be substantially lower under a national VPA scheme compared to importing licensed wood from another FLEGT country or certifying its legality independently (Gooch 2010; Proforest 2010). For each of these reasons, the number of VPA negotiations successfully concluded or nearing completion has spiked sharply since the legislation's passage. The EUTR can thus be understood as a penalty default underpinning the new legality regime. A penalty default, as discussed earlier, is a regulatory measure that is perceived to be so unattractive by the

---

[8] See Commission Delegated Regulation (EU 363/2012) on the procedural rules for the recognition and withdrawal of recognition of monitoring organizations; "Guidance Document for the EU Timber Regulation," 3 Mar. 2013. <http://ec.europa.eu/environment/forests/pdf/Final%20Guidance%20document.pdf>; <http://www.legal-timber.info/en/flegt-eutr/dd/12-menu-anglais/43-due-diligence-mo.html> (accessed May 2013).

[9] <http://www.ettf.info/eutr-implementing-regulation-puts-pressure-monitoring-organisations> (accessed May 2013).

[10] Regulation (EU) 995/2010, arts 10(1) and 10(2). See also Client Earth, <http://www.illegal-logging.info/uploads/1_DueDiligenceintheEUTR.pdf> (accessed May 2013).

addressees that it induces them to cooperate in developing more palatable alternatives.

Together, FLEGT and the EUTR are also likely to have a significant positive impact on private forest certification and third-party legality verification schemes. Most FLEGT VPAs explicitly envisage recognition of private certification schemes in their export licensing system, provided that these incorporate the agreed legality definitions, and subject to regular monitoring and review of their operation and procedures. The due diligence requirement of the EUTR will likewise stimulate forestry firms and importers from non-VPA countries to join private certification and legality verification schemes as a cost-effective alternative to creating and administering their own free-standing risk management systems. It has already spurred significant institutional development by private actors in creating legality verification and certification schemes (Donovan 2010). The implementing regulation specifically encourages the adoption of private certification and legality verification schemes as tools for achieving due diligence, as long as the systems are publicly available, meet the requirements of the legislation, and include appropriate checks, such as field-visits, at regular intervals, no longer than 12 months (European Commission 2012a). The EUTR thus places private certification and legality verification schemes under a measure of public oversight, thereby integrating them into the broader transnational legality assurance regime. But legal liability for effectively excluding illegal timber from the market remains with the operator, not the scheme.

It is possible, of course, that FLEGT and the EUTR could have a negative impact on private certification schemes by spurring both customers and suppliers to shift their energies towards meeting less demanding legality requirements (Bartley 2014; Cashore and Stone 2014). But by reducing a major source of cost pressure on legitimate timber operations, these measures appear likely instead to encourage progression to more ambitious standards of sustainable forestry promoted by private certification schemes like the FSC. The FSC itself is developing a modular, stepwise system in which forest management units would first be certified for legality by accredited auditors, while committing to work towards certification to full sustainability standards at a subsequent stage (Guillery 2011). In the UK, a leader in green procurement policies, FLEGT licenses will be acceptable for public purchases until 2015, when sustainable timber will be required (Brack and Buckrell 2011). Finally, by harmonizing inconsistencies, filling gaps, and resolving conflicts in domestic law, including those concerning customary rights of indigenous communities, the revised legality standards produced through the VPA process will greatly facilitate auditing of compliance by individual FMUs with national legal requirements, which is a core element of all private certification schemes (Proforest 2010).

By placing private forest certification schemes under ongoing scrutiny and review by national and European authorities, FLEGT and the EUTR should push them to ensure that illegal logging is actually detected and corrected on the ground, thereby addressing a key gap in their public accountability. Depending on how they are implemented, the procedures for recognizing monitoring organizations and reviewing their operations under the EUTR may also serve as a mechanism for improving the performance standards of private certification schemes through public comparison and benchmarking for equivalence.

FLEGT and the EUTR go a long way towards the construction of a transnational experimentalist regime for forest sector governance. They demonstrate how such a "common interest regulation" regime, in the language of this volume, can emerge from unilateral initiatives by large developed country jurisdictions, subject to procedural constraints imposed by the rules of multilateral institutions like the WTO. The EU's approach to combating illegal logging appears likely to be accepted as legitimate not only by the WTO but also by developing countries, because it offers them an opportunity to participate in a jointly governed system of legality assurance, while imposing parallel obligations on European timber firms to exercise due diligence in respecting local legal standards. FLEGT VPAs and the inclusive, deliberative negotiation processes leading up to them have already had a major impact in a number of countries in terms of empowering civil society stakeholders, exposing inconsistencies and gaps in existing forest regulation, securing political commitments to legal and governance reform, and measurably reducing illegal logging in anticipation of their implementation (Lawson and MacFaul 2010). The joint governance systems created to oversee these agreements institutionalize key experimentalist principles, including regular review and revision of both the underlying legality standards and the assurance system designed to achieve them through recursive learning by monitoring of implementation experience. The EUTR enhances the incentives for developing country governments to sign VPAs and ensures that wood imports into the European market will not be diverted to countries with weaker legality enforcement standards. Its due diligence requirements are already encouraging importing firms to join private forest certification schemes, while promising to enhance the public accountability and performance standards of these schemes by subjecting them to comparative review and benchmarking for equivalence.

As the original FLEGT Action Plan observed in 2003, the EU is an important but not dominant player in the world wood market. According to an analysis conducted for the OECD, the EU accounted in 2005 for 49 percent of all industrial wood imports, followed by the US at 23 percent, China at 8 percent, and Japan at 7 percent. But the EU accounted for only 24 percent of imports from countries representing a high risk of illegal logging, compared to 23 percent for China and 14 percent for both the US and Japan respectively (Contreras-Hermosilla et al. 2007). Since then, Chinese imports and exports of wood products have both surged dramatically (European Forest Institute 2011b). Hence the global effectiveness of the EU regime for promoting sustainable forestry and combating illegal logging will inevitably depend on its capacity to develop productive interactions with regulatory initiatives in other large importing countries.

10.5 Joining up the Pieces: Transnational Governance Interactions

Beyond FLEGT and the EUTR, the most important recent development in the transnational campaign against illegal logging has been the 2008 extension of the US Lacey Act from fish and wildlife to plants.[11] This amended Act, which dates back originally to 1900, makes it a criminal offense to import, trade, or otherwise handle any timber product harvested in violation of the laws applicable in the country of origin. Penalties, which can include imprisonment, fines, and confiscation of goods, depend on the level of intent of the violator, and the extent to which "due care" was exercised to avoid foreseeable risks of trafficking in illegal products. To facilitate detection of illegal timber, importers are obliged to submit customs declarations with information on the scientific name of the species, the value and quantity of the shipment, and the country of origin.

The amended Lacey Act, which was the product of a "Baptist-bootlegger" coalition of environmental NGOs and domestic forest firms concerned about competition from illegal wood imports (Cashore and Stone 2013), lacks most of the experimentalist features of FLEGT and the EUTR. It takes foreign laws as they stand, without seeking to reconcile ambiguous and contradictory legislation or fill gaps in existing regulations, unlike the updated legality standards produced by FLEGT VPAs. Nor does it engage local forest communities and other domestic stakeholders in the definition of illegal logging, controversies over which have derailed previous US efforts to address this problem in bilateral trade agreements (Brack and Bucknell 2011: 7). US officials, prosecutors, and judges are thus placed in the difficult position of assessing the current state of foreign laws in order to determine whether a given timber shipment has been harvested illegally. Lacey Act enforcement relies

---

[11] Except where otherwise indicated, the analysis in this section is based on the following sources: Brack and Bucknell 2011; Lawson and MacFaul 2010; presentations and discussions at Chatham House and Potomac Illegal Logging Fora, 10–11 Jan. and 4 May 2011.

primarily on spot inspections by US Customs and Fish and Wildlife agents, often based on tipoffs from external competitors or internal whistleblowers. Such inspections and the prosecutions to which they give rise are highly resource-intensive, and hence necessarily infrequent. The US Department of Agriculture Animal and Plant Health Inspection Service (APHIS), the agency responsible for processing declaration forms, reports that it lacks the funds to develop software to enter the information into a database, and to conduct sensitivity analyses which might help it identify high-risk imports.

Given these limits of enforcement capacity, the major impact of the amended Lacey Act is likely to come through the deterrent effect of high-profile prosecutions, which despite their low frequency appear to create strong incentives for larger firms to set up internal legality assurance systems to mitigate the risk of criminal liability and reputational damage.[12] The Act is also likely to stimulate importing firms to enroll in private certification systems as a means of demonstrating "due care" in avoiding illegally logged wood. Unlike the EUTR, Lacey does not explicitly encourage external actors to provide due diligence systems, although participation in private certification schemes may be adduced as evidence of "due care" in avoiding illegally logged wood. Some US NGOs such as the Forest Legality Alliance are entrepreneurially taking on this role by creating online declaration and risk assessment tools, while an alliance of industry associations and environmental NGOs has developed a set of "Lacey Act Due Care Consensus Standards," which encourage producers to adopt FSC, PEFC, or Seneca Creek/AHEC US Hardwood certification programs.[13] The SFI has revised its rules to incorporate the requirements of the Lacey Act, and there has been a significant rise in demand for private certification and legality verification services among US firms since its passage in 2008.

Despite these transatlantic differences in governance architecture, there are significant mutual influences and points of intersection between the US and EU regimes for combating illegal logging. Thus the EU FLEGT Action Plan encouraged US environmental activists to push for the Lacey Act amendment, while the latter helped to build political momentum for the passage of the EU Timber Regulation, and inspired the European Parliament to incorporate an "underlying offense" of handling illegal timber which was absent from the Commission's original proposal (British Woodworking Federation 2010). Conversely, the revised legality standards and export licenses produced by

---

[12] The Justice Department has pursued two cases under Lacey, both against Gibson Guitars, which were settled successfully in Aug. 2012. But these cases relied heavily on tip-offs from competitors with unusual inside knowledge, while the Gibson prosecutions provoked a hostile hearing in the US House of Representatives, which threatened to enact new legislation gutting the enforcement provisions of the Act (Bewley 2012).

[13] <http://www.laceyduecare.com>.

FLEGT VPAs will dramatically simplify the task of US Lacey Act enforcement for imported timber from those countries. EU authorities' monitoring and review of firms' internal risk management systems and private third-party certification schemes could likewise be used as an information platform for improving the effectiveness of the more conventional US enforcement system and adjudicating due care claims in US courts. Dense networks of private activists, public officials, and business people from both jurisdictions meet regularly in illegal logging fora on both sides of the Atlantic to exchange experiences and ideas about how best to exploit opportunities for productive interaction between the US and EU regimes.

But the most powerful synergy between the two regimes is their combined impact on other countries. The US and the EU together account for a majority of the global wood market, which is now formally closed to illegally harvested timber. The Lacey Act amendment has helped to overcome resistance to FLEGT VPAs and stimulate the negotiation of domestic legality assurance systems in countries like Indonesia, where these had previously stalled. The coexistence of Lacey and the EUTR ensures that illegal wood exports from non-VPA countries are not simply diverted from one large northern market to another. Their joint example has stepped up moral and political pressure on other timber-importing economies to adopt similar measures. The EU and US have been "gospelling" the virtues of legality verification models both jointly and separately, encouraging other countries to create similar regulations excluding illegal imports, in order to buttress the broader timber legality regime. These efforts have achieved some significant successes. Most notably, Australia adopted its own Illegal Logging Prohibition Act, which entered into force in November 2012, making it a criminal offense to place illegally sourced timber on the national market. Like the EUTR, this law requires Australian importers to exercise due diligence in avoiding illegally sourced timber. Currently, the government is developing regulations that will detail these requirements, which are expected to be in place by November 2014.[14] In addition, the Trans-Pacific Trade Partnership currently being negotiated between the US and other Pacific rim countries (including Australia, Canada, Chile, Japan, Malaysia, Mexico, New Zealand, Peru, Singapore, and Vietnam) incorporates provisions for developing Lacey-style legislation that would prohibit illegal timber imports (Congressional Research Service 2013).

Crucial to the effectiveness of any transnational regime to combat illegal logging and promote sustainable forestry is the incorporation of China, which has emerged as the world's largest importer of timber from high-risk countries, as well as a leading global exporter of processed wood products

---

[14] <http://www.daff.gov.au/forestry/policies/illegal-logging>; <http://www.iges.or.jp/en/news/press/12_12_19.html> (accessed May 2013).

such as furniture, flooring, plywood, and paper (European Forest Institute 2011b). China now officially increasingly accepts the need for national and international action to combat illegal logging, and has signed bilateral cooperation agreements or memoranda of understanding on FLEG with a number of countries, including the US, the EU, Australia, Indonesia, Russia, and Myanmar. Few tangible steps have thus far been taken to implement these agreements, beyond the issuance of non-binding guidelines for Chinese forest firms abroad. But both the national authorities and forest firms themselves appear to recognize the strategic importance of sustainability certification and legality verification in safeguarding access for Chinese wood exports to Western markets. Thus China has created its own national forest certification scheme, which is now recognized by the PEFC, and is also developing its own legality verification system, which will include chain-of-custody tracking within the country (Bartley 2014; Sun and Canby 2011; Cashore and Stone 2013). The take-up of these schemes and their impact on the behavior of Chinese wood products firms, which often have little internal capacity to monitor and control their supply chains, will depend in no small measure on the rigor with which the US and the EU enforce their due diligence/due care requirements. Critical in this regard will be the EU's approach to recognizing the Chinese national legality verification and certification scheme (European Forest Institute 2011b; Bartley 2011; van der Wilk 2010). Such benchmarking for equivalence of local certification and verification schemes will be equally important for integrating other large producing countries like Russia and Brazil, which are unlikely to sign FLEGT VPAs, into the emergent transnational forestry regime.[15]

10.6 Conclusion

Since 1992, national governments have failed to produce a binding global forest convention. Instead, beset by divergent interests and values, governments have created a weak international public regime that has failed to produce meaningful change on the ground. In response to this impasse, private actors have sought to push the forest governance agenda forward piecemeal. The FSC sidestepped the primary barriers to a global forest convention by balancing the voice of the main stakeholders and taking the discussion outside

---

[15] Russia participates in a FLEG program with the EU funded through the European Neighbourhood and Partnership Instrument (ENPI), www.enpi-fleg.org, and has also been a major growth pole for FSC certification (Malets 2011). Brazil has been rapidly improving its domestic forest governance and enforcement capacity in recent years, while also experiencing significant growth in certification of individual FMUs both through the FSC and through a PEFC-affiliated national scheme (Lawson and MacFaul 2010).

the deadlocked intergovernmental arena. Addressing the voice gap between north and south, bypassing entrenched government actors, and pursuing regulation voluntarily along supply chains and through industry associations, this strategy elicited competing responses from other actors. The FSC was quickly followed by industry imitators with weaker standards, which were broadly adopted and threatened to undermine the nascent experiment in multi-stakeholder forest certification. However, through public comparison and benchmarking for equivalence, the competition between private schemes resulted in mutual adjustment and upward convergence of standards, without completely closing the gap between them. But the most serious limitation was the sluggish uptake of certification in the global south, due to the more difficult conditions faced by developing country producers.

Faced with this lacuna, the EU moved unilaterally to advance a different but complementary approach to transnational forest governance. Inspired by an emerging global consensus on the role of illegal logging in tropical deforestation and disciplined by WTO procedural constraints on import restrictions and requirements for consultation, the EU launched the FLEGT Action Plan. At its heart is a participatory process requiring developing countries to reach consensus on the definition and prevention of illegal logging among domestic stakeholders, combined with external support for the construction and monitoring of export licensing legality assurance systems. Encouraged by the EU initiative, American environmental activists successfully joined with domestic forest firms in persuading the US government to amend the Lacey Act, thereby reinforcing political momentum for passage of the EU Timber Regulation. Despite their architectural differences, the EU and US regimes together close off the world's largest markets to illegally logged wood, build an ongoing platform for transnational exchange of information and implementation experience, and provide a powerful stimulus to participation in forest certification and legality verification schemes by private firms and third-country governments.

Although there is still no global forestry convention, the interaction between these pieces seems to be generating an effective patchwork or joined-up regime, whose core elements have experimentalist characteristics. In particular, by combining local experimentation with performance monitoring, information pooling, and deliberative review of successes and failures, there is increased capacity for coordinated learning from pieces of the regime complex. The rise of private forest certification demonstrated the importance of experimentalist disciplines of participatory goal-setting and comparative performance monitoring, while its own failures pointed to the need to address capacity gaps between north and south to advance a transnational forestry regime complex. FLEGT provided an important pathway for addressing these capacity issues, but also created a platform for learning from comparison of overlapping negotiations in different settings. The VPAs in turn quickly demonstrated both their transformative potential and their limited capacity for autonomous diffusion, which the EUTR and the Lacey Act, as well as the possibility of similar legislation in other countries, go a long way toward redressing. Compared to the weak public international regime built since 1992, this emergent regime complex, which involves a multiplicity of regulatory experiments, monitoring, and revision based on implementation experiences, appears as though it will produce a more comprehensive, strongly recursive policy effort than its individual pieces or stand-alone public or private efforts. Although implementation of many components of this emergent regime is still at an early stage and faces major practical challenges, there is evidence that it has already begun to have a significant and measurable impact on the ground, both in improving domestic forest governance and in reducing illegal logging.[16]

Four major conclusions for transnational regime formation follow from this analysis. First, the chapter shows that there are multiple pathways to the creation of an experimentalist transnational regime, which can be combined in various ways in specific empirical cases. These pathways have different starting points (public/private, national/international), involve different causal mechanisms, and operate at different levels (within and between separate regulatory schemes). But they lead in a common direction: towards the construction of transnational governance regimes with a similar experimentalist architecture, which can be nested within one another vertically and joined up horizontally. Table 10.2 presents in analytical form the four main pathways and associated causal mechanisms through which an experimentalist transnational governance regime has developed in the forest sector over the past two decades. Although the interactions between them analyzed in this chapter are specific to the forestry case, these ideal-typical pathways and mechanisms—and others like them—are general enough to be applicable across many other sectors of transnational governance (cf. Sabel and Zeitlin 2011).

Second, this chapter challenges the view that building an effective transnational regime, capable of common interest regulation in the language of this volume, is possible only under restrictive scope conditions, notably the

---

[16] For a comprehensive overview of accomplishments and challenges facing the emergent forest governance regime, see Overdevest and Zeitlin (2013). An authoritative study by Chatham House of 12 countries which together account for 50 percent of illegal wood trade estimates that they were responsible for a 22 percent reduction in the global incidence of illegal logging between 2002 and 2008, while imports of illegally sourced wood to the countries in the sample had fallen 30 percent from their peak (Lawson and MacFaul 2010). The study covered five producer countries (Brazil, Cameroon, Ghana, Indonesia, Malaysia), two import processing countries (China, Vietnam), and five consumer countries (France, Japan, the Netherlands, the UK, and the US), using a variety of methods including wood-balance analysis and expert surveys.

Table 10.2 Pathways and mechanisms of experimentalist regime formation in the forest sector

Pathway	Mechanism(s)	Case(s)
From multilateral impasse and public inaction to private transnational regime (TRR) formation	• Balanced, multi-stakeholder governance • Vertical diffusion along supply chains • Horizontal diffusion through industry associations	• FSC
From unilateral public (national/regional) regulatory initiatives (TIRs) to transnational joint governance	• Multilateral procedural requirements as reflexive disciplines	• EU FLEGT
Convergence between separate national/regional regimes	• Mutual influence through transnational networks • Exchange of information and experiences • Reciprocal support towards third countries	• Interactions between EU FLEGT/Timber Regulation and US Lacey Act
Joining up competing pieces of regime complexes	• Public comparison and benchmarking for equivalence	• Upwards convergence between FSC and PEFC • Public recognition of private certification schemes

existence of a hegemonic power or broad convergence of interests, values, and beliefs among the parties. The forest governance case is widely discussed precisely because it is beset with interest and value conflicts and the absence of a hegemon. This chapter demonstrates how polyarchy, diversity, and strategic uncertainty can be used productively to promote the formation of a transnational regime based on coordinated learning from decentralized experimentation. Insofar as there has been a partial convergence of policy preferences and beliefs among key actors in the forest sector, which includes developing as well as developed countries, this should be considered as an endogenous *product* of the experimentalist mechanisms we analyze, notably reflexive learning from past failures of both public and private regulation, multilateral procedural constraints on unilateral initiatives, and benchmarking for equivalence of competing schemes, rather than an exogenous *precondition* for the construction of an effective transnational regime. Polyarchy, diversity, and strategic uncertainty characterize many issue areas in global governance today, suggesting the wide applicability of experimentalist approaches to transnational regime formation.

Third, experimentalism provides an analytical framework for evaluating transnational governance interactions in regime complexes. In our view, experimentalism provides a normatively desirable governance architecture for building regimes that respect diversity, address complexity, and respond to change. The four architectural elements of (1) broad participatory goal-setting, (2) decentralized experimentation with alternative implementation approaches, (3) performance monitoring, information pooling, and peer review, and (4) revision of goals, metrics, and procedures based on deliberative comparison of experience, identify a set of governance functions that can be provided through a variety of institutional forms by different combinations of public and private actors. The keys to evaluating the effectiveness of such regime complexes lie in whether progress is made towards achieving the desired performance goals, and whether failures and the inevitable unintended consequences of specific institutional designs are recursively recognized and redressed.

Looking forward, we argue that a key mechanism for realizing the promise of the emergent transnational regime is the experimentalist discipline of benchmarking and public comparison of its components. Benchmarking for equivalence is an important accountability mechanism for polyarchic governance arrangements. Because polyarchic systems, by definition, lack a central authority with the legitimacy to impose its will, the process of publicly comparing nascent experiments constitutes a crucial platform for deliberation and reflexivity. Benchmarking leads to public reflection on successes and failures that creates mutual accountability by obliging actors in the regime to provide persuasive accounts of their performance. Regularly accounting for performance is a central requirement of fully developed experimentalist regimes. To support such accountability, experimentalist regimes must be both performance-based and participatory. In forestry, the nascent transnational regime has been characterized by policy experiments that led to performance assessment, learning from success and failure, and broad stakeholder participation. Introducing more systematic benchmarking both within each component of the regime complex (forest certification schemes, VPAs, legality assurance systems, timber regulations) and between them could thus help to institutionalize a platform from which to continue productive adaptation and elaboration of the emerging experimentalist governance architecture.

11

Regional Integration and Transnational Regulatory Regimes

The Polycentric Architecture of Governance in Latin American Telecommunications

Jacint Jordana and David Levi-Faur

11.1 Introduction

Governance is becoming increasingly transnational. This means inter alia that transnational regulatory spaces are increasingly institutionalized at the regional and global levels as alternative or complementary spaces of regulatory authority. One of the major institutional designs in transnational regulatory spaces is the regulatory network. Neither hierarchies nor markets, networks are major features of any research agenda aiming to better explain the diverse and polycentric institutional architecture of transnational governance. The extent to which networks can develop innovative modes of decision-making, public sphere processes, and strategies of development is highly critical to any viable alternative to hierarchy in global and regional governance. Commentators have high hopes for networks, generated, for example, by Sabel and Zeitlin's theory of experimental governance (2012). This chapter examines networks' contributions and limitations in promoting transnational regulatory governance, with special reference to the case of regional telecommunications networks in Latin America.

As the Introduction noted, this region has transnational integration regimes (TIRs) with weak capacities to help transnational networks to solve their coordination problems. Unlike the EU accession and neighbourhood policies, TIRs in Latin America have extremely limited capacities to frame and assist attempts of transnational regulatory networks at furthering regulatory integration (see the chapter by Andonova and Tuta for a contrasting case).

The telecommunications industry and its governance more generally have experienced radical change since the 1980s. Publicly owned post, telegraph, and telecoms (PTT) corporations, which had been adopted almost universally, were dismantled and privatized. New digital technologies transformed the structure of investment and industrial organization in the sector, and opened it for foreign investment by multinationals. The convergence of telecoms, internet, and computer technologies was a great boon to consumers worldwide, and the coincidence of privatization on the one hand and a booming industry and user-friendly technology on the other made the sector, rightly or wrongly, a great showpiece for neo-liberal policies. It is clear, however, that the policy changes that allowed the growth of the industry consisted of more than deregulation. They did not involve the retreat of the state from the economy via privatization and the removal of legal and regulatory constraints on private actors. Telecoms reforms, in Latin America and in the rest of the world, necessitated reform of the state and the creation of legal and regulatory structures with policy capacities that could enhance, monitor, and enforce a competitive environment (Gutierrez 2003; Jordana 2012). This environment called for more than the protection of property rights or the promotion and enforcement of competition laws. The governance model that emerged in Europe and the OECD countries embodied sector-specific regulation-*for*-competition (Levi-Faur 2003). This model involved the creation of arms-length professional regulatory agencies to govern the sector and a framework of national law credibly committed to competition. At the centre of the day-to-day governance of this model stood national agencies that regulated the telecoms operators on issues ranging from the cost of service to the interconnection and interoperability of networks. Their policy capacities became the *sine qua non* for the successful development of the national telecoms markets.[1]

Regulatory spaces at regional levels, not unlike regulatory spaces at global and national levels, are slowly but surely being institutionalized all over the world. These regulatory spaces are diverse in their institutional designs. At

---

[1] The model of independent regulatory agencies that govern through the promotion of competition is not confined to telecoms. Since the late 1980s, and especially during the 1990s, the number of new regulatory agencies in Latin America exploded (Jordana and Levi-Faur 2005). This growth was particularly important in the utilities, where privatization in many sectors boosted new market regulation, intensifying a process that went beyond the diffusion of privatization itself. In the telecommunications sector, we identify the creation of the first agency in Costa Rica in 1963, and the second in Chile in 1985. A few years later, suddenly, between 1990 and 1996, 13 Latin American countries created regulatory agencies. Three latecomer countries in the region (Brazil, Dominican Republic, and Uruguay) created similar regulatory agencies in the next few years (Jordana and Levi-Faur 2006). By 2002 almost all countries, with the notable exception of Cuba, had established a regulatory agency for telecommunications.

the national level they are often based on the separation of the political from the bureaucratic and the regulatory. The most significant indicator of this development is the global diffusion of regulatory agencies as a form of governance that undermines Weberian forms of bureaucratic control (Jordana et al. 2011). Rule making, monitoring, and enforcement in this process have been traditionally embedded in the national level.

We turn our attention now to the global level. Here one alternative to the limitations of traditional intergovernmental organizations (with their tight political controls) could be the development of global and regional regulatory networks, composed of public and private actors. For many sectors, the shift from government to governance at the national level may also be a shift—or so it seems—from international political institutions to transnational regulatory networks. The ability of these networks to augment capacities and prestige and to become an important mode of governance and regulatory integration—also involving a development program—depends on their environment and on the development of "institutional scripts" that determine their autonomy, mechanisms of decision-making, finance, role, and legitimacy (Bruszt and McDermott in this volume). While regional regulatory networks have emerged in many parts of the world (Berg and Horrall 2008), we explore in detail the case of the establishment of transnational networks in Latin American telecommunications. We aim to provide a systemic account of the abilities of networks to become important components of transnational developmental regimes with regard to four issues: regional regulatory harmonization, asymmetric information exchange, support for dealing with domestic enforcement problems, and common positions in global debates on telecoms policy (cf. Gorp and Maitland 2009).

We raise three questions. First, what are the organizational variations, the external and internal supporters, and the main characteristics of the telecommunications regulatory networks in the region, and which factors facilitate or constrain their promotion of regional governance? Second, how do these networks interact with the political integration initiatives for regional or subregional governance in this sector? Third, to what extent can regional regulatory networks help the developmental role assigned to them by Bruszt and McDermott's (2012) framework of transnational integration regimes as development programs?

11.2 Networks and Institutions as Modes of Transnational Governance in Latin American Telecommunications

A network, considered as an actor in the international context, is "an organizational form capable to achieve significant outcomes" (Kahler 2011) operating on set of relatively stable relationships of a non-hierarchical and interdependent nature, which link a variety of actors (cf. Börzel 1998: 254; Podolny and Page 1998: 58; Ahrne and Brunsson 2011: 6). Unlike international organizations and agencies, networks often do not have principals or strong administrative and independent financial capacities. In some cases, they have formal structures, like associations, just to support the continuity of the network and provide basic resources to their members. In other cases, they are launched or promoted by established international organizations, but operate separately from their hierarchical structures. What are important, however, are the interactions that occur among their members. Also, their decision rules are often flexible and non-binding, and their membership is voluntary.

While the literature often distinguishes networks from markets and hierarchies (Rhodes 1990; Klijn 2008; Sørensen and Torfing 2007) and tends to see networks as stable informal organizations, under certain conditions networks can be transformed, institutionalized, and formalized (Levi-Faur 2011b; Berg and Horrall 2008). There is, though, scant literature on the question of how to encourage, inhibit, accommodate, and challenge the condition of networks and their relations with other networks and institutions. However, the growth of networks at the transnational level attracts more and more attention to them and their strength as a form of governance.

One way to understand the role of networks in governance is to distinguish them from other modes of governance. We define "mode of governance" as the coupling of a decision-making mechanism with a sphere of authority (Levi-Faur 2012). The notion of a sphere of authority draws on Rosenau and indicates the institutions where authority is located (Rosenau 2007). Characterizing the phenomena as spheres helps to separate them from territories, nations, or sovereigns. Authority can be located at the national level and at the transnational level, and at the federal level and at the local level, and it can be private and civil and not only statist. Using the notion of authority instead of sovereignty helps to open up the institutional sphere to wider and more relevant ways of making and changing policies in political space than the ambiguous notion of sovereignty allows. Thus, networks as spheres of authority involve basically the use of persuasion to activate governance functions and facilitate decisions, and the intense flow of information among the members of the network as a catalyst to realize these functions. Fundamentally, persuasion as a decision-making mechanism involves the elaboration of values, preferences, and interests as well as the rationalization and framing of options for action and the exchange of ideas and information in a deliberative manner, to make governance effective. Consequently, these processes may also induce changes in actor preferences and behavior, which in turn can transform policies and regulatory styles in their domestic settings, favoring the development of more integrated regulatory regimes (Bruszt and McDermott in this volume; Andonova and Tuta in this volume).

The primary outputs of regulatory networks are, as identified by Berg and Horrall (2008: 188), "(1) events and meetings; (2) data for benchmarking; (3) public pronouncements; (4) material for stakeholders; (5) capacity-building for professional staff; (6) best practice laws, procedures and rules; (7) regulatory network news; and (8) technical studies". Thus, the network mode of governance involves the use of these instruments, some of them having the character of club goods, while others are pure or impure (excludable) public goods, to fulfill the purposes of the network's members, in particular its sponsors or leading members. Governance functions that we expect can be activated by networks and other entities include norm and agenda setting, consensus building, policy coordination, knowledge production, exchange, and dissemination, and also the use of international reputation for domestic purposes. In our empirical analysis we observe the specific capabilities of the main transnational networks and entities identified in the Latin American regulatory space. While norm and public agenda setting can be promoted by pronouncements or by diffusing best practice laws—which are pure public goods—consensus building, international reputation, and policy coordination basically require investment in events and meetings—which are more akin to club goods—and all functions related to knowledge management require training, studies, benchmarking data, studies, and so on, configuring a mix of different types of goods (Berg and Horrall 2008).

The creation, development, consolidation, stability, and decay of networks as compared with other modes of governance are issues that have attracted little attention in the literature. Why would participants prefer a network mode of governance over markets or over the creation of formal hierarchical organizations? Functional, power-centered, and ideational theories might be useful here. In the functional version, networks would be the preferred mode of governance when the exchange of information is the most valuable and least costly regional public good to pursue, while no capability to produce more public goods exists. Power-centered approaches might focus on the institutional constraints on establishing more hierarchical modes of governance and on the costs of ungoverned markets. Ideational theories tend to emphasize the role of the environment that makes networks and other horizontal modes of governance fit with the ideology of the actors and the logic of appropriateness.

Here we aim to examine regional networks of regulators as a particular mode of transnational governance, and how this sphere of authority interacts in their governance functions with other spheres of authority, for example, intergovernmental public institutions operating on a regional scale. In our case, we find the coexistence of a regulatory network in the region, established shortly after the creation of regulatory agencies in most Latin American countries, with previous institutional structures operating at the regional or subregional level to promote the development of the telecommunications sector. Thus, we have in the region during the 2000s a separation between two different modes of governance, the traditional one (politicians in public institutions) and a new one (professionals in regulatory networks), with different mechanisms of decision-making. This provides an interesting means of determining which modes of governance tend to predominate at the regional level or, more precisely, how they coexist and under which premises.

The study of transnational networks and institutions in the telecoms sector allows us to examine the way they are integrated into the Latin American regulatory space and how they compete and collaborate as modes of governance (Djelic and Sahlin-Andersson 2006; Martinez-Diaz and Woods 2009). Unlike Europe, where elected politicians have to compete with networks of regulatory agencies and the European Commission itself as alternative modes of governance in this sector (Levi-Faur 2011b), in Latin America the institutional landscape is much less crowded and is dominated by traditional intergovernmental institutions such as the regional branch of the International Telecommunication Union (ITU) and the Organization of American States (OAS) and its telecom branch Comisión Interamericana de Telecomunicaciones (CITEL), which also involves the US and Canada as members. The region has no clear supranational institution or intergovernmental center. There is no Commission, no regional directive such as the one issued by the EU institutions, and no Council of Ministers. In short, seen from an institutional perspective, in Latin America the lack of competition among different modes of governance makes networks a more feasible option. Viewed from a functional capacity perspective, the low level of integration when compared with Europe makes networks not only feasible but desirable, in so far as no more sophisticated "aggregation technology" exists to produce a larger offer of regional public goods (Berg and Horrall 2008).

In fact, in Latin America we find a situation in which traditional strategies of regulatory integration have not always been successful in advancing regional convergence of national telecommunications regulatory regimes during recent decades. On the one hand, south–south integration initiatives, basically MERCOSUR (Brazil, Argentina, Uruguay, and Paraguay—Venezuela joined in 2006) and the Comunidad Andina de Naciones (CAN, Andean Community of Nations: Colombia, Peru, Ecuador, and Bolivia), have developed subregional structures to promote dialogue and joint efforts among their members, but the effective results are not particularly striking. On the other hand, north–south initiatives, particularly the North American Free Trade Agreement (NAFTA), involving Mexico, the United States, and Canada, and more recently the Central America Free Trade Agreement (CAFCA), have produced significant regulatory changes in telecommunications for countries like Mexico in the 1990s or Costa Rica during late 2000s. These initiatives have forced open the markets with the establishment of a formal pro-competition regulatory structure. However, such processes of regulative integration have often been highly contested, and neither have led to clear or exceptional improvements in market conditions nor facilitated regulatory harmonization among the countries involved. Thus, it would appear that a window of opportunity opened for a regional network mode of governance in Latin American telecoms during the 2000s, based on regulators' frequent personal exchanges and the sharing of similar values and technical understanding.

To analyse this case in detail, it would be useful to distinguish between different transnational networks and international organizations involved in the governance of Latin American telecommunications. First, those entities relate to intergovernmental and supranational international organizations. To some extent, they are based on command or majoritarian decision-making mechanisms, and are not expected to be fully independent from their principals, although eventually they may develop hybrid modes of governance between hierarchies and networks. Second, independent transnational networks of public regulators are emerging from the bottom-up, and do not have a principal in the form of an established international organization. Third, we find regional transnational organizations of telecom operators. These organizations aim to establish direct interaction with regional governance organizations, and also adopt highly decentralized structures in their internal dynamics, like a hybrid mode of governance, although they are dependent on their principals for funding and general orientation.

11.3 International Telecom Organizations in Latin America

International organizations that operate in Latin America are among the most important sources of support for regional governance of telecoms. Two types are especially important. First are wide-purpose, territorially based international organizations (or multilateral trade agreements) that focus on regional or subregional integration goals. Most important here is the Organization of American States (OAS; Organización de los Estados Americanos, OEA), which was established in 1948 for pan-continental purposes and headquartered in Washington, DC. Second are sectoral-based international organizations such as the Latin American branch of the International Telecommunications Union (ITU), an intergovernmental organization affiliated to the United

Nations that is one of the oldest intergovernmental organizations in the world. In its original form it was established in 1865.

The regional networks that are connected to these international organizations are presented in Table 11.1. One of the most important is the Comisión Interamericana de Telecomunicaciones (CITEL), an entity created by the OEA/OAS; it is an active international organization in this field. Thus, this is a case of a territorially based international organization that has created a subunit specializing in telecoms' regional governance. CITEL, as an OEA branch, was created in 1994, at the highest point of the sector's commitment to market competition and privatization, to promote its governance. It aimed to find a common site for the dialogue between the public and the private sectors, and to contribute to setting new collaborative rules. The organization has two types of membership. On the one side are representatives from the public sector (who now come from 33 countries); they may be from any type of public body, and often ministers are involved. On the other side are associated members from different areas of the private sector, but mainly from regulated firms. This parallel structure aims to promote a network type of organization in order to widen CITEL's governance functions, in particular to expand its core functions and facilitate information exchange.

CITEL's main governance purpose, however, is to focus on pure public goods, promoting agenda and rule setting on the technical and regulatory side of telecommunications, in order to establish common norms, network interoperability, joint use of the radio-electric spectrum, and so forth. During the 2000s CITEL became more and more a place where governmental positions for forthcoming ITU conferences were negotiated, with the aim of reaching consensus for regional strength in global forums. This is particularly true for the United States and Canada, which usually look to conclude hemispheric agreements at CITEL—while striving to establish common regional standards, something strongly contested by several Latin American countries.

CITEL has a complex structure including a rotating board of directors and two specialized committees called "Permanent Consultative Committees" (CCP) in which detailed discussions take place. All these bodies meet at least once a year, and each includes a number of working groups, which include representatives of several countries. They focus on particular topics of telecommunications policy. In these meetings, they discuss different points of view, exchange information, and approach positions regarding their representation in worldwide meetings. In addition to these regular gatherings, CITEL is very active in providing specialized training: it has established a number of training centers in most Latin American countries, it offers a large number of courses, provides grants for course participants, and also coordinates these tasks with the regional branch of the ITU, which is also involved in providing specialized training. CITEL and ITU have also collaborated in a number of technical projects, as for example the creation of a database for the allocation of the radio electric spectrum in the whole region.

CITEL has published reports only since 2003. However, the Blue Book on telecommunications policy prepared by CITEL (2005), which has been updated every few years since 1996, is an interesting example of a collective document that summarizes the main points of consensus among OEA/ CITEL members regarding the regulation and policy of the telecommunications sector in the region. The Blue Book is published jointly with the ITU branch in the Americas, and its contents represent a common understanding about the background of most issues of telecommunications policies and strategies that have been developed in the region since the liberalization of the sector in early 1990s.

The regional office of the ITU, which was opened in 1992, is active in launching programs to provide technical support and promote the advance of telecommunications in the less developed countries in the region. In addition to governmental participation, the regional branch ITU has also expanded its membership to a network-like structure involving 115 organizations, which include firms, NGOs, scientific units, and regional organizations. The network is employed to disseminate information, facilitate meetings, and provide specialized training. In fact, the ITU office is strongly focused on developing policies in the area of telecommunications in the region, providing technical advice on the telecom governance of less developed countries and also coordinating some ICT development projects. This initiative represents a move towards establishing a hybrid mode of regional governance, taking advantage of the characteristics of network-based procedures within a more traditional institution.

In addition to CITEL and the regional branch of ITU, we also find a number of subregional organizations with a similar operating logic (see Table 11.1). These subregional initiatives have a public nature, taking the form of an international treaty or of sectoral initiatives of subregional integration processes. For example, a group of Central American countries established Comisión Técnica Regional de Telecomunicaciones (COMTELCA) in 1966. Originally a network of public operators, COMTELCA is an association of different Central American regulatory agencies that served the purpose of promoting Central American integration processes. Although the organization has not achieved size or regulatory relevance during its long history, it represents a common space for subregional governance involving national authorities and regulatory agencies. Also at the subregional level are other structures that serve some governance functions, mainly consensus building and policy coordination, in other parts of the continent, such as the MERCOSUR Committee for Communications, SGT-1, established in 1995, or the Comite Andino de Autoridades de Telecomunicationes (CAATEL),

Table 11.1 Regional regulatory governance based on international organizations

Name	Sponsoring IO	Type	Year of creation	Organization (secretariat, budget, etc.)	Scope and membership	Main interest
Comité Andino de Autoridades de Telecomunicaciones, CAATEL	Andean Community of Nations (CAN/CAN)	International organization (delegated committee)	1991	Secretariat in Lima, Peru (Secretariat Unit of Comunidad Andina)	5 Regulatory Agencies of 5 countries (also participation of government unit)	Joint representation in international bodies, common agreements in some areas of regulation
Subgrupo de Trabajo 1, Comunicaciones- SGT-1	MERCOSUR	International organization (delegated committee)	1995	Secretariat in Montevideo, Uruguay	(MERCOSUR) 4 RA for 4 countries (+ Venezuela as observer since 2007)	Adopting common regulations in particular areas (roaming, borders, frequencies,...); information and personal exchange
Comisión Técnica Regional de Telecomunicaciones, COMTELCA	Own international agreement	Network of regulatory agencies having also an institutional form	1966	Secretariat in Tegucigalpa, Honduras Budget less than US$250.000	6 RA and 4 public firms, in 6 countries (Central America)	Technical collaboration, based on an international agreement
Eastern Caribbean Telecommunications Authority, ECTEL	Own international agreement	International organization: supranational regulatory agency	2000	Secretariat in Castries, Saint Lucia (offices in each country)	Caribbean—1 RA for 5 countries (with commissions in each one)	Regulatory activity (rule setting, supervision, etc.)
Caribbean Telecommunications Union, CTU		Intergovernmental organization	1989	Secretariat in Port of Spain, T&T	Caribbean—all Caribbean countries, governmental and non-governmental	Coordination, sharing information, training, launching subregional projects

Table 11.1 Continued

Name	Sponsoring IO	Type	Year of creation	Organization (secretariat, budget, etc.)	Scope and membership	Main interest
Comisión Interamericana de Telecomunicaciones, CITEL	OEI/OAS	International organization (delegated committees)	1994	Secretariat in Washington, DC (OEI/OAS)	Pan-American 33 governments from the Americas 110 associated members (mainly sector firms)	Training, public consultations, coordination with IUT, supporting representation in international forums
International Telecommunications Union, Regional Office. Americas	ITU	Regional branch of UN sectoral organization	1992	Brasilia, Brazil (with 3 offices: Barbados, Honduras, Chile)	35 countries from the Americas 115 sector members (firms, NGO, regional networks, scientific org., etc.)	Intra-regional cooperation, training. technical support, development assistance, reports

established in 1991. In addition to its regular interactions, CAATEL was also quite active in taking joint decisions for the regulation of some technical areas (e.g. satellite communications) during the 1990s and early 2000s.

11.4 Regulatory Agency Networks in Telecoms

Transnational regulatory networks can emerge from the bottom up, beginning as occasional encounters of national regulators and developing governance functions at the regional level. Their development can be also nurtured by external actors, both networks and wide-purpose organizations. There are a number of such networks in Latin America, but probably the most relevant is the regional network of telecom regulatory agencies, REGULATEL. Established in 1998 as a forum to facilitate policy coordination in the region among the new regulatory agencies in most Latin American countries, it began to operate after almost all countries had already created their regulatory agencies. The origin of REGULATEL is strongly related to a critical juncture when all Latin American countries sought to have a common position regarding international call termination costs, in opposition to US and Canadian interests that were seeking to quickly reduce their payments for call termination. This cleavage created the need to establish a forum separate from CITEL, centered on regulatory agencies instead of ministerial representatives. This was a real dispute and forged a view of interests to be defended jointly by the Latin American agencies, which all had a responsibility for that issue. REGULATEL rapidly brought together 20 telecommunications regulatory agencies in Latin America (thereafter three European agencies, from Portugal, Spain, and Italy, joined as observers, but Caribbean regulatory agencies were not invited).

Once the termination cost dispute was over, the network was already in operation, and the agencies, most of them still young, expanding organizations, continued to perform some governance activities and tried to keep the network structure functioning under certain limited internal rules. For example, REGULATEL members did not agree to pay any contribution to sustain the network, which created a permanent shortage of resources and the need to look for external support. Resistance in several countries stifled support for this initiative, limiting the possibility to develop a stronger transnational platform and to build up an international reputation for domestic purposes. Within this context, the European Commission supported the consolidation of the network (for example with a grant of €1 million for the period 2008–12 under the @LIS Program to promote development in Latin America).

The presidency of REGULATEL rotates each year among the heads of the 20 regulatory agencies that form the network. There is also a steering committee composed from a smaller number of agencies, and a General Secretary who assures administrative coordination among the members. A significant obstacle to the REGULATEL network becoming more institutionalized is related to the widely varied formal status of the telecom regulatory agencies in Latin America. There is a great diversity of arrangements for distributing responsibilities between the government and the agency: while in some countries all responsibilities are concentrated in the agency, in other countries most of the powers remain with the government. To activate some additional governance functions, REGULATEL has created several working groups that meet informally or interact over virtual spaces, allowing regulators to openly share opinions and exchange information. Three groups were operating in 2011, on broadband, indicators, and politics and regulation. The network operates only as a coordinating body, sharing tasks and responsibilities among its members and having a minimal organizational structure; but it does not operate as an international organization. Its members see the network as a forum, a common space in which to manage knowledge and build consensus: "The Forum operates through an organization that takes advantage of the infrastructure of the regulator of each member country, to carry out exchanges of information and experiences" (REGULATEL 2009). The main objectives are to facilitate the exchange of information and policy coordination, to promote the harmonization of regulation in the region (contributing to regional integration), and to identify and defend the regional interests as a whole, seeking to define common positions to be defended in international forums.

In spite of its limited governance capabilities, we find REGULATEL to be the core regional telecommunications regulatory network, being very active in organizing annual meetings in the region. In addition to its annual conference and several other meetings, it convenes an annual meeting with Asociación Hispanoamericana de Centros de Investigación y Empresas de Telecomunicaciones (AHCIET), a telecom operators group in which companies' professionals and regulators interact openly. To some extent, these periodic exchanges of information are believed to contribute to the harmonization of regulation in the region, facilitating the emergence of learning mechanisms (Zapata 2006). REGULATEL has also organized joint annual meetings since 2001 with the network of European telecoms agencies (BEREC since 2009, IRG before). These meetings bring together national agency representatives from both regions, and also hold high-level seminars in which best regulatory practices are presented and discussed. Because of its nature as a network, and the rotating presidency, REGULATEL does not have a leadership position in most regional integration initiatives. For example,

283

when in 2009 Iniciativa para la Integración de la Infraestructura Regional Suramericana (IIRSA) launched a plan to better coordinate roaming networks in Latin America, REGULATEL was consulted but its role was largely passive, and its participation in this initiative was also less visible than CITEL's (IIRSA 2010).

As for other activities of the network, it is worth mentioning that REGULATEL has produced a limited number of commissioned reports and specialized research publications. Some of these reports had a significant impact in clarifying issues regarding regulatory diversity in the region, as for example a report prepared in 2006 on the provision of universal service (Stern 2009). REGULATEL also produces an electronic bulletin, which details information and news about regulatory activities in telecommunications within the region. REGULATEL has not developed an intensive training program, in spite of occasionally launching various training activities in partnership with international organizations.

A parallel network involving Caribbean utility regulators exists. The Organisation of Caribbean Utility Regulators (OOCUR) was created in 2002 and includes agencies dealing with telecommunications regulation. This is not a formal organization, but a network of regulatory agencies which exchange information, promote joint activities, and facilitate their interactions, similar to REGULATEL but on a smaller scale (see Table 11.2). It is interesting to note that it was created years after the establishment of the Caribbean Telecommunications Union (CTU), and could also represent an attempt to develop a separate structure for regulatory agencies, albeit less formalized, to allow more intensive interaction among the national public regulators.

Table 11.2 Independent bottom-up networks

Name & acronym	Sponsoring organization	Type	Year of creation	Organization (secretariat, budget, etc.)	Scope and membership	Main interest
Foro de Entes reguladores latinoamericanos de Reguladores, REGULATEL	EU funding	Network of regulatory agencies	1998	Secretariat in Bogotá, Colombia	Latin American: 20 Latin Am. RA (+3 European RA as observers)	Regular meetings, professional exchanges, training, sharing research and information
Organization of Caribbean Utility Regulators, OOCUR		Network of regulatory agencies	2002	Secretariat in Port of Spain, Trinidad and Tobago	Caribbean: 11 RA (utilities) from 10 countries (Caribbean)	Research, training, information, collaboration in utilities regulation

11.5 Regional Business Associations in Latin American Telecoms

The third type of transnational structure emerging in regional regulatory governance is organized by regional business associations and non-governmental organizations. We might expect these associations to have as their goal to exert influence on agenda and rule setting, either directly at the regional or subregional level, or indirectly by accessing national regulatory authorities throughout the international arena. Eventually, they might also evolve into forms of private transnational government, providing some regional public goods, for example facilitating knowledge production and diffusion, but this is not usual in the telecoms sector as far as public regulation of market competition limits the potential. However, we find a particular situation in Latin American regarding the associations of telecommunications firms operating in the region. There are two large associations that have their origins in traditional post-colonial links: the Asociación Hispanoamericana de Centro de Investigación y Empresas de Telecomunicaciones (AHCIET), created in 1982 by the then public telecom monopolies in each country and promoted by the Spanish public operator Telefonica at that time, and also the Associação dos Operadores de Correios e Telecomunicações dos Países e Territórios de Língua Oficial Portuguesa (AICEP), originally promoted by the Portuguese government, in a similar way to the Spanish case.

Interestingly, both organizations transformed themselves from semi-governmental organizations during the 1980s and early 1990s, representing public telecom monopolies in each country, into private regional organizations in Latin America, having a mixed membership of privatized operators and new firms active in different subsectors of the telecom markets. These associations lost their semi-governmental nature when public operators were privatized and the newly established regulatory agencies did not join such associations. AHCIET, in particular, has become a very active organization, with an extended membership that creates a privileged space for interactions at regional level among telecom professionals and firms' executives, and it also maintains contacts with regulators and public servants. There is, for example, the organization and coordination of periodic meetings and conferences on different issues, such as various regulatory topics (broadband, international traffic), but also on applications of information and communications technology (ICT) in multiple subjects (such as education, management, and health). Dissemination activities are also important for AHCIET. In addition to providing many online courses, AHCIET produces a large number of reports and studies on telecommunications policy and ICT development in Latin America.

There are also some subregional associations of telecommunications firms, with a similar origin in so far as they were created before the privatization of the sector (see Table 11.3). This is the case of the Caribbean Association of National Telecommunication (CANTO) and Asociación de Empresas de Telecomunicaciones de la Comunidad Andina (ASETA). CANTO was created in 1985 in the Caribbean area and was semi-governmental in nature at the beginning, while the Andean Community created ASETA in 1974. Similar to the previous cases, during the 1990s they transformed themselves into subregional associations of firms, while the newly created public regulatory agencies established their own subregional organizations, as we have already detailed. While CANTO, in the Caribbean, appears to be quite active in promoting the interest of the telecoms operators in the area, ASETA appears to be less active, but still operational, and has included among its services technical advice and specialized consulting for private firms, probably as a way of being more grounded in the particular needs of its members.

Table 11.3 Regional business telecoms associations

Name/Acronym	Type	Year of creation	Organization (secretariat, budget, etc.)	Scope and membership	Main interest
Caribbean Association of National Telecommunication Organizations, CANTO	Network of regulated firms	1985	Secretariat in Port of Spain, Trinidad and Tobago	Caribbean: 113 firms in 31 countries (firms, consultants, etc.)	Information and personnel exchange, influencing policy, regular meetings
Asociación de Empresas de Telecomunicaciones de la Comunidad Andina, ASETA	Network of regulated firms	1974	Secretariat in Quito	Andean: 10 firms from 5 countries (ComAnd)	Training, exchange of information, interaction with regulators
Associação dos Operadores de Correios e Telecomunicações dos Países e Territórios de Língua Oficial Portuguesa, AICEP	Network of RA and regulated firms	1990		Cultural-Portuguese 24 firms (including post services), 5 RA, and 4 public bodies from 9 countries (using Portuguese in 3 continents)	Information exchange, network opportunities, disseminating innovation practices
Asociación Hispanoamericana de Centros de Investigación y Empresas de Telecomunicaciones, AHCIET	Network of regulated firms	1982	Secretariat in Madrid	+50 firms from 20 LatAm countries, + 1 Spanish firm (RA and governments left AHCIET in mid-1990s)	Information exchange, regular meetings, training, research and innovation dissemination, policy positions for technical issues

All these business associations, at regional or subregional level, actively promote the celebration of multiple events around relevant topics. They favour interaction with the governmental side of regulatory governance at the international level—mainly inviting representatives of regulatory agencies to their activities. At the regional level, there has not been much need to exert influence on specific regulatory issues, because these have been little debated at that level so far. However, it is important for business associations to create the conditions to construct the regional agenda, understood as embracing those policy issues and regulatory frameworks that dominate debates in most countries in the region and may also emerge as relevant regulatory issues at the regional level in the near future. All in all, we found some significant contributions to regional public goods from these non-governmental associations, aiming to complement the provision of regional public goods by regulatory networks and intergovernmental organizations in training, opportunities for personal contacts, exchange of information, and reports and analysis on relevant issues for the sector.

11.6 Analysis of the Findings

Our findings so far suggest that the regional regulatory space in Latin American telecoms is characterized by a large number of associative forms, transnational networks, and international organizations. Indeed, it is a larger and more stable configuration than we were expecting when we started this research. Figure 11.1 presents the growth in the number of active transnational networks and organizations in the region. As can be seen, we were able to identify 13 different active transnational entities and networks in operation since the mid-2000s. Overall, the greatest number was established in the 1990s, during the process of market liberalization and the diffusion of privatization in the region. When compared with the structure and dispersion of similar initiatives in Europe, we found that the Latin American telecoms space is more populated and also characterized by more subregional initiatives and stronger fragmentation (Levi-Faur 2003, 2011b; Jordana and Levi-Faur 2005).

The extensive transformation of the telecoms industry and telecoms governance at the national level in Latin America since the 1990s is well-reflected in the organizational development of its transnational regulatory regime in the 2000s. AHCIET became a private operators' network in the mid-1990s; in 1998 a new transnational actor—REGULATEL—appeared, adopting a network structure and aiming to coordinate national regulatory bodies at the regional level. This network was created in order to strengthen the regulatory identity and the independence of telecoms regulatory agencies, setting it apart

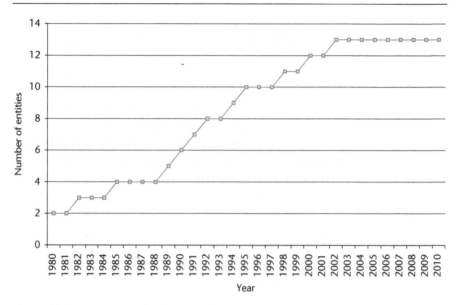

Figure 11.1 Transnational entities and networks in LA

from old and already established identities like AHCIET, in which originally governments were present together with telecom operators. Thereby, a core regulatory network for regional governance in this sector was established. In addition, the ministerial-political point of view remained active and became closely associated with CITEL, which was promoted by the OAS as a way to help Latin American countries to establish telecom markets. Its bilateral relations established during the 2000s suggest that REGULATEL has cooperated regularly with AHCIET, also organizing a joint annual meeting. However, CITEL has not made a similar arrangement with AHCIET; and CITEL and REGULATEL do not have close relations, but interact only in those cases where a third actor intervenes as a convener.

As for the subregional networks, we have identified multiple areas within the region (MERCOSUR, CAN, Caribbean, Central America). It is important, first, to highlight the existence (and persistence) of all cases. Many subregional networks were created originally as associations of public operators in telecommunications, but after the intense process of market liberalization and privatization in the 1990s these structures remained and redefined their nature as associations concerned with subregional interests. Thus, we may observe the persistence of these associations over several decades. It is unclear how these subregional sector regimes have promoted institutional change in their countries. Probably, the amount of change effected is quite limited, such as adjusting some relatively marginal regulatory settings, and providing only weak subregional public goods, like coordination, information exchange, and trust among regulatory bodies, thus reinforcing the circulation of regulatory ideas already existing in regional networks.

What are the three main regional entities doing to promote and articulate regional governance in the telecoms sector? To answer this question, drawing on our previous analysis on governance functions, in Table 11.4 we summarize and compare their performance for each of the eight functions identified. It is important to bear in mind that the assessments of the levels achieved by each entity/network are based on personal interviews and documentation analysis, and should be considered tentative until we provide more research to support this exercise.

Public goods provided by regional networks and associations are not very abundant, in fact. There are some public pronouncements, regulatory studies, best practice rules, and so forth, but these are not provided in great number. However, club goods such as events and meetings on the one side, and capacity building on the other, are more profuse. All networks identified promote a number of meetings and encounters at the regional level. We also find many specialized courses and seminars on telecommunications, for both the regulatory and the technical sides, and with some intensity international organizations and networks collaborate on these tasks. All things considered, there was during the 2000s an important offer of courses and seminars in the region having an international dimension, although with some overlap amongst them.

These findings bring us to the question of why there is more intense provision of club goods than of pure public goods within the regulatory networks in the region. Table 11.4 suggests a tentative answer. As we observed, regional networks perform relatively weak governance functions, and concentrate on knowledge exchange and diffusion, activities that can be performed by means of impure public goods or club goods, including meetings and training. Other governance functions that often require pure public goods—such as consensus building and policy coordination—are not very

Table 11.4 Governance function of three main regional entities/networks

	REGUTEL	CITEL	AHCIET
Norm setting	Inactive	Weak	Inactive
Agenda setting	Weak	Medium	Medium
Consensus building	Weak	Weak	Weak
Policy coordination	Inactive	Weak	Inactive
Knowledge production	Weak	Weak	Weak
Knowledge exchange	Strong	Medium	Medium
Knowledge diffusion	Weak	Weak	Strong
International prestige for domestic purposes	Medium	Weak	Medium

actively performed at all. Thus, might we assume that the network mode of governance is more biased towards developing governance functions that require only excludable goods? Such a result would confirm the expectations of Mancur Olson's logic of collective action (1971): voluntary contributions by network members require excludable benefits, while pure public goods remain scarcely provided. Comparing the governance functions of the three different networks (Table 11.4) confirms the logic of collective action: the more voluntary-based the network is, the more central are governance functions based on club goods (REGULATEL); the stronger the links are with conventional international organizations (CITEL), the more governance capacity based on public goods emerges.

The logic set out suggests that networks as a mode of governance experience difficulties in developing some governance functions, which undermines regulatory governance at the regional level, at least in the case we examine. However, other factors might undermine the performance of telecom regulatory networks in Latin America. In this sense, a common problem in developing a mode of regional governance for this sector in Latin America is that all three entities being studied work under the shadow of external hierarchies. European regulatory agencies, as well as the European Commission, supported the establishment of REGULATEL and its further development. While REGULATEL has stronger European connections, CITET and some subregional organizations (particularly in the Caribbean and Central America) have more North American connections. The role of the United States in CITEL is highly relevant in framing and strengthening stronger hemispheric regulatory relations and moving towards constructing a common regulatory space. The presence as observers of some European regulatory agencies in REGULATEL and the absence of Anglo-Saxon representatives probably introduce a different perspective on the construction of the regulatory space, less connected to the North American regulatory framework and energizing the links with the European regulatory framework. Also, AHCIET was established by an extra-regional initiative on the part of Telefonica, the Spanish public monopoly, during the 1980s. Since North American and European companies are major players in telecommunications markets in the region, we can expect these companies and their governments to be interested in participating in regional networks and sectoral associations. These external influences can also be understood as a manifestation of the global regulatory struggles on standards and policy principles between the US and Europe. In turn it might have exacerbated the difficulties regional networks experienced in successfully performing all the governance functions identified.

When countries in the region have to cooperate to establish common positions in international meetings and conferences, whether of the ITU or other standardization bodies, the already dominant regulatory views in the region influence the decisions taken; also, dominant regulatory frames and principles circulating at the regional level in different networks and meetings can be of greater relevance for domestic regulatory change in the countries of the region. For this reason, creating, sustaining, and promoting ideas and principles on regulation appear to be a major concern of regional governance; yet regulatory networks are not always capable of dealing with it. They are unable to establish coherent development programs, and their serious limitations become evident when more elaborate decision-making procedures are required for regional regulatory governance. For example, they have difficulty coordinating some key issues at the regional scale, such as cellular roaming or digital TV standards, aiming to contribute to a minimum level of regulatory harmonization. Subregional regulatory networks, in fact, replicate at their specific levels such logic of information exchange and value formation, and in most cases are not capable of moving towards common subregional regulatory frameworks.

It is clear that no hierarchical mode of governance exists at the regional level, but only a network mode complemented by different organizations that are more focused on producing typical network public goods than more complex outcomes, such as, for example, regulatory harmonization initiatives. As a consequence, what we observe is an intensive process of diffusion of regulatory ideas, values, and instruments within the Latin American space. This is not a top-down process, and regulatory ideas from different sources compete turbulently at the regional level, circulating over partially overlapping networks and multiple international organizations, to increase the possibility of activating policy learning processes at the domestic level. The extent to which this web of different networks and organizations with various scopes and territorial reach is capable of producing domestic institutional change in the sector remains unclear.

11.7 Conclusions

Our study of Latin American regulatory governance in telecoms suggests that formal networks and hybrid modes of governance that similarly involve network-like activities are indeed important spheres of authority in the region. They are stable features and have a legitimate presence in the transnational regulatory arena. Nonetheless, we find that their presence and functions are more limited than one would expect in light of Slaughter's expectations in her *New World Order* (2004). Networks as a mode of governance also have a long way to go before they become effective instruments for regional development or regional integration as expected by Bruszt and McDermott (in this volume) and probably by all of us. Partly, this is not a problem that is confined to Latin America. Similar challenges can be observed also in European Union networks (Eberlein and Newman, 2008; Coen and Thatcher 2008; Levi-Faur 2011b), although the presence of regional hierarchies in Europe creates a different structure of incentives for transnational networks (Andonova and Tuta in this volume). The existing gaps, however—in strength, effectiveness, perhaps legitimacy, and contribution to the promotion of national policy capacities—are not impossible to fill. The options are still there for the creation of a global template of effective and creative intergovernmental networks, including ways to overcome classical collective action dilemmas.

Problems of collective action undermine the production of pure public goods within regional networks, limiting the effectiveness of networks to particular functions of governance, such as, for example, knowledge exchange and dissemination. However, in the Latin American case we have identified an additional problem limiting the provision of regional public goods by networks, namely the dependent role of the countries in the global political economy of telecommunications and the tensions between different regulatory hegemons in this sector that affect the regional networks. More specifically, our tentative findings so far suggest that network governance in Latin American telecoms provides a limited supply of regional public goods to promote better telecom services. The effects of the regional regulatory networks in telecoms are quite limited. Exchange of information and experiences, formal and informal, is the primary activity of established networks. New ideas circulate over these networks that affect agenda setting at the national level, but only potentially influencing policy developments and regulatory frameworks.

In fact, the major players in the region performing the key governance function of rule setting have been intergovernmental organizations with close ties to national governments, such as the World Trade Organization (liberalization and market opening) and ITU (technical standardization). These organizations, rather than the regional networks and/or regional organizations, often provide the de facto general frameworks for regulatory developments. While Latin American actors have shown some interest, progress in forming a regional bloc, involving other actors, in order to design a more focused developmental program has so far been very limited. What is true at the regional level is also true for the subregional regulatory spaces. At the moment they do not play a significant role in the regulatory governance of telecoms, and remain mainly second-level nodes of interaction for regional networks.

In the end, the constraints on regional regulatory governance developing a more effective regime in Latin American telecoms are both global and domestic. They include a limited regional identity and the weakness of the domestic players (regulatory agencies, business association, and government officials). The road to better and more effective transnational networks and organizations at the regional level is via stronger regional identity, the growth of transnational regional elites, and stronger domestic capabilities to nurture regional collective action. Beyond these "structural" preconditions, it is possible to suggest four immediate causes of the weakness of these networks, which may also explain the polycentric architecture of regional governance: (a) competition among extra-regional interests in influencing countries in the region; (b) lack of a shared institutional framework or general trade agreements among the region's countries; (c) domestic policy processes that are not very responsive to external policy coordination; and (d) transnational networks' lack of resources to strength their dynamic beyond informal coordination based on knowledge.

12

Transnational Regulatory Regimes in Finance

A Comparative Analysis of their (Dis-)Integrative Effects

Katharina Pistor

12.1 Introduction

Financial markets have long been transnational. Indeed, the financing of long-distance trade precedes the emergence of the nation state (Padgett and McLean 2006) with its emphasis on territorially based jurisdiction.[1] As such, finance has always posed critical challenges to effective regulation by nation states. This does not mean, however, that it has been barren of governance. Family and kinship ties as well as close affinity with powerful political elites have played a critical role in enhancing the efficacy of contractual networks plagued by information asymmetries (Greif 2001; Landa 1981).

Attempts to govern them notwithstanding, financial markets have been subject to repeat crises. Even prior to new empirical evidence (Reinhart and Rogoff 2009), it was well established that the history of financial markets is also a history of financial crises (Kindelberger 2005; Neal 1990). Not surprisingly, there have been multiple attempts to govern financial markets both at the domestic and the transnational levels, with one mode of governance replacing another after yet another crisis left the previous governance regime in disarray. Based on this pattern of trial and error, three types of regimes can be identified: a *laissez-faire*, a *coordinative*, and a *centralized* regime. Each

[1] I would like to thank László Bruszt and Gerry McDermott and participants at the TIR workshops at the European University Institute in Florence and the Inter-American Development Bank in Washington, DC, for comments on an earlier version of this chapter. All remaining errors are mine.

depicts difference in the intensity of regulation, the allocation of regulatory powers, and risk.

Reflecting the approach in the Introduction, transnational financial regulatory integration are in many ways combinations of competing TIRs and TRRs, varying not only in the relative roles of public and private actors but the mechanisms used to facilitate domestic institutional changes and cross-border coordination. But the classification suggested in this chapter does not map neatly into other classifications adopted by other authors in this volume. Specifically, at least as of now there is no fully integrated model for transnational finance,[2] although the Eurozone countries are moving more decisively towards such a model (see later, under Centralized Governance). Moreover, what I call *coordinative* governance is not identical to intergovernmental regulatory regimes. Coordinative governance may, but does not have to, be intergovernmental. The Bretton Woods regime can be described as an intergovernmental regime; however, the European Banking Coordinative Initiative established in 2008/9 to protect the countries of Central and Eastern Europe from a meltdown involved private as well as public stakeholders, along with domestic and international agents. Nor do these governance regimes map neatly into stages of economic development with the implication that countries pass through them in a quasi-natural evolutionary fashion. Instead, the choice of governance regimes for finance is driven more by ideology than compatibility with underlying institutional developments, as well as by their varying capacity to cope with the possible fallout from crises. Take laissez-faire governance as an example. It has been tried in the past and failed spectacularly in the boom and bust of financial markets in the late 1920s and the subsequent Great Depression, but was nonetheless tried again with even more vigor after the dismantling of the Bretton Woods regime. That regime stands for *coordinative governance* and proved remarkably successful in promoting economic growth for a while, but was ultimately unsustainable because of the difficulties of coordinating foreign exchange policy in light of structural differences and diverging policy priorities across countries. The same dynamics have challenged attempts in Europe to integrate financial markets, starting first with a coordinated governance regime, the EMS. It fell apart in 1992 and was replaced with full monetary integration in the form of the euro (James 2012). This regime, however, has also come under stress and arguably for very similar reasons. At the national level, *centralized* governance of finance has taken hold even in federal countries like the US, where federal institutions have increasingly asserted regulatory powers over financial markets. At the transnational level this is a more recent

---

[2] See, however, Jordana and Levi-Faur (in this volume), who use this classification in analyzing the Telecom sector in Latin America.

development and largely confined to Europe. Specifically, member countries of the Eurozone are now moving towards a banking union with supervisory powers vested in a special department inside the ECB.

The purpose of analyzing these regimes is not simply to introduce yet another classification of regulatory regimes. Instead, it is to analyze the relative strengths and weaknesses of different governance regimes for the domain of finance. Finance has eluded a stable governance regime. In light of theories that deem finance as *inherently* instable, this is not surprising. But it raises important questions about the ability of standardized regulatory regimes to achieve more than regulatory integration. In the world of finance regulatory integration has only too often resulted in financial and political *disintegration*.

12.2 Regime Typology in Historical and Comparative Perspective

This section introduces a typology of three governance regimes for transnational finance that has been derived from actual practices, past and present. Like any classification it entails a certain level of abstraction. Yet, the historical examples and comparative analysis will hopefully make a convincing case that the three regime types, the laissez-faire, the coordinative, and the centralized, capture core features of real-world transnational governance regimes.

12.2.1 *Laissez-Faire Governance*

The first regime type is the laissez-faire regime. It relies primarily on market self-governance with only little institutional support to reduce information costs and ensure the enforceability of contracts. The laissez-faire model comes in a pure and in a modified form. The pure form was approximated, though arguably never fully reached, from late nineteenth century up until the First World War, and again in its aftermath, and is characterized by free trade and free financial flows under the umbrella of the gold standard. The countries that committed to adhere to the gold standard also agreed, at least in principle, to open trade and capital flows to ensure that any imbalances in trade would be corrected by a readjustment of the flow of gold (Eichengreen 2008). In actual practice the maintenance of the gold standard was more complicated than suggested by theoretical models that laud it as a solution to the problem of increasing imbalances in transnational trade and finance. Because of the repercussions a readjustment in capital and trade flows had on the real economy of the countries involved, their governments frequently sought to mitigate these impacts and increasingly so as they became more democratic and thus dependent on their domestic electorate (Eichengreen 2008). In the end, the gold standard, and the laissez-faire regime associated with it, broke down under the pressure of economic crises that were at least in part caused by financial exuberance in the 1920s. Country after country abandoned the standard and engaged in a vicious cycle of competitive devaluation, dubbed beggar-thy-neighbor policies.

A modified version of the laissez-faire regime evolved in the aftermath of the breakdown of the Bretton Woods system (see later, under Coordinative Regime). It embraces the principle of free capital flows, but seeks to mitigate the propensity of crises by establishing common principles of regulation for countries joining global financial markets and provided for a division of labor between the home and host country regulators of multinational banks. The recognition that some form of governance was needed after the Bretton Woods system had been dismantled came in response to several financial crises: the failure of Germany's Herstatt Bank in 1974 after trading losses incurred by its New York entity, the UK financial crisis of 1976, as well as the growing competition from Japanese banks that threatened the predominance of Western financial intermediaries in global finance (Kapstein 1996). The modified laissez-faire approach rested on two interlinked agreements: one on the appropriate division of labor between so-called "home" and "host" country regulators, the Basel Concordat (1975); and another on the establishment of common regulatory standards for entities that were deemed "banks," the Basel Accord of 1989 with subsequent iterations in 2004 (Basel II) and 2011 (Basel III).

According to the Basel Concordat, home country regulators are in charge of regulating banks they charter domestically as well as their international operations that are carried about in the form of branch offices. In contrast, the country where a subsidiary has been established operates as its home regulator. The reason for that is foreign subsidiaries are independently incorporated and licensed entities. Nonetheless, subsidiaries operate de facto as an integral part of a multinational banking group. Subsequent iterations of the Basel Concordat therefore vested the home regulator of the parent with consolidated supervision of the entire group. The idea behind this arrangement was that someone should supervise the operation of transnational bank groups at a consolidated level and that this task should naturally fall within the jurisdiction of the parent bank's home country regulator. The effect has been to strengthen the role of parent bank regulators over those of the subsidiaries (Pistor 2010).

The relation between parent and subsidiary regulators is governed by memoranda of understanding (MoUs) that are meant to ensure adequate cooperation of regulatory activities, including the sharing of information, notification of enforcement actions, and the like. However, MoUs have rarely worked as anticipated. Regulators of subsidiaries have only limited knowledge of parent–subsidiary relations. Conversely, the parent's regulator lacks familiarity with foreign markets and has few incentives to monitor any negative effects the operation of the parent might have on those markets. In the event of a financial crisis the subsidiary regulator bears the responsibility in accordance with the Basel Accord for providing liquidity for that entity. This is what Herring has called the "nightmare scenario" of subsidiary home country regulators—the possibility that financial practices they do not or cannot effectively regulate can trigger a crisis for which they have to stand in (Herring 2007). The integration of financial markets has made this nightmare scenario quite real for many regulators. The same rules that fostered financial integration in the run-up to a crisis have resulted in disintegration during a crisis, as parent bank regulators seek to protect their own markets and subsidiary regulators lack the capacity to deal with the fallout from the crisis. This scenario reflects the interplay between domestic public and private capacity and regional or supranational power structure depicted in Figure 1.1 and can be located in the upper left corner of that figure.

A good example for this dynamic is the effect the global crisis has had on Central and Eastern Europe (Pistor 2011). The prospective European Union member states had to comply with EU law to be admitted to the club. Unlike the older member states, which had given priority to the liberalization of goods, services, and people while maintaining control over capital flows and their financial sectors for decades, the new member states had to endorse the fourth freedom of the Treaty of Rome, the free flow of capital, upon entry and in fact did so even earlier than that (Pistor 2012b). Moreover, heightened capital adequacy requirements inside the EU forced many local banks into the arms of foreign bank groups as they were unable to meet these requirements on their own. This accelerated foreign bank ownership in the region. By 2007 between 36 and 98 percent of the domestic banking sectors in the new member states were controlled by foreign financial groups, most from old member states of the EU (Enoch 2007). They helped fuel a credit market boom in the years leading up the crisis, mostly by funding themselves on global interbank lending markets and taking advantage of the principle of free capital flow within the EU to lend to borrowers in these countries at a higher yield—and in some countries in foreign currency (Pistor 2012a). This exposed the capital-receiving countries to the threat of rapid capital withdrawal in the midst of the global crisis (Gardor and Martin 2010).

The second pillar of the modified laissez-faire model, the Basel Accord, seeks to create a level playing field for international banks. In a world where capital controls were abandoned there was a substantial threat that financial intermediaries would migrate to low-cost regulatory regimes, thus triggering a regulatory race to the bottom. Under the auspices of the Bank for International Settlement (BIS), central bankers and regulators from the major industrialized countries (the G10) formed the Basel Committee of Banking Supervision (BCBS) and developed common standards for prudential regulation known as Basel I, II, and III (Kapstein 2006). Basel I introduced capital adequacy ratios to ensure that banks would retain some buffer to protect them in the event of a downturn. The ratio was set at 8 percent for all transnationally active banks. Still these standards were never implemented in a uniform manner. The Basel standards are non-binding, although failure to adhere to them may preclude banks from operating in foreign markets. Domestic regulators retain substantial leeway in interpreting the broad standards the Basel Accord establishes (BIS 2005). Not surprisingly, manipulating the assets that count as "Tier-1" capital has become an art form and incentive for financial innovation. Indeed, banks lobbied hard to be released from this single, rigid standard. Basel II effectively acquiesced by allowing sophisticated banks to use their own internal risk management models in lieu of strict compliance with the 8 percent capital adequacy requirement (Danielsson et al. 2001; Simon 2010). Thus, the first attempt to impose rigorous regulatory standards on multinational banks was watered down substantially within 15 years of its introduction. A global integration regime for finance was left to disintegrate under pressure of multinational banks located in countries that are hegemons in the Bruszt/McDermott framework.

The Eastern European countries were not alone in suffering from financial crises as a result of transnational financial integration. Financial liberalization induced rapid financial expansion as it had in earlier periods (Kindelberger 2005). The most important incidents include Mexico's Tequila Crisis in 1994, the East Asian Financial Crisis of 1997/8, Russia's financial crisis of 1998, as well as the financial meltdown in Argentina in 2001 (Reinhart and Rogoff 2009). There is now substantial empirical evidence well beyond these cases in support of a pattern that links financial liberalization to financial crises, even if the causal mechanisms are not fully established (IMF 2009). In fact, in the aftermath of the global crisis, the IMF has backed away from earlier policies, which committed its members to the full liberalization of their capital accounts. It now advocates a more gradual approach. Yet, there is still little clarity about the root causes of financial booms and busts. The most common explanation is that domestic institutions in the capital-receiving countries are not up to the task of dealing with modern financial systems. The remedy therefore is to improve financial regulation and supervision, including the regulatory capacity of local actors (Fratianni and Pattison 2002). Not surprisingly, the response to the global financial crisis has been more of the same. Instead of Basel II we now have Basel III and with a nod to the rise of emerging markets they have now been admitted to the club of regulators by giving them a place at the global regulatory table, the Financial Stability Board (FSB). Yet, at least part of the problem may lie with the laissez-faire governance model and misallocation of regulatory responsibilities under the Basel Concordat. It assumes that financial markets are largely self-regulating, that a one-fits-all model is appropriate, and places more emphasis on protecting the home countries of parent banks from any fallout of a failure of one of its subsidiaries than protecting the countries in which subsidiaries are located from excessive lending practices pushed by the parent bank. As such, the laissez-faire model is not an equalizer, but a governance regime that privileges the banks housed at hegemons at the expense of the economies on the periphery of the transnational or global integration regime.

12.2.2 Coordinated Governance

The second regulatory regime, coordinative governance, also comes in two flavors: an intergovernmental regime based on treaty commitments, and ad hoc regimes typically devised in the context of financial crises. The Bretton Woods system fits the first category, the European Banking Coordination Initiative (EBCI) the second.

The Bretton Woods system was the answer to the lessons learnt from the perceived flaws of the laissez-faire model under the gold standard and its final collapse in the 1930s. It was based on international agreements among the major economic powers of the time, coordinated by the IMF, and supported by a host of domestic institutional arrangements to ensure compliance with the regime. A critical ingredient of the Bretton Woods system was restrictions on capital controls, which were thought to be indispensable for successful coordination. The Bretton Woods system was slow to develop and lasted only until 1971 when the US backed off from the gold standard, forcing other countries to float their currencies as well. Still, frictions in the system had emerged much earlier as it became increasingly clear that the US would not be able to maintain its peg to gold at the agreed rate. This was due in part to changes in trade balances. As Europe recovered from the aftermath of the war it became less import-dependent and in fact, began to export their goods to the US. In addition, the US incurred major military expenditures for peacekeeping as well as war (Vietnam) efforts, which strained its fiscal resources. For a number of years, the countries that participated in the Bretton Woods system played along and pretended that the system was still workable even though changes in the real world made it no longer tenable without major adjustments in the domestic and foreign policies of key countries, which they were unwilling to implement (Gavin 2004).

In short, the Bretton Woods regime as designed proved unsustainable in the absence of a political will to elevate this regime over other domestic policy concerns. Perhaps it could have been replaced by a regime that would have introduced greater flexibility for the US but still maintained a commitment to coordination. That, however, did not happen. Instead, it gave way to another round of financial liberalization—precisely the policies that the Bretton Woods system had meant to forestall.

The first region of the world that was directly affected by the new wave financial liberalization in the aftermath of the demise of the Bretton Woods system was Latin America. It benefited from rapid financial expansion as Western banks channeled Eurodollars—deposits denominated in US dollars held by banks outside the US and primarily in London at the time—to governments in the region. However, when debt levels became unsustainable, capital flows were cut back and the region plunged into a sovereign debt crisis. The response to the Latin American debacle did not spur renewed attempts to coordinate global finance. To the contrary, the lessons drawn by policy-makers in Washington was that liberalization, including the further liberalization of capital accounts, was the appropriate remedy for what were perceived to be governmental failures in the region (Williamson 1990). Thus, the Latin American debt crisis gave rise to the Washington consensus—the short-hand for laissez-faire policies (Ocampo 2001).

Subsequent crises in Latin America in the 1990s (Mexico, Argentina), followed by the East Asian financial crisis in 1998, with spillovers in other emerging markets (Russia, and again Latin America), were interpreted as revealing institutional flaws in these countries—not as indicative of problems in regional or global integration regimes. The International Monetary Fund's "International Financial Architecture" called for standardizing regulatory practices to make finance safe for the world (IMF 2003)—using the regulatory standards of the financial hegemons (US and UK) as a benchmark. This, of course, amounted to a full endorsement of the modified laissez-faire policy. One would have thought that the global financial crisis, which erupted in 2007 in the US—the country that had served as a model for the standardization of regulatory practices—would shed some doubts on the accuracy of this diagnoses. However, little rethinking has occurred. The IMF has become more tolerant of selective capital controls (IMF 2011), but has made no attempt to organize a concerted effort towards establishing a better-coordinated governance regime for global finance.

A rather different approach to coordinating transnational finance can be discerned from an ad hoc governance regime that emerged in response to the threat that the global financial crisis would bring down the financial systems in Central and Eastern Europe with possible repercussions for the rest of Europe. The "Vienna Initiative" (Pistor 2011), later relabeled the European Banking Coordination Initiative (EBCI), was comprised of a series of stakeholder meetings with involvement of several multilateral organizations, including the European Banking for Reconstruction and Development (EBRD). The EBCI is an open forum, not a closed club. Stakeholders in the pan-European financial system can participate, whether or not they or their home countries are members of the European Union. This feature pays tribute to the fact that the actual scope of the region's financial system is not confined to the current boundaries of the EU, but encompasses prospective member states (such as Serbia, Croatia, or Bosnia-Herzegovina) and potentially other countries as well.[3] By the same token it raises a fundamental question about regulatory integration, namely whether formal institutions that make regulatory standardization stand in the way of building effective governance regimes if and when the domain to be governed only partially overlaps with the political institutions.

The EBCI is different from the EU mode of governance also in other respects. All participants were given a voice, at least in the initial negotiations.[4] Instead of being on the receiving end of countless European legal acts and accountable for their implementation without having participated in their design, the new member states were present. They together with old member states developed strategies aimed at safeguarding the financial system that linked their respective national regulatory domains. Moreover, rather than relegating banks to commentators on draft regulations and implementing guidelines, they participated directly in the negotiations of crisis solutions. And instead of hashing out specific interventions on a country-by-country basis, as is typically the case in IMF rescue packages, the IMF participated with other international financial institutions (IFIs) in the development of a regional, pan-European strategy. They were subsequently implemented at the country level to take account of the region-wide implications of country-level crises. Last but not least, the coordination effort was orchestrated by an actor with a decisively regional perspective that was respected by the key stakeholders and had the requisite convening power to bring them to the negotiation table. This actor was the EBRD, which was supported in its efforts by the IMF, the World Bank, and the European Commission (Pistor 2011).

The apparent success of the EBCI notwithstanding, it may not be sustainable or serve as a model for transnational financial governance more generally. Critical for this kind of coordination is a shared will to cooperate and to engage in a give and take to find common solutions—notwithstanding competing political and commercial interests. National politics can easily get in the way of such coordination if the costs imposed on some stakeholders

---

[3] In fact, the Vienna Initiative sought to incorporate Ukraine into early negotiations, which ultimately did not work out, mostly due to domestic circumstances in the Ukraine—not due to artificial territorial boundaries of the governance regime.

[4] For a critical perspective on the Vienna Initiative, see Lütz and Kranke 2010.

appear too high, as the difficulties incurred in resolving the sovereign debt crisis within the Eurozone demonstrates only too vividly. A major lesson that can be learned from the EBCI is that coordination is likely to be most successful when mediated by a neutral agent that has a stake in the outcome but does not directly compete with any of the other stakeholders (Pistor 2011). The EBRD was uniquely well placed in taking up such a role, not the least because its own structure and mission had allowed it to build close relations not only with governments but also with the financial sector throughout the region. This may hold important lessons for future attempts to build coordinated governance regimes: They require a mediator with convening power over all relevant stakeholders, public and private, within and beyond established governance or integration regimes.

12.2.3 Centralized Governance

Centralized governance is a fairly new concept for transnational financial markets. Finance directly touches upon issues of national sovereignty. Banks and other financial intermediaries may be private, but their failure has major repercussions for affected countries—their real economies and the solvency of their governments. Not surprisingly, the EU stopped short of a centralized governance regime for its increasingly integrated financial markets until the financial crisis (Garcia and Nieto 2005). Indeed, the reforms enacted in response to the global crisis reaffirmed that EU-level financial regulation would not impede the fiscal sovereignty of member states.[5]

This position appears increasingly untenable at least within the Eurozone. The evolution from a private credit crisis into a sovereign debt and ultimately a currency crisis has demonstrated that the resolution of financial crises cannot be shifted to the national level when countries are part of a currency union. Nor can the currency be sustained without some backstopping mechanism to address illiquidity and insolvency, both of which are bound to arise in financial markets no matter how well regulated. To this date, five Eurozone countries have requested EU financial rescue packages: Greece, Ireland, Portugal, Spain, and Cyprus. These rescue packages must be funded somehow, but the EU has no taxing authority. Several strategies have been advanced to try to square the circle. A first attempt was the creation of the European Financial Stability Facility. It was structured as a corporate entity incorporated under the laws of Luxemburg with several EU member states as

---

[5] See, the recital 5 to Regulation (EU) No. 1093/2010 of the European Parliament and of the Council of 24 November 2010 establishing a European Supervisory Authority (European Banking Authority), amending Decision No. 716/2009/EC and repealing Commission Decision 2009/78/EC, which explicitly states that measures taken by the European financial supervisors "shall not impinge on the fiscal responsibilities of Member States."

its shareholders.[6] This arrangement had two advantages: It did not require a Treaty change and helped maintain the appearance that fiscal sovereignty of the member states was still adhered to. This principle is still being upheld in principle—mostly by Germany—even as the EU is moving towards further centralization of financial governance especially in the area of banking. Still, at a summit on 28/9 June 2012, the member states of the Eurozone agreed to form a banking union attached to the European Central Bank.[7] This was a precondition for Germany to agree that funds of the yet to be established European Stability Mechanisms (ESM) can be used to directly capitalize banks in member countries rather than limiting support to governments, as its predecessor, the European Financial Stability Facility (EFSF) had done.

The commitment to establish a common supervisory unit at the ECB is a significant departure from previous governance arrangements within the EU, which rely for the most part on centrally coordinated, yet decentralized governance. EU-level directives set broad standards, which were fine tuned by EU-level committees, but which are ultimately implemented by member states (Vander Stichele 2008). In the immediate aftermath of the financial crisis, the EU enacted a New European Financial Stability System (EFSS). It elevated the committees to "authorities" and added macro-prudential risk monitoring to the task of European regulation, but did not touch the sovereignty of member states in fiscal affairs or the regulation of their financial system. At least in the area of banking this may now be changing, although it remains to be seen how far the powers of the new ECB unit will reach and what control national bank regulators will retain.

Centralization or full regulatory integration of transnational financial governance has some appealing features. Most importantly, it aligns at least in principle regulatory powers with the allocation of risk in a financial crisis. If domestic banks are to be rescued with resources pooled at the European level, it makes sense to ensure that control over these institutions is also shifted to the European level. This argument, of course, assumes that the root cause for the failure of intermediaries lies with the individual intermediaries and their domestic regulators, not with the structure of transnational financial markets. The PIGS (Portugal, Ireland, Greece, and Spain) are not the only euro member states that witnessed the near collapse of financial institutions in the aftermath of the global financial crisis. The region's hegemon, Germany, rescued several of its own domestic banks (Aareal Bank, Comerzbank, Deutsche Pfandbriefbank, Hypo Real Estate Holding, West

---

[6] For details, see the Framework Agreement between Belgium, Germany, Ireland, Spain, France, Italy, Cyprus, Luxembourg, Malta, the Netherlands, Austria, and Portugal, and the European Financial Stability Facility of 7 June 2010.

[7] See Euro Area Summit Statement, 29 June 2012, available at <http://www.consilium.europa.eu/uedocs/cms_data/docs/pressdata/en/ec/131359.pdf> (accessed June 2012).

LB); and so did other European countries with and without euro member-ship. This suggests that the crisis in countries on the periphery of the EU can hardly be explained by domestic factors alone, such as some countries' inability to properly regulate their financial markets. The major difference between these countries and those currently caught in the euro crisis is that the former had sufficient resources to bail out their financial sectors without putting their sovereign solvency at risk, while the latter do not. The former also happen to be home to multinational banks with extensive operations in the latter and operated as major creditors to private and public borrowers in the countries in the run-up to the crisis.

To be successful, the move towards centralized governance therefore needs to do more than simply improve the governance of regulators in countries that were hit hardest by the crisis. It also has to address the governance of regulators responsible for multinational bank groups that participated in the credit boom, which preceded the crisis. Finally, it is critical to ensure that the centralized governance regime is sufficiently insulated from attempts of multinational groups to bend regulatory standards to their advantage, as happened with Basel II. Perhaps a centralized governance regime attached to the ECB will be able to retain a greater arms-length relation to powerful financial intermediaries than most domestic regimes have proven capable of. But there is no guarantee that it will. Financial intermediaries will be certain to regroup. It was no coincidence that the major international lobby-ing organization for banks, the Institute of International Finance, was estab-lished at the time the first Basel Accord, nor that it is located in Washington, DC, in the capital of the country with the greatest sway over standards set by the BSBC (Mattli and Woods 2009; Simmons 2001). A European Banking Association already exists with headquarters in Paris.[8] It is anyone's guess, how quickly it will relocate to Frankfurt (perhaps even Berlin) once the new powers of the ECB are institutionalized. There is thus a non-negligible danger that not all stakeholders in the pan-European TIR will get equal voice in this new centralized structure. Not surprisingly, the Polish and Czech govern-ments have already voiced concern about a centralized European bank regu-lator, fearing that their predicament as countries with high concentrations of foreign-owned subsidiaries may not be sufficiently recognized.[9] Experience with centralized banking supervision elsewhere is not encouraging. After the US dismantled restrictions for the mobility of banks across state lines, it witnessed a major consolidation of the banking industry with branches and subsidiaries of these conglomerates now crisscrossing the country (Wilmarth

---

[8] <https://www.abe-eba.eu/Home-N=HomeEBA-L=EN.aspx>.
[9] See Jan Cienski and Neil Buckley, "Warsaw and Prague Warn on Bank Union Plan," *Financial Times*, 27 June 2012, available at <www.ft.com> (accessed July 2012).

2002). As a result, federal regulation of the financial sector became much more prominent. That, however, did not prevent the financial crisis of 2007; nor did it ensure that states with rapidly building asset bubbles (Florida foremost among them) would be adequately protected against an unsustainable credit and asset boom. There is therefore no good reason to believe that the EU will fare much differently.

12.2.4 Summary

The previous sections discussed three different governance regimes for transnational finance—laissez-faire, coordination, and centralization. They have been tried and tested in different contexts and all have failed at one point or another. This leads to the deeper question, namely why effective governance of finance has been so elusive. The following section will seek to answer this question by drawing on financial theories that have been largely forgotten in contemporary discourse.

12.3 Financial Instability and Regulatory Integration: Theoretical Perspective

Dominant economic theories tend to depict markets as stable. If property rights are clearly delineated and protected and transaction costs kept at a minimum, competitive market processes are supposed to produce efficient, i.e. stable, equilibrium outcomes (De Alessi 1983). Importantly, this was said to be true in finance as in other markets (Fama 1970; Gilson and Kraakman 1984), with no clear distinction drawn between the two (see Minsky 1986). Yet, casual observation of real-world financial markets suggests that they tend to be volatile, prone to instability and frequent collapse (Reinhart and Rogoff 2009). Different theories have come up with different explanations, some invoking complexity theory (Sornette 2003), others the core features of the capitalist system and its reliance on finance (Keynes 1964; Minsky 1986). Those arguing that financial systems are inherently instable point to two interrelated factors to explain this phenomenon. First, fundamental uncertainty, which implies that those who allocate society's resources by investing make bets on the future, which is unknown and unknowable (Keynes 1964; Knight 1921). In other words, markets in general and financial markets in particular are beset by "imperfect knowledge" (Frydman and Goldberg 2011). Second, any adjustment of investment strategies in light of changes in the real world alters expectations about the viability of investment projects and places the financial system under strain. This is true in particular for projects that rely on refinancing, because they do not expect to generate sufficient income to pay bills from income as they become due. Downward adjustments of future earning affect the willingness of creditors to refinance, or only at rates the borrower may not be able to afford. The more investors cut back, the more projects will experience liquidity shortages and some will become insolvent. Once insolvencies become widespread, a fire sale of assets will occur, transmitting the financial into an economic crisis (Mehrling 2011; Minsky 1986).

The possibility of instability is an ever-present danger in financial markets. According to Minsky, competitive pressures tend to push every system *endogenously* towards ever more risky modes of financing (Minsky 1986). Even if at the outset institutions are created that favor conservative financing practices based on the expectation that future payments will be paid from actual income, these institutions will erode over time. The ability to profit from a shift to "speculative financing," which implies that refinancing is likely, or even "Ponzi financing," which implies that refinancing is affirmatively expected, destabilizes a system over time by pushing more and more competitors to adopt such practices. The result is an expansion of liquidity as more borrowers take on credit in the expectation that refinancing will be available at affordable rates in the future, which in turn fuels asset booms. If and when the costs of refinancing increase, because investors begin to harbor doubts about the viability of many projects to ever pay up their debt, liquidity dries up and the system goes into reverse (Mehrling 2011).

Minsky elaborated this dynamic of financial development, its booms and busts, using the US financial system as an example. Yet, the same dynamics he outlined also apply to transnational finance. The crises in Central and Eastern Europe, Ireland, Spain, and Portugal have followed a very similar pattern. The liberalization of financial markets and the low borrowing costs banks in these countries faced fueled an expansion of credit in countries that had relatively underdeveloped financial markets and offered higher yields to foreign banks than did their own home markets. As long as interbank lending markets offered easy access to refinancing, the game continued. When Lehmann Brothers, the US investment bank, collapsed in September 2008 and these markets froze in response, this was no longer possible. More and more intermediaries were unable to balance their assets and liabilities by relying on repo markets and cut credits from their own borrowers, who themselves had relied on refinancing that now was no longer available (Mehrling 2011).

The inherent instability of financial markets certainly helps explain why none of the governance models discussed has proved to be successful in stabilizing them once and for all. One might conclude from this analysis that financial crises are inevitable and attempts to govern financial markets therefore futile (Gordon and Muller 2011). That, however, would be in direct contradiction to Minsky's own analysis; he argued that the financial markets are a product of institutional and organizational choice.[10] They may be inherently instable, but their relative instability is determined by institutional choice—i.e. by regulatory regimes. For the purpose of the analysis presented in this chapter this raises the question, which of the three governance models discussed is likely to contribute most to the relative stability of markets—and which are more likely to increase instability and thereby indirectly lead to the disintegration of financial markets. Including a time dynamic perspective is critical in light of the fact that financial markets are all about making bets about a future that is unknown. Effective governance must therefore incorporate a process for adapting existing governance regimes in response to changes in the real world.

Laissez-faire models of governance, which are built on the assumption that markets will trend towards equilibrium outcomes, are in direct conflict with theories that posit that financial markets are inherently instable. From the perspective of the latter, markets will not self-regulate, but destabilize themselves in an endogenous process driven by the profit motive. Regulatory intervention that seeks to put markets back on a more stable track is therefore indispensable. Moreover, it is not sufficient to design such institutions once. They need to be adapted and reinvented in response to actual market developments. The major goal of regulation must be to disrupt the endogenous drive towards instability, to put "speed bumps" and "trip wires" in place (Krippner 2011). They may take the form of capital adequacy rules, or structural reforms that separate banking operations with explicit or implicit government guarantees from high-risk financial activities. The precise measures may well vary from market to market depending on its exposure to the risk of destabilization. Indeed, there are good reasons to believe that, if stability is the overriding goal, regulatory integration is not an ideal mode of governance. This is because not all markets have the same implicit insurance of a lender of last resort that is actually capable of stabilizing a financial system in crisis. As the experience with the financial crisis has demonstrated, Iceland, Ireland, and Spain clearly were unable to cope with the collapse of a financial system that had ballooned in the years preceding the crisis. This stands in contrast to Germany regionally or the US globally with its privileged position as the issuer of the global reserve currency (Eichengreen 2011). This also suggests that the modified laissez-faire approach is doomed as well. As practiced over the past several decades it presumes that standardizing regulation around the globe is the surest way to financial stability, mostly because

---

[10] "Economic systems are not natural systems. An economy is a social organization created either through legislation or by an evolutionary process of invention and innovation" (Minsky 1986: 7).

intermediaries would not be able to exploit differences in regulation to their advantage. What this view overlooks, however, is that the standardization of laws has created a virtual highway for regulatory arbitrage. Indeed, the rules that have been standardized at the regional or global levels—such as capital adequacy rules—have become prime targets for lobbying, regulatory arbitrage as well as financial innovation, as individual intermediaries have much to gain from reducing their individual regulatory burden.

Centralized governance of financial markets may appear as the right antidote to the problem of differentiated implementation of common standards. If regulation is not only made, but also implemented by centralized institutions, stability should ensue, or so it seems. Much, however, depends on how centralization is conducted. Centralized monitoring of the interdependent global system may be a good, indeed much warranted improvement over the hands-off policies that characterized the pre-crisis era (Shin 2011). Moreover, if capital is allowed to flow freely within an integrated market or currency union, it makes sense to mutualize the liability for the failure of such a system. What is less clear, however, is whether centralized monitoring should be paired with the standardization of rules and their implementation. If the argument is correct that markets *are* different and face different risk exposure because of their relative distance to a resourceful lender of last resort, then a differential approach that is sensitive to the effects of financial collapse is preferable. Otherwise there is a clear danger that the regional hegemons will set the rules of the game based on their own risk perception. That, however, is most likely shaped by the explicit and implicit guarantees available to them, which may not be available to actors further on the periphery, if only because they are not of systemic importance to the larger system. Put differently, the same rules and regulations may have very different implications for different actors depending on their location in the interdependent financial system. The rules that may be sufficient for those at the core may put at risk those on the periphery.

The need to scale the regulatory regime for interdependent markets to the relative risk of different market participants suggests that coordinative governance may be a superior solution. It would allow for a flexible arrangement with commonly agreed goals, but differential applications. Moreover, rather than placing the emphasis on streamlining governance based on a set of fixed principles, it may encourage decentralized learning and experimentation (Sabel 1995). That of course assumes that all critical stakeholders in the interdependent financial market place are willing to cooperate and engage in such a mutual learning process. The EBCI suggests that, at least in the context of a crisis, this is not infeasible. However, as has been pointed out, for this governance arrangement to work in light of the conflicting interests of different participants, a third party that mediates competing positions and ensures that participants do not lose sight of the common goal may be critical. This would require a major overhaul or reinvention of international and regional actors; it would also require a reconceptualization of the very meaning of regulatory integration: not standardization *cum* centralization but variation *cum* coordination. Yet, this may well be worth the effort given the shortcomings of laissez-faire and centralized governance.

12.4 Concluding Comments

As the previous discussion suggests, different models for governing transnational finance have been tried and tested in the past or are being put to a test, namely the new centralized approach to governing the Eurozone's financial market. As the analysis in this chapter suggests, current governance structures are ill equipped to deal with the dynamic, volatile systems that form the interdependent, transnational marketplace. Too much emphasis is placed on the ability of markets to achieve stability on their own. More specifically, extensive financial liberalization has left prudential regulation as the only critical governance tool. It has turned out to be a rather weak one in light of the forces of instability. Moreover, the quest to standardize has introduced a level of rigidity to financial regulation—it takes years, if not decades, from agreeing principles of regulation in Basel to their implementation in countries around the world—that is counterproductive when the object of regulation is a highly dynamic system with strategic actors seeking to avoid the regulatory costs imposed on them. The rapid development of financial markets requires instead a flexible response system, not a set of predetermined rules that are difficult to reform once they have been standardized globally.

This leaves a return to coordinative governance in the realm of finance. The Bretton Woods system was such a system. So was the EU prior to the new trend towards centralization. Sadly, neither has offered sustainable solution. Indeed, the comparison between the formal coordinative governance of the EU and the informal, ad hoc regime of the EBCI poses an interesting puzzle. Why have the formal structures of the EU been so ill equipped to deal with the financial crisis as a transnational problem that requires transnational solutions, whereas the ad hoc regime of the EBCI offered regional problem-solving that included not only countries that had not even joined the EU but also private actors? Or more specifically, what specific structures of the formal EU have made a more flexible response strategy to the crisis impossible? Answering this question will require much more in-depth research. However, some insights can be drawn from the foregoing analysis.

First, the global crisis exposed once more the fallacy of the idea that regulatory integration is sufficient or even desirable for stabilizing financial markets. In practice, the standardized rules became the major focal point for regulatory arbitrage and financial innovation that endogenously destabilizes the financial system over time. Ex ante rules are by definition powerless to counter these trends.

Second, the fact that the EU has created EU-level governance structures in the form of EU-level committees did not guarantee that they conducted their work in the spirit of the transnational European project. Instead, EU committees are only too often the place where national priorities are staked out and bargained over. This structure is not conducive to a common crisis response.

Third, a transnational project needs its own independent advocate lest it be subordinated to national interests. In theory, the newly created position of "president" of the EU should have given the EU its own voice. The fact that member states decided to fill the position with a rather weak representative strongly signaled that ultimately governance in the EU has remained intergovernmental. In contrast, the EBRD played quite a different and arguably a much more influential role in crisis management under the umbrella of the EBCI. It assumed the role of convener and arbiter of all relevant stakeholders in the pan-European financial crisis. Having built close relations with both government and industry in Central and Eastern Europe during the transition process equipped this institution with the trust and authority to convene critical stakeholders in the midst of the crisis. This takes time and cannot be easily replicated by existing institutional arrangements that have created very different sets of incentives. Still, the EBCI holds important lessons for structuring coordinative governance for the instable interdependent financial markets that resulted from decades of (modified) laissez-faire governance.

Bibliography

Abbott, K. W. 2000. "NAFTA and the Legalization of World Politics: A Case Study." *International Organization*, 54(3): 519–47.

Abbott, K. W., and D. Snidal. 2001. "International 'Standards' and International Governance." *Journal of European Public Policy*, 8(3): 345–70.

Abbott, K. W., and D. Snidal. 2009a. "The Governance Triangle: Regulatory Standards Institutions and the Shadow of the State." In W. Mattli and N. Woods (eds), *The Politics of Global Regulation*, 44–88. Princeton: Princeton University Press.

Abbott, K. W., and D. Snidal. 2009b. "Strengthening International Regulation through Transnational New Governance: Overcoming the Orchestration Deficit." *Vanderbilt Journal of Transnational Law*, 42(2): 503–77.

Abbott, K. W., and D. Snidal. 2010. "International Regulation without International Government: Improving IO Performance through Orchestration." *Review of International Organisations*, 5: 315–44.

Abel, Andrea, and Marico Sayoc. 2006. "North American Development Bank: An Institution Worth Saving." Center for International Policy, 6 June. Cited at <http://americas.irc-online.org/am/3307>. Accessed June 2009.

Adamov, T. C., and M. I. Iancu. 2009. "Tendencies and Perspectives of the Romanian Milk Market." *Lucrări Ştiinţifice* (seria Agronomie), 52: 125–30.

ADEFA. 2010. *Historia de la industria automotriz en la Argentina*. Munro, Buenos Aires: Grupo Maori.

AgriPolicy. 2006. "Structure and Competitiveness of the Milk and Dairy Supply Chain in Poland." <http://www.europartnersearch.net/countries/country. php?p=29>. Accessed July 2012.

Ahrne, G., and N. Brunsson. 2011. "Organization Outside Organizations: The Significance of Partial Organization." *Organization* 18(1): 83–104.

Alcalde, Arturo. 2006. "El sindicalismo, la democracia, y la libertad sindical." In José González and Antonio Gutiérrez (eds), *El Sindicalismo en México: Historia, Crisis y Perspectivas*,161–76. Mexico City: Plaza y Valdés.

Alcalde, Arturo. 2012. "Peña Nieto frente a los trabajadores." *La Jornada,* 1 Dec.

Alcantar, M. 2010. "Las innovaciones tecnologicas en el sector horticola del noroeste de Mexico." Doctoral Thesis, Programa de Doctorado en Ciencias Económicas, Facultad de Economía y Relaciones Internacionales, UABC.

Alegre, S., I. Ivanova, and D. Denis-Smith. 2009. *Safeguarding the Rule of Law in an Enlarged EU: The Cases of Bulgaria and Romania*. Brussels: Centre for European

Policy Studies Special Report. Available at: <http://www.ceps.eu/book/safeguarding-rule-law-enlarged-eu-cases-bulgaria-and-romania>.

Almeida, Manuseto. 2007. *Beyond Informality: Understanding How Law Enforcers and Economic Development Agents Promote Small and Medium Firms' Growth under the Law.* Washington, DC: World Bank.

Alonso, Fernando, and Gustavo Idigoras. 2011. *Incidencia de los estándares privados voluntarios en el sector frutícola del Mercosur.* Montevideo, Uruguay: Proyecto UE-Mercosur SPS, Convenio ALA/2005/17887.

Alter, Karen. 2007. "Jurist Social Movements in Europe: The Role of Euro-Law Associations in European Integration (1953–1975)." *EUSA Review,,* 20(4): 6–12.

Alter, K. J., and S. Meunier. 2009. "The Politics of International Regime Complexity." *Perspectives on Politics,* 7(1): 13–24.

Alvarez, R. 2006. "The Transnational State and Empire: U.S. Certification in the Mexican Mango and Persian Lime Industries." *Human Organization,* 65(1): 35–45.

Amengual, M. 2010. "Complementary Labor Regulation: The Uncoordination Combination of State and Private Regulators in the Dominican Republic." *World Development,* 38(3): 405–14.

Anastasakis, O. 2008. "The EU's Political Conditionality in the Western Balkans: Towards a More Pragmatic Approach." *Southeast European and Black Sea Studies,* 8(4): 365–77.

Andonova, L. B. 2004. *Transnational Politics of the Environment: The European Union and Environmental Policy in Central and Eastern Europe.* Cambridge, MA: MIT Press.

Andonova, L. B. 2010. "Public-Private Partnerships for the Earth: Politics and Patterns of Hybrid Authority in the Multilateral System." *Global Environmental Politics,* 10: 25–53.

Andonova, L. B., M. Betsill, and H. Bulkeley. 2009. "Transnational Climate Governance." *Global Environmental Politics,* 9(2): 52–73.

Andreev, S. A. 2009. "The Unbearable Lightness of Membership: Bulgaria and Romania After the 2007 EU Accession." *Communist and Post-Communist Studies,* 42(3): 375–93.

Andriamananjara, Soamiely. 2003. "On the Relationship between Preferential Trade Agreements and the Multilateral Trading System." Remarks prepared for the PECC Trade Forum Meetings at the Institute for International Economics, Washington, DC, 22 Apr.

Angelleli, Pablo, Rebecca Moudry, and Juan Jose Llisterri. 2006. *Institutional Capacities for Small Business Policy Development in Latin America and the Caribbean.* Washington, DC: IDB.

APHIS. 2008a. *Five-Year Strategic Plan 2008–2013 for Fruit Flies of Mexico.* Washington, DC: USDA; available at: <http://www.aphis.usda.gov/plant_health/plant_pest_info/fruit_flies>.

APHIS. 2008b. *United States, Mexico, and Guatemala Fruit Fly Emergence and Release Facilities Review.* Washington, DC: USDA.

Arias, Javier, O. Azuara, P. Bernal, J. Heckman, and C. Villarreal. 2010. *Policies to Promote Growth and Economic Efficiency in Mexico.* IZA Discussion Paper, 4740. Bonn: Institute for the Study of Labor.

Aspinwall, Mark. 2013. *Side Effects: Institutional Design Capacity-Building and Socialization in NAFTA's Labor and Environmental Accords*. Palo Alto, CA: Stanford University Press.

Auld, G., B. Cashore, C. Balboa, L. Bozzi, and S. Renckens. 2010. "Can Technological Innovations Improve Private Regulation in the Global Economy?" *Business and Politics*, 12(3): art. 9.

AutoData. 2012a. "Argentina restringe ainda mais importação de autopeças." *Boletim Autodata*. 31 Jan.

AutoData. 2012b. "Uruguai poderá romper acordo automotivo com a Argentina." *Boletim Autodata*. 30 June.

Avendaño, B., and R. Rindermann, 2005. "Factores de competitividad en la producción y exportación de hortalizas: El caso del valle de Mexicali." *Problemas del Desarrollo*, 36(140): 165–92.

Avendaño, B., R. Rindermann, S. Lugo Morones, and A. M. Lagarda. 2006. *La Inocuidad Alimentaria en México*. Mexico: Universidad Autónoma de Baja California.

Avendaño, B., C. Narrod, and M. Tiongco. 2009. Food Safety Requirements for Cantaloupe Exports from Mexico and their Impact on Small Farmers' Access to Export Markets. Washington, DC: IFPRI Discussion Paper, May.

Avendaño B., C. Narrod, and M. Tiongco. 2013. "The Role of Public-Private Partnerships on the Access of Smallholder Producers of Mexican Cantaloupe to Fresh Produce Export Markets." In Wayne Ellefson, L. Zach, and D. Sullivan (eds), *Improving Food Import Safety*, 65–86. London: Wiley-Blackwell Publishers.

Avramov, Stefan. 2010. *Natura 2000 Implementation Fact Sheet Bulgaria*, accessed via <http://www.ceeweb.org/workinggroups/natura2000/resources/Updated_Factsheet_2010/Fact%20sheets_BG_updated.pdf>, Jan. 2012.

Balcet, Giovanni, and Aldo Enrietti. 1998. *Regionalisation and Globalisation in Europe: The Case of Fiat Auto Poland and its Suppliers*. Working Paper. Turin: University of Turin.

Baldwin, R. 2011. "*Trade and Industrialisation After Globalisation's 2nd Unbundling: How Building and Joining a Supply Chain are Different and Why it Matters*. Cambridge, MA: NBER Working Paper, 17716, Dec.

Baldwin, R. 2012. *WTO 2.0: Global Governance of Supply-Chain Trade*. CEPR Policy Insight, 64. London: Centre for Economic Policy Research.

Balkan Insight. 2013. "Germany Pushes Serbia Hard on Kosovo." 20 Mar. Available at: <http://www.balkaninsight.com/en/article/germany-pushes-serbia-to-normalise-relations-with-kosovo>.

Barbosa, Rubens. 2009. *MERCOSUL e a integração regional*. São Paulo: Imprensa Oficial do Estado de São Paulo.

Barov, Boris. 2006. "Legal Instruments for Site Protection in the EU." BSPB presentation at CEEweb Academy.

Bartley, T. 2007. "Institutional Emergence in an Era of Globalization: The Rise of Transnational Private Regulation of Labor and Environmental Conditions." *American Journal of Sociology*, 113(2): 297–351.

Bartley, T. 2010. "Transnational Private Regulation in Practice: The Limits of Forest and Labor Standards Certification in Indonesia." *Business and Politics*, 12(3): article 7. doi: 10.2202/1469-3569.132.

Bartley, T. 2011. "Transnational Governance as the Layering of Rules: Intersections of Public and Private Standards." *Theoretical Inquiries in Law*, 12: 517–42.

Bartley, T. 2014. "Legality, Sustainability and the Future of Transnational Forest Governance." *Regulation and Governance*, 8(1): 93–109.

Bartley, T., and S. Smith. 2010. "Communities of Practice as Cause and Consequence of Transnational Governance." In Marie-Laure Djelic and Sigrid Quack (eds), *Transnational Communities: Shaping Global Economic Governance*, 347–74. Cambridge: Cambridge University Press.

Bassuener, K., and B. Weber. 2013. "House of Cards: The EU's "Reinforced Presence" in Bosnia and Herzegovina." Democratization Policy Council, May. Available at: <http://democratizationpolicy.org/images/policynote/may.pdf>.

Batista, Cornelio. 2007. "Decenas van a gobernaci ón en busca de Empleo." *Diario Libre*, 29 Nov.

Baz, Verónica, M. C. Capelo, R. Centeno, and R. Estrada. 2010. *Productive Development Policies in Latin America and the Caribbean: The Case of Mexico*. Washington, DC: IDB.

BECC and NADB. 2008. *Joint Status Report,* 30 June. Ciudad Juarez and San Antonio.

Beeko, C., and B. Arts. 2010. "The EU-Ghana VPA: A Comprehensive Policy Analysis of its Design." *International Forestry Review*, 12(3): 221–30.

Bensusán, Graciela. 2006a. "Relación Estado-sindicatos: Oportunidades para la renovación durante el primer gobierno de alternancia." In José González and Antonio Gutiérrez (eds), *El Sindicalismo en México: Historia, Crisis y Perspectivas*, 253–79. Mexico City: Plaza y Valdés.

Bensusán, Graciela. 2006b. "Diseño legal y desempeño real: México." In Graciela Bensusán (ed.), *Diseño legal y desempeño real: Instituciones laborales en América Latina*, 313–409. Mexico City: Miguel Angel Porrúa.

Bensusán, Graciela. 2008. *Regulaciones Laborales, Calidad de los Empleos y Modelos de Inspección: México en el Contexto Latinoamericano*. Mexico City: CEPAL.

Berg, V. S., and J. Horrall. 2008. "Networks of Regulatory Agencies as Regional Public Goods." *Review of International Organizations*, 3(2): 179–200.

Berlinski, J. 2003. "GATS Commitments and Policy Issues of MERCOSUR and NAFTA Countries." In F. Lorenzo and M. Vaillant (eds), *MERCOSUR and the Creation of the Free Trade Area of the Americas*. Washington, DC: Woodrow Wilson Center Report on the Americas, #14.

Bernaciak, Magdalena, and Vera Scepanovic 2010. "Challenges of Upgrading: The Dynamics of East Central Europe's Integration into the European Automotive Production Networks." *Industrielle Beziehungen*, 17(2):123–46.

Bernstein, S., and B. Cashore. 2004. "Non-State Global Governance: Is Forest Certification a Legitimate Alternative to a Global Forest Convention?" In J. J. Kirton and M. J. Trebilcock (eds), *Hard Choices, Soft Law: Voluntary Standards in Global Trade, Environment and Social Governance*, 33–63. Aldershot: Ashgate.

Betsill, Michele M., and Harriet Bulkeley. 2004. "Transnational Networks and Global Environmental Governance: The Cities for Climate Protection Program." *International Studies Quarterly*, 48(2): 471–93.

Bewley, E. 2012. "House Panel Considers Lacey Act Changes." *USA Today,* 8 May. <http://usatoday30.usatoday.com/news/washington/story/2012-05-08/lacey-act-house/54845078/1> (accessed June 2013).

Bezerra, Carlos Alberto Mendes, and Eduardo Campos de São Thiago. 1993. 'O Mercosul e as normas técnicas.' *Ciência da Informação,* 22(1): 68–70.

Bieber, F. 2011. "Building Impossible States? State-Building Strategies and EU Membership in the Western Balkans." *Europe-Asia Studies,* 63(10): 1783–1802.

BirdLife International. 2008. *Bulgarian SPA Designation and Protection.* Accessed via <http://www.birdlife.org/eu/pdfs/Nature_Directives_material/Bulgaria_brief_for_EC_180608.pdf>, July 2012.

BIS. 2005. *International Convergence of Capital Measurement and Capital Structures.* Basel: Bank for International Settlement.

Black, J. 2008. "Constructing and Contesting Legitimacy and Accountability in Polycentric Regulatory Regimes." *Regulation and Governance,* 2: 137–64.

Block, Greg. 2003. "Trade and Environment in the Western Hemisphere: Expanding the North American Agreement on Environmental Cooperation into the Americas." *Environmental Law,* 33: 501–46.

Bluhm, Katharina. 2007. *Experimentierfeld Ostmitteleuropa? Deutsche Unternehmen in Polen und der Tschechischen Republik.* Wiesbaden: VS Verlag.

Bolle, Mary Jane. 2007. *Trade Promoition Authority (TPA)/Fast-Track Renewal: Labor Issues.* Washington, DC: Congressional Research Service.

Börzel, T. A. 1998. "Organizing Babylon: On the Different Conceptions of Policy Networks." *Public Administration,* 76: 253–73.

Börzel, T. 2000. "Improving Compliance through Domestic Mobilization? New Instruments and the Effectiveness of Implementation in Spain." In C. Knill and A. Lenschow (eds), *Implementing EU Environmental Policy: New Approaches to an Old Problem,* 222–50. Manchester: Manchester University Press.

Börzel, T. 2010. "Why You Don't Always Get What You Want: EU Enlargement and Civil Society in Central and Eastern Europe." *Acta Politica,* 45: 1–10.

Börzel, T. 2011. *Comparative Regionalism: A New Research Agenda.* Kolleg-Forschergruppe (KFG) Working Paper Series, The Transformative Power of Europe, 28. Berlin: University of Berlin.

Börzel, T., and Aron Buzogàny. 2010a. "Environmental Organizations and the Europeanisation of Public Policy in Central and Eastern Europe: The Case of Biodiversity Governance." *Environmental Politics,* 19(5): 708–35.

Börzel, T., and Aron Buzogàny. 2010b. "Governing EU Accession in Transition Countries: The Role of Non-State Actors." *Acta Politica,* 45: 158–82.

Börzel, T., T. Hoffmann, D. Panke, and C. Sprungk. 2010. "Obstinate and Inefficient: Why Member States Do Not Comply with European Law." *Comparative Political Studies,* 43(11): 1363–90.

Bourget, Ann. 2004. *Ten Years of the North American Commission for Environmental Cooperation's Joint Public Advisory Committee.* Document published on the website of the Commission for Environmental Cooperation, Montreal. <www.cec.org/files/pdf/JPAC/CCPM-AnnBourget-June-2004_en.pdf>. Accessed Oct. 2008.

Bouzas, José. 2006. "Los contratos de protección y el sindicalismo mexicano." In José González and Antonio Gutiérrez (eds), *El Sindicalismo en México: Historia, Crisis y Perspectivas*, 115–30. Mexico City: Plaza y Valdés.

Bouzas, R., and J. M. Fanelli. 2001. *Mercosur: Integración y Crecimiento*. Buenos Aires: Fundación OSDE.

Bouzas, Roberto. 2001. "MERCOSUR Ten Years After: Learning Process or Deja-vu?" In Joseph Tulchin (ed.), *Paths to Regional Integration: The Case of Mercosur*, 115–34. Washington, DC: Wilson Center.

Brack, D. 2009. *Combating Illegal Logging: Interaction with WTO Rules*. Illegal Logging Briefing Paper, 2009/01. London: Chatham House.

Brack, D., and J. Buckrell. 2011. *Controlling Illegal Logging: Consumer-Country Measures*. Illegal Logging Briefing Paper, 2011/01. London: Chatham House.

Braithwaite, John, and Peter Drahos. 2000. *Global Business Regulation*. Cambridge: Cambridge University Press.

Braithwaite, John. 2008. *Regulatory Capitalism: How it Works, Ideas for Making it Work Better*. Cheltenham and Northampton, MA: Edward Elgar.

Bravo, Gonzalo. 2008. "Comisión de Cooperación Ecológica Fronteriza: La COCEF y la Participación Comunitaria." *Derecho Ambiental y Ecología*, 5(27) (Oct.—Nov.): 41–5.

Bredahl, M., and E. Holleran. 1997. "Technical Regulations and Food Safety in NAFTA." In R. M. A. Loyns, R. D. Knutson, K. Meilke, and D. Sumner (eds), *Harmonization/Convergence/Compatibility in Agricultureand Agri-Food Policy: Canada, United States and Mexico*, 71–85. Winnipeg: Friesen Printers.

British Woodworking Federation. 2010. "European Parliament Agrees Timber Due Diligence Regulation." 23 June, <http://www.bwf.org.uk/help/news/news/date/2010/07/13/european-parliament-passes-due-diligence-legislation>.

Bruszt, L., and B. Greskovits. 2010. "Transnationalization, Social Integration, and Capitalist Diversity in the East and the South." *Studies in Comparative International Development*, 44: 411–34.

Bruszt, L., and G. A. McDermott. 2012. "Integrating Rule Takers: Transnational Integration Regimes Shaping Institutional Change in Emerging Market Democracies." *Review of International Political Economy*, 19(5): 742–78.

Bruszt, L., and D. Stark. 2003. "Who Counts? Supranational Norms and Societal Needs." *East European Politics and Societies*, 17(1): 74–82.

Bruszt, László, and B. Vedres. 2013. "Associating, Mobilizing, Politicizing: Local Developmental Agency from Without." *Theory and Society*, 42(1): 1–23.

Bryla, P. 2004. "The Impact of SAPARD on the Behaviour of Farms and Food-Processing Enterprises in the Lodz Region." Paper prepared for presentation at the 94th EAAE Seminar "From Households to Firms with Independent Legal Status: The Spectrum of Institutional Units in the Development of European Agriculture," Ashford (UK), 9–10 Apr. 2005.

Bulgarian Chamber of Chemical Industry (BCCI). 2011. *Annual Report 2010–11*. Accessed via <www.bcci2001.com>, July 2011.

Bulgarian Society for the Protection of Birds (BSPB). 2011. *Annual Report*. Accessed via <http://bspb.org/bg/documents/3.html>, Feb. 2014.

Bulgarian Society for the Protection of Birds (BSPB). 2012. *Guide for Natura 2000.* Accessed via <http://bspb.org/category.php?chPage=1&menu_id=83>, July 2012.

Burgess, Katrina. 2010. "Global Pressures, National Policies, and Labor Rights in Latin America." *Studies in Comparative International Development*, 45: 198–224.

Burley, Anne-Marie, and Walter Mattli. 1993. "Europe Before the Court: A Political Theory of Legal Integration." *International Organization*, 47(1): 41–76.

Büthe, Tim, and Walter Mattli. 2011. *The New Global Rulers: The Privatization of Regulation in the World Economy.* Princeton: Princeton University Press.

Cafaggi, F. 2010. *Private Regulation, Supply Chain and Contractual Networks: The Case of Food Safety.* Florence: EUI Working Papers, Robert Schuman Center for Advanced Studies, Private Regulation Series-03.

Cafaggi, F. 2011. "New Foundations of Transnational Private Regulation." *Journal of Law and Society*, 38(1): 20–49.

Cafaggi, F., and A. Janczuk. 2010. "Private Regulation and Legal Integration: The European Example." *Business and Politics*, 12(3): 1–40.

Calvin, L. 2003. "Produce, Food Safety, and International Trade: Response to U.S. Foodborne Illness Outbreaks Associated with Imported Produce." In J. Buzby (ed.), *International Trade and Food Safety: Economic Theory and Case Studies*, 74–96. Washington, DC: United States Department of Agriculture, Agricultural Economic Report, 828.

Calvin, L., and V. Barrios. 1998. "Marketing Winter Vegetables from Mexico." In *Vegetables and Specialties Situation and Outlook Report*, Washington, DC: USDA, ERS, VGS-274, Apr., 29–38.

Calvin, L., B. Avendaño, and R. Schwentesius. 2004. *The Economics of Food Safety: The Case of Green Onions and Hepatitis A Outbreaks.* Outlook Report VGS-305-01, Electronic Outlook, Washington, DC: USDA-ERS. <www.ers.usda.gov/publications/vgs/nov04/VGS30501>.

Camarena, Salvador. 2012. "La reforma laboral en México deja en entredicho a Peña Nieto." *El País*, 1 Oct.

Cameron, D. 2007. "Post-Communist Democracy: The Impact of the European Union." *Post-Soviet Affairs*, 23(3):185–217.

Campos, Jesús. 2009. *Historia Oral de una Vida en Defensa de los Trabajadores.* Mexico City: Eduardo Solís Impresores.

Cardoso, Fernando Enrique, and Enzo Faletto. 1979. *Dependency and Development in Latin America.* Berkeley, CA: University of California Press.

Carmin, JoAnn. 2010. "NGO Capacity and Environmental Governance in Central and Eastern Europe." *Acta Politica*, 45(1/2): 183–202.

Carmin, JoAnn, and Adam Fagan. 2010. "Environmental Mobilization and Organizations in Post-Socialist States." *Environmental Politics*, 19(5): 689–707.

Carmin, JoAnn, and Barbara Hicks. 2002. "International Triggering Events, Transnational Networks, and the Development of Czech and Polish Environmental Movements." *Mobilization: An International Journal*, 7(3): 305–24.

Carmin, JoAnn, B. Hicks, and A. Beckman. 2003. "Leveraging Local Action: Grassroots Initiatives and Transnational Collaboration in the Formation of the White Carpathian Euroregion." *International Sociology*, 18(4): 703–25.

Carothers, T. 2003. *Promoting the Rule of Law Abroad: The Problem of Knowledge.* Rule of Law Series Working Paper, 34. Washington, DC: Carnegie Endowment for International Peace.

Casella, Paulo Borba. 2007. "Pequenas e médias empresas e integração no Mercosul." In Maristela Basso (ed.), *Mercosul—Mercosur: Estudos em homenagem a Fernando Henrique Cardoso,* 273–93. São Paulo: Editora Atlas.

Cashore, B., and M. Stone. 2013. "Can Legality Verification Promote "Good Forest Governance?": Lessons from Indonesia, Malaysia, and Brazil." Presented at the International Studies Association Annual Meeting, San Francisco, Apr.

Cashore, B. and Stone, M. W. (2014), Does California need Delaware?Explaining Indonesian, Chinese, and United States support for legality compliance of internationally traded products..Regulation & Governance, 8: 49–73. doi: 10.1111/rego.12053

Cashore, B., G. Auld, and D. Newsom. 2004. *Governing through Markets: Forest Certification and the Rise of Non-State Authority.* New Haven, CT: Yale University Press.

Cashore, B., G. Auld, S. Bernstein, and C. McDermott. 2007. "Can Non-State Governance 'Ratchet Up' Global Environmental Standards? Lessons from the Forest Sector." *Review of European Community and International Environmental Law,* 16: 158–72.

Cason, Jeffrey. 2011. *The Political Economy of Integration: The Experience of Mercosur.* New York: Routlege.

Caswell, J. A., and D. Sparling. 2005. "Risk Management in the Integrated NAFTA Market: Lessons from the Case of BSE." In K. M. Huff, K. D. Meilke, R. D. Knutson, R. F. Ochoa, J. Rude, and A. Yunez Naude (eds), *North American Agrifood Market Integration: Situation and Perspectives,* 141–72. Winnipeg: Friesens Printers. Available at <http://naamic.tamu.edu/cancun/caswell.pdf>.

Caulfield, Norman. 2010. *NAFTA and Labor in North America.* Champaign, IL: University of Illinois Press.

CEC. 2001. Mesa Redonda sobre Oportunidades y Desafíos del Registro de Emisiones y Transferencias de Contaminantes de México, Mexico City, 5 Mar.

CEC. 2002. Bringing the Facts to Light (Montreal). Cited at <www.cec.org/files/pdf/SEM/BringingFacts-Jun02_en.pdf>. Accessed Dec. 2008.CEC. 2007. Factual Record. ALCA-Iztapalapa II Submission (SEM 03-004) Montreal.

CEEweb. 2006. "Strengthening Civil Participation in the Implementation of EU Nature Conservation Directives through the Experiences Gained by the 10 New Member States." CEEWEB Academy Agenda, <http://www.ceeweb.org/members/capacity-building/academy_3_n2k/>. Accessed Jan. 2012.

CEFIC (European Chemical Industry Council). 1998. *Impact of the Commission's White Paper on the Chemical Industry in CEE Countries.* Executive Summary. Brussels: CEFIC-PHARE.

Ceka, B. 2013. "The Perils of Political Competition: Explaining Participation and Trust in Political Parties in Eastern Europe." *Comparative Political Studies,* 46(12): 1610–35.

Centre for the Study of Democracy (CSD). 2010. "The Cooperation and Verification Mechanism Three Years Later: What has been Done and What is Yet to Come." Available at: <http://www.csd.bg/artShow.php?id=15187>.

Cervantes-Godoy, M. 2007. *The Growth of Supermarkets in Mexico: Impact on Production and Transaction Costs of Small-Scale Farmers.* University of Guelph, Doctoral Dissertation.

Cervantes-Godoy, M., D. Sparling, B. Avendaño, and L. Calvin. 2008. "North American Retailers and their Impact on Food Chains." In K. M. Huff, K. D. Meilke, R. D. Knutson, R. F. Ochoa, and J. Rude (eds), *Contemporary Drivers of Integration*, 113–46. College Station, TX: College Station, TX: Texas A&M University, University of Guelph, Instituto Interamericano de Cooperacion para la Agricultura-Mexico.

Chavez, M. 2009. "Asymmetry of Resources, Access to Information, and Transparency as Structural Development Challenges in Rural Areas." In J. Rivera, S. Whiteford, and M. Chavez (eds), *NAFTA and the Campesinos: The Impact of NAFTA on Small-Scale Agricultural Producers in Mexico and the Prospects for Change*, 21–42. Chicago: University of Scranton Press.

CITEL (Comisión Interamericana de Telecomunicaciones). 2005. *Libro Azul: Políticas de Telecomunicaciones para las Américas.* Washington, DC: CITEL-ITU.

Claridades. 2006. *Los organizaciones economicas del sector rural.* Mexico City: Claridades, SAGARPA.

COEMEL. 2005. *De la cadena del sistema product melón.* Colima, Mexico: Diagnostico, SAGARPA.

Coen, D., and M. Thatcher. 2008. "Network Governance and Multi-Level Delegation: European Networks of Regulatory Agencies." *Journal of Public Policy*, 28(1): 49–71.

Cohn, Theodore H. 2007. *Global Political Economy Theory and Practice.* New York: Pearson Longman.

Compa, Lance. 1999. "El ACLAN: Un recuento de tres años." In Graciela Bensusán (ed.), *Estandares Laborales después del TLCAN*, 73–96. Mexico City: Plaza y Valdés Editores.

Compa, Lance. 2001. "NAFTA's Labor Side Agreement and International Labor Solidarity." *Antipode*, 33(3): 451–67.

Congressional Research Service. 2013. *The Trans-Pacific Partnership Negotiations and Issues for Congress.* Washington, DC: CRS Report for Congress R42694, 15 Apr.

Contreras-Hermosilla, R., R. Doornbusch, and M. Lodge. 2007. *The Economics of Illegal Logging and Associated Trade.* Paris: OECD, SG/SD/RT(2007)1/REV.

Contiero, Marco. 2006. *Toxic Lobby: How the Chemical Industry is Trying to Kill REACH.* Report of Greenpeace International. Retrieved: <http://www.greenpeace.org/raw/content/international/press/reports/toxic-lobby-how-the-chemical.pdf>, May 2008.

Coolidge, Jacqueline. 2006. *Reforming Inspections.* World Bank Public Policy for the Private Sector, Note 308. Washington, DC: World Bank.

Coraci, Ioan Cezar. 2006. "Employers' Federation of Romanian Chemistry and Petrochemistry." Retrieved: <http://www.emcef.org/committees/SD/Che/20060529/presentations/Coraci_Fepachim_en.PPT>, Apr. 2011.

Coslovsky, Salo. 2009. *Compliance and Competitiveness: How Prosecutors Enforce Labor and Environmental Laws and Promote Economic Development in Brazil.* MIT, Ph.D dissertation.

Cruz Vargas, Juan Carlos. 2012. "Envía México 'señales positivas' con Reforma Laboral: Hacienda." *Proceso*. 1 Oct. <www.proceso.com.mx/?p=321364>.

Cruz, M. A., and R. Rindermann. 2009. "NAFTA's Impacto n Mexican Agriculture: An Overview." In J. Rivera, S. Whiteford, and M. Chavez (eds), *NAFTA and the Campesinos: The Impact of NAFTA on Small-Scale Agricultural Producers in Mexico and the Prospects for Change*, pp. 1–20. Chicago: University of Scranton Press.

Danielsson, Jon, Paul Embrechts, Charles Goodhart, Con Keating, Felix Muennich, Olivier Renault, and Hyun Song Shin. 2001. *An Academic Response to Basel II*. Special Paper LSE Financial Markets Group. London: LSE.

Dannenmaier, E. 2005. *The JPAC at Ten: A Ten-Year Review of the Joint Public Advisory Commission of the North American Free Trade Agreement*. Montreal: NAFTA Commission on Environmental Cooperation, Mar.

De Alessi, Louis. 1983. "Property Rights, Transaction Costs, and X-Efficiency: An Essay in Economic Theory." *American Economic Review*, 73(1): 64–81.

De Bree Simon. 1995. "Global Industry Perspective." Paper presented at the conference on competing in the new Europe: strategies for the Central and Eastern European chemical industry.

De Buen Unna, Carlos. 1999. "Mexican Unionism and the NAALC." unpublished paper, Mexico City.

de Búrca, G. 2010. "The EU in the Negotiation of the UN Disability Convention." *European Law Review*, 35(2): 174–97.

de Búrca, G., R.O. Keohane, and C. Sabel. 2013. "New Modes of Pluralist Global Governance." *NYU Journal of International Law and Politics*, 45(3): 723–86.

de Melo, Adriano Braga, and Fernando Goulart. 2003. "A eliminação de barreiras técnicas no Mercosul: O papel do INMETRO no SGT Nº3." *Ponto Focal de Barreiras Técnicas às Exportações* (Fevereiro). Sao Paulo, Brazil. <www.inmetro.gov.br/barreirastecnicas>.

de Tappatá, A. R. 2003. *Fruticultura de Exportación, Pomáceas y Citricos Dulces Estudios Sectoriales*. Estudio 1.EG.33.6. Buenos Aires: CEPAL.

DG DEVCO, European Commission. 2011. *FLEGT 6th Annual Coordination Meeting 12–14 January Final Report*, <http://www.euflegt.efi.int/portal/documents/?did=240>.

Díaz, Luis Miguel. 2004. "Propuesta para enmendar la ley laboral mexicana." *University of Detroit Mercy Law Review*, 81(4:555–69.

Dimitrova, A. 2010. "The New Member States of the EU in the Aftermath of Enlargement: Do New European Rules Remain Empty Shells?" *Journal of European Public Policy*, 17(1): 137–48.

Dimitrova, Antoaneta. 2002. "Governance by Enlargement? The Case of the Administrative Capacity Requirement in the EU's Eastern Enlargement." *West European Politics*, 25: 4.

Dimitrova, Snezhanka. 2007. "First National Cooperation Pact Signed in Chemicals Sector." Eurofound, Retrieved from: <http://www.eurofound.europa.eu/eiro/2007/06/articles/bg0706019i.htm>. Accessed Apr. 2011.

Djelic, Marie-Laure, and Sigrid Quack. 2010. *Transnational Communities: Shaping Global Economic Governance*. Cambridge: Cambridge University Press.

Djelic, Marie-Laure, and Kerstin Sahlin-Andersson (eds). 2006. *Transnational Governance: Institutional Dynamics of Regulation*. Cambridge: Cambridge University Press.

Doctor, Mahrukh. 2012. "Prospects for Deepening Mercosur Integration: Economic Asymmetry and Institutional Deficits." *Review of International Political Economy* 20(3): 515–40.

Doktor, Frantisek. 2002. "Outcome of the ChemFed and ChemLeg projects." Presentation prepared for the conference on making the enlarged internal market for chemicals a reality, DG Enterprise, 21–2 Nov.

Dolan, C., and J. Humphrey. 2004. "Changing Governance Patterns in the Trade in Fresh Vegetables between Africa and the United Kingdom." *Environment and Planning A*, 36(3): 491–509.

Dolenec, D. 2013. *Democratic Institutions and Authoritarian Rule in Southeast Europe*. Colchester: ECPR Press.

Dombalova, Liliana. 2011. *Responsible Care Implementation in Bulgaria*. Accessed via <http://www.bcci2001.com>, July 2012.

Donovan, R. Z. 2010. *Private Sector Forest Legality Initiatives as a Complement to Public Action*. Richmond, VT: Rainforest Alliance. <http://www.google.com/url ?sa=t&rct=j&q=&esrc=s&frm=1&source=web&cd=1&ved=0CC0QFjAA&url=ht tp%3A%2F%2Frainforest-alliance.org%2Fsites%2Fdefault%2Ffiles%2Fpublicati on%2Fpdf%2Fforest_products_legality_by_r_donovan_march_2010.pdf&ei=N Ma4UYqoK4LU9ASt54HgBg&usg=AFQjCNGA06tJvSMkuTeLL8Xz_MvpTqHV0A &sig2=TSmOycuTJg7L1deUQ04o3g&bvm=bv.47810305,d.eWU>. Accessed June 2013.

Drahokoupil, Jan. 2008. *Globalisation and the State in Central and Eastern Europe*. London: Routledge.

Drezner, Daniel W. 2007. *All Politics is Global: Explaining International Regulatory Regimes*. Princeton: Princeton University Press.

Dries, L. 2004. "Vertical Coordination and Foreign Direct Investment: A Comparative Study of the Dairy Chains in Bulgaria, Poland, and Slovakia." Paper prepared for the World Bank (ECSSD) project "Dynamics of Vertical Coordination in ECA Agrifood Chains: Implications for Policy and Bank Operations" (EW-P084034-ESW-BB).

Dries, L., and J. F. M. Swinnen. 2004. "Foreign Direct Investment, Vertical Integration, and Local Suppliers: Evidence from the Polish Dairy Sector." *World Development*, 32(9):1525–44.

Duina, Francesco G. 2006. *The Social Construction of Free Trade: The European Union, Nafta, and Mercosur*. Princeton: Princeton University Press.

Dunn, E. C. 2003. "Trojan Pig: Paradoxes of Food Safety Regulation." *Environment and Planning A*, 35(8): 1493–511.

Dussel Peters, Enrique. 2001. "Condiciones y retos de las pequeñas y medianas empresas en México: Estudio de casos de vinculación de empresas exitosas y propuestas de política." In Enrique Dussel Peters (ed.), *Claroscuros: Integración exitosa de las pequeñas y medianas empresas en México*, 43–78. Mexico City: CNIT.

Dussel Peters, Enrique. 2009. "The Mexican Case." In R. Jenkins and E. Dussel Peters (eds), *China and Latin America: Economic Relations in the Twenty First Century*, 279–385. Bonn: German Development Institute.

Dussel Peters, Enrique, Michael Piore, and Clemente Ruiz Duran. 2002. "Learning and the Limits of Foreign Partners as Teachers." In G. Gereffi, D. Spener, and J. Bair (eds), *Free Trade and Uneven Development: The North American Apparel Industry after NAFTA*, 224–45. Philadelphia: Temple University Press.

Džihić, V., and A. Wieser. 2011. "Incentives for Democratisation? Effects of EU Conditionality on Democracy in Bosnia and Hercegovina." *Europe-Asia Studies*, 63(10): 1803–25.

Easterly, W. R. 2006. *The White Man's Burden: Why the West's Efforts to Aid the Rest have Done So Much Ill and So Little Good*. New York: Penguin Press.

Eberlein, B., and A. L. Newman. 2008. "Escaping the International Governance Dilemma? Incorporated Transgovernmental Networks in the European Union." *Governance*, 21: 25–52.

Eberlein, B., K. W. Abbott, J. Black, E. Meidinger, and S. Wood. 2013. "Interactions in Transnational Business Governance: Mapping and Conceptualizing a Terrain." *Regulation and Governance*. doi: 10.1111/rego.12030, first published online: 22 July 2013.

Eichengreen, Barry. 2008. *Globalizing Capital: A History of the International Monetary System*. 2nd edn. Princeton and Oxford: Princeton University Press.

Eichengreen, Barry. 2011. *Exorbitant Privilege: The Rise and Fall of the Dollar and the Future of the International Monetary System*. Oxford: Oxford University Press.

El Economista. 2013. "Multan a empresas con 1 mdp por ley laboral." 15 July. <http://eleconomista.com.mx/industrias/2013/07/15/empresas-pierden-hasta-1-millon-multas-coparmex>.

El Informador. 2012. "STPS anuncia inspecciones a carboníferas." 21 Dec. <http://www.informador.com.mx/economia/2012/425642/6/stps-anuncia-inspecciones-a-carboniferas.htm>.

El Informador. 2013. "Peña destaca las reformas aprobadas, pero van por más." 3 Jan. <http://www.informador.com.mx/mexico/2013/427797/6/pena-destaca-las-reformas-aprobadas-pero-van-por-mas.htm>.

El Universal. 2013. "STPS: resultados de reforma laboral, en nueve meses." 2 Jan. <http://www.eluniversal.com.mx/notas/893408.html>.

Enoch, Charles. 2007. "Credit Growth in Central and Eastern Europe." In Charles Enoch and Inci Ötker-Robe (eds), *The Causes and Nature of the Rapid Growth of Bank Credit in the Central, Eastern and South-Eastern European Countries*, 3–12. New York: Palgrave Macmillan.

Epstein, R. A., and U. Sedelmeier. 2008. "Special Issue—Beyond Conditionality: International Institutions in Postcommunist Europe After Enlargement." *Journal of European Public Policy*, 15(6): 795–955.

Estevadeordal, A., B. Frantz, and T. Nguyen (eds). 2004. *Regional Public Goods*. Washington, DC: Inter-American Development Bank.

Estevadeordal, A., K. Suominen, and R. The. 2009. *Regional Rules in the Global Trading System*. New York: Cambridge University Press.

European Commission. 1997. *Regular Report from the Commission on Hungary's Progress towards Accession.* Brussels: European Commission.

European Commission. 2001. *Regular Report on Romania's Progress to Accession.* 13 Nov. SEC(2001) 1753. Brussels: European Commission.

European Commission. 2002a. *Regular Report on Hungary's Progress to Accession.* Brussels: European Commission.

European Commission. 2002b. *Regular Report on Romania's Progress to Accession.* 9 Nov. Brussels: European Commission.

European Commission. 2003a. *Communication from the Commission to the Council, the European Parliament and the European Economic and Social Committee on a Comprehensive EU Policy Against Corruption.* COM(2003) 317 final, 28 May.

European Commission. 2003b. *Forest Law Enforcement, Governance and Trade (FLEGT): Proposal for an EU Action Plan.* COM (2003) 251 final, 21 May. Brussels: European Commission.

European Commission. 2003c. *Regular Report on Romania's Progress to Accession.* 8 Nov. Brussels: European Commission.

European Commission. 2005. *Romania Comprehensive Monitoring Report.* SEC (2005) 1354, 25 Oct. Brussels: European Commission.

European Commission. 2007. *Report from the Commission to the European Parliament and the Council on Progress in Bulgaria under the Cooperation and Verification Mechanism.* COM(2007) 377 final, 27 June. Brussels: European Commission.

European Commission. 2008. *Report from the Commission to the European Parliament and the Council on Progress in Romania/Bulgaria under the Cooperation and Verification Mechanism.* COM(2008) 494/495 final, 23 July. Brussels: European Commission.

European Commission. 2009. *Report from the Commission to the European Parliament and the Council on Progress in Bulgaria/Romania under the Cooperation and Verification Mechanism.* COM(2009) 402 final, 22 July. Brussels: European Commission.

European Commission. 2010. *Report from the Commission to the European Parliament and the Council on Progress in Bulgaria/Romania under the Cooperation and Verification Mechanism.* COM(2010) 400/401 final, 20 July. Brussels: European Commission.

European Commission. 2011a. *Commission Decision of 6.6.2011 Establishing an EU Anti-Corruption Reporting Mechanism for Periodic Assessment: EU Anti-Corruption Report.* COM(2011) 3673 final. Brussels: European Commission.

European Commission. 2011b. *EU Dairy Farms Report.* Brussels: European Commisson.

European Commission. 2011c. *Report from the Commission to the European Parliament and the Council on Progress in Bulgaria/Romania under the Cooperation and Verification Mechanism.* COM(2011) 459/460 final, 20 July. Brussels: European Commission.

European Commission. 2012a. *Implementing Regulation No. 607/2012 of 6 July 2012 on the Detailed Rules Concerning the Due Diligence System and the Frequency and Nature of the Checks on Monitoring Organisations as Provided for in Regulation (EU) No*

995/2010 of the European Parliament and of the Council Laying down the Obligations of Operators Who Place Timber and Timber Products on the Market. Brussels: European Commission.

European Commission. 2012b. *Interim Report from the Commission to the European Parliament and the Council on Progress in Romania/Bulgaria under the Cooperation and Verification Mechanism.* COM(2012) 56/57 final, 8 Feb. Brussels: European Commission.

European Commission. 2013a. *Report from the Commission to the European Council and the Parliament on Progress in Romania under the Cooperation and Verification Mechanism.* COM(2013) 47 final, 30 Jan. Brussels: European Commission.

European Commission. 2013b. *Steps Toward Joining.* Available at: <http://ec.europa.eu/enlargement/policy/steps-towards-joining/index_en.htm>.

European Commission. Opinions and Regular Reports. Various years and countries. <http://ec.europa.eu/enlargement/archives/enlargement_process/past_enlargements/eu10/index_en.htm>.

European Council. 1993. "Conclusion of the Presidency." 21–2 June 1993, Copenhagen. *Bulletin of the European Communities,* 26(6): 2–45.

European Forest Institute. 2011a. *Final Report, Support Study for Development of the Non-Legislative Acts Provided for in the Regulation of the European Parliament and of the Council Laying Down the Obligations of Operators Who Place Timber and Timber Products on the Market,* <http://ec.europa.eu/environment/forests/timber_regulation.htm>.

European Forest Institute. 2011b. *Baseline Study 1, China: Overview of Forest Governance, Markets and Trade,* <http://www.euflegt.efi.int/portal/documents/?did=271>.

Evans, P. B. 1995. *Embedded Autonomy: States and Industrial Transformation.* Princeton: Princeton University Press.

Evans, Peter B. 2004. "Development as Institutional Change: The Pitfalls of Monocropping and the Potentials of Deliberation." *Studies in Comparative International Development,* 38(4): 30–52.

Fagan, Adam. 2006. "Transnational Aid for Civil Society Development in Post-Socialist Europe: Democratic Consolidation or a New Imperialism?" *Journal of Communist Studies and Transition Politics,* 22(1): 115–34.

Falkner, Gerda. 2000. "Policy Networks in a Multi-Level System: Convergence towards Moderate Diversity?" *West European Politics,* 23(4): 94–119.

Falkowski, J. 2012. "Dairy Supply Chain Modernization in Poland: What about Those Not Keeping Pace?" *European Review of Agricultural Economics,* 39(3): 397–415.

Fama, Eugene. 1970. "Efficient Capital Markets: A Review of Theory and Empirical Work." *Journal of Finance,* 25: 383–417.

FAO. 2005. "Informe de Evaluación Nacional Subprograma de Inocuidad de Alimentos." *FAO-SAGARPA Evaluación de Alianza para el Campo,* 12 Oct. Rome: FAO.

FAO. 2006. "Informe de Evaluación Nacional de Programa de Sanidad e Inocuidad Agroalimentaria." *FAO-SAGARPA Evaluación de Alianza para el Campo,* 25 Sept. Rome: FAO.

FAO. 2007. "Informe de Evaluación Nacional: Subprograma de Sanidad Vegetal." *FAO-SAGARPA Evaluación de Alianza para el Campo*, Sept. Rome: FAO.

FAO. 2012. *Diagnostico del Sector Rural y Pesquero de Mexico*. Mexico City: SAGARPA. <http://www.fao-evaluacion.org.mx/cuestionario_final/diagnostico/index.php>.

Farina, Elizabeth M. M. Q., and Thomas Reardon. 2000. "Agrifood Grades and Standards in the Extended Mercosur: Their Role in the Changing Agrifood System." Principal paper for presentation at the annual meetings of the American Agricultural Economics Association, Tampa, FL, 1 Aug.

FAS. 2003. *Dairy Production in Selected Countries*. Washington, DC: Foreign Agricultural Service, United States Department of Agriculture.

Federação das Indústrias do Estado de São Paulo. 2012. "Na Argentina, Paulo Skaf busca solução para restrições aos importados." Fiesp, <http://www.fiesp.com.br/noticias/na-argentina-paulo-skaf-busca-solucao-para-restricoes-aos-importados>. Accessed Feb. 2012.

Fenianos, Eduardo. 2009. *Volkswagen Brasil*. 2nd edn. São Paulo: Editora Univer Cidade.

Ferman, Ricardo K. S. 2006. "O processo de elaboração de normativas técnicas Mercosul: O caso das negociações sobre produtos elétricos." *Revista Brasileira de Política Internacional*, 49(1):117–30.

FERN. 2013. *Improving Forest Governance: A Comparison of FLEGT VPAs and Their Impact*. Brussels: FERN, Feb.

Fernholz, K., J. Howe, S. Bratkovich, and J. Bowyer. 2010. *Forest Certification: A Status Report*. Minneapolis, MN: Dovetail Partners, Inc.

Flores, Zenyazen. 2012. "STPS multó con 680 mdp a empresas: Rafael Avante." *El Financiero*. 24 July.

Flores, Zenyazen. 2013. "Avanza a paso lento y parcial la reforma laboral." *El Financiero*, 17 June.

Florescu, Florentina. 2009. *WWF Danube-Carpathian Programme Office (DCPO)- Implementing Natura 2000: Status—Problems—Practical Solutions in Romania* (on file).

Fortwengel, Johann. 2011. "Upgrading through Integration? The Case of the Central Eastern European Automotive Industry." *Transcience Journal*, 2(1):1–25.

Fox, Jonathan. 2004. "The Politics of North American Economic Integration." *Latin American Research Review*, 39(1): 254–72.

Fratianni, Michele, and John Pattison. 2002. "International Financial Architecture and International Financial Standards." *Annals, AAPSS* 579: 183–99.

Freedom House. 2010. *Nations in Transit*. Washington, DC: Freedom House.

Frundt, Henry. 1998. *Trade Conditions and Labor Rights: U.S. Initiatives, Dominican and Central American Responses*. Gainesville, FL: University Press of Florida.

Frydman, Roman, and Michael Goldberg. 2011. *Beyond Mechanical Markets: Asset Price Swings, Risk, and the Role of the State*. Princeton: Princeton University Press.

FSC. 2004. *FSC Principles and Criteria for Forest Stewardship*. FSC-STD-01-001, Apr. 2004, <www.fsc.org>.

FunBaPa. 2010. *Evaluación del Impacto del Programa Nacional de Supresión de Carpocapsa en la fruticultura de pepita de los valles irrigados de la Norpatagonia*. FunBaPa ediciones, available at FunBaPa's web page.

Fundación Exportar. 2009. *Informe Estadístico Intercambio comercial Argentina–Mercosur.* Dec. <http://www.exportar.org.ar/informes_estadisticos.html>.

GAIN Report. 2011. *Argentina: Fresh Deciduous Semi-Annual.* Prepared by Maria Julia Barbi. Washington, DC: USDA Foreign Agricultural Service.

Gallagher, Kevin. 2004. *Free Trade and the Environment: Mexico, NAFTA and Beyond.* Stanford, CA: Stanford University Press.

Ganev, V. 2007. *Preying on the State: The Transformation of Bulgaria after 1989.* Ithaca, NY: Cornell University Press.

Ganev, V. 2013. "Post-Accession Hooliganism: Democratic Governance in Bulgaria and Romania After 2007." *East European Politics and Societies,* 27(1): 26–44.

GAO. 1997. *North American Free Trade Agreement: Impacts and Implementation.* Washington, DC: GAO, Sept.

GAO. 2000. *U.S.-Mexico Border: Despite Some Progress, Environmental Infrastructure Challenges Remain.* Washington, DC: GAO. Mar., GAO-00-26.

Garcia, Gillian G. H., and Maria J. Nieto. 2005. "Banking Crisis Management in the European Union: Multiple Regulators and Resolution Authorities." *Journal of Banking Regulation,* 6: 206.

Garcia-Johnson, Ronie. 2000. *Exporting Environmentalism: U.S. Multinational Chemical Corporations in Brazil and Mexico.* Cambridge, MA: MIT Press.

Gardini, Gian Luca. 2011. "MERCOSUR: What You See is Not (Always) What You Get." *European Law Journal,* 17(5): 683–700.

Gardor, Sandor, and Reiner Martin. 2010. *The Impact of the Global Economic and Financial Crisis on Central, Eastern and South-Eastern Europe: A Stock-Taking Exercise.* Occasional Paper Series, 114. Frankfurt: European Central Bank.

Garver, Geoff. 2001. "Ayudó el expediente de hechos de Cozumel, dice el peticionario." *Trio* (Summer), cited at <www.cec.org/trio/stories/index.cfm?varlan=espanol&ed=4&ID=50>, accessed Dec. 2008.

Gavin, Francis J. 2004. *Gold, Dollars, and Power: The Politics of International Monetary Relations, 1958–1971.* Chapel Hill, NC, and London: North Carolina University Press.

Gereffi, G., and J. Lee. 2009. *A Global Value Chain Approach to Food Safety and Quality Standards.* Global Health Diplomacy for Chronic Disease Prevention Working Paper Series. Durham, NC: Duke University.

Gil, Miguel Ángel. 2007. *Crónica Ambiental: Gestión Pública de Políticas ambientales en México.* México, DF: Instituto Nacional de Ecología.

Gilbreath, John. 2003. *Environment and Development in Mexico.* Washington, DC: CSIS.

Gilbreath, J., and J. Ferretti. 2004. "Mixing Environment and Trade Policies Under Nafta." In S. Weintraub (ed.), *NAFTA's Impact on North America,* 93–121. Washington, DC: CSIS.

Gilson, Ronald, and Reinier Kraakman. 1984. "The Mechanisms of Market Efficiency." *Virginia Law Review,* 70: 549.

Giménez, Luis Emilio. 2007. *Transparencia y Derechos Laborales.* Mexico City: IFAI.

Giorgi, L., and L. Lindner Friis. 2009. "The Contemporary Governance of Food Safety: Taking Stock and Looking Ahead." *Quality Assurance and Safety of Crops and Foods,* 1(1): 36–49.

Giuzio, Graciela, and Natalia Colotuzzo. 2011. "Cuestionario sobre el tema I: La eficacia de la legislación laboral y el papel de la inspección del trabajo: Informe de Uruguay." XX Congreso Mundial de Derecho de Trabajo y de la Seguridad Social.

Gobierno de Chile. 2011."Ministra Matthei detalla los objetivos de su gestión tras reunión con Presidente Piñera." 18 Jan.

Goetz, K. H. 2005. "The New Member States and the EU: Responding to Europe." In S. Bulmer and C. Lequesne (eds), *The Member States of the European Union*, 254–80. New York: Oxford University Press.

Goldstein, Judith, Miles Kahler, Robert O. Keohane, and Anne-Marie Slaughter. 2000. "Introduction: Legalization and World Politics." *International Organization*, 54(3): 385–99.

Gooch, L. 2010. "Loggers Seek Green Lane into EU." *International Herald Tribune*, 10-11 Apr.

Gordon, Jeffrey N., and Christopher Muller. 2011. "Confronting Financial Crisis: Dodd-Frank's Dangers and the Case for a Systemic Emergency Insurance Fund." *Yale Journal on Regulation*, 28(1): 151–212.

Gorp, A. van, and C. Maitland. 2009. "Comparative Research on Regional Regulators' Associations: A Theory-Driven Path for Progress." *Telecommunications Policy*, 33(1): 41–53.

Gould, J. 2004. "Out of the Blue? Democracy and Privatization in Post-Communist Europe." *Comparative European Politics*, 1(3): 277–311.

Grabbe, H. 2006. *The EU's Transformative Power: Europeanization through Conditionality in Central and Eastern Europe*. London: Palgrave.

Graubart, Jonathan. 2005. " 'Politicizing' a New Breed of 'Legalized' Transnational Political Opportunity Structures: Labor Activists Uses of NAFTA's Citizen-Petition Mechanism." *Berkeley Journal of Employment and Labor Law*, 26(1): 97–142.

Green Balkans. 2008. *Official Complaint to the European Commission*. Ref. No 200/21.05.2008, accessed via <http://www.greenbalkans.org/article_files/12157024290.pdf>, Jan. 2012.

Green Balkans. 2011. *Natura 2000*. Accessed via <www.greenbalkans.org>, Jan. 2012.

Green, T., L. Hanson, L. Lee, H. Fanghanel, and S. Zahniser. 2006. "North American Approaches to Regulatory Coordination." In K. Huff, K. Mielke, R. Knutson, R. Ochoa, and J. Rude (eds), *Agrifood Regulatory and Policy Integration Under Stress*, 9–48. College Station, TX: Texas A&M.

Greif, Avner. 2001. "Impersonal Exchange and the Origins of Markets: From the Community Responsibility System to Individual Legal Responsibility in Pre-Modern Europe." In Masahiko Aoki and Yujiro Hayami (eds), *Communities and Markets in Economic Development*, 3–41. Oxford: Oxford University Press.

Grzymala-Busse, A. 2007. *Rebuilding Leviathan: Party Competition and State Exploitation in Post-Communist Democracies*. Cambridge: Cambridge University Press.

Guillery, P. 2011. FSC Presentation to 4th Potomac Forum on Illegal Logging, Washington, DC, 4 May (not available online).

Gulbrandsen, L. H. 2011. "Private and Public Governance Interactions: State Influences in Forest and Fisheries Certification Programs." Paper for Transnational

Governance Interactions workshop, European University Institute, Florence, 23–4 May.

Gutierrez, L. 2003. "Regulatory Governance in the Latin American Telecommunications Sector." *Utilities Policy*, 11: 225–40.

Haas, Ernst B. 1958. *The Uniting of Europe: Political, Social and Economic Forces.* Redwood City, CA: Stanford University Press.

Haas, Peter M. 1989. "Do Regimes Matter? Epistemic Communities and Mediterranean Pollution Control." *International Organization*, 43(3): 377–403.

Hall, P. A., and Soskice, D. (eds). 2001. *Varieties of Capitalism: The Institutional Foundations of Comparative Advantage.* Oxford: Oxford University Press.

Hämäläinen, Päivi, K. Leena, and J. Takala. 2009. "Global Trend According to Estimated Number of Occupational Accidents and Fatal Work-Related Diseases at Region and Country Level." *Journal of Safety Research*, 40: 125–39.

Hanf, J. H., and A. Pieniadz. 2007. "Quality Management in Supply Chain Networks: The Case of Poland." *International Food and Agribusiness Management Review*, 10(4): 102–28.

Hanf, J. H., and A. Pieniadz. 2006. "Quality Management in Strategic Networks: Is There Any Relevance in the Polish Dairy Sector?" In M. Fritz, U. Rickert, and G. Schiefer (eds), *Trust and Risk in Business Network*, 459–67. Bonn: University Bonn-ILB Press.

Hanson, Gordon. 2010. "Why isn't Mexico Rich?" *Journal of Economic Literature*, 48: 987–1004.

Hasenclever, A., P. Mayer, and V. Rittberger. 2000. "Integrating Theories of International Regimes." *Review of International Studies*, 26(1): 3–33.

Haughton, T. 2007. "Half Full But Also Half Empty: Conditionality, Compliance and the Quality of Democracy in Central and Eastern Europe." *Political Studies Review*, 5(2): 233–46.

Helleiner, E., and S. Pagliari. 2011. "The End of an Era in International Financial Regulation? A Post-Crisis Research Agenda." *International Organization* 65: 169–200.

Henson, S., and J. Humphrey. 2009. "The Impacts of Private Food Safety Standards on the Food Chain and on Public Standard-Setting Processes." Paper prepared for FAO/WHO Codex Alimentarius Commission, May.

Henson, S., and T. Reardon. 2005. "Private Agri-Food Standards: Implications for Food Policy and the Agrifood System." *Food Policy*, 30: 241–53.

Herrera, Juan. 2008. "Law Clinics in the Context of the Citizen Submission Mechanism." unpublished paper, Autonomous University of Tamaulipas.

Herring, Richard J. 2007. "Conflicts between Home and Host Country Prudential Supervisors." #07-33 Financial Institutions Center, Wharton School, University of Pennsylvania.

Herzenberg, Stephen. 1996. *Calling Maggie's Bluff: The NAFTA Labor Agreement and the Development of an Alternative to Neoliberalism.* Canadian-American Public Policy, 28. Sept. Paper provided by author.

Hirschman, Albert O. 1981. *Essays in Trespassing: Economics to Politics and Beyond.* New York: Cambridge University Press.

Hockmann, H., and A. Pieniadz. 2006. "Is the Full Diffusion of EU Standards Optimal for the Development of the Food Sectors in the CEEC? The Case of the Polish Dairy Sector." *Cahiers Options Méditerranéennes*, 64: 179–96.

Hoekman, Bernard. 2013. *New Approaches to Support Transatlantic Trade Integration*. Working Paper. Florence: European University Institute and CEPR.

Hollingsworth, J. Rogers, Philippe C. Schmitter, and Wolfgang Streeck (eds). 1994. *Governing Capitalist Economies: Performance and Control of Economic Sectors*. Oxford: Oxford University Press.

Hooghe, Liesbet, and Gary Marks. 2001. *Multi-Level Governance and European Integration*. Lanham, MD: Rowman & Littlefield.

Hooghe, Liesbet and Gary Marks. 2003. "Unravelling the Central State, But How? Types of Multi-Level Governance." *American Political Science Review* 97(2): 233–43.

Huerga, Miguel, and Sebastián San Juan. 2004. *Report: El control de las plagas en la agricultura argentina*. Buenos Aires: Estudio Sectorial Agrícola Rural, Banco Mundial y Centro de Inversiones FAO, Argentina.

Humphrey, J., N. McCulloch, and M. Ota. 2004. "The Impact of European Market Changes on Employment in the Kenyan Horticulture Sector." *Journal of International Development*, 16: 63–80.

Humphreys, D. 2006. *Logjam: Deforestation and the Crisis of Global Governance*. London: Earthscan.

Hunek, T. 1994. *Reorienting the Cooperative Structure in Selected Eastern European Countries*. Rome: Food and Agriculture Organization of the United Nations.

Idigoras, Gustavo, Alejandro Fried, and Pablo Lara. 2011. *Incidencia de los requisitos privados para alimentos en el Cono Sur*. San Jose: Estudio sobre cadenas bovinos de carne. IICA y CVP, Programa de Inserción Agrícola.

IIRSA (Iniciativa para la Integración de la Infraestructura Regional Suramericana). 2010. *Iniciativas para la mejora del Mercado sudamericano de servicios de roaming. Análisis y Recomenaciones*. Buenos Aires: BID-CAN-Fonplata.

IMF. 2003. *International Standards: Strengthening Surveillance, Domestic, Institutions, and International Markets*. Washington, DC: International Monetary Fund.

IMF. 2009. *Global Financial Stability Report*. Washington, DC: International Monetary Fund.

IMF. 2011. *Global Financial Stability Report*. Washington, DC: International Monetary Fund.

International Labour Organization. 2004. *Statistical Activities of the International Labour Organization*. Geneva: ILO.

International Labour Organization. 2006a. *Strategies and Practice for Labour Inspection*. Geneva: ILO.

International Labour Organization. 2006b. *Labour Overview: Latin America and the Caribbean*. Geneva: ILO.

International Labour Organization. 2012. Committee on Freedom of Association. <http://www.ilo.org/dyn/normlex/en/f?p=1000:20060:0::NO:20060::>.

Ismail, F. 2007. "Aid for Trade." *World Economics*, 8(1): 15–45.

Istvan, P., Volkan Ildiko Reka, and Tamas Ervin. 2009. *Assessment of the Competitiveness of the Dairy Food Chain in Romania*. AgriPolicy Enlargement

Network for Agripolicy Analysis. Cluj, Romania: Babes Bolyai University Cluj-Napoca.

Jacoby, Wade. 2004. *The Enlargement of the European Union and NATO: Ordering from the Menu in Central Europe.* New York: Cambridge University Press.

Jacoby, Wade. 2010. "Managing Globalization by Managing Central and Eastern Europe: The EU's Backyard as Threat and Opportunity." *Journal of European Public Policy,* 17(3): 416–32.

James, Harold. 2012. *Making the European Monetary Union.* Cambridge, MA: Belknap Press of Harvard University Press.

Jatib, Inés. 2003. "Food Safety and Quality Assurance Key Drivers of Competitiveness." *International Food and Agribusiness Management Review,* 6(1): 38–56.

Jesse, E. V., J. R. Bishop, W. D. Dobson, G. G. Frank, and M. Sznajder. 2005. *The Dairy Sector of Poland: A Country Study.* Babcock Institute Discussion Paper, 3. Madison, WI: University of Wisconsin, Babcock Institute for International Dairy Research and Development.

Jordan, Andrew (ed.). 2005. *Environmental Policy in the European Union: Actors, Institutions and Processes.* 2nd edn. London: Earthscan.

Jordana, J. 2012. "The Institutional Development of Latin American Regulatory State." In D. Levi-Faur (ed.), *Handbook on the Politics of Regulation,* 156–170. Cheltenham: Edward Elgar Publishing.

Jordana, J., and D. Levi-Faur (eds). 2004. *The Politics of Regulation: Institutions and Regulatory Reforms for the Age of Governance.* CRC Series on Competition, Regulation and Development. Cheltenham and Northampton, MA: Edward Elgar Publishing.

Jordana, J., and D. Levi-Faur. 2005. "The Diffusion of Regulatory Capitalism in Latin America: Sectorial and National Channels in the Making of New Order." *Annals of the American Academy for Political and Social Sciences,* 598: 102–24.

Jordana, J., and D. Levi-Faur. 2006. "Towards a Latin American Regulatory State? The Diffusion of Autonomous Regulatory Agencies across Countries and Sectors." *International Journal of Public Administration,* 29(4–5): 335–66.

Jordana, J., D. Levi-Faur, and X. Fernández. 2011. "The Global Diffusion of Regulatory Agencies: Channels of Transfer and Stages of Diffusion." *Comparative Political Studies,* 40(10): 1343–69.

Jürgens, Ulrich, and Martin Krzywdzinski. 2009. "Work Models in the Central Eastern European Car Industry: Towards the High Road?" *Industrial Relations Journal,* 40(6): 471–90.

Kahler, M. (ed.). 2011. *Networked Politics: Agency, Power and Governance.* Ithaca, NY: Cornell University Press.

Kahler, Miles, and David A. Lake. 2009. "Economic Integration and Global Governance: Why So Little Supranationalism?" In Walter Mattli and Ngaire Woods (eds), *The Politics of Global Regulation,* 242–75. Princeton: Princeton University Press.

Kaminski, Bartlomiej. 2001. *The EU Factor in Trade Policies of Central European Countries.* Washington, DC: World Bank Paper.

Kandell, Jonathan. 2012. "Back to the Future for Mexico." *Institutional Investor,* 46(5):19.

Kaplan, David, and Joyce Sadka. 2008. "Enforceability of Labor Law: Evidence from a Labor Court in Mexico." Paper presented at the American Law and Economics Association Annual Meetings.

Kapstein, Ethan B. 1996. *Governing the Global Economy: International Finance and the State.* Cambridge, MA: Harvard University Press.

Kapstein, Ethan B. 2006. *Architects of Stability? International Cooperation among Financial Supervisors.* Basel: BIS Working Papers, 199.

Kaufman, Herbert. 1960. *The Forest Ranger: A Study in Administrative Behavior.* Washington, DC: Resources for the Future.

Kaufmann, D., A. Kraay, and M. Mastruzzi. 2010. *Governance Matters VIII: Aggregate and Individual Governance Indicators, 1996–2009.* World Bank Policy Research Working Paper, 4978. Available at: <http://ssrn.com/abstract=1424591>.

Kay, Tamara. 2011. *NAFTA and the Politics of Labor Transnationalism.* Cambridge: Cambridge University Press.

Keck, Margaret. 1995. "Social Equity and Environmental Politics in Brazil: Lessons from the Rubber Tappers of Acre." *Comparative Politics,* 27(4): 409–24.

Keck, Margaret, and Kathryn Sikkink. 1998. *Activists Beyond Borders: Transnational Advocacy Networks in International Politics.* Ithaca, NY: Cornell University Press.

Kelley, J. 2004a. *Ethnic Politics in Europe: The Power of Norms and Incentives.* Princeton: Princeton University Press.

Kelley, J. 2004b. "International Actors on the Domestic Scene: Membership Conditionality and Socialization by International Institutions." *International Organization,* 58 (Summer): 425–57.

Kelman, Steven. 1981. *Regulating Sweden, Regulating America: A Comparative Study of Occupational Safety and Health Policy.* Cambridge: MIT Press.

Keohane, R., and E. Ostrom, E. (eds). 1995. *Local Commons and Global Interdependence: Heterogeinty and Cooperation in Two Domains.* London: SAGE.

Keohane, R. O., and D. G. Victor. 2010. *The Regime Complex for Climate Change.* Discussion Paper 10-33, Harvard Project on International Climate Agreements. Cambridge, MA: Belfer Center for Science and International Affairs, Harvard Kennedy School.

Keohane, R. O., and D. G. Victor. 2011. "The Regime Complex for Climate Change." *Perspectives on Politics,* 9(1): 7–21.

Keohane, R. O., A. Moravcsik, and A.-M. Slaughter. 2000. "Legalized Dispute Resolution: Interstate and Transnational." *International Organization,* 54(3): 457–88.

Ketzer, Christian. 2013. Interview by authors. Munich, 30 July.

Key, N., and D. Runsten. 1999. "Contract Farming, Smallholders, and Rural Development in Latin America: The Organization of Agroprocessing Firms and the Scale of Outgrower Production." *World Development,* 27(2): 381–401.

Keynes, John Maynard. 1964. *The General Theory of Employment, Interest and Money.* Orlando, FL: Harcourt, Inc.

Kindelberger, Charles. 2005. *Mania, Panics, and Crashes: A History of Financial Crises.* 5th edn. New York: John Wiley & Sons.

Klijn, E.-H. 2008. "Governance and Governance Networks in Europe: An Assessment of Ten Years of Research on the Theme." *Public Management Review,* 10(4): 505–25.

Knight, Frank H. 1921. *Risk, Uncertainty and Profit.* Boston: Houghton Mifflin.

Knill, C., and A. Lenschow. 2005. "Compliance, Communication and Competition: Patterns of EU Environmental Policy Making and their Impact on Policy Convergence." *European Environment,* 15(2): 114–28.

Knill, C. and J. Tosun. 2009. "Hierarchy, Networks, or Markets: How Does the EU Shape Environmental Policy Adoptions within and beyond its Borders?" *Journal of European Public Policy,* 16(6): 873–94.

Knutson, R. 2009. *Assessment of Mexico's Sanitary, Phytosanitary, and Food Safety Policies and Programs and their Implementation: Diagnosis and Proposals for Reforms.* Mexico City: Policy Evaluation Document, Centro de Estudios para el Desarrollo Rural Sustentable y la Soberania Alimentaria.

Kobrin, S. J. 2002. "Economic Governance in an Electronically Networked Global Economy." In R. B. Hall and T. J. Biersteker (eds), *The Emergence of Private Authority: Forms of Private Authority and their Implications for Global Governance,* 43–75. Cambridge: Cambridge University Press.

Konitzer, A. 2011. "Speaking European: Conditionality, Public Attitudes and Pro-European Party Rhetoric in the Western Balkans." *Europe-Asia Studies,* 63(10):1853–88.

Koutalakis, Charalampos. 2010. "Enabling Harmonization: Business Actors and the Eastern Enlargement of the EU." *Acta Politica,* 45(1): 247–67.

Krippner, Greta A. 2011. *Capitalizing on Crisis.* Cambridge, MA: Harvard University Press.

Landa, Janet T. 1981. "A Theory of the Ethnically Homogeneous Middleman Group: An Institutional Alternative to Contract Law." *Journal of Legal Studies,* 10: 349–62.

Langbein, J. 2011. *Organizing Regulatory Convergence Outside the EU: Setting Policy-Specific Conditionality and Building Domestic Capacities.* KFG Working Paper Series, 33, Research College "Transformative Power of Europe." Berlin: Freie Universität Berlin.

LaSala, Barry. 2001. "NAFTA and Worker Rights: An Analysis of the Labor Side Accord After Five Years of Operation and Suggested Improvements." *The Labor Lawyer,* 16(3): 319–48.

Lawson, S., and L. MacFaul. 2010. *Illegal Logging and Related Trade: Indicators of the Global Response.* London: Chatham House.

Leal Riesco, I., and S. Ozinga. 2010. "Forest Watch Special—VPA Update October 2010." EU Forest Watch, Oct., <www.fern.org>.

Leavy, Sebastián, and Francisco Fabián Saez. 2010. "Debilidades en la armonización de medidas santiarias y fitosanitarias en el Mercosur," *Densidades* (Buenos Aires), 5 (Aug.): 19–37.

Lederman, D., W. F. Maloney, and L. L. Servén. 2005. *Lessons from NAFTA for Latin America and the Caribbean.* Washington, DC: World Bank; Stanford, CA: Stanford University Press.

Lee, J., Gereffi, G., and J. Beauvais. 2012. "Global Value Chains and Agrifood Standards: Challenges and Possibilities for Smallholders in Developing Countries." *Proceedings of the National Academy of Science of the United States of America*, 109(31): 12326–31.

Lehman, John. 2001. *US-Mexico Border Five-Year Outlook*. San Antonio, TX: North American Development Bank.

Lengyel, Miguel (ed.), Valentina Delich, and Violeta Angel. 2009a. *Report. Adhesión de nuevos miembros a los esquemas de integración. El caso de las medidas sanitarias y fitosanitarias en la Unión Europea y el MERCOSUR. 11 de diciembre*. Buenos Aires: Proyecto UE Mercosur SPS, Convenio ALA 2005/17887.

Lengyel, Miguel (ed.), Valentina Delich, and Violeta Angel. 2009b. *Report. Obligaciones multilaterales en materia de transparencia. El caso de las medidas sanitarias y fitosanitarias en la Unión Europea y en el Mercosur. 11 de diciembre* Buenos Aires: Proyecto UE Mercosur SPS, Convenio ALA 2005/17887.

Lengyel, Miguel (ed.), Valentina Delich, and Violeta Angel. 2010. *Report. Mecanismos de Monitoreo. El caso de las medidas sanitarias y fitosanitarias en el Mercosur. 30 de abril*. Buenos Aires: Proyecto UE Mercosur SPS, Convenio ALA 2005/17887.

Lengyel, Miguel (ed.), Valentina Delich, and Violeta Angel. 2011. *Report. Los capítulos sanitarios y fitosanitarios en las negociaciones comerciales. Análisis comparativo*. Buenos Aires: Proyecto UE Mercosur SPS, Convenio ALA 2005/17887.

Levi-Faur, D. 2003. "The Politics of Liberalisation: Privatisation and Regulation—for—Competition in Europe's and Latin America's Telecoms and Electricity Industries." *European Journal of Political Research*, 42(5): 705–40.

Levi-Faur, D. 2011. "Regulatory Networks and Regulatory Agencification." *Journal of European Public Policy*, 18(6): 810–29.

Levi-Faur, D. 2012. "'Big Government' to 'Big Governance'?" In D. Levi-Faur (ed.), *Oxford Handbook of Governance*, 3–18. Oxford: Oxford University Press.

Levitsky, S., and L. Way. 2010. *Competitive Authoritariansim*. New York: Cambridge University Press.

Levitz, P., and G. Pop-Eleches. 2009. "Why No Backsliding? The EU's Impact on Democracy and Governance Before and After Accession." *Comparative Political Studies*, 43(4): 457–85.

Levitz, P., and G. Pop-Eleches. 2010. "Monitoring, Money and Migrants: Countering Post-Accession Backsliding in Bulgaria and Romania." *Europe-Asia Studies*, 62(3): 461–79.

Levy, Santiago. 2007. *Can Social Programs Reduce Productivity and Growth? A Hypothesis for Mexico*. IPC Working Paper Series, 37. 8th Global Development Conference. Beijing: Global Development Network.

Lipsky, Michael. 1980. *Street-Level Bureaucracy: Dilemmas of the Individual in Public Services*. New York: Russell Sage Foundation.

Locke, R. M. 2013. *The Promise and Limits of Private Power: Promoting Labor Standards in a Global Economy*. New York: Cambridge University Press.

Locke, Richard. 2013. *Promoting Labor Rights in a Global Economy*. Cambridge: Cambridge University Press.

Luca, L. 2007. "Romania: Large Semi-Subsistence Farm Sector, Result of Wrong Strategic Approach?" Paper prepared for presentation at the 104th (joint) EAAE-IAAE Seminar Agricultural Economics and Transition: "What was expected, what we observed, the lessons learned," Corvinus University of Budapest (CUB), Budapest. 6–8 Sept.

Luca, L., C. Alexandri, and M. Grodea. 2010. "The Adjustment Factors of the Dairy Farm Sub-Sector in Romania." *Lucrări Ştiinţifice* (seria Agronomie), 53(1): 371–6.

Lütz, Susanne, and Matthias Kranke. 2010. *The European Rescue of the Washington Consensus? EU and IMF Lending to Central and Eastern European Countries.* LEQS Paper 22. London: London School of Economics.

McDermott, C. L., B. Cashore, and P. Kanowski. 2009. "Setting the Bar: An International Comparison of Public and Private Forest Policy Specifications and Implications for Explaining Policy Trends." *Journal of Integrative Environmental Sciences,* 6(3): 217–37.

McDermott, Gerald A. 2007. "The Politics of Institutional Renovation and Economic Upgrading: Recombining the Vines that Bind in Argentina." *Politics and Society,* 35(1): 103–43.

Maggetti, Martino, and Fabrizio Gilardi. 2011. "The Policy-Making Structure of European Regulatory Networks and the Domestic Adoption of Standards." *Journal of European Public Policy,* 18(6): 830–47.

Majone, Giandomenico. 1996. *Regulating Europe.* London: Routledge.

Malamud, Andrés. 2005. "Mercosur Turns 15: Between Rising Rhetoric and Declining Achievement." *Cambridge Review of International Affairs,* 18(3): 421–36.

Malets, O. 2011. *From Transnational Voluntary Standards to Local Practices: A Case Study of Forest Certification in Russia.* MPIfG Discussion Paper, 11/7. Cologne: Max Planck Institute for the Study of Societies.

Małysz, J. 1996. "Procesy integracyjne w agrobiznesie." *Wieś I rolnictwo,* 99(2): 19–44.

Mann, M. 1984. "The Autonomous Power of the State: Its Origins, Mechanisms and Results." *Archives Européennes de Sociologie,* 25(2): 185–213.

MARD. 2000. *Sapard: Operational Programme for Poland.* Warsaw: Ministry of Agriculture and Rural Development.

MARD. 2006. *National Plan for Agriculture and Rural Development over the 2000–2006 Period under the EU Special Accession Program for Agriculture and Rural Development (SAPARD).* Bucarest: Ministry of Agriculture and Rural Development of Romania.

Marin, Simeon. 2006. "Creation of Natura 2000 Network—Preparation Procedure in Bulgaria." Green Balkans Presentation, CEEweb Academy III, Kiten, Aug.

Marks, Gary, and Doug McAdam. 1996. "Social Movements and the Changing Structure of Political Opportunity in the European Union." *Journal of West European Politics,* 19: 249–78

Martinez-Diaz, L., and N. Woods. 2009. *Networks of Influence? Developing Countries in a Networked Global Order.* Oxford: Oxford University Press.

Mattli, Walter, and Ngaire Woods. 2009a. "In Whose Benefit? Explaining Regulatoroy Change in Global Politics." In Walter Mattli and Ngaire Woods (eds), *The Politics of Global Regulation,* 1–43. Princeton: Princeton University Press.

Mattli, Walter, and Ngaire Woods. 2009b. *The Politics of Global Regulation.* Princeton: Princeton University Press.

Mayntz, R. 2004. "Mechanisms in the Analysis of Social Macro-Processes." *Philosophy of the Social Sciences*, 34(2): 237–59.

Mazey, Sonia, and Jeremy Richardson. 2005. "Environmental Groups and the European Community: Challenges and Opportunities." In A. Jordan (ed.), *Environmental Policy in the European Union: Actors, Institutions and Processes*, 106–21. 2nd edn. London: Earthscan.

MECON. 2011. *Complejo Frutícola: Manzana y Pera. Serie: Producción Regional por Complejos Productivos*. Buenos Aires: Dirección de Información y Análisis Regional y Sectorial.

Medve-Balint, Gergo. 2014. "The Role of the EU in Shaping FDI Flows to East Central Europe." *Journal of Common Market Studies*, 52(1): 1–17.

Mehrling, Perry. 2011. *The New Lombard Street: How the Fed Became the Dealer of Last Resort*. Princeton: Princeton University Press.

Ministerio de Trabajo, Empleo, y Previsión Social (Bolivia). 2012. <http://www.mintrabajo.gob.bo/PersonalDependiente.asp>. Accessed Feb. 2012.

Ministro de Relaciones Laborales (Ecuador). 2011. "Inspecciones laborales avanzan a ritmo acelerado." 9 June. <http://www.mrl.gob.ec>.

Minsky, Hyman P. 1986. *Stabilizing an Unstable Economy*. New Haven, CT: Yale University Press.

Monroy Gallego, Luis Humberto. 2011. "Tema I: La eficacia de le legislación laboral y el papel de la inspección del trabajo en Colombia." XX Congreso Mundial de Derecho de Trabajo y de la Seguridad Social.

Moreno-Brid, Juan Carlos, and Jaime Ros. 2009. *Development and Growth in the Mexican Economy: A Historical Perspective*. Oxford: Oxford University Press.

Moschen, Valesca Raizer Borges. 2006. "Aspectos Institucionais do MERCOSUL: 11 anos do Protocolo de Ouro Preto." In Kai Ambos and Ana Cristina Paulo Pereira (eds), *MERCOSUL e União Européia: Perspectivas da integração regional*, 1–17. Rio de Janeiro: Editora Lumen Juris.

Murillo, M. Victoria, Lucas Ronconi, and Andrew Schrank. 2011. "Latin American Labor Reforms: Evaluating Risk and Security." In J. A. Ocampo and J. Ros (eds), *Oxford Handbook of Latin American Economics*, 790–812. Oxford: Oxford University Press.

Natura. 2000. NGO Coalition Romania, Coalition Statute, accessed via <http://www.natura2000.ro/_files/public/content/coalitia/aderare/Regulament.Coalitie.pdf>, Jan. 2012.

Navarro, Marcelo Julio. 2011. "La eficacia de la legislacion laboral y el pael de la inspección de trabajo—Republica Argentina." XX Congreso Mundial de Derecho de Trabajo y de la Seguridad Social.

Neal, Larry. 1990. *The Rise of Financial Capitalism*. Cambridge: Cambridge University Press.

Neumayer, Eric. 1999. "Multilateral Agreement on Investment: Lessons for the WTO from the Failed OECD-Negotiations." *Wirtschaftspolitische Blätter*, 46(6): 618–28.

Niel, Maurício. 2012. Interview by authors. São Paulo, 11 Dec.

Bibliography

Niemann, A. and P. C. Schmitter. 2009. "Neo-Neo-Functionalism." In Antje Wiener and Thomas Diez (eds), *European Integration Theory*, 45–66. Oxford: Oxford University Press.

Nivar, Amilcar. 2010. "Dicen que entidades del gobierno no cumplen con ley de las Mipymes." *Listín Diario*, 24 Nov.

Nolan García, Kimberly A. 2011. "Transnational Advocates and Labor Rights Enforcement in the North American Free Trade Agreement." *Latin American Politics and Society*, 53(2): 29–60.

Noriega, Sofía. 2011. "Continúa el riesgo para mineros." *El Diario de Coahuila*, 18 Feb.

North American Agreement on Labor Cooperation. 1993. North American Agreement on Labor Cooperation Between the Government of the United States of America, the Government of Canada and the Government of the United Mexican States, 13 Sept.

Noutcheva, G. 2012. *European Foreign Policy and the Challenges of Balkan Accession: Conditionality, Legitimacy and Compliance*. London: Routledge.

Noutcheva, G., and S. Aydin-Düzgit. 2011. "Lost in Europeanization: The Western Balkans and Turkey." *West European Politics*, 35(1): 59–78.

Noutcheva, G., and D. Bechev. 2008. "The Successful Laggards: Bulgaria and Romania's Accession to the EU." *East European Politics and Societies*, 22(1): 114–44.

Oberto, T., K. Oliveira, and N. Goizueta. 2011. "Cuestionario sobre el Tema 1: La eficacia de la legislación laboral y el papel de la Inspección del Trabajo. (Venezuela)." XX Congreso Mundial de Derecho de Trabajo y de la Seguridad Social.

Ocampo, Jose Antonio. 2001. *Recasting the International Financial Agenda*. G-24 Discussion Paper Series, 13. New York and Geneva: United Nations.

Olson, M. 1971. *The Logic of Collective Action: Public Goods and the Theory of Groups*. Cambridge, MA: Harvard University Press.

Orenstein, M., S. Bloom, and N. Lindstrom (eds). 2008. *Transnational Actors in Central and East European Transitions*. Pittsburgh, PA: University of Pittsburgh Press.

Organisation for Economic Co-operation and Development. 2011. *Employment Outlook 2011: How does Mexico Compare?* Paris: OECD.

Organización Internacional de Trabajo. 2011. *Resumen Ejecutivo: Informe de Verificación de la Implementación de las Recomendaciones del Libro Blanco. Periodo Agosto 2010–Diciembre 2010*. Geneva: OIT.

Overdevest, C. 2004. "Codes of Conduct and Standard Setting in the Forest Sector: Constructing Markets for Democracy?" *Industrial Relations/Relations Industrielles*, 59(1): 172–98.

Overdevest, C. 2005. "Codes of Conduct and Standard Setting in the Forest Sector: Constructing Markets for Democracy?" Ph.D thesis, University of Wisconsin-Madison.

Overdevest, C. 2010. "Comparing Forest Certification Schemes: The Case of Ratcheting Standards in the Forest Sector." *Socio-Economic Review*, 8(1): 47–76.

Overdevest, C., and J. Zeitlin. 2013. "Constructing a Transnational Timber Legality Assurance Regime: Architecture, Accomplishments, Challenges." *Forest Policy and Economics,*, iFirst http://dx.doi.org/10.1016/j.forpol.2013.10.004, published online 9 Dec. 2013.

Padgett, J., and C. Ansell. 1993. "Robust Action and the Rise of the Medici, 1400–1434." *American Journal of Sociology*, 98(6): 1259–320.

Padgett, John F., and Paul D McLean. 2006. "Organizational Invention and Elite Transformation: The Birth of Partnership Systems in Renaissance Florence." *American Journal of Sociology*, 11: 1463–568.

Papp, Dorottya, and Csaba Tóth. 2007. "Natura 2000 Site Designation Process with a Special Focus on the Biogeographic Seminars." Accessed via <http://www.ceeweb.org/publications/english/biogeo_booklet_2007.pdf>, Jan. 2012.

Parau, Cristina E. 2009. "Impaling Dracula: How EU Accession Empowered Civil Society in Romania." *West European Politics*, 32(1):119–41.

Parsons, T. 1960. *Structure and Process in Modern Societies*. Glencoe, IL: Free Press.

Pavlínek, Petr. 2008. *A Successful Transformation? Restructuring of the Czech Automobile Industry*. Berlin: Springer Verlag.

Pavlínek, Petr, Bolesław Domański, and Robert Guzik. 2009. "Industrial Upgrading through Foreign Direct Investment in Central European Automotive Manufacturing." *European Urban and Regional Studies*, 16(1): 43–63.

Pelovski, Yoncho. 2006. "Bulgarian Chemical Industry from Economic and Social Point of View." Presentation at the Chemicals Policy, REACH and Health and Safety in the Candidate Countries Conference, Bucharest, Romania, 29–30 May. Retrieved from <http://www.emcef.org/euproj.asp?job=re>, Aug. 2007.

Peña, C., and R. Rozemberg. 2005. "MERCOSUR ¿Una experiencia de desarrollo institucional sustentable?" *Revista de Comercio Exterior e Integración* (Mar.): 45–62.

Perez-Aleman, P. 2011. "Collective Learning in Global Diffusion: Spreading Quality Standards in a Developing Country Cluster." *Organization Science*, 22(1): 173–89.

Petrova, Tsveta, and Sidney Tarrow. 2007. "Transactional and Participatory Activism in the Emerging European Polity: The Puzzle of East-Central Europe." *Comparative Political Studies*, 40(1): 74–94.

Pevehouse, Jon. 2002. "Democracy from the Outside-In? International Organizations and Democratization." *International Organization*, 56(3): 515–49.

Pevehouse. J. C. 2005. *Democracy from Above: Regional Organizations and Democratization*. New York: Cambridge University Press.

Pieniadz, A., J. H. Hanf, S. Wegener, and D. M. Voicilas. 2010. "Vertical Coordination as a Driving Force for Structural Change in the Romanian Dairy Market." *Studies in Agricultural Economics*, 111: 23–36.

Pietrobelli, C., and Rabellotti, R. 2011. "Global Value Chains Meet Innovation Systems: Are there Learning Opportunities for Developing Countries?" *World Development*, 39(7): 1261–9.

Piore, Michael. 2011. "Beyond Markets: Sociology, Street-Level Bureaucracy and the Management of the Public Sector." *Regulation and Governance*, 5(1): 145–64.

Piore, Michael, and Andrew Schrank. 2006. "Trading Up." *Boston Review* <http://bostonreview.net/michael-piore-andrew-schrank-trading-up-embryonic-model-for-easing-human-costs-of-free-market>.

Piore, Michael, and Andrew Schrank. 2008. "Toward Managed Flexibility: The Revival of Labour Inspection in the Latin World." *International Labour Review*, 147(1): 1–23.

Pires, Roberto. 2008. "Promoting Sustainable Compliance: Labor Inspections and Compliance Outcomes in Brazil." *International Labour Review*, 147(2–3): 199–229.

Pistor, Katharina. 2010. "Host's Dilemma: Rethinking EU Banking Regulation in Light of the Global Crisis." In Harald Baum, B. Haar, H. Merkt, and P Mülbert (eds), *Festschrift für Klaus J. Hopt*, 239–66. Berlin: de Gruyter.

Pistor, Katharina. 2011. "Governing Interdependent Financial Systems: Lessons from the Vienna Initiative." *Globalization and Development*, 2(2): 1–23.

Pistor, Katharina. 2012a. "Real vs. Imagined Markets: The Regulatory Challenge." Presented at Paradigm Lost, Institute for New Economic Thinking, Berlin.

Pistor, Katharina. 2012b. "Into the Void: The Governance of Finance in Central and Eastern Europe." In Gerard Roland (ed.), *Reflections on Transition: Twenty Years After the Fall of the Berlin Wall*, 134–52. New York: Palgrave.

Podolny, J. M., and K. L. Page. 1998. "Network Forms of Organization." *Annual Review of Sociology*, 57–76.

Polaski, Sandra. 2006. "Perspectivas sobre el futuro del TLCAN: La mano de obra mexicana en la integración de América del Norte." In Monica Gambrill (ed.), *Diez Años del TLCAN en Méxic*, 35–56. Mexico City: UNAM.

Pollack, Mark A., and Gregory C. Shaffer (eds). 2001. *Transatlantic Governance in the Global Economy*. Lanham, MD: Rowman & Littlefield.

Pop-Eleches, G. 2013. "Learning from Mistakes: Romanian Democracy and the Hungarian Precedent." *Newsletter of the European Politics and Society Section of the American Political Science Association* (Winter), 9–12.

Pop-Eleches, G., and J. Tucker. 2011. "Communism's Shadow: Postcommunist Legacies, Values, and Behavior." *Comparative Politics*, 43(4): 379–408.

Prakash, Aseem, and Matthew Potoski. 2006. *The Voluntary Environmentalists: Green Clubs, ISO 14001, and Voluntary Environmental Regulations*. Cambridge: Cambridge University Press.

Preiss, Osvaldo, and Nora Diaz. 2003. *Exportaciones de Pera y Manzana de Rio Negro y Neuquén: Inserción en el mercado mundial y factores que condicionan su competitividad*. Documento de Trabajo. Comahue, Argentina: PIEA.

Primatarova, A. 2010. "On High Stakes, Stakeholders and Bulgaria's EU Membership." Unpublished paper, Centre for European Policy Studies, Brussels.

Proforest. 2010. *FLEGT Licensed Timber and EU Member State Procurement Policies*, <http://www.proforest.net/publication/results?tag=8455ca0687aa85008263b3163a1193df>.

Pronatura. 2007. *Informe Annual 2007*. Mexico City: Pronatura.

Puig, Maximilano. 2010. "Las MIPYMEs y las Políticas Públicas de Empleo." Ponencia en el Tercer Congreso Nacional del PROMIPYME, 24 Nov.

Raustiala, K., and D. Victor. 2004. "The Regime Complex for Plant Genetic Resources." *International Organization*, 58(2): 277–309.

Reardon, T., and C. B. Barrett. 2000. "Agroindustrialization, Globalization and International Development: An Overview Of Issues, Patterns and Determinants." *Agricultural Economics*, 23: 195–205.

Reardon, Thomas, Jean-Marie Codron, Lawrence Busch, James Bingen, and Craig Harris. 2001. "Global Change in Agrifood Grades and Standards: Agribusiness

Strategic Responses in Developing Countries." *International Food and Agribusiness Management Review,* 2(3–4): 421–35.

REGULATEL. 2009. *Foro latinoamericano de entes reguladores de telecomunicaciones. 11 años promoviendo el intercambio de información y las experiencias reguladoras en la región.* Annual Report, Jan. <http://www.regulatel.org/info/ANTECEDENTES/el_foro.pdf>.

Reid, Donald. 1986. "Putting Social Reform into Practice: Labor Inspectors in France, 1892–1914." *Journal of Social History,* 20(1): 68–72.

Reimann, Kim D. 2006. "A View from the Top: International Politics, Norms and the Worldwide Growth of NGOs." *International Studies Quarterly,* 50: 45–67.

Reinhart, Carmen, and Kenneth S. Rogoff. 2009. *This Time is Different: Eight Centuries of Financial Folly.* Princeton: Princeton University Press.

Resource Extraction Management. 2010. *Independent Monitoring of Forest Law Enforcement and Governance and Timber Legality Verification Systems within VPAs.* <www.rem.org>.

Rhodes, R. A. W. 1990. "Policy Networks: A British Perspective." *Journal of Theoretical Politics,* 2(3): 292–316.

Rhys, Garel. 2004. "The Motor Industry in an Enlarged EU." *World Economy,* 27(6): 877–900.

Risse, Thomas, and Kathryn Sikkink. 1999. "The Socialization of International Human Rights Norms into Domestic Practices: Introduction." In T. Risse, S. Ropp, and K. Sikkink (eds), *The Power of Human Rights: International Norms and Domestic Change,* 1–38. Cambridge: Cambridge University Press.

Risse, T., S. Ropp, and K. Sikkink (eds). 1999. *The Power of Human Rights. International Norms and Domestic Change.* Cambridge: Cambridge University Press.

Ristei, M. 2010. "The Politics of Corruption: Political Will and the Rule of Law in Post-Communist Romania." *Journal of Communist Studies and Transition Politics,* 26(3): 341–62.

Rivas, Juan José Natera, and Ana Ester Batista Zamora. 2010. "El Complejo agroindustrial limonero de la provincia de Tucumán (Argentina): Ejemplo de producciones no tradicionales y de desaparición de los pequeños productores." *Boletín de la Asociación de Geógrafos Españoles,* 53: 67–88.

Romero Gudiño, Alejandro. 2008. "Inspección Federal del Trabajo en México." *Revista Latinoamericana de Derecho Social.* 6(Jan.–June): 113–43.

Rosado Marzán, César. 2010. "Of Labor Inspectors and Judges: Chilean Labor Law Enforcement After Pinochet (And What the United States Can Do to Help)." *Saint Louis University Law Journal,* 54: 497.

Rosenau, J. N. 2007. "Governing the Ungovernable: The Challenge of a Global Disaggregation of Authority." *Regulation and Governance,* 1: 88–97.

Rosendal, G. K. 2001. "Overlapping International Regimes: The Case of the Intergovernmental Forum on Forests (IFF) between Climate Change and Biodiversity." *International Environmental Agreements,* 1: 447–68.

Ruggie, J. 1982. "International Regimes, Transactions, and Change: Embedded Liberalism in the Postwar Economic Order." *International Organization,* 36(2): 379–415.

Ruiz Durán, Clemente. 2009. *México: Las dimensiones de la flexiguridad laboral.* Mexico City: CEPAL.

Ruiz Durán, Clemente. 2012. *Mexico: Buenas practices para impulsar el trabajo decente (un acercamiento a traves de casos).* Ginebra: Oficina International de Trabajo.

Ruiz, A. 2001. "Sustainable Development and Rural Poverty: A Mexican Perspective." SAGARPA, Subsecretaria de Desarrollo rural, presented at the Woodrow Wilson Center, Washington, DC, 24 May.

Russo, Mark. 2002. "NAALC: A Tex-Mex Requiem for Labor Protection." *University of Miami Inter-American Law Review,* 34(1): 51–120.

Sabel, C. F. 1994. "Learning by Monitoring: The Institutions of Economic Development." In N. Smelser and R. Swedberg (eds), *Handbook of Economic Sociology,* 137–65. Princeton: Princeton University Press; New York: Russell Sage Foundation.

Sabel, C. 1995. "Learning by Monitoring: The Institutions of Economic Development." In Neil J. Smelser and Richard Svedberg (eds), *Handbook of Economic Sociology,* 137–65. Princeton: Princeton University Press.

Sabel, C. F., and J. Zeitlin. 2008. "Learning from Difference: The New Architecture of Experimentalist Governance in the European Union." *European Law Journal,* 14(3): 271–327.

Sabel, C. F., and J. Zeitlin (eds). 2010. *Experimentalist Governance in the European Union: Towards a New Architecture.* Oxford: Oxford University Press.

Sabel, C. F., and J. Zeitlin. 2011. *Experimentalism in Transnational Governance: Emergent Pathways and Diffusion Mechanisms.* GR:EEN (Global Reordering: Evolution through European Networks) Working Paper, 3, <http://www2.warwick.ac.uk/fac/soc/csgr/green/papers/workingpapers/sabel_and_zeitlin_exp._in_tran._gov.pdf>.

Sabel, C. F., and J. Zeitlin. 2012. "Experimentalist Governance." In D. Levi-Faur (ed.), *The Oxford Handbook of Governance,,* 169–83. Oxford: Oxford University Press.

Saltini, Marco Antonio. 2012. Interview by authors. São Paulo, 4 Jan.

Samford, Steven, and Priscila Ortega Gómez. 2012. "Subnational Politics and Foreign Direct Investment in Mexico." *Review of International Political Economy,* 21(2): 467–96.

Sánchez Reaza, Javier, and Andrés Rodriguez-Pose. 2002. "The Impact of Trade Liberalization on Regional Disparities in Mexico." *Growth and Change,* 33: 72–90.

Santana, Aurélio. 2012. Interview by authors. São Paulo, 12 Dec.

Santos, Alvaro. 2009. "Labor Flexibility, Legal Reform and Economic Development." *Virginia Journal of International Law,* 50(1): 34–106.

SAR (Romanian Academic Society). 2011. "Beyond Perception: Has Romania's Governance Improved After 2004?" <http://www.sar.org.ro>.

Sasse, G. 2008. "The Politics of Conditionality: The Norm of Minority Protection Before and After EU Accession." *Journal of European Public Policy,* 15(6): 842–60.

Scepanovic, Vera. 2011. *Institutional Configurations and Industrial Dynamics in the Central and East European Automotive Sector.* Paris: ICATSEM Working Paper.

Schamp, Eike. 2005. "Die Autoindustrie auf dem Weg nach Europa." *Geographischer Rundschau,* 57(12):12–19.

Schimmelfennig, F., and U. Sedelmeier. 2004. "Governance by Conditionality: EU Rule Transfer to the Candidate Countries of Central and Eastern Europe." *Journal of European Public Policy*, 11(4): 661–79.

Schimmelfennig, Frank, and Ulrich Sedelmeier (eds). 2005. *The Europeanization of Central and Eastern Europe*. Ithaca, NY: Cornell University Press.

Schmitter, Philippe C., and Wolfgang Streeck. 1999. *The Organization of Business Interests: Studying the Associative Action of Business in Advanced Industrial Societies*. Working Paper. Cologne: Max Planck Institute for the Study of Societies.

Schneider, B. 2004. *Business Politics and the State in 20th Century Latin America*. New York: Cambridge University Press.

Schrank, A. 2005. "Conquering, Comprador, or Competitive? The National Bourgeoisie in the Developing World." In F. Buttel and P. McMichael (eds), *Research in Rural Sociology and Development, vol. 11. New Directions in the Sociology of Global Development*, 91–120. Amsterdam: JAI/Elsevier Science.

Schrank, A. 2009. "Professionalization and Probity in a Patrimonial State: Labor Law Enforcement in the Dominican Republic." *Latin American Politics and Society*, 51(2): 95–115.

Schrank, A. 2013a. "From Disguised Protectionism to Rewarding Regulation: The Impact of Trade-Related Labor Standards in the Dominican Republic." *Regulation and Governance*, 7(3): 299–320.

Schrank, A. 2013b. "Rewarding Regulation in Latin America." *Politics and Society*, 41(4): 487–95.

Scott, J. 2007. *The WTO Agreement on Sanitary and Phytosantiary Measures: A Commentary*. Oxford: Oxford University Press.

Secretaría de Trabajo e Previsión Social. 2010. "Necesario reforzar mecanismos preventivos para fortalecer seguridad y salud en el trabajo: Javier Lozano Alarcón." *Boletín*, 73. México City, 28 Apr. 2010, <www.stps.gob.mx>.

Secretaría del Trabajo y Previsión Social. 2013. "Centra la Secretaría del Trabajo y Previsión Social Sus Labores de Inspección En Empresas Con Mayor Peligrosidad." *Boletín de Prensa: Dirección General de Comunicación Social*. Mexico City, 28 Oct.

Sedelmeier, U. 2008. "After Conditionality: Post-Accession Compliance with EU Law in East Central Europe." *Journal of European Public Policy*, 15(6): 806–25.

Sedelmeier, U. 2011a. "Europeanisation After Accession: Leaders, Laggards, and Lock-In." *West European Politics*, 35(1): 20–38.

Sedelmeier, U. 2011b. *Europeanisation in New Member and Candidate States*. Living Reviews in European Governance (LREG). Available at: <http://europeangovernance.livingreviews.org/Articles/lreg-2011-1>.

Sedelmeier, U. 2014. "Anchoring Democracy from Above? The European Union and Democratic Backsliding in Hungary and Romania." *Journal of Common Market Studies*, 52(1): 105–21.

Selin, Henrik. 2007. "Coalition Politics and Chemicals Management in a Regulatory Ambitious Europe." *Global Environmental Politics*, 7(3): 63–93.

Šelo Šabić, S. 2003. *State Building under Foreign Supervision: Bosnia-Herzegovina 1996–2003*. Florence: European University Institute.

SEMARNAT. 2000. *La gestión ambiental en México*. Mexico City: SEMARNET.

SEMARNAT. 2001. *Programa nacional de medio ambiente y recursos naturales, 2001–2006*. Mexico City: SEMARNAT.

SEMARNAT. 2004. *Guía ciudadana para el acceso a la información ambienta*. Mexico City: SEMARNAT.

SEMARNAT. 2007. *Programa sectorial de medio ambiente y recursos naturales, 2007–2012*. Mexico City: SEMARNAT.

Severino, Jairon. 2010. "Conep y Codopyme piden reglamentos de Ley 488-08." *Listín Diario*, 18 Aug.

Shadlen, Kenneth. 2004. *Democratization without Representation: The Politics of Small Industry in Mexico*. University Park, PA: Penn State Press.

Shadlen, Kenneth. 2005. "Exchanging Development for Market Access? Deep Integration and Industrial Policy under Multilateral and Regional-Bilateral Trade Agreements." *Review of International Political Economy*, 12: 750–75.

Shapiro, Helen. 1994. *Engines of Growth: The State and Transnational Auto Companies in Brazil*. New York: Cambridge University Press.

Shin, Hyun Song. 2011. "Macroprudential Policies beyond Basel III." In BIS (ed.), *Macroprudential Regulation and Policy*, 5–15. Seoul: Bank of Korea.

Sikkink, Kathryn. 2005. "Patterns of Dynamic Multilevel Governance and the Insider-Outsider Coalition." In Donatella della Porta and Sidney Tarrow (eds), *Transnational Protest and Global Activism*, 151–73. Lanham, MD: Rowman & Littlefield.

Silbey, Susan. 2011. "The Sociological Citizen: Pragmatic and Relational Regulation in Law and Organizatons." *Regulation and Governance*, 5(1): 1–13.

Silvan, Laura. 2004. "CEC Makes a Difference in Mexico by Fostering Public Participation." accessed on the CEC website, May 2005. <www.cec.org/files/pdf/JPAC/CEC-Mexico-LauraSilvan-June-2004_en.pdf>.

Simmons, Beth A. 2001. "The International Politics of Harmonization: The Case of Capital Market Regulation." *International Organization*, 55(3): 589–620.

Simon, William H. 2010. "Optimization and its Discontents in Regulatory Design: Bank Regulation as an Example." *Regulation and Governance*, 4(3): 3–21.

Sissenich, Beate. 2008. "Cross-National Policy Networks and the State: EU Social Policy Transfer to Poland and Hungary." *European International Relations Journal*, 14(3): 455–87.

Sissenich, Beate. 2010. "Weak States, Weak Societies: Europe's East-West Gap." *Acta Politica*, 45(1/2): 11–40.

Slaughter, Anne-Marie. 2004. *A New World Order*. Princeton: Princeton University Press.

Snyder, R. 1999. "After Neoliberalism: The Politics of Reregulation in Mexico." *World Politics*, 51(2): 173–204.

Sørensen, E., and J. Torfing (eds). 2007. *Theories of Democratic Network Governance*. Basingstoke: Palgrave Macmillan.

Sornette, Didier. 2003. *Why Stock Markets Crash*. Princeton: Princeton University Press.

Spendzharova, A. 2008. "For the Market or 'For our Friends'? The Politics of Banking Sector Legal Reform in the Post-Communist Region after 1989." *Comparative European Politics*, 6(4): 432–62.

Stanford, L. 2002. "Constructing 'Quality': The Political Economy of Standards in Mexico's Avocado Industry." *Agriculture and Human Values*, 19: 293–310.

Sterian, Maria G. 2013. "WTO: Reform it or Change it?" *Annals of Faculty of Economics, Romanian-American University*, 1(1): 347–56.

Stern, P. A. 2009. "Objetivos y obligaciones de acceso universal en el sector de las telecomunicaciones en América Latina." In J. Calzada, A. Costas, and J. Jordana (eds), *Más allá del mercado: Las políticas de servicio universal en América Latina*, 177–214. Barcelona: CIDOB.

Stiglitz, J. E., and A. Charlton. 2006. "Aid for Trade." *International Journal of Development Issues*, 5(2): 1–41.

Štiks, I. 2013. "'We are all in this together': A Civic Awakening in Bosnia-Herzegovina." openDemocracy, 12 June. At: <http://www.opendemocracy.net/igor-Štiks/'we-are-all-in-this-together'-civic-awakening-in-bosnia-herzegovina>.

Stone Sweet, A., and W. Sandholtz. 1997. "European Integration and Supranational Governance." *Journal of European Public Policy*, 4(3): 297–317.

Stoychev, Stoycho, and Danko Poliyakov. 2009. "Establishment of Natura 2000 Network in Bulgaria: Common Challenge for Hunting and Conservation Organizations." Presentation at the seminar Promoting Nature 2000 and Sustainable Wildlife Use, DG Environment, Brussels, Nov.

Streeck, Wolfgang. 1997. "Beneficial Constraints: On the Economic Limits of Rational Voluntarism." In R. Boyer and J. Rogers Hollingsworth (eds), *Contemporary Capitalism: The Embeddedness of Institutions*, 197–219. Cambridge: Cambridge University Press.

Studer, I., and C. Wise (eds). 2007. *Requiem or Revival? The Promise of North American Integration*. Washington, DC: Brookings Institution Press.

Subotic, J. 2010. "Europe is a State of Mind: Identity and Europeanization in the Balkans." *International Studies Quarterly*, 55(2): 309–30.

Sun, X., and K. Canby. 2011. *Baseline study 1, China: Overview of Forest Governance, Markets and Trade*. Kuala Lumpur: Forest Trends for FLEGT Asia Regional Programme, June.

Sunstein, C. 1990. *After the Rights Revolution*. Cambridge, MA: Harvard University Press.

Suprema Corte. 2008. *Contradicción de Tesis 74/2008-SS*. Mexico City: Suprema Corte de la Justicia de la Nación, 10 Sept.

Suwa-Eisenmann, A., and T. Verdier. 2007. "Aid and Trade." *Oxford Review of Economic Policy*, 23(3): 481–507.

Szajner, P. 2009. *Assessment of the Competitiveness of the Dairy Food Chain in Poland*. AgriPolicy, Enlargement Network for Agripolicy Analysis, Working Paper, 2. <www.agripolicy.net>.

Takala, Jukka. 1999. "Global Estimates of Fatal Occupational Accidents." *Epidemiology*, 10(5): 640–6.

Tallberg, J. 2002. "Paths to Compliance: Enforcement, Management, and the European Union." *International Organization*, 56(3): 609–43.

Teague, Paul. 2002. "Standard-Setting for Labour in Regional Trading Blocs: The EU and NAFTA Compared." *Journal of Public Policy*, 22(3): 325–48.

Tendler, J. 1997. *Good Government in the Tropics*. Baltimore, MD: Johns Hopkins University Press.

Thelen, K. 2003. "How Institutions Evolve: Insights from Comparative Historical Analysis." In J. Mahoney and D. Rueschemeyer (eds), *Comparative Historical Analysis in the Social Sciences*, 208–40. New York: Cambridge University Press.

Torres, Blanca. 2002. "The North American Agreement on Environmental Cooperation: Rowing Upstream." In Carolyn Deere and Daniel Esty (eds), *Greening the Americas: NAFTA's Lessons for Hemispheric Trade*, 201–20. Cambridge, MA: MIT Press.

TRAC. 2004. *Ten Years of North American Environmental Cooperation: Report of the Ten-Year Review and Assessment Committee*. Montreal: Commission for Environmental Cooperation, 15 June.

Trauner, F. 2009. "Post-Accession Compliance with EU Law in Bulgaria and Romania: A Comparative Perspective." *European Integration Online Papers*, 13(2): art. 21.

Triches, Divanildo. 2003. *Economia política do Mercosul e aspectos monetários, cambiais e o Euro em perspectiva*. Caxias do Sul, RS: Editora da Universidade de Caxias do Sul.

US Department of Labor, Bureau of International Labor Affairs, and US Embassy. 2002. *Foreign Labor Trends*. Report 02-08. Mexico City: US Department of Labor and US Embassy.

US Department of Labor. 2005. *North American Agreement on Labor Cooperation: A Guide*. Washington, DC: US National Administrative Office-Bureau of International Labor Affairs, US Department of Labor, Oct. <http://www.dol.gov/ilab/media/reports/nao/naalcgd.htm>.

UNECE (United Nations Economic Commission for Europe) and FAO (Food and Agriculture Organization). 2012. *Forest Products Annual Market Review 2011–2012*. New York and Geneva: United Nations.

United Nations Economic Commission for Latin America and the Caribbean. 2009. *Economic Survey of Latin America and the Caribbean 2008–09: Policies for Creating Quality Jobs*. Santiago: UNECLAC.

US Department of Labor, Bureau of International Labor Affairs. 2010. Status of Submissions under the NAALC. <http://www.dol.gov/ilab/programs/nao/status.htm>.

US Department of State. 2010. *2010 Findings on the Worst Forms of Child Labor*. Panama and Washington, DC: GPO.

US NAO. 2007. *Public Report of Review of NAO Submission No. 2005-03*. Washington, DC: International Labor Affairs Bureau, Department of Labor. 31 Aug.

Vachudova, M. A. 2005. *Europe Undivided: Democracy, Leverage, and Integration After Communism*. Oxford: Oxford University Press.

Vachudova, M. A. 2008. "Tempered by the EU? Political Parties and Party Systems Before and After Accession." *Journal of European Public Policy*, 15(6): 861–79.

Vachudova, M. A. 2009. "Corruption and Compliance in the EU's Post-Communist Members and Candidates." *Journal of Common Market Studies*, 47: 43–62.

Valadez, Blanca. 2012. "PGR y Trabajo revisarán minas en tres entidades." *Milenio*, 21 Dec.

Van Berkum, S. 2004. *Dynamics in Vertical Coordination in the Romanian Dairy Sector.* Report for the World Bank Study on Dynamics of Vertical Coordination in ECA Agrifood Chains: Implications for Policy and Bank Operations. The Hague/Wageningen: LEI-WUR.

Van Berkum, S. 2009. *Assessment of the Competitiveness of the Dairy Supply Chain in New Member States, Candidate and Potential Candidate Countries.* Brussels: AgriPolicy Network, Final Report.

Vander Stichele, Myriam. 2008. *Financial Regulation in the European Union: Mapping EU Decision Making Structures on Financial Regulation and Supervision.* Report Commissioned by the Bretton Woods Project, available at <http://www.eurodad.org/uploadedfiles/whats_new/reports/eumapping_financial_regulation_final.pdf>. Accessed Mar. 2014.

van der Wilk, N. 2010. "China and the EU's Normative Approach to Africa: Competitor or Collaborator? A Case Study of Forest Law Enforcement, Governance and Trade (FLEGT)." MA thesis, University of Amsterdam.

VanDeveer, Stacy D. 2011. "Networked Baltic Environmental Cooperation." *Journal of Baltic Studies*, 42(1): 37–55.

Van Koppen, C. S. A., and W. T. Markham (eds). 2007. *Protecting Nature: Organizations and Networks in Europe and the USA.* Cheltenham: Edward Elgar.

Vargas, Lucinda. 1999. *NAFTA's First Five Years (Part 1).* El Paso Business Frontier, 2. Dallas: FRB.

Vaughan, Scott. 2003. "The Greenest Trade Agreement Ever? Measuring the Environmental Impacts of Agricultural Liberalization." In John Audley, Demetrios Papademetriou, Sandra Polaksi, and Scott Vaughan (eds), *NAFTA's Promise and Reality: Lessons from Mexico for the Hemispher,* 61–82. Washington, DC: Carnegie Endowment for International Peace.

Vaz, Alcides Costa. 2003. *Trade Strategies in the Context of Economic Regionalism: The Case of Mercosur.* CLAS Working Paper Series, 4 (June). UC Berkeley: Center for Latin American Studies.

Veiga, Pedro da Motta. 2004. "Regional and Transregional Dimensions of Brazilian Trade Policy." In Vinod Aggarwal, Ralph Espach, and Joseph Tulchin (eds), *The Strategic Dynamics of Latin American Trade,,* 175–89. Stanford, CA: Stanford University Press.

Vergara del Río, Mónica, and María Ester Feres. 2011. "Informe de Chile: Tema I: La eficacia de le legislación laboral y el papel de la inspección del trabajo." XX Congreso Mundial de Derecho de Trabajo y de la Seguridad Social.

Vogel, David. 1995. *Trading Up: Consumer and Environmental Regulation in a Global Economy.* Cambridge, MA: Harvard University Press.

Vogel, David. 2008. "Private Global Business Regulation." *Annual Review of Political Science*, 11: 261–82.

Vogel, David, and European Community Studies Association. 1997. *Barriers or Benefits? Regulation in Transatlantic Trade.* Washington, DC: Brookings Institution Press.

Walter, M. 2011. *Analysis of the PEFC System for Forest Management Certification using the Forest Certification Assessment Guide (FCAG).* WWF International, <http://assets.panda.org/downloads/2008_11_17_final_fcag_assessment_.pdf>.

Wapner, Paul. 1995. "Politics beyond the State: Environmental Activism and World Civic Politics." *World Politics*, 47(3): 311–40.

Weatherspoon, D. D., and T. Reardon. 2003. "The Rise of Supermarkets in Africa: Implications for Agrifood Systems and the Rural Poor." *Development Policy Review*, 21(3): 333–56.

Weber, M. 1978. *Economy and Society*. Berkeley, CA: University of California Press.

Weinstein, M. M., and S. Charnovitz. 2001. "The Greening of the WTO." *Foreign Affairs*, 80(6): 147–56.

Wendler, F. 2008. "The Public-Private Regulation of Food Safety through HACCP: What does it Mean for the Governance Capacity of Public and Private Actors?" In E. Vos (ed.), *European Risk Governance: its Science, its Inclusiveness and its Effectiveness*, 223–56. Mannheim: CONNEX.

Wilkin, J., Dominika Milczarek-Andrzejewska, Agata Malak-Rawlikowska, and Jan Falkowski. 2006. *The Dairy Sector in Poland. Regoverning Markets Agrifood Sector Study*. London: Sustainable Markets Group IIED.

Williamson, John. 1990. "What Washington Means by Policy Reform." In John Williamson (ed.), *Latin American Adjustment: How Much has Happened?*, 5–20. Washington, DC: Institute for International Economics.

Wilmarth, Arthur E. 2002. "The Transformation of the U.S. Financial System: Competition, Consolidation, and Increased Risk." *University of Illinois Law Review*, 2: 215–476.

Winter, Johannes. 2010. "Upgrading of TNC Subsidiaries: The Case of the Polish Automotive Industry." *International Journal of Automotive Technology and Management*, 10(2/3): 145–60.

World Bank. 1996–2009. "World Government Indicators (WGI)." Available at: <http://info.worldbank.org/governance/wgi/index.asp>.

World Bank. 2011–13. "World Development Indicators (WGI)." Available at: <http://info.worldbank.org/governance/wgi/index.asp>.

WTO. 2007. *Las normas privadas y el Acuerdo SMF: Nota de la Secretaria*. Geneva. G/SPS/GEN/746.

WWF Danube Carpathian Programme (DCPO). 2012. *Bulgarian Protected Areas Campaign*. Accessed: <http://wwf.panda.org/what_we_do/where_we_work/black_sea_basin/danube_carpathian/our_solutions/forests_and_protected_areas/protected_areas/bulgaria_protected_areas_campaign>, Jan. 2012.

WWF Danube Carpathian Programmme (DCPO). 2008. "Destruction of Bulgarian Parks Continue." Accessed: <http://wwf.panda.org/what_we_do/where_we_work/black_sea_basin/danube_carpathian/news/?uNewsID=147121>, Jan. 2012.

WWF Romania. 2007–2009. Activity Reports (on file).

Young, O. R. 2006. *Institutional Dynamics: Emergent Patterns in International Environmental Governance*. Cambridge, MA: MIT Press.

Zangrando, Carlos. 2011. "Cuestionario sobre el tema I: La eficacia de le legislación laboral y el papel de la inspección del trabajo." Brazil. XX Congreso Mundial de Derecho de Trabajo y de la Seguridad Social.

Zapata, E. G. 2006. "Entrevista al Secretario General de Regulatel, Gustavo Peña." *Revista AHCIET: Revista de Telecomunicaciones*, 106: 2–4.

Zepeda, Eduardo, Timothy A. Wise, and Kevin P. Gallagher. 2009. *Rethinking Trade Policy for Development: Lessons from Mexico under NAFTA*. Washington, DC: Carnegie Endowment for International Peace Policy Outlook.

Žilović, M. 2011. "Dissolution, War, Sanctions, and State-Building in the Post-Yugoslav Region." *Western Balkan Security Observer*, 21: 91–103.

Bibliography

Index